Lecture Notes in Computer Science   11104

Commenced Publication in 1973
Founding and Former Series Editors:
Gerhard Goos, Juris Hartmanis, and Jan van Leeuwen

Editorial Board

More information about this series at http://www.springer.com/series/7411

Nicolas Montavont · Georgios Z. Papadopoulos (Eds.)

Ad-hoc, Mobile, and Wireless Networks

17th International Conference on Ad Hoc
Networks and Wireless, ADHOC-NOW 2018
Saint-Malo, France, September 5–7, 2018
Proceedings

 Springer

Editors
Nicolas Montavont
IMT Atlantique, IRISA
Cesson Sevigne Cedex
France

Georgios Z. Papadopoulos
IMT Atlantique, IRISA
Cesson Sevigne Cedex
France

ISSN 0302-9743 ISSN 1611-3349 (electronic)
Lecture Notes in Computer Science
ISBN 978-3-030-00246-6 ISBN 978-3-030-00247-3 (eBook)
https://doi.org/10.1007/978-3-030-00247-3

Library of Congress Control Number: 2018953178

LNCS Sublibrary: SL5 – Computer Communication Networks and Telecommunications

This Springer imprint is published by the registered company Springer Nature Switzerland AG
The registered company address is: Gewerbestrasse 11, 6330 Cham, Switzerland

Preface

The International Conference on Ad-Hoc Networks and Wireless (AdHoc-Now) is one of the most popular series of events dedicated to research on ad-hoc, mobile and wireless sensor networks, and computing. Since its inception in 2002, the conference has been held 16 times in 6 different countries and the 17th edition in 2018 was held in Saint-Malo, France, during September 5–7.

We wish to thank all of the authors who submitted their work. This year, AdHoc-Now received 52 submissions and 21 papers were accepted for presentation as full contributions after a rigorous review process involving the Technical Program Committee (TPC) members, some external reviewers, and the TPC chairs. Moreover, due to the high quality of the received submissions, 6 papers were accepted as short contributions. Finally, AdHoc-Now 2018 had two papers by invited speakers.

The AdHoc-Now 2018 program was organized in six sessions grouping the contributions into the following topics: Routing in Low Power Networks; 5G and mmWave; Low Power Wide Area Networks; Mobile Communications and Networks; Distributed Systems and Architectures; Testbeds and Real-World Deployments. In each of these sessions, new ideas and directions were discussed among attendees from both academia and industry, thus, providing an in depth and stimulating view on the new frontiers in the field of mobile, ad hoc and wireless computing.

The conference was also enriched by the following six distinguished keynote speakers that completed a high-level scientific program: Pascal Thubert, George Oikonomou, Laurent Toutain, Luigi Alfredo Grieco, Antonio Skarmeta, Marc-Oliver Pahl.

We would like to thank all of the people involved in AdHoc-Now 2018. First of all, we are grateful to the TPC members and the external reviewers for their help in providing detailed reviews of the submissions, to Maddalena Nurchis, our proceedings chair, to Xenofon Fafoutis, Julien Montavont, Georgios Z. Papadopoulos, Tanguy Ropitault and Marc-Oliver Pahl, our TPC chairs, to Yann Busnel and Periklis Chatzimisios, our publicity chairs, to Tanguy Kerdoncuff and Remous-Aris Koutsiamanis, our web, submission and registration chairs. A special thanks goes to Frédéric Weis for his valuable support in the local organization and the arrangements of the event. We also thank the team at Springer for their great support throughout the entire process, from the submission till the proceedings production.

Finally, the organization was made possible through the strong support of our sponsors: IMT Atlantique Bretagne Pays de la Loire, IRISA research center, Technical University of Munich (TUM), German-French Academy for the Industry of the Future, Texas Instruments (TI), Springer and Springer's *Lecture Notes in Computer Science* (*LNCS*), Administrative Region of Brittany, France, Pracom, Université Bretagne Loire. A special thank you goes to them.

September 2018   Nicolas Montavont
                                                                               Georgios Z. Papadopoulos

Organization

ADHOC-NOW 2018 was organized by IMT Atlantique, France.

General Co-chairs

Nicolas Montavont   IMT Atlantique, France
Georgios Z. Papadopoulos   IMT Atlantique, France

Technical Program Committee Chairs

Xenofon (Fontas) Fafoutis   University of Bristol, UK
Julien Montavont   University of Strasbourg, France
Georgios Z. Papadopoulos   IMT Atlantique, France
Tanguy Ropitault   National Institute of Standards and Technology, USA
Marc-Oliver Pahl   Technische Universität München, Germany

Publicity Arrangements Chairs

Yann Busnel   IMT Atlantique, France
Periklis Chatzimisios   Alexander Technological Educational Institute
                       of Thessaloniki, Greece

Proceedings Chair

Maddalena Nurchis   University of Pompeu Fabra, Spain

Submission and Registration Chairs

Tanguy Kerdoncuff   IMT Atlantique, France
Remous-Aris Koutsiamanis IMT Atlantique, France

Local Arrangements Chair

Frédéric Weis   IUT de Saint-Malo, France

Web Chairs

Tanguy Kerdoncuff   IMT Atlantique, France
Remous-Aris Koutsiamanis IMT Atlantique, France

Technical Program Committee Members

Mohamed Aymen Chalouf	IRISA, France
Eleni Stai	National Technical University of Athens, Greece
Francesco Longo	University of Messina, Italy
Pierre Leone	University of Geneva, Switzerland
Nathalie Mitton	Inria Lille Europe, France
James Pope	University of Bristol, UK
Ivan Mezei	University of Novi Sad, Serbia
Giovanni Stea	University of Pisa, Italy
Fabrice Theoleyre	University of Strasbourg, France
Marco Lucio Scarpa	University of Messina, Italy
Symeon Papavassiliou	National Technical University of Athens, Greece
Eirini Eleni Tsiropoulou	University of New Mexico, USA
Juan Carlos Cano Escribá	Universitat Politècnica de València, Spain
Flávio Assis	Federal University of Bahia, Brazil
Carlo Puliafito	University of Pisa, Italy
Fabio Postiglione	University of Salerno, Italy
Tayeb Lemlouma	IRISA, France
Jacek Cichoń	Wrocław University of Science and Technology, Poland
Ralf Klasing	CNRS and University of Bordeaux, France
Atis Elsts	University of Bristol, UK
Xenofon (Fontas) Fafoutis	University of Bristol, UK
Remous-Aris Koutsiamanis	IMT Atlantique, France
Georgios Z. Papadopoulos	IMT Atlantique, France
Nicolas Montavont	IMT Atlantique, France
Dimitrios Zorbas	University of Piraeus, Greece
Konrad Wrona	NCI Agency, The Netherlands
Carlo Vallati	University of Pisa, Italy
Rustem Dautov	Kazan Federal University, Russia
Chrysa Papagianni	University of Maryland, USA
Carlos Miguel Tavares Calafate	Universitat Politècnica de València, Spain
Francisco J. Martinez	University of Zaragoza, Spain
Weifa Liang	Australian National University, Australia
German Castignani	Motion-S and Université de Luxembourg, Luxembourg
Andreas Herkersdorf	Technische Universität München, Germany
Jose M. Barcelo-Ordinas	Polytechnic University of Catalonia, Spain
Vasileios Karyotis	National Technical University of Athens, Greece
Alessandra De Paola	Università degli Studi di Palermo, Italy
Violet Syrotiuk	Arizona State University, USA
Qin Xin	University of the Faroe Islands, Faroe Islands
Julien Montavont	University of Strasbourg, France
Thomas Noel	University of Strasbourg, France
Giovanni Merlino	University of Messina, Italy

Contents

Distributed Systems and Architectures

Testbeds and Real-World Deployments

Routing in Low Power Networks

Adaptive k-cast Scheduling
for High-Reliability and Low-Latency
in IEEE802.15.4-TSCH

Inès Hosni[1] and Fabrice Théoleyre[2(✉)] [ID]

[1] LSC, University of Tunis El Manar, Tunis, Tunisia
ines.hosni@hotmail.fr
[2] ICube lab, CNRS/University of Strasbourg, Strasbourg, France
theoleyre@unistra.fr

Abstract. The Industrial Internet of Things tends now to emerge as
a key paradigm to interconnect a collection of wireless devices. However, most industrial applications have strict requirements, especially
concerning the reliability and the latency. IEEE802.15.4-TSCH represents currently a promising standard relying on a strict schedule of the
transmissions to provide such guarantees. The standard ISA-100.11a-
2011 has proposed the concept of duocast, where a pair of receivers are
allocated to the same transmission opportunity to increase the reliability.
In this paper, we generalize this approach to involve k different receivers,
and we explore the impact of this technique on the performance of the
network. We propose an algorithm assigning several receivers for each
transmission to increase the probability that at least one device receives
correctly the packet. By exploiting a multipath topology created by the
routing layer, we are able to reduce the number of transmissions while
still achieving the same reliability. We consequently increase the network
capacity, and reduce significantly the jitter. Our simulation results highlight the relevance of this k-cast technique in TSCH for the Industrial
Internet of Things.

Keywords: IEEE802.15.4-TSCH · k-cast transmissions · Duocast
Scheduling algorithms · High-reliability · Low jitter

1 Introduction

Industry 4.0 is promised as the next industrial revolution, where digital automation aims to reduce the cost and to maximize the flexibility [11]. In particular,
the Industrial Internet of Things (IIoT) aims to connect a large set of industrial
objects to the Internet. In this context, a real-time infrastructure has to provide
high-reliability for the wireless transmissions.

While the Internet of Things focused so far on *best-effort* solutions, industrial
applications have often strict requirements concerning the reliability and the
delay [2]. We need consequently specific MAC protocols able to provide strict

© Springer Nature Switzerland AG 2018
N. Montavont and G. Z. Papadopoulos (Eds.): ADHOC-NOW 2018, LNCS 11104, pp. 3–14, 2018.
https://doi.org/10.1007/978-3-030-00247-3_1

guarantees. Deterministic approaches are particularly relevant, allocating a fixed bandwidth to each device or flow. These solutions can provide also flow isolation, where each flow receives a certain bandwidth, dedicated for *its* transmissions.

IEEE802.15.4-TSCH relies on channel hopping to increase the robustness to external interference and fading [1]. TSCH adopts a deterministic approach, and schedules carefully the transmissions to avoid the collisions. More precisely, it allocates a set of different *cells* for interfering transmitters to reduce the contention while still avoiding collisions. A cell is defined by a pair of timeslot and channel offset. The channel offset is translated into a physical frequency at the beginning of the timeslot, to follow a pseudo-random sequence.

Many centralized and distributed scheduling algorithms [6] have been proposed so far for TSCH. To cope with unreliable links, the scheduling process often uses overprovisionning, and reserves several of cells so that a packet can be retransmitted. Unfortunately, more cells mean that the delay and the jitter may increase [13]. This over-provisioning also reduces the network capacity if the traffic is large and/or the links are very unreliable because of e.g. external interference.

IEEE802.15.4-TSCH is largely inspired from ISA-100.11a-2011 [9]. ISA has proposed a *duocast* mechanism to increase the reliability: two receivers are assigned to a given transmission. A transmission is considered a failure only if *both* receivers failed to decode correctly the packet.

In this paper, we aim to investigate the relevance of using k-cast scheduling, i.e. a cell is assigned to one transmitter, and k possible receivers (ordered by their priority). Subslots allow each receiver to acknowledge the transmission if none of the receivers with a larger priority sent an ack. The contributions of this paper are threefold:

1. We propose a scheduling algorithm tailored for k-cast transmissions. We propose to minimize the energy consumption for both transmitting and receiving the packets. Each node selects the set of parents to assign to a given cell to minimize this energy consumption;
2. We investigate the impact of the k-cast technique on the amount of duplicated packets. Indeed, the receivers may receive all the packets, but not the ack they transmit. In this case, the packets are duplicated wasting energy and bandwidth;
3. We implemented our scheduling algorithm and the k-cast technique to evaluate its performance. We highlighted this technique helps to improve the reliability with a limited impact on the energy consumption.

2   Related Work

IEEE 802.15.4-2015 has proposed the TSCH mode, which relies on a strict schedule of the transmissions [1]. The *slotframe* contains a fixed number of timeslots, during which at most one frame and its acknowledgment are transmitted. Each timeslot is labelled with an Absolute Sequence Number (ASN) which counts the number of timeslots since the PAN coordinator started. Based on the schedule, a node can decide its role (transmitter/receiver/sleeping mode) at the beginning of each timeslot.

IEEE 802.15.4-2015 TSCH implements a channel hopping approach to combat external interference and signal fading and, thus, to achieve high reliability [18]. For this purpose, each *cell* in the schedule is defined by a pair of timeslot and channel offset. At the beginning of each timeslot, the actual frequency to use is derived from the channel offset and the ASN.

IEEE802.15.4-TSCH supports two medium access approaches:

Shared cells are allocated to a group of nodes (e.g. for broadcast). A packet is for the first time transmitted without contention. If it corresponds to a unicast packet, and no `ack` is received, a random backoff is then used. This backoff corresponds to the number of cells to *skip* before the retransmission;

Dedicated cells are allocated to non-interfering transmitters. Thus, the transmitter just starts the transmission after a fixed offset from the beginning of the timeslot.

2.1 Improving the Reliability

Several techniques have been proposed to improve the reliability in this kind of deterministic architecture. Over-provisioning consists in reserving additional cells to retransmit the packets if the transmission has failed. For instance, the number of cells may be inversely proportional to the Packet Delivery Ratio for the considered radio link [16]. Dobslaw *et al.* [3] propose rather to fortify a centralized schedule by allocating additional cells to the most unreliable links until the deadline constraint cannot be anymore respected. Hashimoto *et al.* [5] propose to allocate shared cells for the retransmissions. However, shared cells are prone to collisions, impacting negatively the reliability of retransmissions.

Multipath also helps to improve the end-to-end reliability [10]. Papadopoulos *et al.* [13] propose to use multiple parents, replicating the packets over the two paths. With overhearing, several receivers try to decode a packet, increasing the reliability. A node which receives several times the same packet (identified with a sequence number) must drop the subsequent copies. However, the authors focus on a fault-tolerance scenario: the link quality drops suddenly on the primary path. We propose rather to address the *normal* case, where radio links may be unreliable *on average*.

Opportunistic routing consists in choosing several next hops. The destination address is transformed in anycast so that the same transmission can be received by any receiver. Typically, opportunistic routing helps to improve the efficiency in asynchronous wireless networks [17]. In IEEE802.15.4-TSCH, all the receivers wake-up synchronously. However, opportunistic routing is still efficient to improve the reliability: it is sufficient that *one* of the receivers decodes correctly the packet. Huynh *et al.* demonstrated that opportunistic scheduling helps to improve theoretically the reliability when exploiting a Rayleigh fading channel [7].

2.2 6TiSCH

6TiSCH has defined a set of protocols to execute IPv6 above IEEE802.15.4-TSCH. It relies on RPL (Routing over Low-Power Lossy Networks) to construct the routing topology [15]. A node uses a link quality metric and the rank of its parent to compute its own rank, denoting its virtual distance from the sink. Typically, the link quality is estimated via ETX (Expected Transmission Count), the average number of transmissions before the packet is acknowledged by the receiver. By default, RPL uses only one preferred parent (next hop toward the sink), but has been extended to support also multi-parent routing [8].

Scheduling the transmissions has attracted much attention in the past [6]. The 6P protocol [14] is in charge of negotiating the cells to use. The transmitter sends a request to the receiver to decide how many, and which cells to use. Then, 6TiSCH relies on a so-called Scheduling Function (SF) to decide which and how many cells to use between each pair of nodes. 6TiSCh supports both centralized (e.g. TASA [12]) and distributed (e.g. SFx [4]) scheduling algorithms. For instance, SFx [4] maintains the number of cells at least equal to the number of packets to forward, and relies on an hysteresis function to limit the number of oscillations.

3   k-cast Scheduling: Choosing the Right Set of Parents

Let us consider the example illustrated in Fig. 1. A node A has two ordered parents P_1 and P_2. During the first timeslot, P_1 receives correctly the packet and acknowledges it. During the second one, the transmission to P_1 fails, but P_2 is able to decode the packet: it should be able to acknowledge it to avoid another transmission. Typically, the ack of P_2 is transmitted if the medium is still idle after a timeout: it means P_1 is not currently transmitting an ack.

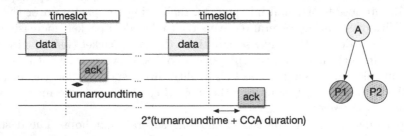

Fig. 1. Duocast transmission (with two different parents)

We aim here to investigate which strategy to adopt to assign several receivers to the same cell (k-cast) to improve the reliability. With perfect links, k-cast transmissions are useless since the primary parent *always* receives the packet correctly. The other parents will have to awaken to receive the packet although they are useless. On the other hand, unreliable links may be combatted when several receivers can all decode the same packet.

Besides, opportunistic scheduling would be inefficient if the radio link *among* parents is very unreliable. In that case, a parent may not hear that a previous parent is currently transmitting an `ack`: it will start to transmit its own `ack`, which will create a collision, and retransmissions. Moreover, both parents are convinced they both have to forward the packet: a *duplicated* packet has been created.

3.1   Number of Cells to Provision for a Given Set of Parents

Let us first compute the number of cells a node has to reserve with its parent. We rely on RPL to construct the routes [15] (cf Sect. 2.2). Then, the scheduling algorithm has to decide how many cells to reserve with its parent. We decide here to minimize the energy consumption, i.e. energy for reception and transmission so that at least one parent has received correctly the data packet.

Let denote by $\mathcal{P}$ the set of parents selected by the node n to forward its packets. We compute the Packet Delivery Ratio (PDR) for this node, i.e. average number of transmissions before one parent has acknowledged correctly the packet. In most implementations, each node divides the number of packets it transmits by the number of acks it receives. When a packet is transmitted to several receivers/parents, the transmission has failed if none is able to send an ack:

$$PDR_{n \to \mathcal{P}} = 1 - \prod_{p \in \mathcal{P}} (1 - PDR(p)) \qquad (1)$$

where $PDR(p)$ denotes the average Packet Delivery Ratio toward the parent p, i.e. ratio of unicast packets received correctly by p.

We force the scheduling function to reserve a sufficient number of cells to achieve a given minimum reliability (e.g. $PDR_{th} = 99\%$) within the current slotframe. The number of transmission opportunities $(n_{txop}(n \to \mathcal{P}))$ We denote by $n_{txop}(n \to \mathcal{P})$ the number of transmission opportunities to reserve to guarantee a minimum reliability. Typically, $n_{txop}(n \to \mathcal{P})$ must contain one copy and all its retransmissions to have a minimum Packet Delivery Ratio:

$$1 - (1 - PDR_{n \to \mathcal{P}})^{n_{txop}(n \to \mathcal{P})} \geq PDR_{th} \qquad (2)$$

$$n_{txop}(n \to \mathcal{P}) = \frac{log(PDR_{th})}{log(1 - (1 - PDR_{n \to \mathcal{P}}))} \qquad (3)$$

Finally, we have to provision enough cells to forward **all** the packets:

$$nbCells = n_{txop}(n \to \mathcal{P}) * n_{pkts}(n \to \mathcal{P}) \qquad (4)$$

where $nbCells$ denotes the number of cells reserve from n to its parents, and $n_{pk}(n \to \mathcal{P})$ denotes the average number of packets that the node n has to forward to its parents within a slotframe.

Cells are then removed and inserted dynamically in the schedule to respect this reliability. To avoid oscillations, we use an hysteresis function, similarly to the scheduling function SFx [4].

3.2   Energy Consumption to Choose the Right Set of Parents

We should not allocate systematically all the parents to a given cell. Indeed, medium link qualities do not require to have so many receivers: only the first parents will be actually useful, the other ones will waste their energy for idle listening. Inversely, allocating an insufficient number of receivers has a negative impact on the reliability and the delay: the source node needs more retransmissions to deliver the packet and to receive an `ack`.

Let us compute the energy consumption associated to a correct reception of a packet transmitted by a node n. For a sake of simplicity, a node assumes the link quality with its different parents may differ, but all the parents have paths with similar qualities toward the border router. $\mathcal{P}$ keeps on denoting the set of parents selected by the node n to forward its packets.

Thus, the energy consumption (in transmission mode) is finally:

$$E_{tx}(n) = n_{txop}(n \rightarrow \mathcal{P}) * E_{tx} \qquad (5)$$

where E_{tx} denotes the energy in TX mode for one cell.

Each parent has to be awake during all these cells. However, only some of them are actually busy, the other ones only correspond to idle listening. Thus, the energy to receive the packets of n can be estimated as:

$$E_{rx}(n) = n_{pkts}(n \rightarrow \mathcal{P}) * E_{rx} + (nbCells - n_{pkts}(n \rightarrow \mathcal{P})) * E_{idle} \qquad (6)$$

where E_{rx} (resp. E_{idle}) denotes the energy in RX (resp. IDLE) mode for one cell.

We have consequently to compute the set of parents which minimizes the energy consumption

$$E_{total}(n) = E_{rx}(n) + E_{tx}(n) \qquad (7)$$

Thus, the energy consumed by a node depends on the Packet Delivery Ratio toward its parents, and on the number of cells to provision to guarantee a given reliability. Inserting more parents increases the Packet Delivery Ratio and thus decreases the energy to transmit one packet. On the contrary, it also increases the energy consumed to receive the packets (idle and rx) for the parents. We will propose in the next section a strategy to decide which and how many parents to select.

3.3   Adaptive and Localized Scheduling Strategy

We propose here a scheduling algorithm adapted for k-cast. In particular, we have to decide how many and which parents should be allocated for each transmitting cell. Using a bad link instead of a good link is never relevant: a node should always use its best parents.

We propose a greedy approach to decide which cells to schedule (Algorithm 1). A node n applies the following approach:

1. n ranks its parents according to their PDR in descending order (line 2);
2. greedily, it inserts the next best parent in the list of forwarders (lines 5–6);

Algorithm 1. Parent Selection for Scheduling

    Data: set of parents (*Parents*)
    Result: set of forwarders (*FW*)
    `// initialization`
1 $FW \leftarrow \emptyset$;
2 rank(*Parents*, PDR);
3 *energy* $\leftarrow \infty$;
    `// adds a new parent in the forwarder set`
4 **repeat**
       `// picks the first parent in the list`
5      $p \leftarrow popFirst$(Parents);
6      $FW \leftarrow FW \cup \{p\}$;
       `// updates the energy cost according to eq. 7`
7   *energyOld* $\leftarrow$ *energy*;
8   *energy* $\leftarrow$ *computeEnergy*(FW);
       `// repeat until the energy starts to increase`
9 **until** *energy* > *energyOld*;
    `// removes the last forwarder added in the list`
10 *removeLast*(FW);
11 **return** (*FW*);

---

3. if the energy consumption (for both RX and TX) is reduced, then we continue the greedy allocation, and we consider the next parent. Else, the node n finally assigns the current list of forwarders (except the last parent) to its cells.

In other words, the algorithm stops when a local minimum is achieved. To decide how many cells have to be allocated, the node n uses the Eq. 4.

Theorem 1. *This greedy strategy allocates the set of parents which minimizes the energy consumption.*

Proof. Let us follow here a proof by contradiction. We order the parents by their decreasing PDR value. Our algorithm terminates with the set P. If the set P is not optimal, we replace one parent p of P by another parent p' with a smaller energy consumption. The reception energy of p is at least equal to those of p' since the number of cells with p' cannot be smaller (Eq. 6) since p' provides a larger PDR than p.

We can prove similarly that when the algorithm discards the kth parent because it starts to increase the energy consumption, another parent with a lower PDR cannot decrease further the energy consumption. □

4   Performance Evaluation

We evaluate here the performance of IEEE802.15.4TSCH with k-cast relying on openwsn[1]. We re-use here the approach of SFx [4] to define how many cells

---

[1] http://openwsn.org provides an opensource implementation of IEEE802.15.4-TSCH.

Table 1. Default values of the parameters in our simulations.

Parameter	Default value
Duration	60 s
Traffic type	100 packets
Data packet size	127 bytes
Number of nodes	20 nodes
Number of receivers	2 parents (in the same slot)
Destination	1 sink (convergecast)
MAC layer	IEEE802.15.4-TSCH
Schedule	Distributed
Time slot duration	15 ms
Slotframe length	101 slots
PHY model physical PDR	Fixed physical PDR for each radio link uniformly picked between 20 and 90%

have to be reserved. Each node computes dynamically the number of cells to use according to the number of packets to forward, and the Packet Delivery Ratio in the cells. Then, we decide how many parents have to be allocated to a given cell. Our implementation is fully available at https://github.com/ineshos/6TSCH/tree/master/python/ScheduleSimulator/simulator.

We rely here on simulations, and control the physical Packet Delivery Ratio (complement of the PER) of the links (Table 1). We assume the physical PDR remains fixed for the whole simulation. We first focus on a simple topology to evaluate the behavior of one flow, and then we study the performance in a random topology.

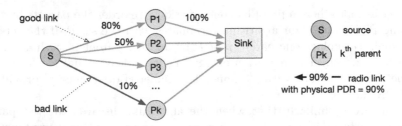

Fig. 2. Simple topology with multiple forwarding nodes with different link qualities.

4.1 Simple Forwarding Scenario

We first consider the topology illustrated in Fig. 2, where the physical Packet Delivery Ratio (i.e. the complement of the Packet Error Rate) has been fixed statically. The source generates 100 packets for the sink, 2 hops away.

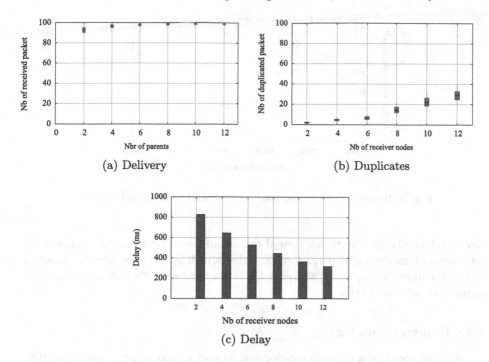

Fig. 3. Performance of a source with multiple parents with different link qualities.

Using more parents allows the network to increase the reliability: a single transmission may be received by any of the parents (Fig. 3a). However, using more than 6 parents seems to be inefficient. Indeed, the bad parents have only a marginal impact: they receive seldom the packets correctly. Besides, such parents would forward a packet only if all the previous parents (with a better link quality) have not transmitted an ack. This will occur very infrequently, and their impact on the reliability is very limited.

Figure 3b illustrates the number of duplicated packets (the packets which are received several times by the sink). With only two receivers, the amount of duplicates can be neglected (less than 2% of the packets). With many receivers, the number of duplicates becomes significant, and has a negative impact on the energy consumption: redundant and useless packets are forwarded by the different parents.

Figure 3c illustrates the delay. Because of the anycast transmission, we let *any* receiver forward the packet. Thus, the delay decreases with more receivers. Selecting many receivers has always a positive impact on the delay, even if it also increases the energy consumption.

Finally, we measured the number of cells that SFx reserves in the schedule (Fig. 4). The number of shared cells varies between 12 and only 3 cells for the whole network (20 devices), depending on the volume of traffic to forward. We remind that using dedicated cells requires to reserve at least one cell for each

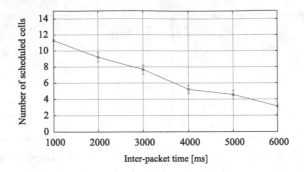

Fig. 4. Impact of the traffic load on the number of allocated cells.

device (thus 20 cells). Some additional cells would even be required to cope with retransmissions with non perfect radio links, which is the case here for most of the radio links. Thus, using shared cells is particularly efficient to reduce the number of allocated cells.

4.2   Random Topology

We now consider a random topology of 20 nodes, and assign a physical PDR to each radio link, uniformly distributed between 20 and 90%. This way, we verify that k-cast transmissions help to improve the efficiency even in more complex topologies.

We first measure the number of packets received when transmitting 100 packets (Fig. 5a). We make the same remarks as for the simple topology case: k-cast keeps on improving the reliability, to the same extent. Thus, the k-cast approach helps to improve globally the network-layer PDR: almost all packets are correctly delivered to the sink.

We measure then the amount of duplicated packets with a variable traffic (Fig. 5b). The amount of duplicated packets is linear with the inter-packet time. Thus, the solution is scalable and robust to the traffic conditions.

Finally, we consider the energy consumption in Fig. 5c. Using more receivers decreases at the beginning the energy consumption since less retransmissions are required to deliver a packet. In particular, selecting 3 parents allows the network to reduce its energy consumption by almost 30% compared with the unicast approach. On the contrary too many receivers means that we increase idle listening, which has a negative impact on the energy consumption when the parent has a marginal contribution on the delivery (i.e. it is seldom involved in the transmission). We obtain the optimal energy efficiency with 5 parents. Obviously, this optimal number of receivers depends on the ability of the device to turn fast its radio off when a cell is unused. Thus, it depends on the radio chipset specifications.

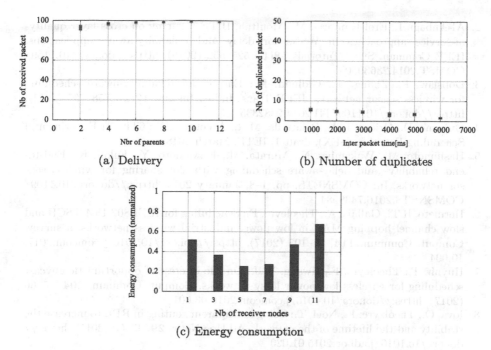

(a) Delivery

(b) Number of duplicates

(c) Energy consumption

Fig. 5. Random topology – 20 nodes, physical PDR picked uniformly between 10 and 90%.

5   Conclusion and Perspectives

We propose a distributed algorithm to exploit k-cast scheduling: several receivers are assigned to the same transmission, to improve the probability of success. Our algorithm computes the set of parents to schedule so that the energy consumption is minimized, considering both the RX and TX mode. Our simulations show k-cast helps to improve the reliability with a low energy consumption. The amount of duplicated packets is reasonable when a small number of parents (e.g. 2 or 3) are assigned to the same cell.

In the future, we plan to investigate the actual cost of implementing such k-cast feature in TSCH. In particular, a larger number of acks means often a longer timeslot, which may waste energy. Besides, we also plan to investigate the number of duplicated packets which may be generated by complex topologies (hidden terminals, asymmetrical links, etc.)

References

1. IEEE Standard for Low-Rate Wireless Personal Area Networks (LR-WPANs). IEEE Std 802.15.4-2015 (Revision of IEEE Std 802.15.4-2011), April 2016. https://doi.org/10.1109/IEEESTD.2016.7460875

2. Al-Anbagi, I., Erol-Kantarci, M., Mouftah, H.T.: A survey on cross-layer quality-of-service approaches in WSNs for delay and reliability-aware applications. IEEE Commun. Surv. Tutorials **18**(1), 525–552 (2016). https://doi.org/10.1109/COMST.2014.2363950
3. Dobslaw, F., Zhang, T., Gidlund, M.: End-to-end reliability-aware scheduling for wireless sensor networks. IEEE Trans. Indus. Inform. **12**(2), 758–767 (2014). https://doi.org/10.1109/TII.2014.2382335
4. Dujovne, D., Grieco, L.A., Palattella, M.R., Accettura, N.: 6TiSCH Experimental Scheduling Function (SFX). draft 1, IETF, March 2018
5. Hashimoto, M., Wakamiya, N., Murata, M., Kawamoto, Y., Fukui, K.: End-to-end reliability- and delay-aware scheduling with slot sharing for wireless sensor networks. In: COMSNETS, pp. 1–8, January 2016. https://doi.org/10.1109/COMSNETS.2016.7439984
6. Hermeto, R.T., Gallais, A., Theoleyre, F.: Scheduling for IEEE802.15.4-TSCH and slow channel hopping MAC in low power industrial wireless networks: a survey. Comput. Commun. **114**, 84–105 (2017). https://doi.org/10.1016/j.comcom.2017.10.004
7. Huynh, T., Theoleyre, F., Hwang, W.J.: On the interest of opportunistic anycast scheduling for wireless low power lossy networks. Comput. Commun. **104**, 55–66 (2017). https://doi.org/10.1016/j.comcom.2016.06.001
8. Iova, O., Theoleyre, F., Noel, T.: Using multiparent routing in RPL to increase the stability and the lifetime of the network. Ad Hoc Netw. **29**, 45–62 (2015). https://doi.org/10.1016/j.adhoc.2015.01.020
9. ISA-100.11a-2011: Wireless systems for industrial automation:process control and related applications. International Society of Automation (ISA) Std. 1, May 2011
10. Kafi, M.A., Othman, J.B., Badache, N.: A survey on reliability protocols in wireless sensor networks. ACM Comput. Surv. **50**(2), 31:1–31:47 (2017). https://doi.org/10.1145/3064004
11. Li, X., Li, D., Wan, J., Vasilakos, A.V., Lai, C.F., Wang, S.: A review of industrial wireless networks in the context of Industry 4.0. Wireless Netw. **23**(1), 23–41 (2017). https://doi.org/10.1007/s11276-015-1133-7
12. Palattella, M.R., Accettura, N., Grieco, L.A., Boggia, G., Dohler, M., Engel, T.: On optimal scheduling in duty-cycled industrial IoT applications using IEEE802.15.4e TSCH. IEEE Sens. J. **13**(10), 3655–3666 (2013). https://doi.org/10.1109/JSEN.2013.2266417
13. Papadopoulos, G., Matsui, T., Thubert, P., Watteyne, T., Montavont, N., Texier, G.: Leapfrog collaboration: toward determinism and predictability in industrial-IoT applications. In: ICC, pp. 1–6. IEEE (2017). https://doi.org/10.1109/ICC.2017.7997160
14. Wang, Q., et al.: 6top protocol (6p). draft 12, IETF, June 2018
15. Winter, T., et al.: Rpl: Ipv6 routing protocol for low-power and lossy networks. rfc 6550, IETF (2012). https://doi.org/10.17487/RFC6550
16. Theoleyre, F., Papadopoulos, G.Z.: Experimental validation of a distributed self-configured 6TiSCH with traffic isolation in low power lossy networks. In: MSWiM, pp. 102–110. ACM (2016). https://doi.org/10.1145/2988287.2989133
17. Wang, X., Wu, X., Zhang, X.: Optimizing opportunistic routing in asynchronous wireless sensor networks. IEEE Commun. Lett. **21**(10), 2302–2305 (2017). https://doi.org/10.1109/LCOMM.2017.2729557
18. Watteyne, T., Mehta, A., Pister, K.: Reliability through frequency diversity: why channel hopping makes sense. In: PE-WASUN, pp. 116–123. ACM (2009). https://doi.org/10.1145/1641876.1641898

Multi-path Selection in RPL Based on Replication and Elimination

Tomás Lagos Jenschke[✉], Remous-Aris Koutsiamanis,
Georgios Z. Papadopoulos, and Nicolas Montavont

IMT Atlantique, Irisa, UBL, Cesson-Sévigné, France
{tomas.lagos-jenschke,remous-aris.koutsiamanis,georgios.papadopoulo,
nicolas.montavont}@imt-atlantique.fr

Abstract. IPv6 Routing Protocol for Low-Power and Lossy Networks
(RPL) is a distance vector routing protocol especially designed for the
Internet of Things (IoT). RPL uses broadcast DODAG Information
Object (DIO) messages to build a Destination Oriented Directed Acyclic
Graph (DODAG) toward a root. Each node selects a parent node toward
the root using a common Objective Function (OF). However, the use of a
single route can affect the network reliability and the end-to-end latency.
In this study, we propose to employ the Packet Replication and Elimination (PRE) principles to use parallel paths toward the DODAG root, over
the IEEE 802.15.4 Time-Slotted Channel Hopping (TSCH) as a medium
access. To this aim, we propose number of algorithms to select the second
or the alternative parent in RPL. Furthermore, we study the advantages
of using overhearing feature over correlated paths. Our simulation campaign conducted over Cooja, the simulator of Contiki OS, demonstrate
that the use of overhearing in conjunction with PRE in RPL considerably improves the robustness of a wireless network by providing greater
opportunity to a packet to reach its destination.

Keywords: Multi-path routing · RPL · TSCH
Leapfrog collaboration

1 Introduction

The IoT are set of standards and technologies developed to connect embedded
and smart objects to the Internet. Its low cost, environment adaptability and
easy development have allowed the massive integration of these technologies in
different application domains, such as the smart grid, Intelligent Transport System (ITS) or the Industry 4.0. The use of the IoT in these various applications
however requires different quality of service, which is not an inherent features
provided by IoT technologies. For example, the Industry 4.0 is especially concerned with the deterministic nature of the network, i.e., to rely on bounded
delay and very high delivery ratio.

Many standard solutions have appeared during the last decade for wireless
technologies for embedded devices. IEEE 802.15.4 [4] is a standard for low energy

© Springer Nature Switzerland AG 2018
N. Montavont and G. Z. Papadopoulos (Eds.): ADHOC-NOW 2018, LNCS 11104, pp. 15–26, 2018.
https://doi.org/10.1007/978-3-030-00247-3_2

power devices focused on the industry. This standard is historically based on Time Division Multiple Access (TDMA) and Frequency Division Multiple Access (FDMA). Few years ago, the concept called TSCH [1] has emerged, which reduces the Multi-path fading by using frequency hopping. For extended networks where a destination node is out of the radio range of the source node, a routing protocol might be used on top of the Layer 2 technology. RPL is one of the most popular routing protocol for the IoT and is a distance vector routing protocol, which distributes the nodes within a tree hierarchy called DODAG. By default, each node has an option (route) to transmit a packet to a preferred node until it reaches the target. However is has been shown that reliability performance can be mitigated in real environment, and the retransmission schemes employed when a packet is loss introduce significant delay and jitter. In our previous works, we introduced Leapfrog Collaboration (LFC) [3,7] which allows nodes to select additional parents to create alternate paths. To do so, we used the PRE concept, in which several copies of a data packet are introduced in a network to increase the probability of reception at the root node. In this paper, we further investigate LFC and study the effect of the parent selection algorithm. We introduce five algorithms for a node to select alternate parents, and compare their performance in the Cooja simulator.

The document is organized into five sections as follows. In Sect. 2 the RPL protocol, TSCH technique and the PRE mechanism are briefly explained. In Sect. 3, the different techniques proposed for the Alternative Parent (AP) selection to be evaluated are explained. In Sect. 4 contains the results obtained from the different methods proposed in Sect. 3. In Sect. 5, we find the different works carried out on multi-path in RPL before our work. Finally, Sect. 6 concludes our paper.

2 Background

2.1 IEEE802.15.4

TSCH is a recent channel access technique developed for IEEE 802.15.4. Its main objective is to reduce the impact of wireless fading on a network transmission. TSCH is composed of many timeslots that, in turn, are grouped into slotframes. In order to make this work, TSCH schedules a node to do what it has to do in a timeslot. The formula that uses TSCH to do its channel hopping is represented in the Eq. 1.

$$f = F(ASN + chOF) \bmod n_{ch} \tag{1}$$

where ASN is the slot offset, $chOF$ is the channel offset, F is the channel input and f is the resultant frequency. TSCH is focused exclusively on the MAC layer, allowing the adjustment of time intervals in a wide range of protocols enabled for IPv6. IEEE802.15.4e currently defines the mechanisms necessary to carry out a communication through TSCH but does not establish the construction and maintenance policies of this, so there is a free interpretation.

2.2 RPL

RPL is a distance vector routing protocol designed and developed by the IETF working group ROLL [11]. This protocol organizes the nodes in a DODAG to allow upward traffic from leafs to sensors, and propose different options for the downward routes. To build a DODAG, a DODAG root sends multicast DIO packets with the necessary information so that a node can join the network. A unicast DODAG Advertisement Object (DAO) message is sent upward to propagate destination information and construct downward routes. Within a RPL instance, there is an OF which defines how to combine different metrics to perform parent selection, i.e. choose which neighbor will be the default relay node toward the root. By default, a node has a single Preferred Parent (PP) selected from its parent list. Different metrics can be used:

- Hop Counting (HC): This metric consists of the minimum amount of hops necessary for the message to reach its destination. In contiki OS [6], the OF0 is designed to find the nearest root. i.e, the minimum number of relay nodes.
- Expected Transmission Count (ETX): ETX consists of a link quality metric, based on the average number of retransmissions needed to reach a given neighbor. This does not mean that it will be the shortest route, but it ensures the quality of the transmission links. To reach this objective, the OF uses the following formula defined by [9]:

$$ETX_{ij} = \frac{|N_{tx_{data}}|}{|N_{rx_{data}}|} \times \frac{|N_{tx_{ACK}}|}{|N_{rx_{ACK}}|} = \frac{|N_{tx_{data}}|}{|N_{rx_{ACK}}|} \qquad (2)$$

Where $N_{tx_{data}}$ is the number of transmitted messages, $N_{rx_{data}}$ is the number of received messages, $N_{tx_{ACK}}$ is the number of transmitted ACKs and $N_{rx_{data}}$ is the number of received ACKs.

2.3 6TiSCH

The IETF working group 6TiSCH [10] is in charge of the interworking between the IEEE802.15.4 TSCH and the IETF upper stack 6LoWPAN, RPL and CoAP. To make this possible, they are implementing an extra layer over TSCH MAC layer to adapt the scheduling technique to the specificities and requirements of the upper layers. As is explained in [10] LLN needs to:

1. Provide a mechanism for two devices to negotiate the allocation and deallocation of cells between them.
2. Provide a mechanism for the device to monitor and manage the capabilities of a node several hops away.
3. Define a mechanism for these different scheduling mechanisms to coexist in the same network.

In this paper we assume a centralized scheduling where controller establishes the transmission and reception slots for all RPL nodes.

2.4   PRE

We previously proposed LFC which increases the reliability and the determinism feature of a multi-hop network by using PRE concept. Replication means that several copies of a single packet are generated in the network (either by the source, by intermediate nodes, or both), and Elimination means that each node that receives a duplicates will discard it. In RPL, by default, a node can have one preferred route identified by its PP. To do the replication, LFC adds the use of an alternative route by choosing an AP from its parent set except for its chosen PP.

Once a node has chosen two PPs, it duplicates a packet to both its parents, and then send two copies of the same data packets. Note that the two parents may benefit from overhearing the transmission to the other parent, ever increasing the probability of receiving the packet. A node may select its PP in many different ways, and in the next sections we present five possible algorithms.

3   Algorithms for Multiple Parent Selection

By default, RPL performs routing by forwarding packets via the selected PP. The selection of a PP amongst multiple candidate parents is made through its OF. This selection consists mainly of the ranking hierarchy, which increases as the DODAG tree becomes deeper. This type of selection avoids communication loops because a node can be a possible PP, if and only if, its rank is lower than that of its children. To find the most suitable route, there are different types of selection metrics, of which we chose to use ETX.

In this section we define different types of AP selection for Multi-path transmission. Note that if none of the potential parents of a node matches the selection process, or if several nodes do, then the one with the second best ETX will be chosen. It is also possible that no AP is selected in the case where a node has only one parent.

3.1   Overhearing

To take advantage of the nature of the wireless medium, nodes close to a transmission can overhear a packet. We implemented this feature, that we call *overhearing*, to let a potential parent receive a packet sent from a child to another parent. This allows a second opportunity for the information to reach its destination.

Within this work, the use of overhearing was incorporated into LFC, i.e., in all cases of Multi-path selection. In addition, we developed another algorithm where we only add the Overhearing to RPL (i.e., RPLO) without doing any duplication.

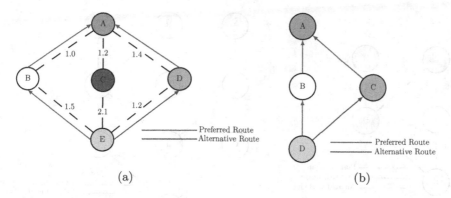

Fig. 1. (a) 2ETX illustration (b) CA illustration

3.2   Second Best ETX (2ETX)

This algorithm consists of obtaining an AP by selecting the node that has a lower ranking than the current node and that has the best link quality among the set of possible parents. In Fig. (1a) a selection example is shown by the use of 2ETX where if we define the rankings such as R and link quality as M:

- $A_R < B_R$ and $A_R < C_R$ and $A_R < D_R$
- $E_R > B_R$ and $E_R > C_R$ and $E_R > D_R$

$$E_M + B_M + A_M = 2.5_{ETX}$$
$$E_M + C_M + A_M = 3.1_{ETX} \qquad (3)$$
$$E_M + D_M + A_M = 2.6_{ETX}$$

Since 2.5_{ETX} is the lowest value, node B will be the PP of node E and node D will be the AP of node E because $2.6_{ETX} < 3.1_{ETX}$.

3.3   Common Ancestor (CA)

A node will select a node as its AP if it has a common ancestor with the PP. It means that the AP and the PP should have a common PP in their Metric Container (MC) [2]. If multiple potential parents exhibit the same characteristic, the one with the best ETX will be selected. Minet et al. in [5] call this algorithm the "Triangle Pattern". They also present the "Braided patter" which works similarly to the triangle pattern with the main difference being that the AP also has the chance to have an AP too. In our previous work [7], we used this algorithm.

Figure (1b) shows an example of CA where node C is the AP of node D and A is the common ancestor (potential parent) of node D and C. In order to implement this algorithm, a node should advertise its list of potential parents to its children. The IETF draft [2] provides a proposal and defines a "Type-Length-Value" (TLV) field within the "Node State and Attribute" (NSA) object type in the MC of DIO packets to carry this information.

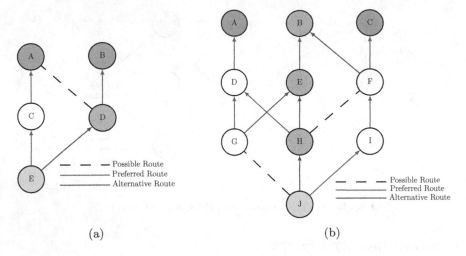

Fig. 2. (a) NCPA illustration (b) Disjoint illustration

3.4 Non-common Preferred Ancestor (NCPA)

A node is selected as an AP if it has a different PP than the PP one. This selection mechanism works by storing in the DIO MC the PP address and the receiving child just has to compare the PP address of its potential parents. Figure (2a) illustrates the NCPA operation where node A is the preferred grandparent of node E and node B is the PP of node D. Because A is different from B, D will be the AP of node E.

3.5 Non-common Ancestor (Disjoint)

This algorithm consists in the selection of an AP if the current PP has a PP and AP different than the PP and AP from the potential node. In this way, the composition of a triangular pattern through an alternative node is deactivated, which allows the generation of one or several disjoint patterns according to the built network topology. Like the other selection techniques, the node will classify and select its potential AP ordered by the ETX metric. The Fig. (2b) illustrates the operation of the Disjoint selection.

4 Performance Evaluation

4.1 Simulation Environment

In this study, we employed the COOJA network simulator for Contiki OS [6] to perform the performance evaluation campaign. To this aim, we defined three types of topology illustrated in Fig. 3 and configured as shown in Table 1.

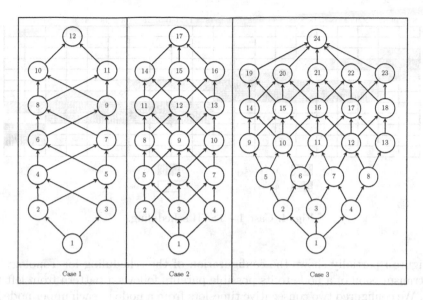

Fig. 3. Case 1: topology with 12 nodes. Case 2: topology with 17 nodes. Case 3: topology with 24 nodes.

Table 1. Simulation setup.

	Topology 1	Topology 2	Topology 3
Topology	Multi-hop	Multi-hop	Multi-hop
Number of nodes	12	17	24
SlotFrame length	53	86	121

Duration	until 120 packets	**EB period**	$4sec$
Traffic	$1pkt/5sec$	**TimeSlot length**	$10ms$
Routing	RPL	**Number of source**	1
MAC	TSCH	**Number of channels**	1

- Topology 1 - simple use-case, where each node has two potential parents: 12 nodes, where leaf node 1 will be the transmitter and node 12 will be the DODAG root.
- Topology 2 - wider network, where each node has three potential parents: 17 nodes, where leaf node 1 will be the transmitter and node 17 will be the DODAG root.
- Topology 3 - dense network, where a node can have up to four siblings: 24 nodes, where leaf node 1 will be the transmitter and node 24 will be the DODAG root.

The simulation consists in the transmission of 120 packets every 5 s. We ran 10 trials for each algorithm and we tested six algorithms: default RPL, RPLO, 2ETX, CA, NCPA and Disjoint described in Sect. 3.

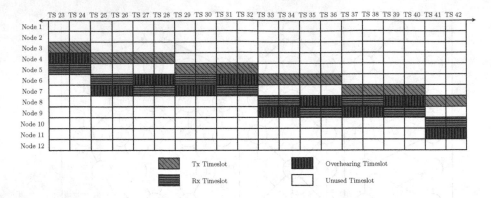

Fig. 4. Case 1 - TSCH scheduling.

Figure 4 partially shows the configuration of the scheduling for Topology 1. The transmission of a node to its possible parents follows a pattern from left to right. We configured two consecutive timeslots from a node to each upper node in the topology to allow the transmission of one data packet plus a retransmission if this first attempt failed. For some algorithms, we also defined overhearing timeslots, where a node will listen a transmission intended to another node. For example, in timeslot 33, node 6 is sending to node 8, and node 9 is also listening the transmission. The same pattern is also applied for Topology 2 and 3.

4.2   Results

Packet Delivery Ratio. We first measure the average Packet Delivery Ratio (PDR), i.e., the percentage of packets that arrive at the DODAG root. As shown in Fig. 5, except for RPL, topologies 2 and 3 reach almost 100% PDR while in the case of Topology 1 they approach 95% PDR. Stock RPL does not perform well with around 50% of PDR in all topologies. This highlights the improvement provided by the use of Multi-path and overhearing with respect to the standard implementation.

Delay and Jitter. As shown in Fig. 3, Topology 1 consists of 12 nodes where each of these has a set of two possible parents with the exception of the last hop. Considering that each timeslot lasts 10 ms, the approximate delay can be calculated with the Eq. 4:

$$(((P_2 \times N_{ps2}) + (P_3 \times N_{ps3}) + 1) \times TR) - T = min_{delay}$$
$$((P_2 \times N_{ps2}) + (P_3 \times N_{ps3}) + N_{sp}) \times TR = max_{delay}$$

(4)

where P is the parent set, N_{ps} are the nodes that have more than a single parent, N_{sp} are the node that have only a single parent, T is the timeslot duration and R is the amount of transmissions plus retransmissions per attempt.

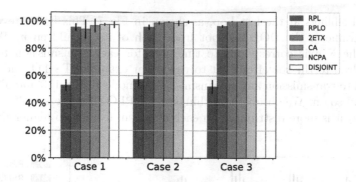

Fig. 5. Packet Delivery Ratio (PDR): percentage of received packets.

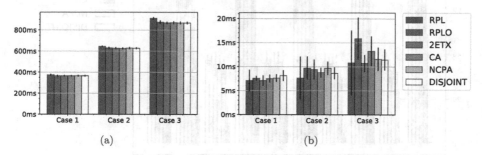

Fig. 6. (a) Packet delay: time for a packet to cross the network (b) Packet jitter: delay variation.

The minimum and maximum delay for the first, second and third topologies are shown in the Eqs. 5, 6 and 7, respectively.

$$
\begin{aligned}
(((2 \times 9) + 1) \times 20) - 10 &= 370\,\text{ms} \\
((2 \times 9) + 2) \times 20 &= 400\,\text{ms}
\end{aligned}
\tag{5}
$$

$$
\begin{aligned}
(((2 \times 8) + (3 \times 5) + 1) \times 20) - 10 &= 630\,\text{ms} \\
((2 \times 8) + (3 \times 5) + 3) \times 20 &= 680\,\text{ms}
\end{aligned}
\tag{6}
$$

$$
\begin{aligned}
(((2 \times 11) + (3 \times 7) + 1) \times 20) - 10 &= 870\,\text{ms} \\
((2 \times 11) + (3 \times 7) + 5) \times 20 &= 960\,\text{ms}
\end{aligned}
\tag{7}
$$

Figure (6a) shows the average delays obtained during the simulations where all tend to present minimum delay, while in Fig. (6b) the average of the standard deviation (Jitter) between packets is shown.

As it can be observed that the algorithms have a similar pattern when their results are compared. The main difference is found in Fig. (6b), Topology 3, where the jitter of the RPLO and CA algorithms are more important than the others. In RPLO, a node never duplicates packets, but several copies of each data packets are still created because there are multiple receivers for each transmission (due to the overhearing). This results in a more uniform distribution of the copies between all siblings at the last hop, as shown in Fig. 7. This figure reveals the reception traffic of the DODAG root from each of its 5 children in Topology 3, where the X axis corresponds to timeslots for each transmission from the root's children to the root from left to right. For example, TS 111 and TS 112 correspond to transmission and retransmission of node 19, TS 113 and TS 114 of node 20 and so on. We observe two things: *(i)* RPLO shows less traffic on each children *(ii)* it is more distributed on each children, leading to higher jitter.

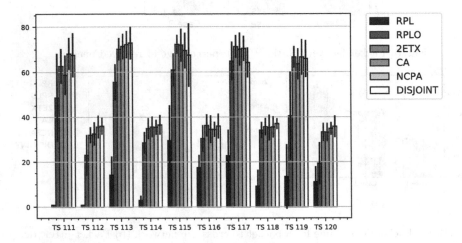

Fig. 7. Percentage of packets that follow a path.

Figure 8 represents the percentage of packets received for the first time in each timeslot. Thus, it represents a CDF, i.e., the proportion of packets received in all possible timeslots. We can see that the distribution is concentrated in TS 111 or node 19, which corresponds to a jitter = 0. This phenomenon is due to the nature of the static scheduling. The traffic will behave like a priority queue, since, for each loss within a timeslot, the next attempt is made in the following timeslot. This explains the low jitter variance between the algorithms and the low delay for each of the transmissions.

Because default RPL does not have Multi-path and overhearing, its information receptions are not subject to TS 111 since it is unidirectional. In the case of RPLO and CA, their distribution is focused on the overhearing nodes because RPLO only follows the route of its PP and CA makes its way based on a triangular pattern. If we analyze Fig. 8, we can observe a small variation of reception in TS 113 and TS 115 respectively, due to the distributive nature of these two algorithms.

In the case of 2ETX, this can be totally variable because its distribution focuses on the selection of the best link quality, while NCPA and Disjoint seek to expand as much as possible within the DODAG tree. This tends to happen across all the nodes and, in turn, to TS 111.

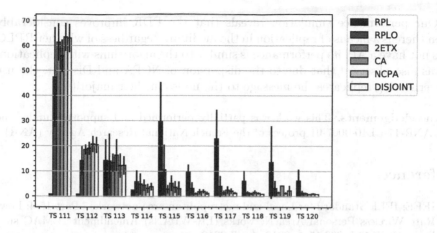

Fig. 8. Path of the first copy received by the DODAG root.

5   Related Work

A number of works related with multi-path in RPL have been conducted in the literature, focusing either on improving energy consumption or network reliability. However, to the best of our knowledge, there is no work that investigated the alternative parent and route selection for the Multi-path objective.

In [8], they propose the construction of a scheduling architecture to allow the transmission of multiple routes between a node and its different route options. To reach this goal, they adapt the transmit scheduling to resend the data packet to its different neighbors by choosing a randomly free slot and retrieving the used slots of their neighbors nodes. RPL is adapted also to take into account the delay and the packet delivery before a deadline. This is done with the purpose of handling the deadline transmission at each hop that the packet does.

In [5] the authors propose and analyze three different types of patterns. Each pattern is intended to increase the reliability of the communication by using an alternative route in addition to its preferred route. The result of each pattern is the duplication of packets in each node given more chances that the message reaches its destination. Consequently, the increase in reliability is proportional to the number of available paths that the node posses to transmit a packet. The drawbacks of the increase in possible paths is a higher networking overhead and a higher energy consumption.

6   Conclusion

In this work, we investigated the potentials of PRE scheme over parallel paths towards the DODAG root. To do this aim, we proposed four algorithms, the 2ETX, CA, NCPA and Disjoint where overhearing function was employed, and we compared them against default RPL and RPLO.

Our performance simulation reveals that the PDR improves considerably when there is a means of replication in the medium. Regardless of whether RPLO does not have a AP, its performance is similar to the algorithms with replication. It was also observed that due to the dispersion of NCPA and Disjoint, the use of overhearing replicates the message to the nodes in their majority.

Acknowledgements. This work was partially performed and supported under the TPI ANR-17-CE10-0007-01 project of the French National Research Agency (ANR).

References

1. IEEE: IEEE Standard for Local and metropolitan area networks - Part 15.4: Low-Rate Wireless Personal Area Networks (LR-WPANs) Amendment 1: MAC sublayer. IEEE Std. 802.15.4e-2012, April 2012
2. Koutsiamanis, R., et al.: RPL DAG Metric Container (MC) Node State and Attribute (NSA) object type extension. draft-koutsiamanis-roll-nsa-extension-01, IETF, roll, January 2018
3. Koutsiamanis, R.A., Papadopoulos, G.Z., Fafoutis, X., Fiore, J.M.D., Thubert, P., Montavont, N.: From best-effort to deterministic packet delivery for wireless industrial IoT networks. IEEE Trans. Indus. Inform. (2018)
4. Kurunathan, H., et al.: IEEE 802.15.4e in a nutshell: survey and performance evaluation. IEEE Commun. Surv. Tutorials (2018)
5. Minet, P., et al.: Increasing reliability of a TSCH network for the industry 4.0. In: 16th IEEE International Symposium on Network Computing and Applications, November 2017
6. Contiki OS. Contiki: The Open Source OS for the Internet of Things, March 2018. http://www.contiki-os.org
7. Papadopoulos, G.Z., Matsui, T., Thubert, P., Texier, G., Watteyne, T., Montavont, N.: Leapfrog collaboration: toward determinism and predictability in industrial-IoT applications. In: Proceedings of the IEEE International Conference on Communications (ICC) (2017)
8. Pavković, B., et al.: Multipath opportunistic RPL routing over IEEE 802.15.4. In: International Conference on Modeling, Analysis and Simulation of Wireless and Mobile Systems, October 2011
9. Rajalingham, G., et al.: Quality of service differentiation for smart grid neighbor area networks through multiple RPL instances Gowdemy. In: Proceedings of the 10th ACM Symposium on QoS and Security for Wireless and Mobile Networks - Q2SWinet 2014, September 2014
10. Watteyne, T., et al.: Using IEEE 802.15.4e Time-Slotted Channel Hopping (TSCH) in the Internet of Things (IoT): Problem Statement. IETF, RFC 7554, October 2015
11. Winter, T., et al.: RPL: IPv6 Routing Protocol for Low-Power and Lossy Networks. IETF, RFC 6550, March 2012

Performance Evaluation of a RPL Hybrid Objective Function for the Smart Grid Network

François Lemercier[1]([✉]) [iD] and Nicolas Montavont[2]

[1] Itron, IMT Atlantique, IRISA, UBL, 2 rue de la Châtaigneraie,
35576 Cesson Sevigné, France
francois.lemercier@imt-atlantique.fr
[2] IMT Atlantique, IRISA, UBL, 2 rue de la Châtaigneraie,
35576 Cesson Sevigné, France
nicolas.montavont@imt-atlantique.fr

Abstract. Multiple heterogeneous communication technologies offer great opportunities in Smart grid network by using wire, wireless and optic fiber. Most of future smart meters will use Powerline Communication (PLC) technology in addition to one or more wireless interfaces to tackle the physical constraints and failure of the PLC network. When a smart meter is connected using two different technologies, choosing the best relay node and the best link to transmit the message is a key decision to provide a good quality of service and increase the reliability of the communication network. In this paper, we propose an algorithm to manage multiple interfaces at the routing level (using RPL), and a re-transmission scheme to improve the reliability of the network when a PLC interface fails.

Keywords: RPL · LLN · Hybrid routing · Smart grid
Heterogeneous networks

1 Introduction

The new services of the electricity grid require a communication network capable of high bandwidth, high reliability and secure exchange [1]. To tackle the technological evolution of this demand, the internet of things (IoT) is one of the sources of inspiration. The Automatic Meter Reading (AMR) uses the Power Line Communication (PLC) network to enable automatic and remote electric and gas meter readings. The smart grid is the new generation of the electric grid that provides a two-way communication between providers and consumers using an electric power distribution network based on Advanced Metering Infrastructure (AMI). However, PLC communication networks are subject to high sensitivity to interference. Errors in such PLC systems come especially from background noise, impulsive noise and narrow-band interference (NBI) [2].

A MAC protocol is required to face the high variation of available bandwidth due to the severe noise condition, which is common in PLC networks. Although

© Springer Nature Switzerland AG 2018
N. Montavont and G. Z. Papadopoulos (Eds.): ADHOC-NOW 2018, LNCS 11104, pp. 27–38, 2018.
https://doi.org/10.1007/978-3-030-00247-3_3

such a dynamic adaptive solution exists, several alternative communication technologies are considered, such as Wireless Sensor Network, Mesh, cellular, Wimax, IoT Long Range, etc. Most of them are also highly sensitive to noise and may not work in specific environments, those technologies are consequently considered Low Power and Lossy network (LLN). In order to enhance the communication capabilities, a commonly used solution consists in mixing multiple heterogeneous technologies to cope with all possible scenarios and interference levels. When one technology is not working well in a specific case, most of the time another technology can be used instead. For these reasons, most of future smart meters will embed several heterogeneous communication technologies to ensure a certain quality of service. However, supporting these multiple interfaces is a challenge. Most of these technologies are short range, and nodes must collaborate to reach a destination that require multiple hops. Routing protocols play a central role by optimizing the selected paths according to application requirements and field specificity.

RPL [3] is the most popular routing protocol in the IoT community. Unlike AODV [4] or LOAD [5], RPL is a proactive protocol based on distance vector. RPL builds a DODAG rooted at a sink by leaving each node to choose its next hop toward the root. The selection of the preferred parent is based on an Objective Function (OF) that determines the best relay node and computes the node rank. The rank represents more or less the distance from the root.

RPL is mostly used on homogeneous network and has been designed to operate on single communication network. Few solutions exists to handle multiple interfaces nodes with RPL, most of the solutions presented in the related work section propose to create an abstraction layer between RPL and MAC layers that is in charge of providing metrics and low layers information as a unified interface for RPL. In order to simplify exchanges between low layers and RPL, we extended RPL as it could see all the interface and manage all the metrics provided by the respective MAC layers.

In [6] we present three different concepts to modify RPL to take advantage of a hybrid network. One of the presented solution, called Parent Oriented (PO), merges the characteristics of the heterogeneous interfaces to provide a single virtual link with a neighbor in order to compare potential parent during the RPL selection operation.

In this paper, we show how the Parent Oriented solution could increase the network performance by handling two interfaces of a smart meter, under a PLC smart grid application scenario. The main contribution of this paper is an extension to RPL routing protocol, which uses the diversity of communications technologies to construct the routing graph.

The remainder of the paper is organized as follows. We describe the routing protocol RPL and related works in Sect. 2, before presenting our interface management methods in Sect. 3. We present our evaluation platform and results in Sect. 4, before concluding in Sect. 5.

2   Related Works

RPL [3] is a routing protocol that organizes the network topology in a Directed Acyclic Graph (DAG). Vertices between nodes have a direction and a "non-circular" property. The routing graph must have at least one root, which is a node with no outgoing edge, because of the acyclic characteristic of the DAG. To construct the topology, RPL uses the destination oriented DAG (DODAG) where only one root is defined. A rank is assigned to each node in the DAG to indicate a virtual position in the topology. Each node in the network sends periodic messages to notify routing information such as the rank or the DODAGID to other nodes using the 'DODAG Information Object' (DIO).

A node can determine whether it is up or down in the DODAG thanks to the rank contained in the DIO. If it is down, which means the received rank is smaller than the rank of the receiver node, it may select the sender as a preferred parent and computes its own rank by deriving the rank advertised in the DIO. In RPL, the Objective Function (OF) manages the parent selection and the rank computation. A set of routing metrics are proposed in [7], and the OF defines how to convert those metrics into a rank value. Note that during the lifetime of the network, a node will receive many DIO messages, which allow updating the structure of the network. A new node may be selected as preferred parent at any time, if link qualities change over time, or whether nodes appear or disappear in the topology. While many contributions on RPL and its performance over a (single interface) wireless network exist, only few works have studied RPL over a PLC network, which has its own specific characteristics [8]. Moreover, only few works have been done using both PLC and wireless communications in a RPL network.

Ben Saad et al. [9] present a heterogeneous architecture based on RF-PLC gateways to make a cooperation between RF-only and PLC-only sensors at the network level. Such an architecture gives improvements in network lifetime and reliability in small topology but could cause severe congestion around gateways in large scale scenario. Ben-Shimol et al. [10] propose an evaluation of RPL in large scale PLC networks using field measurement to configure the simulation channel. They propose a modified RPL OF in order to improve the rank computation to address the constrains of the PLC network. Their contribution shows improvements in the DODAG formation, using more control messages for DODAG maintenance, which raises the issue of large scale PLC networks. In the same context, but in a hybrid network this time, Pignolet et al. [11] present an extension of the contiki network stack to handle multiple interfaces. They propose to use one instance per technology for the routing operation but the interface management is not addressed. A smart grid scenario is also studied in Cooja simulator to test the repair mechanism benefits of having two interfaces nodes. While those works are mainly based on the multiple instance feature of RPL, we propose in the next section an objective function that deal with multiple interface by using only one RPL instance. Ropitault et al. [12] present some recommendations for RPL parameters for smart grid networks. They show that RPL parameters selection has to be carefully set for narrow-band PLC networks as well as IEEE 802.15.4 multihop AMI networks. This shows that carefully set parameters for each networks, by using multiple instance, or using an hybrid objective function, could lead to better results than a trade of between the two networks characteristics.

3   Hybrid Objective Function

In this section, we present the link evaluation process, two parent selection algorithms and a re-transmission scheme to manage multiple interfaces nodes. We consider that every nodes in the network may have a PLC and a RF interface and is potentially able to communicate via those two heterogeneous interfaces, each having their own link qualities with their neighbors. A node stores in a neighbor table the list of its neighbor with the evaluated link quality, as explained below. The selection of a path is performed in two steps. First the routing layer, RPL, selects the next hop, and second the MAC layer selects the interface and/or the modulation to communicate with that next hop.

3.1   Link Evaluation

Both PLC and radio interfaces can support multiple modulations. The modulation is chosen by the MAC layer depending on the link quality. The better the link quality, the faster the modulation. Neighbors periodically exchange messages to constantly supervise the link quality. Packets are sent using each modulation and statistics allow to determine which modulations are possible. Once all media are evaluated, the metrics about the link quality (SNR, ETX, etc.) in addition to the best modulation are updated in the neighbor table, for each interface of a given neighbor. These metrics are also updated when a data traffic is exchanged between a node and its neighbors.

3.2   The Parent Oriented (PO) Solution

The objective of the PO solution is to make a single DODAG in a single RPL instance, by merging the capabilities of the heterogeneous interfaces. We propose to modify the RPL parent selection by considering a node ability to communicate with multiple interfaces in the OF. When the network starts, nodes send DIO using both interfaces. If no metrics are available to determine the modulation to use (e.g. the link evaluation returned no results, or has failed), a default modulation is used, which should be the slowest available.

During the selection of the preferred parent among a parent set, potential parents that have only one active interface will be downgraded comparing to multi-interfaces candidates. To do so, we compute an hybrid metric when the OF is called to calculate the rank of the node. If the neighbor is accessible only with one technology (either because it is out of range, or because it is not an hybrid node), the missing metric will be set to a default value, similar to a broken link. Consequently, the node is penalized since it cannot offer the benefit of

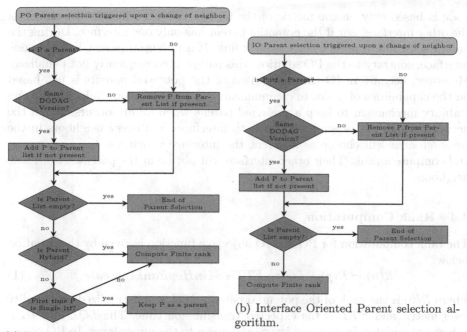

(a) Parent Oriented Parent selection algorithm

(b) Interface Oriented Parent selection algorithm.

Fig. 1. Parent selection algorithms of PO and IO objective functions.

heterogeneous communication. To increase the stability of the DODAG, when a preferred parent node looses one of its interface because of a failure, we propose to keep it as the preferred parent until the OF is called again for a parent selection. Consequently, we keep a track of hybrid parent in the routing table, and if a preferred parent that just become single interface is compared to other node in the parent set, the parent selection algorithm will keep the previous metrics and therefore, the rank is not altered. At the next OF call, this preferred parent is compared to other node in the parent set without any stability privilege, it means that unless its metrics are better than other potential parents, it will result in a parent switch. Once the hybrid parent is chosen, it has the possibility to forward message on either of the two available interfaces. If a node can communicate with a potential parent through a hybrid link, the node will select the interface with the best metric for the forwarding.

3.3 The Interface Oriented (IO) Solution

The purpose of the IO solution is to make a DODAG in a single RPL instance by considering each link with a neighbor in a given technology as an independent potential parent. In that way, the objective function always chose the potential parent with the best link as the preferred parent. The rank computation of a node is based only on the metric of the best interface no matter the metric of the other interface, nor if the potential parent has only one interface. During the parent selection, a node evaluates each link. If a potential parent has only one interface, contrary to the PO solution, this parent is consequently not penalized. Moreover, because in IO the comparison of the potential parents is not based on the capabilities of nodes to communicate via heterogeneous links, there is no stability mechanism to keep a preferred parent when failure occurs. When the network starts, nodes send DIO on both interfaces and every neighbors in the coverage area will choose as a parent the interface which has the best metric and compute a rank. Their other interface will not be in the parent set of those neighbors.

3.4 Rank Computation

The rank computation for PO and IO objective function is given by the equation below:

$$R(n) = R(p) + LQL * ETT * MinHopRankIncrease \tag{1}$$

where $R(p)$ is the rank of the potential parent, LQL is a normalized link quality level metric and ETT is the expected transmission time. The LQL and ETT values are updated by the mac layers and given to the upper layer. In PO objective function, the LQL value of a link with a potential parent is the average value of the two interfaces LQL. The LQL value of a penalized interface is set to the lowest quality level (7) when an interface fails. In IO objective function, the LQL and ETT values of the selected interface are used to compute the rank.

3.5 Re-transmission

To overcome a transmission failure on hybrid nodes, we propose an algorithm that is applicable to both PO or IO solutions. Let us consider a node with two interfaces, interface A which has the best metric, (thus it will be chosen for the transmission) and interface B the other one. If the node sends a packet with interface A and this attempt fails, the first re-transmission happens by changing to the interface B with the highest modulation registered in the neighbor table. If this second attempt fails

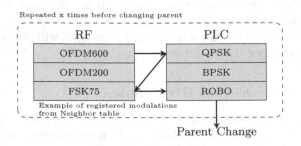

Fig. 2. Re-transmission scheme example.

again, the node will change again to interface A and select the lowest modulation registered for this interface. In case of another fail, the node will make a last change to interface B and select the lowest transmission available.

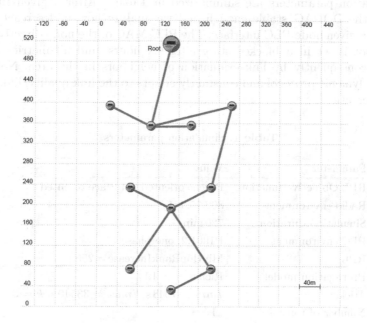

Fig. 3. Hybrid topology example

4   Performance Evaluation

In this section, we describe our simulation platform and the different parameters used to see how much the network could benefit from having two interfaces using the PO and IO solutions comparing to a single PLC interface network.

4.1   Simulation

We have created a smart grid scenario that consists of a simple data collecting application. We have developed a new framework in the Riverbed Modeler 18.5 network simulator. After the initialization phase where all nodes define their preferred parent toward the root, each node periodically sends data packets to the root (every minutes). Our evaluation model considers hybrid nodes with a network layer, where RPL operates, that shares two separate MAC/Physical layers. Thus, the node could send and receive message via PLC and Wireless 802.15.4e/g. The propagation model used in our RF model is a Rician fading and interference are set as probabilistic drops related to used modulation and *RSSI*. The RF range distance limit is set to 850m. We use a smart controller between the MAC and the network layer that is in charge of the radio and PLC link evaluation and the retransmission policy scheme. Each scenario consists of a topology made of eleven routers. The PLC has an attenuation of 9dB/m and 3db at derivations and the PLC topology is given in Fig. 3.

Simulation parameters are summarized in Table 1. After a given time, we consider the DODAG stable enough and we analyze how nodes react to the failure of a given node PLC interface. The PLC MAC of the node directly linked to the root is set in a blocked state after six hours, and all metrics will be updated consequently by link evaluation of neighbors in the area. Note that RPL is a dynamic protocol and constantly adapts to the link quality, link failure and link creation.

Table 1. Simulation parameters

Parameter	Value
RPL Objective function	Parent oriented/interface oriented
Radio environment	802.15.4e/g
Simulation duration	720 min
PLC environment	P1901.2, one phase
RPL	MinHopRankIncrease $= 256$
Propagation model	Rician, $k = 10$
Trickle	$Imin = 1048\,\text{s},\ Imax = 33540\,\text{s},\ k = 3$
Number of routers	11
Distance between routers	80 to 120 m
Runs	100
Traffic type, rate	MP2P, 1 pkt/min

4.2   Results

Figure 4a shows the average of the number of parent changes that occur in the whole DODAG. As the Parent Oriented (PO) solution keeps a parent even if it loses an interface, it offers the best stability comparing to the IO solution. The low number of parent changes of the single PLC scenario is mainly due to the fact that nodes have less possibility to change parent, having less potential parents in the parent set. The Interface Oriented (IO) solution, selecting the best metric without considering the heterogeneous nature of a node results in an unstable DODAG. However, as the parent selection is also governed by a rank stretching to lower the parent switching phenomenon, carefully selecting the rank stretching value could increase the stability of the DODAG at the cost of keeping a parent with the non optimal metric. In Fig. 4b, we study the average end-to-end delay of each solution around the failure occurring after six hours of simulation. We can observe that both PO and IO solutions give similar results, the failure having no consequences on the average end-to-end delay: after the failure the average end-to-end delay remains around 1 s. Concerning the single PLC scenario, the failure of the interface results in a slight increase of the end-to-end delay.

In Fig. 5a we analyze the number of sent DIO messages to maintain the DODAG. We show that hybrid networks considerably reduce the number of RPL DIO messages in this scenario, taking benefit from the stability of the radio network. The low number of sent DIO compared to the high number of Parent Change of the IO solution is counter-intuitive. This result is due to the way parent changes are counted in IO solution. When a parent node stays parent but change interface, this count as a parent change, where in PO solution, it does not. Figures 5b and 6a show the packet delivery ratio (PDR) at the root. We can observe that the median value of the single PLC scenario PDR is around 50% because of many re-transmission and packet losses. The PO solution offers the best PDR taking benefit from the stability of the DODAG, where the instability of IO solution leads to more packet losses. In Fig. 6b we analyze the global number of hops for every packets received by the root. In smart grid networks, the number of hops is critical as it should result in more delay or more hidden nodes.

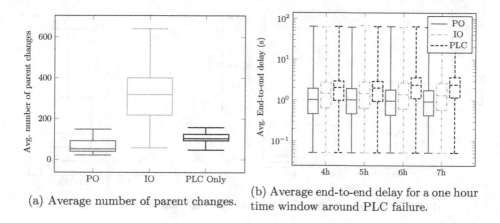

(a) Average number of parent changes.

(b) Average end-to-end delay for a one hour time window around PLC failure.

Fig. 4. Parent change and end-to-end delay for 12 h simulation.

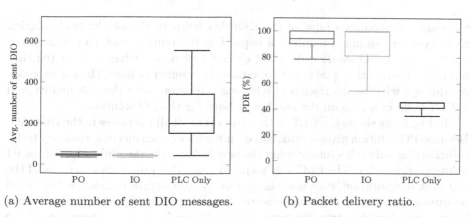

(a) Average number of sent DIO messages.

(b) Packet delivery ratio.

Fig. 5. DIO messages and packet delivery ratio for 12 h simulation.

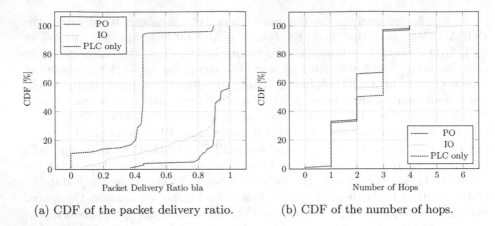

(a) CDF of the packet delivery ratio.   (b) CDF of the number of hops.

Fig. 6. Packet delivery ratio and number of hops for 12 h simulation.

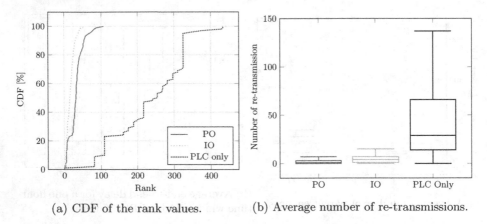

(a) CDF of the rank values.   (b) Average number of re-transmissions.

Fig. 7. Rank and re-transmissions for 12 h simulation.

Showing the maximum hops of the DODAG helps to choose the best solution that gives the minimum number of hops. The IO solution shows a maximum of six hops where PO solution does not exceed four hops. It has to be noted that our objective function goal is not to reduce the number of hops, the consequence of adding a wireless interface and selecting the parent over the link quality and *ETT* results in a gain on the number of hops for the PO solution.

In Fig. 7a we shows the CDF of the rank values of all the nodes in the DODAG. Because PO solution gives a rank based on both interface metrics, contrary to IO solution that only takes into account the best link metric, the rank values of the IO solution are smaller. The PLC only scenario gives high rank values because of the PO rank computation, each node is seen as a single interface node. In Fig. 7b we monitored the number of re-transmissions for each solution. The PLC only scenario shows a number of re-transmissions which indicates that the performance of the network is more impacted by the failure than the other solution.

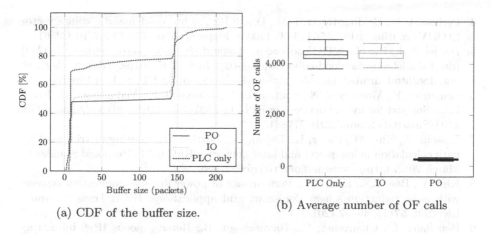

(a) CDF of the buffer size.

(b) Average number of OF calls

Fig. 8. Buffer size and OF calls for 12 h simulation.

5 Conclusion

In this paper, we presented two solutions to manage hybrid network in RPL for smart grids. Using the straightforward IO solution, which selects the preferred parent by only looking for the best link, we could observe a major improvement comparing to a single interface PLC network. Using the Parent Oriented solution, we compare potential parents and promote the selection of hybrid nodes as preferred parent. For nodes which have a single interface, we increase the merged link quality with that neighbor in order to decrease its attractiveness. We also presented a re-transmission scheme that takes into account the number of interfaces of a node, to help a node not to change its preferred parent too frequently. By means of simulations using realistic PLC and RF channels, we showed that PO and IO solution perform systematically better than a single interface network. A future direction of this work is to implement a multiple DODAG/Instance algorithm to have a specific Objective Function for each network specificity. Another concern would be also to fully use the potential of the hybrid network by sending duplicate data on both interfaces in order to improve latency and reliability.

References

1. Hauser, C.H., Bakken, D.E., Bose, A.: A failure to communicate: next generation communication requirements, technologies, and architecture for the electric power grid. IEEE Power Energy Mag. **3**(2), 47–55 (2005). https://doi.org/10.1109/MPAE.2005.1405870
2. de Oliveira, L.G., Colen, G.R., Ribeiro, M.V., Vinck, A.J.H.: Narrow-band interference error correction in coded OFDM-based PLC systems, pp. 13–18, March 2016. https://doi.org/10.1109/ISPLC.2016.7476279
3. Winter, T., et al.: RPL: IPv6 routing protocol for low-power and lossy networks. RFC 6550 (Proposed Standard), Mar 2012

4. Perkins, C.E., Belding-Royer, E.M., Das, S.R.: Ad hoc on-demand distance vector (AODV) routing. RFC **3561**, 1–37 (2003). https://doi.org/10.17487/RFC3561
5. Daniel Park, D.: 6LoWPAN ad hoc on-demand distance vector routing (LOAD) (draft-daniel-6lowpan-load-adhoc-routing-03), June 2007. https://datatracker.ietf.org/doc/html/draft-daniel-6lowpan-load-adhoc-routing-03, work in Progress
6. Lemercier, F., Montavont, N., Toutain, L., Vijayasankar, K., Vedantham, R., Itron, P.C.: Support for hybrid network in RPL, pp. 527–532 (2016). https://doi.org/10.1109/SmartGridComm.2016.7778815
7. Vasseur, J., Kim, M., Pister, K., Dejean, N., Barthel, D.: Routing metrics used for path calculation in low-power and lossy networks. RFC 6551 (Proposed Standard), March 2012. http://www.ietf.org/rfc/rfc6551.txt
8. Kim, Y., Bae, J.N., Kim, J.Y.: Performance of power line communication systems with noise reduction scheme for smart grid applications. IEEE Trans. Consum. Electron. **57**(1), 46–52 (2011)
9. Ben Saad, L., Chauvenet, C., Tourancheau, B.: Heterogeneous IPv6 infrastructure for smart energy efficient building, September 2011. https://hal.inria.fr/hal-00646061
10. Ben-Shimol, Y., Zohar, Y.: Routing in large realistic PLC smart-grids, pp. 1–6, April 2017. https://doi.org/10.1109/ISPLC.2017.7897115
11. Pignolet, Y.A., Rinis, I., Dzung, D., Karaagac, A.: Heterogeneous multi-interface routing: networking stack and simulator extensions, pp. 1–6 (2012). https://doi.org/10.1109/MASS.2012.6708526
12. Ropitault, T., Lampropulos, A., Pelov, A., Toutain, L., Vedantham, R., Chiumiento, P.: Doing it right - recommendations for RPL in PLC-based networks for the smart grid, pp. 452–457 (2014). https://doi.org/10.1109/SmartGridComm.2014.7007688

Latency and Lifetime Optimization for k-Anycast Routing Algorithm in Wireless Sensor Networks

Lucas Leão[✉] and Violeta Felea

FEMTO-ST Institute, University of Bourgogne Franche-Comté, CNRS,
DISC, 16 route de Gray, 25030 Besançon, France
{lucas.leao,violeta.felea}@femto-st.fr

Abstract. Wireless Sensor Network (WSN) applications frequently require different objectives, such as reliability, timely communication and longevity. To cope with that, a WSN can be conceived with multiple sinks and routing protocols designed over different communication schemes. In this paper, we address the communication latency and the network lifetime issues in Multi-Sink WSN deployment. We propose GeoK, a k-anycast geographic routing protocol that considers a linear combination of network metrics during the decision process of the next hop. Packets are forwarded over exactly k sinks, with targets and duplications being defined on the fly. Simulation results show a better performance for GeoK, with improvements of approximately 13% for the average latency, and 30% for the maximum energy consumption, compared to existing work.

Keywords: Wireless Sensor Networks · Routing · k-anycast
Latency · Network lifetime · Geographic routing

1 Introduction

The Multi-Sink Wireless Sensor Network (MS-WSN) is a particular case of the WSN containing multiple sinks. Compared to Single Sink solutions, the use of several sinks normally leads to better network performance. On top of that, it also improves the network manageability, providing more flexibility and continuity [8]. By increasing the number of sinks, the number of hops a packet has to travel before reaching any of the sinks is decreased. It has a direct impact on the performance of metrics such as energy consumption and latency.

There are different communication schemes in MS-WSN implementations. **Unicast:** a path towards one of the sinks is defined and reused for future communications. **Anycast:** data is addressed to a group of sinks. It can be 1-anycast, when data is forwarded to anyone of the sinks, or k-anycast when data must reach any k sinks. **Multicast:** information is routed towards all sinks.

The k-anycast is a flexible communication scheme. A k-anycast routing protocol may behave as 1-anycast routing solution when $k = 1$ or even as a multicast

© Springer Nature Switzerland AG 2018
N. Montavont and G. Z. Papadopoulos (Eds.): ADHOC-NOW 2018, LNCS 11104, pp. 39–50, 2018.
https://doi.org/10.1007/978-3-030-00247-3_4

routing protocol when k equals the number of all sinks. However, the complexity of the algorithm increases, specially when the target sinks and duplications are decided on the fly, during the packet forwarding. In those cases, the packet is not addressed to one specific sink, but to a group of sinks, and the final destination is decided on the way based on the network metrics at each hop.

In this paper we propose GeoK, a k-anycast geographic routing algorithm focused on network lifetime and latency optimizations, capable of assuring the packet routing to exactly k different sinks. Our algorithm differs from the literature by combining several techniques to reduce both the latency and the maximum energy consumption. The next hop decision is taken using a linear combination of network metrics, along with dynamic weights. The metrics weights vary according to the ratio of k and the available sinks. Because of that, the paths are constantly changed during the lifetime of the network, which balances the energy consumption. Both duplication and target sinks are decided on the fly. We also combine and adapt two different void handling techniques, making use of the face routing and the passive participation [3]. Finally, when packets must be duplicated, we benefit from MAC-level information to create an ordered sending list based on the duty-cycle schedule of the neighbor nodes participating in the forwarding task.

The remainder of this paper is organized as follows. Section 2 presents a brief discussion on the existing works in MS-WSN adressing k-anycast routing. Section 3 traces our assumptions and the system model. The description of our solution is detailed in Sect. 4, along with the testing scenarios and the discussion of the performance evaluation in Sect. 5. We conclude the paper in Sect. 6 with the future perspectives.

2   Related Works

The number of works dedicated to k-anycast routing is limited. Most of the solutions are designed as 1-anycast routing protocols. Nevertheless, an 1-anycast routing solution could be used as k-anycast if we assume that packets are duplicated at source and forwarded in sequence. The problem with this strategy is that there is no guarantee that k different sinks will be reached. Depending on the forwarding criteria, chances are that the k packets will be forwarded to the exactly same sink. In that sense, k-anycast solutions are essentially different from 1-anycast protocols, with added complexity and special objectives.

The authors in [2] propose RelBAS, a data gathering algorithm with a fault recovery scheme specially designed to assure reliability. The algorithm considers the construction of disjoint trees, rooted at each sink. However, the sensor nodes serving as forwarders are also disjoint, meaning that a node serves as forwarder to exactly one tree. In order to improve reliability, the solution considers forwarding the packet to exactly k sinks, which are decided in advance. The nodes are always part of exactly k trees, in order to forward the packet to the k sinks.

In [5] we find RPKAC, a routing protocol for Rechargeable MS-WSN designed to reduce network latency and optimize the energy consumption, but focused on assuring the delivery by forwarding the packets to k sinks. The algorithm builds spanning trees rooted at the source node, with nodes sending route request messages in order to define the routing path. The neighbor nodes reply with their cost to reach a sink, and the current node decides to join an existing path with the lowest cost. The cost is calculated based on the linear combination of four metrics: hop count to sink, latency, energy cost and energy replenish rate.

The main objective in KanGuRou [7] is to guarantee the packet delivery to exactly k sinks and at the same time reduce the overall energy consumption. The strategy considers a geographic routing towards a set of sinks. The path is constructed in a greedy way. The current node builds a spanning tree to k sinks with minimum cost. The next hop is decided based on the cost of the energy-weighted shortest path (ESP). The solution assumes an adaptable transmission range in order to reduce the energy cost. At each hop, the algorithm calculates the cost over progress and decides to duplicate the packet towards different paths in order to reach k sinks. When a packet is duplicated, it is targeted to a set of specific sinks, in order to assure the reception by k-sinks. The void areas are handled using a recovery mode with face routing.

Routing solutions [2,5] are based on the hop-count distance to the sinks. This strategy implies either higher network topology knowledge or an important setup phase, with nodes discovering their hop-count distance to each sink. In [7] the focus is on reducing the energy consumption, favoring transmissions to closer nodes. Since the transmission range is variable, the energy cost to transmit a packet to a closer node is reduced. However, the number of hops is increased and consequently the latency.

3   System Model and Assumptions

We represent a MS-WSN as a graph $G = (V, E)$, where V represents the set of all nodes and E the set of existing wireless links. Each $e \in E$ corresponds to a pair of nodes (i, j) as long as i and j, with $i, j \in V$, are within each other's transmission range (symmetric link). The set of neighbors of i is represented by V_i. We also specify that $V = \{S \cup N\}$ where S represents the set of sink nodes and N the set of sensor nodes, with $S \cap N = \emptyset$. The number of sinks to be reached is denoted by k, with $0 < k \leq |S|$.

We assume that every node is aware of its own geographic position and the geographic position of all sinks. For simplification, the geographic positions are represented by the Cartesian coordinates (x, y), and the distance is always the euclidean distance represented as $|ij|$ with $i, j \in V$. We also assume that packets are generated by sensor nodes only, and that k is given and remains constant for each packet generation. For the energy consumption, we follow the radio model in [6], which considers distance and packet size for the dissipated energy during transmission and reception.

We consider two types of networks: with void areas and without void areas. A network with void areas is defined by the existence of a specific node out of the transmission range of a particular sink and for which there is no other neighbor node that presents a better geographic progress towards that sink than the node itself. In summary, $\exists\{n, s_i\}, n \in V, s_i \in S, (n, s_i) \notin E$ such that $|ns_i| < |v_j s_i|$ for all $v_j \in V_n$. In a MS-WSN it is possible for a node to be in the void area of one or more sinks. The amount of void areas is a fixed number based on a particular node and the set of sinks. However, since k sinks must be reached, the probability of entering a void area increases with a higher k. It is because the selection of a sink is a conditional event that depends on the previous selection.

4   Geographic k-Anycast Routing

We propose GeoK, a geographic routing protocol for MS-WSN that assures the packet routing to exactly k sinks using a k-anycast communication scheme, focused on reducing the overall latency and maximizing the network lifetime. The next hop is selected by the current node based on the calculation of weighted metrics. The selection of the targeted sinks is done based on the ordered list of energy cost to reach each of the available sinks. The algorithm can be divided into three steps with a preprocessing at the beginning of the algorithm, and the actual routing at the end. The preprocessing is responsible for retrieving the packet information and triggering the GeoK processing. We denote the current value of k as k_{curr} and the set of available sinks as S_a. The first processing step is responsible for filtering the neighbor nodes, in order to create a list of candidate forwarders. The filtering takes place by eliminating the neighbor nodes with negative progress and neighbors in void areas. If no neighbor is found, the recovery mode is triggered and a neighbor is selected using a void handling technique. The second processing step is dedicated to effectively selecting the forwarders. The candidates are evaluated based on the weighted metrics, and a forwarder is selected for each sink, respecting the size of k_{curr}. The third processing step is triggered only if $k_{curr} < |S_a|$, and it is responsible for distributing the remaining sinks throughout the selected forwarders. Finally, the actual routing is responsible for the packet transmission and an eventual duplication.

Preprocessing. The solution starts at the current node with the execution of the pre-processing whenever a new packet is generated or received and has to be forwarded. The first step is to check if the current node is a sink itself and if it is in the list of target sinks. If the current node is one of the target sinks, the k_{curr} must be decremented, and the current node must be removed from the list of available sinks. If k_{curr} is still greater than zero, the multi-hop process continues with the selection of the new forwarder with the Algorithm 1.

First Step: Candidates Filtering. The candidate filtering step is responsible for creating a list L of candidate forwarders. The list can be composed entirely of candidates with positive progress, candidates issued from the recovery mode, or a mixed list, with candidates presenting positive progress and candidates issued from the recovery mode. Since the algorithm has to find a suitable forwarder for each packet, it is possible that for networks with void areas, only part of the k can be covered by candidates with positive progress. Because we need to assure the delivery to exactly k sinks, it is necessary to complete the candidate list with the neighbor nodes issued from the recovery mode. The filtering process is described in Algorithm 1.

The filtering starts by checking if the node itself offers a positive progress in relation to the previous hop (line 3). If the current node n progress to the set of available sinks (S_a) is smaller than the value from the previous hop, it means that the packet was in recovery mode and no positive progress was yet found. In this case, the packet must keep the recovery mode status and the next hop is selected using the face routing [3]. The recovery algorithm follows the same principles of

---

Algorithm 1. $[F, p_{new}] = GeoK(n, k_{curr}, S_a, V_n, H, p_{prev})$

Input: n: current node, k_{curr}: current number of sinks to be reached, S_a: set of available sinks, V_n: set of neighbors of n, H: set of neighbor nodes in void areas for a set of sinks, p_{prev}: previous value for the packet progress towards S_a

Output: F: forwarders with the sinks and k, p_{curr}: current progress towards S_a

1: $F \leftarrow \emptyset; L \leftarrow \emptyset$ /* Set of pairs [candidate, sink] */
2: $p_{new} \leftarrow ProgressTowards(n, S_a)$
3: **if** $p_{new} > p_{prev}$ **then**
4:     $S' \leftarrow \emptyset$ /* Set of found sinks */
5:     **for all** $v_j \in V_n$ **do**
6:         **for all** $s_i \in S_a$ **do**
7:             **if** $dist(n, s_i) > dist(v_j, s_i)$ **and** $\{[v_j, s_i]\} \notin H$ **then**
8:                 $L \leftarrow L \cup \{[v_j, s_i]\}$
9:                 **if** $S' \cap \{s_i\} = \emptyset$ **then**
10:                     $S' \leftarrow S' \cup \{s_i\}$
11:                 **end if**
12:             **end if**
13:         **end for**
14:     **end for**
15:     $k' \leftarrow |S'|$
16:     **if** $k' < k_{curr}$ **then**
17:         /* Lack of candidates, void handling is triggered */
18:         **if** $k' > 0$ **then**
19:             $F \leftarrow Fwd(n, L, S', k')$ /* Select the forwarders among the candidates */
20:             $k_{curr} \leftarrow k_{curr} - k'$
21:         **end if**
22:         $S' \leftarrow S_a \backslash S'$
23:         $SendVoidNotification(n, V_n, S')$
24:         $L = Recovery(V_n, S', k_{curr})$ /* Recovery mode using face routing */
25:     **end if**
26: **else**
27:     /* Current node does not offer a positive progress */
28:     $L = Recovery(V_n, S_a, k_{curr})$ /* Recovery mode using face routing */
29:     $p_{new} \leftarrow p_{prev}$
30: **end if**
31: $F \leftarrow F \cup Fwd(n, L, S_a, k_{curr})$
32: **return** $[F, p_{new}]$

---

the work in [7]. If the current node offers a positive progress in relation to the previous hop, the normal candidate selection is started. The algorithm selects only the neighbor nodes with positive progress to at least one sink, and excludes the neighbors that have already announced being in a void area (line 7). The values in H represent the set of pairs $[v_j, s_i]$ having the neighbor node in a void area for a given sink. The algorithm creates a second sink list, with the sinks for which a neighbor with positive progress was detected (line 10). The size of this list represents the maximum possible k'. If k' is smaller than the k_{curr}, it means that it was not possible to find a positive progress towards all necessary sinks (line 18). In this case, the algorithm tries to create a preliminary list of forwarders for the found sinks and neighbors (line 19), and completes the list with the candidates issued from the recovery mode (line 24). At the same time, and for the set of sinks the algorithm cannot find a suitable neighbor candidate, the void announcement is triggered (line 23). The algorithm creates a list of sinks for which the current node is in a void area, and a broadcast message is sent with the list in order to inform the neighbor nodes. Each node receiving the broadcast message updates its own H set with the information from n.

Second Step: Forwarders Selection. The forwarders selection stage is focused on selecting the most suitable forwarders (the F list) based on the decision metrics (distance, consumed energy and duplication avoidance) and the defined weights for each metric. Each entry in the F list represents a different

---

Algorithm 2. $F = Fwd(n, L, S_a, k_{curr})$

Input: n: current node, L: set of candidate forwarders with respective sinks, S_a: set of available sinks, k_{curr}: number of sinks to be reached

Output: F: list with the set of forwarders with the respective sinks and k

1: $F \leftarrow \emptyset$; $S_{used} \leftarrow \emptyset$ /* Set of selected target sinks */
2: $p_k \leftarrow k_{curr}/|S_a|$ alg:forwarders:4
3: $S' \leftarrow OrderSinksByEnergyCost(n, S_a)$ alg:forwarders:1 /* S': sinks ordered by energy cost */
4: **for all** $s_i \in S'|i \leq k_{curr}$ **do**
5:     $S_{used} \leftarrow S_{used} \cup \{s_i\}$; $R \leftarrow \{v_j|[v_j, s_i] \in L\}$
6:     $v \leftarrow SelectForwarder(n, R, F, s_i, p_k)$
7:     $f \leftarrow find(F, v)$ /* returns the index of the position of v or −1 if nonexistent */
8:     **if** $f < 0$ **then**
9:         $f \leftarrow |F|$
10:     **end if**
11:     $F[f].neighbor \leftarrow v$; $F[f].sinks \leftarrow F[f].sinks \cup \{s_i\}$; $F[f].k \leftarrow F[f].k + 1$
12: **end for**
13: $S'' \leftarrow S'\backslash S_{used}$ /* S'': set of other possible target sinks */
14: **if** $S'' \neq \emptyset$ **then**
15:     /* Distributes the remaining sinks based on the energy cost */
16:     $F = DistributeRemainingSinks(F, S'')$
17: **end if**
18: **return** F

---

forwarder for the packet. It means that if $|F| > 1$ a duplication takes place. The F list contains a structure with the neighbor node responsible for the forwarding task, the list of target sinks and the size of the new k (k_{new}). The list of target sinks may contain exactly k_{new} sinks or more. It depends on the number of available sinks in comparison to k_{curr} and the proximity of the already selected target sink (S_{used}) in relation to the ones not yet selected (S'').

The target sinks must be chosen in a way to reduce the energy consumption and the packet latency. To cope with that, the solution creates an ordered list of sinks based on the energy cost (Algorithm 2, line 3). The first iteration of the ascending ordering process considers the energy cost from the current node to the closest sinks. The energy cost is calculated and the sink having the smallest value is inserted in the list. Then, the next sink is selected based on the minimum energy cost to either the current node or the already selected sink. This process is repeated iteratively until all the available sinks are inserted in the ordered list.

Once the sink list is created, the algorithm starts the process of searching for the most suitable forwarder. The set of candidates having the sink s_i as target is extracted from L (Algorithm 2, line 5), and the selection of the forwarder v is started (Algorithm 2, line 6).

The selection of the most suitable forwarder is executed using the decision metrics and their respective weights. The weights vary according to the ratio between the k_{curr} and the number of available sinks $|S_a|$. Initially, the value of the aggregated metric $\omega[v_j, s_i]$ is computed using the process in 1.

$$\alpha \times \frac{D[v_j, s_i] - min(D[*, s_i])}{max(D[*, s_i]) - min(D[*, s_i])} + \beta \times \frac{E[v_j] - min(E)}{max(E) - min(E)} + \delta \times G(v_j) \quad (1)$$

where D is the list of distances, E is the list consumed energy, G represents a function that returns 0 if the neighbor v_j is already a forwarder and 1 otherwise, α represents the relative weight for the distance metric, β represents the relative weight for the consumed energy metric and δ represents the relative weight for the duplication avoidance metric. Each metric has a different objective. As for instance, the distance metric is focused on selecting the candidate with the highest positive progress towards the target sink. This is important in order to reduce the overall hop count and consequently the latency. The consumed energy metric regards the selection of the node with the smallest consumption, which in time balances the energy consumption, prolonging the network lifetime. Finally, the duplication avoidance accounts for both latency and energy consumption, since the increase of packets in the network not only intensifies the energy consumption, but also multiplies the possibility of congestion and delays. As already mentioned, the weights for each metric are dynamic and adjustable depending on the situation. For a scenario where k is much lower than S, only few duplications may be triggered, and the focus must be on progressing towards the closest sinks, so the weights for the distance metric and energy consumption are higher. On the other hand, if $k = |S|$ the objective changes, and avoiding duplications becomes more important.

The aggregated decision metric ω is calculated using the weighted relative values of the metrics from each candidate. The node having the smallest ω is selected as forwarder. If the selected forwarded v is already part of the forwarders list F, the k value of the existing entry is incremented and the target sink s_i is added to the list of sinks. Otherwise, a new entry is created in F with the new forwarder, which ultimately triggers a duplication (Algorithm 2, lines 7 to 11).

Third Step: Sink Distribution. Since k may be smaller than $|S|$, the destination sink is not fixed, and it may change during the packet forwarding. Even if the forwarders selection makes use of a particular sink as destination to decide on the most suitable forwarder, there are cases where it changes, as for instance when the packet encounters a void area. The change is only possible if $|S_a| > k_{curr}$. In this case, after the forwarders selection, not all sinks are used as destinations $\{S_a \backslash S_{used}\} \neq \emptyset$, and there are remaining sinks to be distributed over the forwarders in F. The distribution process considers the same principle of the sink list ordering, assigning each of the remaining sinks to the forwarder containing the neighbor node or the sinks with the smallest energy cost.

For a remaining sink $s_r \in \{S_a \backslash S_{used}\}$, the algorithm calculates the transmission energy cost E_{tx} from s_r to the forwarder $f_i.neighbor$ where $f_i \in F$ and each of the sinks in $f_i.sinks$. Then, the remaining sink s_r is included in the sink list of the f_i that presents the lowest E_{tx}.

Routing. The actual routing takes place after the forwarders selection. During the actual routing, the packet is duplicated if $|F| > 1$, and it is updated with the forwarder address, the data of the new list of available sinks and the corresponding k. Also as part of the routing process, and for the case a duplication is necessary, the sending order is decided based on the duty cycle of the selected forwarders. The first packet to be sent is the one of the first forwarder to wake-up. The algorithm makes use of the duty-cycle schedule information from the neighbor nodes to determine the encounter moment in order to define the sending order.

5   Simulation and Results

GeoK protocol was developed using Contiki OS [4] and evaluated through simulations using Cooja [4]. The performance of our solution was compared to an existing approach (KanGuRou) [7], that was adapted to Contiki OS and tested with Cooja under the same configurations. The simulation environment and details are outlined in Table 1.

As in Eq. (2) in Table 1, when the number of deployed nodes changes, and if the network area is kept the same, the network deployment density changes. Since we want to keep a similar deployment density over all variations of $|V|$, we make the network area vary with the number of deployed nodes.

The solution performance is evaluated by observing the average latency, defined by the average time a packet takes to be routed from the source to each of the sinks, and the maximum energy consumption, which gives an indication of the network lifetime. As per explanation, we consider a network to be alive as long as all nodes have some energy. Therefore, network lifetime is considered to be the earliest moment at which a node's battery is completely depleted.

Table 1. Configuration for the simulations

Simulation settings	
Deployment density (d)	8 neighbors (on average)
Network area (variable)	$\frac{\pi \times r^2}{d} \times |V|$ (2)
Comm. range (r)	50 m
# of sensors ($|N|$)	50, 100, 150, 200, 250, 300
# of sinks ($|S|$)	10% of the # of sensors
k	20% to 100% of the # of sinks
# of gen. networks	300 with voids / 300 without voids
Packet size	240 bytes
Packet generation	20% chance at every minute for each sensor
Radio type	802.15.4
MAC protocol	CX-MAC, modified version of [1]
Execution time	120 min

The simulation considered two main network scenarios: with void areas and without void areas. The simulation outcome is given likewise considering two series of results. One with a fixed number of sensors and sinks with a variation of k, in order to evaluate the performance of the solution when k increases, reaching $k = |S|$. And the other where the relative k value is fixed and the number of sensors and sinks varies, in order to evaluate the solution scalability.

5.1   Fixed Number of Sensors and Sinks

Networks Without Void Areas: For the scenario with no void areas and a fixed number of nodes and sinks, we can see in Fig. 1a that GeoK shows a better latency performance in relation to KanGuRou, with a growing gain with the increase of k. Although for a small k the options of sinks are better, with nodes being able to choose the closest sinks, the performance of the two solutions are relatively close, with a gain of approximately 4% in favor of GeoK. When k becomes larger, the options of sinks become limited, and the packet must be forwarded to sinks that are much farther. In those scenarios, GeoK shows an improvement of over 10% in relation to KanGuRou. It is explained by the fact that for farther sinks our algorithm is able to find better routes, performing in average 20% fewer hops to reach the more distant sinks. Regarding the maximum energy consumption, we can see in Fig. 1b that GeoK has also a better performance when compared to KanGuRou. We can notice a maximum gain of almost 30% and a minimum of approximately 13%. That is explained by the nature of our solution that is designed in a way to use different routes during the protocol execution. It means that the energy consumption is distributed, which reduces the chances of nodes depleting their batteries in early stages. Contrarily to the average latency, the performance gain of the maximum energy consumption eases with the increase of k. It is justified by the increase of packets being forwarded.

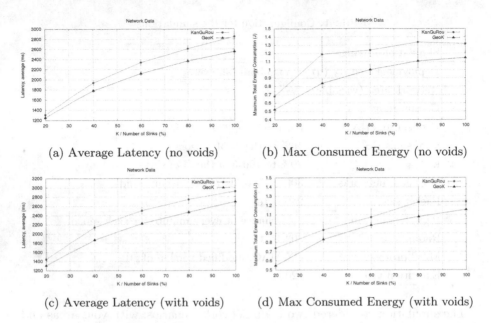

(a) Average Latency (no voids)   (b) Max Consumed Energy (no voids)

(c) Average Latency (with voids)   (d) Max Consumed Energy (with voids)

Fig. 1. 300 sensors, 30 sinks and k varying with a step of 20% of the sinks

When k is larger, it means that at some point the packet is duplicated. Since there are more packets circulating in the network, the energy consumption raises and the performance decreases. In average, packet duplication is in 30% higher with GeoK when compared to KanGuRou. In order to have a faster progress towards a sink, GeoK is constrained to diverge the path in a earlier stage of the forwarding process, so duplications take place more frequently.

Networks with Void Areas: When the network with void areas are considered for the same number of sensors and sinks, we can also notice a good performance for GeoK. For the latency, we can see in Fig. 1c that GeoK has even better results when compared to KanGuRou. That is explained by the void announcement strategy. Since nodes in void areas advertise on their situation, the neighbor nodes may avoid forwarding packets through the problematic area, resulting in better delivery time. However, the performance gain decreases with the increase of k. That happens because with the increment of k the possibility of entering in a void area grows as well. Packets must enter in Recovery Mode more frequently, which increases the hop count. Nevertheless, similarly to the case without void areas, the average hop count for GeoK is smaller than KanGuRou, resulting in lower latencies. GeoK presents a maximum gain of almost 13% and a minimum of approximately 8%.

In terms of maximum energy consumption, GeoK also performed better than KanGuRou, with a maximum gain of almost 26% and a minimum of approximately 7%, as displayed in Fig. 1d. The same tendency observed in the scenario without void areas is noticed when void areas are present. The gain is reduced with the increase of k. Once again, it can be justified by the fact

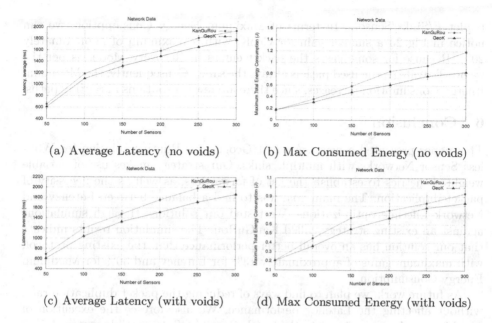

(a) Average Latency (no voids)   (b) Max Consumed Energy (no voids)

(c) Average Latency (with voids)   (d) Max Consumed Energy (with voids)

Fig. 2. 50 to 300 sensors, sinks as 10% of sensors and k as 40% of sinks

that more duplications are necessary, increasing the number of packets in the network. When a void area is detected for a specific sink, the node may decide to split the packet in different ways, so the void area is bypassed.

5.2   Variable Number of Sensors and Sinks

Networks Without Void Areas: With the relative k fixed to 40% of the sinks, and the number of sensors and sinks varying, we intend to analyze the behavior of the solution in terms of scalability. For the scenario without void areas, we can notice that GeoK has better performances for both average latency and maximum energy consumption, as in Figs. 2a and b respectively. The increase in network size translates to even better results for GeoK in terms of maximum energy consumption, with a gain of approximately 30%, and a moderate improvement of the Latency of 7% on average. By increasing the network size, the possibilities of different paths is also increased. The packets are able to alternate through different route paths, leading to better energy balance and consequently a smaller maximum energy consumption. However, the gain on the average latency performance becomes stable, even with the increase of the network size. It is because the ratio k/sinks/sensors is kept the same. The k is a ratio of the number of sinks, and the number of sinks is a ratio of the number of sensors.

Networks with Void Areas: for the case with void areas, we can also notice a performance gain of approximately 12% for the Average Latency, as shown in Fig. 2c. The better results for GeoK are again due to the void announcements strategy. And the stability of the gain comes from the proportionality of the triplet k/Sinks/Sensors. In terms of Maximum Energy Consumption, we can notice in Fig. 2d a smaller gain for GeoK, with a maximum of approximately 20%. Because for some cases the packet enters in Recovery Mode, as per the recovery strategy, the used path is always the same. Consequently, the Maximum Energy Consumption increases, since there are fewer variations in routing paths.

6   Conclusion

This paper presented a new k-Anycast Geographic Routing solution for Wireless Sensor Networks with multiple sinks. Our strategy makes use of variable weighted metrics to establish the list of forwarders, as well as the necessity of packet duplication. The main goal was to find a balance between Latency and Network Lifetime optimizations. We tested our solutions through simulations against an existing strategy called KanGuRou. The simulation results indicate that our solution has an overall better performance than the existing protocol, with maximum gains of approximately 13% for Latency and 30% for Maximum Energy Consumption.

As future work, we plan to find ways of reducing the packet duplication rate, without affecting the Latency performance. We also foresee the execution of real-life experiments using a testbed with Contiki OS compatible motes.

Acknowledgments. This work was partially supported by the Brazilian National Council for Scientific and Technological Development (CNPq). Computations were performed on the supercomputer facilities of the Mésocentre de calcul de Franche-Comté.

References

1. Buettner, M., Yee, G.V., Anderson, E., Han, R.: X-MAC: a short preamble MAC protocol for duty-cycled wireless sensor networks. In: Proceedings of the 4th International Conference on Embedded Networked Sensor Systems, pp. 307–320. ACM (2006)
2. Chakraborty, S., Chakraborty, S., Nandi, S., Karmakar, S.: Fault resilience in sensor networks: distributed node-disjoint multi-path multi-sink forwarding. J. Netw. Comput. Appl. **57**, 85–101 (2015)
3. Chen, D., Varshney, P.K.: A survey of void handling techniques for geographic routing in wireless networks. IEEE Commun. Surv. Tutor. **9**(1), 50–67 (2007)
4. Contiki OS: The OS for the IoT. http://www.contiki-os.org/. Accessed 20 Mar 2018
5. Gao, D., Lin, H., Liu, X.: Routing protocol for k-anycast communication in rechargeable wireless sensor networks. Comput. Stand. Interfaces **43**, 12–20 (2016)
6. Heinzelman, W.R., Chandrakasan, A., Balakrishnan, H.: Energy-efficient communication protocol for wireless microsensor networks. In: 33rd Annual Hawaii International Conference on System Sciences, pp. 1–10. IEEE (2000)
7. Mitton, N., Simplot-Ryl, D., Voge, M.-E., Zhang, L.: Energy efficient k-anycast routing in multi-sink wireless networks with guaranteed delivery. In: Li, X.-Y., Papavassiliou, S., Ruehrup, S. (eds.) ADHOC-NOW 2012. LNCS, vol. 7363, pp. 385–398. Springer, Heidelberg (2012). https://doi.org/10.1007/978-3-642-31638-8_29
8. Poe, W.Y., Schmitt, J.B.: Self-organized sink placement in large-scale wireless sensor networks. In: IEEE International Symposium on Modeling, Analysis & Simulation of Computer and Telecommunication Systems, pp. 1–3. IEEE (2009)

5G and mmWave

A City-Scale ITS-G5 Network
for Next-Generation Intelligent
Transportation Systems: Design Insights
and Challenges

Ioannis Mavromatis(✉), Andrea Tassi, Robert J. Piechocki, and Andrew Nix

Department of Electrical and Electronic Engineering,
University of Bristol, Bristol, UK
{ioan.mavromatis,a.tassi,r.j.piechocki,andy.nix}@bristol.ac.uk

Abstract. As we move towards autonomous vehicles, a reliable Vehicle-to-Everything (V2X) communication framework becomes of paramount importance. In this paper we present the development and the performance evaluation of a real-world vehicular networking testbed. Our testbed, deployed in the heart of the City of Bristol, UK, is able to exchange sensor data in a V2X manner. We will describe the testbed architecture and its operational modes. Then, we will provide some insight pertaining the firmware operating on the network devices. The system performance has been evaluated under a series of large-scale field trials, which have proven how our solution represents a low-cost high-quality framework for V2X communications. Our system managed to achieve high packet delivery ratios under different scenarios (urban, rural, highway) and for different locations around the city. We have also identified the instability of the packet transmission rate while using single-core devices, and we present some future directions that will address that.

Keywords: Connected and Autonomous Vehicles · CAVs
IEEE 802.11p/DSRC · V2X · Real-world field trials · VANET

1 Introduction

The Automotive Industry is progressively commercialising several advanced features such as lane-keeping assistance, forward collision braking, etc. Even the most pessimistic market analysis envisage that fully autonomous vehicles will flood the global market by 2025 [22]. Autonomous vehicles are expected to be equipped with several sensors that will assist their autonomous functionalities [14]. However, the most critical enabler of the full autonomy will be the communication framework [9] among the vehicles, i.e. Vehicle-to-Vehicle (V2V), and between the vehicles and the infrastructure network, i.e. Vehicle-to-Infrastructure (V2I).

The communication framework is essential as the information exchanged can increase the vehicle safety, provide new services, reduce traffic jams improving the

© Springer Nature Switzerland AG 2018
N. Montavont and G. Z. Papadopoulos (Eds.): ADHOC-NOW 2018, LNCS 11104, pp. 53–63, 2018.
https://doi.org/10.1007/978-3-030-00247-3_5

fleet routing, etc. For these reasons, 75 MHz of the spectrum have been allocated in the 5.9 GHz band for Dedicated Short Range Communication (DSRC) to be used for the Cooperative Intelligent Transportation Systems (C-ITSs). The DSRC radio technology was standardized by IEEE in the 802.11p standard [5], describing the PHY and the MAC layer of the framework, as well as in [6,7] describing the networking services and the multi-channel operation respectively.

Performance enhancement of DSRC communications is a hot research topic. The development of a robust Vehicle-to-Everything (V2X) communication framework, able to guarantee the exchange of information between the Connected and Autonomous Vehicles (CAVs), remains a challenge. Most of the research activities on Vehicular Ad-Hoc Networks (VANETs) and the DSRC focus on computer simulations and theoretical models (e.g. [12,21]). The importance of simulations, as well as their limitations, were discussed in [15] showing that, in larger scale scenarios, the existing simulation frameworks lack in accuracy and realism. To that extent, we will focus our research on building and deploying a real-world large-scale testbed for V2I and V2V communications that could offer:

- Continuous availability for delay-critical applications.
- Full-stack system implementation to support various vehicular applications.
- Centralised coordination via a Software-Defined Networking (SDN)-like framework.
- Open-source operating system for customisability and compatibility with Fog and Cloud Computing architectures [11].
- Reduced cost for large-scale deployments.

Our experimental testbed is currently deployed in the City of Bristol, UK. Similar activities can be found in the literature (e.g. [8,10,13]), however, only [8] considered a V2V communication framework. The systems mentioned above mainly rely on Commercial Off-the-Self (COTS) implementations and license-based products. Our prototyped system relies on open-source firmware and low-cost hardware components. Besides, to the best of our knowledge, none of the existing works considered integration with the Fog Computing paradigm. Finally, throughout our three days of field trials, we logged the messages that we generated and exchanged in a V2I and V2I fashion. Our dataset is freely available and can be downloaded from [1]. Later in this work, we will further explain our experimental setup and the messages exchanged.

This paper is organized as follows. In Sect. 2 we present our testbed architecture and describe our prototyped setup in terms of the hardware and the software used. Section 3 describes the testbed deployed around the City of Bristol, UK as well as the field trials that we conducted using this experimental setup. This section also introduces the initial performance investigation of our system. Based on the knowledge acquired from the aforementioned field trials, we later identify the drawbacks that should be addressed in the future. Finally, in Sect. 4 we summarise our key findings, we comment on the knowledge acquired from this real-world experimentation, and we introduce some ideas for future research.

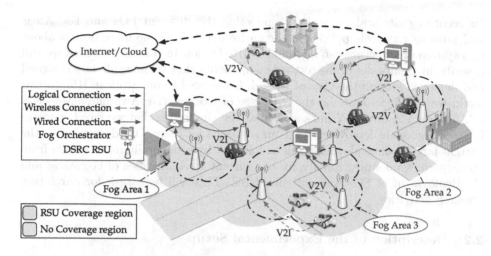

Fig. 1. A general overview of the considered system model. The C-ITS design framework ensures V2X connectivity and a NFV architecture in the infrastructure domain.

2 Experimental Testbed Architecture

2.1 Description of the System Architecture

Our developed experimental VANET testbed consists of different devices and entities. Each one will play a significant role in the operation of our system. An ideal design paradigm can be found in Fig. 1. The different devices that will form our system paradigm are the following:

- *Road Side Units (RSUs):* Network infrastructure devices, mounted on several building, and connected to a centralised control plane to provide V2I connectivity.
- *On-Board Units (OBUs):* Devices installed in the vehicles, able to exchange safety critical messages with the RSUs and other vehicles.
- *Fog Orchestrators (FOs):* Devices that centrally manage the different clustered management areas, called *Fog Areas*, ideally with one-hop distance from the RSUs to reduce the end-to-end delay.

As shown in Fig. 1 the RSUs and OBUs will be connected to each other using IEEE 802.11p/DSRC links. In our system, vehicles can connect to another vehicle (when driving at no coverage regions) or to RSUs (when within the RSU coverage range). In our system paradigm, we assume that our infrastructure network is clustered in different management areas called *Fog Areas*. FOs manage each Fog Area and share a wired connection with the different RSUs. Being one-hop away from the RSUs, they can be used to process all the time-critical information received or generated at the infrastructure side with reduced end-to-end delay. Finally, our system will interact with a cloud-based city-wide connection, interfacing with the different FOs. The cloud-based service will be responsible for recording city-scale data, interconnecting the different FOs and Fog Areas and pushing city-scale policies in the entire network. Some more details about this system architecture can be found in [16–18,20]. In the next section, we will describe in greater detail the testbed components that we have already designed and deployed around the City of Bristol. Compared to our work in [15], in this work, we will focus more on the exchange of Cooperative Awareness Messages (CAMs) on V2I and V2V links as well as the challenges that we faced concerning the large-scale deployment and our solutions for them. Our discussion on the current large-scale deployment will be followed by some preliminary results from our experimental study. Finally, for our current work, the idea of Fog Areas and the deployment of FOs was not considered. This will be a task for our future research activities.

2.2 Description of the Experimental Setup

For our experimental validation, we prototyped an open-source IEEE 802.11p/DSRC testbed (Fig. 2). Our devices, under ideal-like Line-of-Sight (LOS) conditions, were able to achieve good performance and high Packet Delivery Rate (PDR) for distances up to 700 m (as proven in [15]).

The devices were designed to be used as both RSUs and OBUs (Figs. 2a and b). They were equipped with a Mikrotik RB433 single-board computer (CPU 300 MHz, 64 MB RAM, 64 MB storage space, x3 Ethernets, x3 MiniPCI slots) [4]. Also, two wireless IEEE 802.11a NICs were used for redundancy, one regarded as High Power (HP) and the second one regarded as Low Power (LP). The wireless interfaces of the RSUs and the OBUs in our system are accompanied by different antennas as shown in Figs. 2a and c, one bolted on the RSUs and the second magnetically attached to the roof of our vehicles. Our RSU devices were powered up via Power-over-Ethernet (PoE), while a battery pack was used for the OBUs to avoid the voltage spikes experienced when using a lighter inverter within the vehicle. All the device and the key driver characteristics can be found in Table 1.

OpenWRT[1], a low-latency Linux distribution, was used as the operating system for both devices. Both drivers (Table 1) and the Linux kernel modules were modified accordingly to enable IEEE 802.11p compatibility (Fig. 3). The 5.9 GHz band was added to the regulatory domain and the Outside the Context of a BSS (OCB) mode was enabled in the MAC layer, to allow NICs to operate without being associated. The values for the contention windows and the Modulation and Coding Rates (MCSs) were chosen to follow the regulation for the ITS-G5 standard specification. Integration with a GPS dongle via a USB interface was enabled. A beaconing interface was also developed that generates IEEE 802.11p DSRC CAMs and broadcasts them in the network. More details about the modifications can be found in [15].

---

[1] OpenWRT Barrier Breaker Release no. 14.07 - https://openwrt.org/.

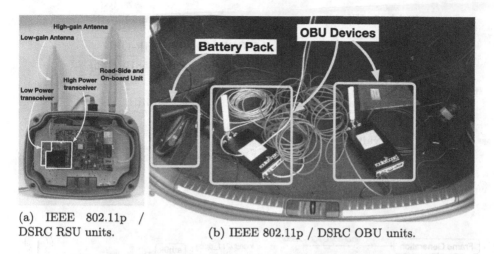

(a) IEEE 802.11p / DSRC RSU units.

(b) IEEE 802.11p / DSRC OBU units.

(c) OBU antenna mounted on the roof of the car.

Fig. 2. Our experimental setup. We prototyped both RSUs and OBUs units, equipped them with different antennas and conducted our trials around the City of Bristol.

The GPS coordinates, the speed, the heading and the timestamp of the GPS are being encapsulated within the transmitted CAMs. A logging interface was designed that logs all the packets generated, transmitted and received. An example of the packets exchanged can be found in Fig. 4. At the TX side, the acquired GPS coordinates are represented as *GpsLongitude*, *GpsLatitude*, being respectively the longitude and latitude values. The *InterLongitude* and *InterLatitude* values are the interpolated values based on the acquired GPS coordinates. The *SeqNum* is the sequence number of the packet generated (starting at zero when the device boots up). The *GpsSpeed* and *InterSpeed* are the acquired values from the GPS dongle and the interpolated value respectively. Finally, the *Timestamp* is the time that the packet is generated, given in Unix Epoch format. The rest of the fields are used for debugging purposes only.

At the RX side, the *RxMAC* is logged at first, which is the MAC address of the device transmitted the packet. *RxLongitude* and *RxLatitude* are the GPS coordinates encapsulated in the transmitted packet. Finally, the *InterLongitude*

Table 1. Wireless network interface controller characteristics

	LP-RSU	LP-OBU	HP-RSU	HP-OBU
Model	Mikrotik R52H [2]		Mikrotik R5SHPn [3]	
TX Power	25 dBm		29 dBm	
Antenna gain	7 dBi	5 dBi	9 dBi	5 dBi
Linux driver	ath5k		ath9k	
Bandwidth	10 MHz			
Frequency	5.89 GHz		5.9 GHz	
CW_{min}, CW_{max}	[15, 1023]			
MCS	QPSK$^{1/2}$			

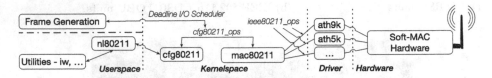

Fig. 3. Linux kernel modules modified to enable the IEEE 802.11p/DSRC capabilities in our system.

and *InterLatitude* values represent the current longitude and latitude of the receiver, acquired from the GPS dongle and interpolated later. The remaining values are similar to the transmitted packet. The above system is highly customisable, and in the future, more features extracted from different sensors can be encapsulated in the exchanged frames to introduce different vehicular applications and expand the cooperative awareness of a vehicle.

3   Field Trials and Preliminary Results

The testbed mentioned above was evaluated under a city-scale deployment during three days of field trials. Throughout the entire evaluation process, we tested various vehicular communication scenarios (both V2V and V2I) under various conditions (urban, rural, highway). The idea behind these field trials was to test the performance of our devices, identify the limitations of our system and find ways to overcome them, and finally get a more in-depth understanding for how a massive city-scale deployment should be approached in the future. In this work, firstly we will investigate the Key Performance Indicators (KPIs) from the perspective of the first car and the RSUs, while the second vehicle acts as an interferer when being within coverage. Secondly, we will present a V2V scenario.

Three RSUs were deployed at first at three locations around the City of Bristol, UK (as shown in Fig. 5a). *Hydrogen-RSU* was mounted at the height of around ~8 m, on a curvy, narrow road very close to a blind T-junction. The second one (*Helium-RSU*) was installed on the wall of a building next to a

TX-REQ-CAM ; Protocol;1 ; StationID;3608578767 ; SeqNum;1000 ; GpsLongitude;-2.6025489 ; GpsLatitude;51.4558020 ;
InterLongitude;-2.6025490 ; InterLatitude;51.4558020 ; GpsSpeed;4.3320000 ; InterSpeed;0.0000000 ;
Timestamp;1519032043343 ;
TX-MSG-LENGTH;107;

RX ; RxMAC;4c:5e:0c:84:35:f6;107 ; RX-CAM ; Validation;1 ; Protocol;1 ; StationID;3608578767; SeqNum;32563 ;
RxLongitude;-2.6031772 ; RxLatitude;51.4563665 ; RxSpeed;28.3320000 ; SpeedConf;3 ; RxHeading;3222 ; InterLongitude;-
2.6025490 ; InterLatitude;51.4558020 ; InterSpeed;12.9980000; Timestamp;1519035271768;

Fig. 4. Example of the log file generated at the transmitter and the receiver side.

straight road with some foliage at the sides at ~5 m. Finally, *Lithium-RSU* was placed on the balcony of a tall building (at ~25 m height), next to a wide road, providing the most LOS coverage compared to the other RSUs. The different locations and buildings were chosen to evaluate how the position of a RSU can affect the performance of the network.

Two vehicles (as in Fig. 2c), equipped with one OBU each, were driving randomly around the city. The second OBU unit shown in Fig. 2b was there for backup purposes only. All the devices in our system generated and transmitted a CAM per NIC every 10 ms. Each CAM, encapsulating the information described in Sect. 2.2, was logged at the transmitter and the receiver side. The log files generated were used later to produce the results that will be described in the next section.

In the next section, we will present our preliminary results. We will focus our performance investigation on some meaningful KPIs related to our research and will try and comprehend the different advantages and drawbacks of our system analysing our findings. Throughout the three days of field trials, we exchanged ~50 million CAMs. Some of our results will use a subset of these exchanged messages. Our entire dataset is available for download in [1]. To the best of our knowledge is one the largest data repositories focused on V2X communications.

3.1 Preliminary Results

Firstly, we start with the V2I scenario. Figure 5 presents the heatmap results for the PDR from all CAMs transmitted from a RSU and received at the vehicle side. The results present the PDR for the vehicle no. 1. Vehicle no. 2 acts as an interferer, as mentioned before, when both vehicles are within the same RSU coverage range. Finally, the red crosses, show the position of a vehicle when a CAM broadcast was successfully received at the RSU side.

Figures 5a and b show the PDR results when both vehicles were driving within the coverage regions of the RSUs. Figures 5c and d show the results when only vehicle no. 1 was within coverage. As described, the DSRC CAMs are being broadcast from all NICs every 10 ms without having any coordination on the channel usage. As shown, there is a significant PDR difference of 30% between the different scenarios, for both the HP and LP transceivers. This is because, the second vehicle, acting as an interferer, led to a big number of frame collisions and longer MAC-layer contention intervals at the receiver side.

(a) Both Vehicles within RSU coverage - HP transceiver.

(b) Both Vehicles within RSU coverage - LP transceiver.

(c) Only Vehicle 1 within RSU coverage - HP transceiver.

(d) Only Vehicle 1 within RSU coverage - LP transceiver.

Fig. 5. Heatmap results for different V2I scenarios (HP and LP NICs). (Color figure online)

The difference can be observed at the RSU side as well. As shown, the heatmap data overlap with the red crosses in Figs. 5c and d, while they do not precisely match the heatmap in the first two figures. This means that when the interfering vehicle was present, vehicle no. 1 was not always able to establish a bidirectional communication link with the RSUs.

In Fig. 6, we present the frequencies of the transmission interval between two DSRC CAM. This is an example from Hydrogen-RSU for all CAMs transmitted throughout one day of field trials. The remaining devices and days produced similar results, therefore will not presented in this work. As shown, even though the CAM transmission interval was set at 10 ms, our testbed generates frames at a different rate. Most of the frames are generated and exchanged either every 12 ms or 14 ms. This was expected as our devices are built upon a single-core CPU, which executes tasks with the same priority according to the Linux *Deadline I/O Scheduler*. To that extent, the CPU cannot fetch/push CAMs streams towards the transceivers at a constant I/O rate. These inconsistencies should be taken into account when designing vehicular applications with strict latency requirements. Generating and processing the packets at a stronger Fog node computer, and using the transceivers as the medium to exchange the packets, will significantly improve the consistency of the transmission rate.

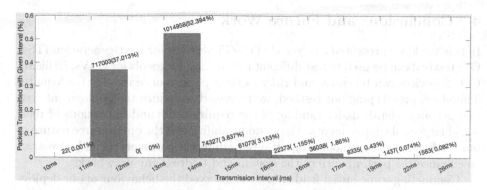

Fig. 6. Transmission intervals between two DSRC CAMs.

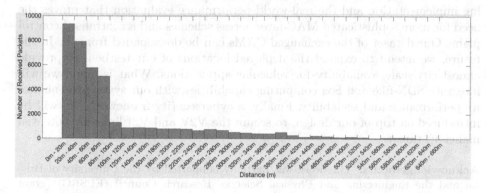

Fig. 7. Awareness horizon for the V2V scenario - HP transceiver.

Finally, Fig. 7 presents the awareness horizon for the V2V scenario, i.e. the Euclidean distance between the vehicles when a CAM is received. For this experiment, two vehicles were driving at opposing directions on a highway section of the road exchanging CAMs every time they were crossing paths. As shown in Fig. 6 most packets are being transmitted every 12 ms or every 14 ms. Given that the vehicles drive at a constant speed, we can estimate that a similar number of packets was exchanged at every distance interval. We observe that when the vehicles are in close proximity, a bigger number of packets is being received compared to longer distances. When the vehicles are more than 80 m apart, most of the packets are never delivered. Similar performance can be observed in the rural and urban trials conducted. From the above, we can observe that using the previously described setup, we can achieve adequate V2V communications for up to about 80 m. For sensor features exchange at longer distances, a multi-hop communication using V2V or V2I links is necessary.

4   Conclusions and Future Work

In this work, we presented a city-scale ITS-G5 network for next-generation ITSs. Our testbed can be used to test different networking protocols for CAVs. Utilising COTS devices can be costly and risky as their performance may be inadequate. Therefore, prototyping our testbed, we managed to reduce the deployment cost and get an in-depth understanding of the requirements and limitations of real-world large-scale deployments. The customisability and the open-source nature of our testbed are of paramount importance as different parameters can be tweaked to enhance the performance of the system and address any drawbacks.

Conducting some initial field trials, we observed the behaviour of our deployment under different conditions and scenarios. Some critical observations can be the inconsistency at the data generation, proving the necessity for a Fog computing implementation and the real-world performance evaluation that proves the need for more sophisticated MAC-layer access schemes and a centralised control plane. Our dataset of the exchanged CAMs can be downloaded from [1]. In the future, we intend to expand the deployed locations of our testbed, to provide almost-city-scale availability for vehicular applications. What is more, we will integrate SDN-like and Fog computing capabilities with our system to enhance its performance and scalability. Finally, a cybersecurity framework [19] will be introduced on top of our design, to secure the V2V and V2I links for potential malicious threats.

Acknowledgements. This work was partially supported by the University of Bristol and the Engineering and Physical Sciences Research Council (EPSRC) (grant EP/I028153/1). It is also supported in part by the Innovate UK FLOURISH project under Grant no. 102582.

References

1. FLOURISH Car Trials - Dataset of three days of field trials. https://seis.bristol.ac.uk/~eerjp/v2xtrials/. Accessed 04 July 2018
2. Mikrotik R52H Data Sheet. https://mikrotik.com/product/R52H
3. Mikrotik R5SHPn Data Sheet. https://routerboard.com/R5SHPn
4. Mikrotik RB433 Data Sheet. https://mikrotik.com/product/RB433
5. IEEE standard for wireless LAN medium access control (MAC) and physical layer (PHY) specifications - amendment 6: wireless access in vehicular environments. IEEE Std. 802.11p-2010, July 2010. https://doi.org/10.1109/IEEESTD.2010.5514475
6. IEEE standard for wireless access in vehicular environments (WAVE) - multi-channel operation. IEEE Std. 1609.4-2016, pp. 1–94, March 2016. https://doi.org/10.1109/IEEESTD.2016.7435228
7. IEEE standard for wireless access in vehicular environments (WAVE) - networking services. IEEE Std. 1609.3-2016, pp. 1–160, April 2016. https://doi.org/10.1109/IEEESTD.2016.7458115
8. Ameixieira, C., et al.: Harbornet: a real-world testbed for vehicular networks. IEEE Commun. Mag. **52**(9), 108–114 (2014). https://doi.org/10.1109/MCOM.2014.6894460

9. Demestichas, P., Georgakopoulos, A., Tsagkaris, K., Kotrotsos, S.: Intelligent 5G networks: managing 5G wireless/mobile broadband. IEEE Veh. Technol. Mag. **10**(3), 41–50 (2015). https://doi.org/10.1109/MVT.2015.2446419
10. Eriksson, J., Balakrishnan, H., Madden, S.: Cabernet: vehicular content delivery using WiFi. In: Proceedings of the 14th ACM International Conference on Mobile Computing and Networking, MobiCom 2008, pp. 199–210. ACM, New York (2008). https://doi.acm.org/10.1145/1409944.1409968
11. Fantacci, R., Tarchi, D., Tassi, A.: A novel routing algorithm for mobile pervasive computing. In: Proceedings of IEEE 2010, December 2010. https://doi.org/10.1109/GLOCOM.2010.5683765
12. Fazio, P., Rango, F.D., Sottile, C.: A predictive cross-layered interference management in a multichannel MAC with reactive routing in VANET. IEEE Trans. Mob. Comput. **15**(8), 1850–1862 (2016). https://doi.org/10.1109/TMC.2015.2465384
13. Hull, B., et al.: CarTel: a distributed mobile sensor computing system. In: Proceedings of 4th ACM SenSys. Boulder, November 2006
14. Levinson, J., et al.: Towards fully autonomous driving: systems and algorithms. In: IEEE Intelligent Vehicles Symposium IV, pp. 163–168, June 2011. https://doi.org/10.1109/IVS.2011.5940562
15. Mavromatis, I., Tassi, A., Piechocki, R.J., Nix, A.: Agile calibration process of full-stack simulation frameworks for V2X communications. In: Proceedings of IEEE VNC 2017, pp. 89–96 (2017). https://doi.org/10.1109/VNC.2017.8275604
16. Mavromatis, I., Tassi, A., Rigazzi, G., Piechocki, R.J., Nix, A.: Multi-radio 5G architecture for connected and autonomous vehicles: application and design insights. EAI Trans. Ind. Netw. Intell. Syst. (2018). https://doi.org/10.4108/eai.20-3-2018.154368
17. Mavromatis, I., Tassi, A., Piechocki, R.J., Nix, A.: MmWave system for future ITS: a MAC-layer approach for V2X beam steering. In: Proceedings of IEEE VTC-Fall 2017, September 2017. https://doi.org/10.1109/VTCFall.2017.8288267
18. Mavromatis, I., Tassi, A., Piechocki, R.J., Nix, A.: Efficient V2V communication scheme for 5G MmWave hyper-connected CAVs. In: Proceedings of IEEE ICC 2018, May 2018
19. Rigazzi, G., Tassi, A., Piechocki, R.J., Tryfonas, T., Nix, A.: Optimized certificate revocation list distribution for secure V2X communications. In: Proceedings of IEEE VTC-Fall 2017, September 2017. https://doi.org/10.1109/VTCFall.2017.8288287
20. Tassi, A., Egan, M., Piechocki, R.J., Nix, A.: Modeling and design of millimeter-wave networks for highway vehicular communication. IEEE Trans. Veh. Technol. **66**(12), 10676–10691 (2017). https://doi.org/10.1109/TVT.2017.2734684
21. Tong, Z., Lu, H., Haenggi, M., Poellabauer, C.: A stochastic geometry approach to the modeling of DSRC for vehicular safety communication. IEEE Trans. Intell. Transp. Syst. **17**(5), 1448–1458 (2016). https://doi.org/10.1109/TITS.2015.2507939
22. Walker, J.: The self-driving car timeline - predictions from the top 11 global automakers. https://www.techemergence.com/self-driving-car-timeline-themselves-top-11-automakers/. Accessed 27 March 2018

The Potential of mmWaves in Smart Industry: Manufacturing at 60 GHz

Chiara Pielli[1]([✉])[iD], Tanguy Ropitault[2][iD], and Michele Zorzi[1][iD]

[1] University of Padova, 35131 Padova, Italy
{piellich,zorzi}@dei.unipd.it
[2] NIST, Gaithersburg, MD 20899, USA
tanguy.ropitault@nist.gov

Abstract. Industry is experiencing a new evolution phase where manufacturing is going through a process of digitalization, with every step of the production chain becoming smart. The emergence of IoT technologies and the fasted-paced evolution in advanced computing capabilities enable a pervasive monitoring and rapid data processing, unleashing new applications, e.g., real-time error-correction and fault-detection, remote robot control, intelligent logistics. The flexibility and low cost of wireless solutions makes them appealing with respect to wired connections, but current wireless technologies operate at sub-6-GHz bands and are not able to meet the reliability, latency, and data rate demands of novel applications. In this paper, we give an overview of the main limits of current technologies and discuss the role that mmWaves may play in guaranteeing ultra reliable and low latency wireless communication in smart industry. We especially focus on the IEEE 802.11ad and 802.11ay standards for communication at 60 GHz. A factory work-cell is used as an illustrative example to explore the potential of mmWaves and how they could contribute to the realization of a resilient smart factory.

Keywords: mmWaves · Smart industry · Beamforming · MAC layer

1 Introduction

The explosion of the Internet of Things (IoT) may lead to a major breakthrough in industries: the capillary deployment of sensors, coupled with advanced analytics capabilities, can enable automatized and flexible processes that can be monitored in real time, reducing production and maintenance costs and unproductive downtime. Production processes have been constantly changing towards an increasingly automatized profile, with some milestones, i.e., mechanization, mass production, and computerization, that are commonly known as industrial revolutions 1, 2 and 3 [1]. The fourth revolution, Industry 4.0, is not related to the introduction of disruptive technologies, but rather to the *digitalization* of the manufacturing sector, with the ultimate goal of optimizing existing operations and creating the so-called *smart factory*. Key enablers of Industry 4.0 are big

N. Montavont and G. Z. Papadopoulos (Eds.): ADHOC-NOW 2018, LNCS 11104, pp. 64–76, 2018.
https://doi.org/10.1007/978-3-030-00247-3_6

data analytics, machine learning, cloud computing, robotics, and artificial intelligence [1]. Manufacturing systems go beyond simple connectivity, and use the collected information to drive further intelligent actions and meet the demands for higher productivity, green production, higher market share and flexibility.

Communication is a major component of Industry 4.0: it enables the connectivity between the devices and a continuous exchange of data that can be used to make the production process smart, flexible and adaptive. Wired technologies have been used for decades in industry but there is a growing interest in the deployment of wireless solutions, because they are much easier to install, upgrade and reconfigure. While several wireless technologies are available, their adoption in industry is still hindered by key technical challenges, including communication reliability and timeliness, security, interoperability and energy sustainability, and by the presence of proprietary and fragmented solutions [2]. New communication technologies could enable pervasive and continuous feedback inside the industry environments, allowing to achieve new industrial automation capabilities, such as intelligent logistics, real-time fault detection, asset tracking, remote visual monitoring, and remote robot control. These new applications could push the Quality of Service (QoS) requirements to extreme values, targeting, e.g., Packet Error Rate (PER) of 10^{-9} and latency below 1 ms [3]. Traditional technologies are not able to achieve such performance, and it is common belief that new communication strategies and protocols are needed [2].

There are multiple candidate technologies for Industry 4.0 and debates are ongoing about which one should be the key players. In this paper, we explore the potential of millimeter waves (mmWaves) in smart industry, focusing on the IEEE 802.11ad standard for communication at 60 GHz, and on its recent evolution, 802.11ay. The spectrum scarcity at 2.4 and 5 GHz and the resulting congestion have pushed a growing interest in the Extremely High Frequency (EHF) band, where the very large amount of bandwidth available greatly increases the system capacity and flexibility [4]. Despite its high potential, the use of mmWaves in smart factory is yet to explore. The peculiar characteristics of signal propagation at EHF, like the strong attenuation and sensitivity to blockage, raise novel issues that need to be solved, and new mechanisms such as beamforming are needed to provide efficient mmWave communication. In this paper, we describe a work-cell scenario to explain the role that mmWaves may play in Industry 4.0, and the main areas of research for the development of an effective industrial mmWave network.

The rest of the paper is organized as follows. Section 2 describes the characteristics of industrial automation scenarios, and provides an overview of the currently used technologies and their limitations. Section 3 introduces mmWaves and the 802.11ad/ay standards, while Sect. 4 discusses the potential and the areas of research to integrate mmWaves in smart industry through the example of a factory work-cell. Finally, Sect. 5 concludes the paper.

2   Smart Manufacturing Now

In the following, we first describe the manufacturing communication requirements, and then introduce the wireless technologies mostly used at the moment, and discuss their limitations in providing the QoS of Industry 4.0.

2.1   Networking Requirements in Industries

At its most fundamental level, industrial automation is historically divided into two main categories that include most of its typical applications: *Process Automation* (PA) and *Factory Automation* (FA) [5]. PA concerns the automatic control of a continuous process, like heating, cooling, stirring, and pumping procedures; usually the monitored values change relatively slowly and have no stringent requirements (latency larger than 100 ms [5]), and the typical communication range is about 100–500 m. FA instead refers to the automation of operations in the production of items such as cars and electronics. FA applications may generate bursty data and typically have stricter requirements than PA ones (latency of 1–50 ms [5]), and shorter communication range, in the order of tens of meters. Within these two macrocategories, there are a large variety of industry environments, which differ for application requirements (latency, PER, scalability, security, data rate, field coverage, etc.) and network characteristics (data size, topology, device mobility profile, etc.).

A major focus in Industry 4.0 is to achieve very low latency and high reliability communication to enable smooth and efficient operation and fast response to warnings and failures. Applications like control systems (for both PA and FA), automated guided vehicles, asset tracking and remote control robots may require a PER in the order of 10^{-9}, and end-to-end latencies in the range of 0.5–5 ms [3, Table 1]. The ability to handle heterogeneous application requirements and device capabilities is also a key requirement.

2.2   Current Wireless Technologies

Although wired communications have been traditionally adopted for use in industrial systems because they provide direct and reliable connections, they also have their own limitations: poor scalability, very limited reconfigurability, minimal flexibility, and physical degradability [6]. Moreover, the increasing presence of moving machines and robots pose a challenge to the use of wired cables. To overcome these issues, wireless communications have become popular in factory plants, but at the cost of reduced reliability and timeliness. Currently, industry automation is spangled with standards and proprietary solutions. Table 1 reviews the core features of the main wireless networking technologies currently employed in industry automation: WirelessHART, ISA100.11a, the Wireless networks for Industrial Automation-Process Automation (WIA-PA) standard, and Wireless Interface for Sensors and Actuators (WISA), which has partly been standardized in Wireless Sensor Networks for Industrial Automation - Factory Automation

Table 1. Overview of current technologies.

	WirelessHART	ISA100.11a	WIA-PA	WISA/WSAN-FA
Target scenario	PA			FA
PHY layer	802.15.4	802.15.4	802.15.4	802.15.1
# of channels	15	16	16	5
Medium access	TDMA and CSMA	TDMA and CSMA	Hybrid TDMA/CSMA	TDMA FDD
Frequency hopping	✓ + blacklisting	✓ + blacklisting	✓	✓ + blacklisting
Superframe structure	Collection of slots	Collection of slots	802.15.4 superframe structure	Collection of slots
Timeslot duration	10 ms	10–14 ms (configurable)	10 ms	128 μs UL 64 μs DL

(WSAN-FA). Interested readers can refer to [5–7] for thorough descriptions and comparisons of these standards.

WirelessHART, ISO100.11a and WIA-PA target PA applications and are based on the IEEE 802.15.4 standard. They use a Time Division Multiple Access (TDMA) schedule, with slots that can either be used in a dedicated way or shared among users, and communication is made more robust thanks to the frequency hopping mechanisms. These standards generally provide good performance in monitoring and control applications, but are not able to guarantee the ultra-high reliability and ultra-low latency required by emerging applications such as smart manufacturing and remote robot control. In particular, a major limitation is the slot duration of 10 ms, which prevents the deployment of WirelessHART, ISA100.11a and WIA-PA for time critical applications.

Protocols for FA are instead typically designed to support real-time requirements and provide latencies of few milliseconds, to avoid interruptions in the manufacturing process. WISA, for example, targets sensor and actuator devices on the field level and has very short slots, which yield a typical latency on the air interface of 5 ms but also limits the system capacity to 64 bits per time slot. Moreover, WISA is not recommended for energy-constrained applications, because it relies on the IEEE 802.15.1 standard, which has high power consumption. WISA is not able to support QoS and security over heterogeneous network segments [6] and is proprietary, thus lacking openness and interoperability. This last issue can be overcome by using the WSAN-FA standard, based on WISA.

Although current wireless technologies are suitable for some of the applications of Industry 4.0, clearly no solution can serve all the disparate possible scenarios, and the capabilities of new available technologies need to be investigated [2]. In the next sections, we will explore the potential use of mmWaves.

3   Communication at mmWaves

Millimeter waves commonly denote the portion of spectrum between 30 and 300 GHz, which corresponds to wavelengths in the range from 1 to 10 mm. mmWaves have been gaining a lot of momentum in telecommunications thanks to the large band of spectrum available; for example, there are 7 GHz of continuous spectrum (from 57 to 64 GHz) in the 60 GHz frequency band. This large bandwidth has the potential to eliminate many of the issues of the overcrowded sub-6-GHz bands and allows for channels with larger bandwidth and, thus, higher capacity.

The propagation environment in the mmWave spectrum is significantly different from that at sub-6-GHz frequencies, and is characterized by a high propagation loss and a significant sensitivity to blockage. However, the high attenuation may be an advantage for applications with short range, since it makes interference from adjacent transmissions negligible. Moreover, the coverage ranges can be increased through beamforming, by focusing the power (both in transmission and in reception) towards the chosen direction yielding a so-called directional link. This can obtained by properly steering the antenna elements of the antenna arrays, which, thanks to the short wavelengths, can be extremely compact and easily embedded into sensors and handsets. The small form factors also facilitate the deployment of Multiple-Input Multiple-Output (MIMO) systems.

Directional transmission opens up new possibilities. With all the power focused in a specific direction, the gain in the other directions is low: this significantly reduces interference among concurrent transmissions, which is one of the main issues in the overcrowded sub-6-GHz bands. The consequent high potential for spatial reuse can boost the network performance. Notice, however, that beamforming is a delicate process. First, beamforming training is necessary to establish a directional link (avoiding the use of inefficient quasi-omnidirectional communication), then beam tracking is needed to maintain the communication link. Beam misalignment may prevent communication, resulting in the so-called *deafness* issue, and poorly trained beams lead to extreme throughput drops of up to 6.5 Gbps in 802.11ad [8]. Extensive research is ongoing to develop mechanisms for efficient beamforming training and beam tracking [9,10].

Because of the peculiar characteristics of the signal propagation at EHF, protocols designed for lower frequencies cannot simply be transposed to the mmWave band, but major design changes are required for both PHY and Medium Access Control (MAC) layers. This pushed a standardization effort from several international organizations. In this paper, we focus on the IEEE 802.11ad and 802.11ay standards, which operate in the 60 GHz unlicensed band.

3.1   802.11ad

Ratified in December 2012, the 802.11ad amendment to the IEEE 802.11 standard targets short range mmWave communication in local area networks [11]. Since it can also be used in Personal Basic Service Sets (PBSSs) (i.e., network architectures for ad hoc modes), the central coordinator of 802.11ad networks

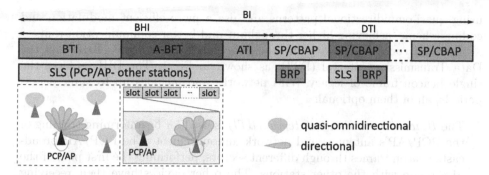

Fig. 1. Structure of a BI. Green boxes correspond to beamforming training operations. The BHI is used for SLS with the PCP/AP: during the BTI, the PCP/AP trains its transmitting antenna pattern; during the A-BFT the other stations train their transmitting or receiving antenna patterns in dedicated slots. During the DTI, stations can perform both SLS and BRP phases with the PCP/AP and with other stations. (Color figure online)

can be either a PBSS Control Point (PCP) or an Access Point (AP); accordingly, it is generally denoted as PCP/AP to include both infrastructures.

In the following, we give an overview of the PHY layer and the main aspects of the MAC layer, i.e., the beamforming protocol to manage directional transmissions and the hybrid medium access.

PHY Layer. The nominal channel bandwidth is 2.16 GHz, and there are up to 4 channels in the ISM band around 60 GHz, although channel availability varies from region to region. Only one channel at a time can be used for communication. There are 32 different modulation and coding schemes available, grouped into three different PHY layers, which differ for robustness, complexity, and achievable data rates (up to 6.75 Gbps).

MAC Layer. Medium access time is divided into Beacon Intervals (BIs), which are used to establish a directional communication link through beamforming training, and for data transmission. The maximum duration of a BI is 1 s, but it is typically chosen around 100 ms. 802.11ad introduces the concept of antenna sectors, which correspond to a discretization of the antenna space and reduces the number of possible beam directions to try. Beamforming training is realized in two subsequent stages: the Sector-Level Sweep (SLS) phase and the Beam Refinement Protocol (BRP) phase. The SLS is necessary to set up a link between the involved stations, with one station sequentially trying different antenna sector configurations while the other station has its antennas configured in a quasi-omnidirectional pattern. Notice that both the transmitting and the receiving antenna patterns can be trained. This determines the best coarse-grained antenna sector configuration. The BRP is then used to fine-tune this configuration using narrower beams and, possibly, to optimize the antenna weight vectors in case of phased antenna arrays. Since a directional link has already been established previously during the SLS phase, in BRP stations can avoid using quasi-omnidirectional patterns and use a more efficient modulation and coding scheme, achieving higher throughput and better communication range.

Each BI consists of two parts: the Beacon Header Interval (BHI) and the Data Transmission Interval (DTI), as shown in Fig. 1. The BHI replaces the single beacon frame of legacy WiFi networks and includes up to three access periods, all of them optional:

– The *Beacon Transmission Interval (BTI)* is used for beamforming training of the PCP/AP's antennas and network announcement. The PCP/AP broadcasts beacon frames through different sectors, performing the first part of the SLS phase with the other stations. The other devices have their receiving antennas configured in a quasi-omnidirectional pattern.
– The *Association-Beamforming Training (A-BFT)* is divided into slots during which stations separately train their antenna sectors for communication with the PCP/AP, and provide feedback to the PCP/AP about the sector to use for transmitting to them. This completes the SLS phase started in the BTI to establish a link with the PCP/AP.
– The *Announcement Transmission Interval (ATI)*, used to exchange management information between the PCP/AP and associated and beamtrained stations, such as resource requests and allocation information for the DTI.

The DTI is used for data transmission. Prior to any additional frame exchange between stations, it is necessary to establish a link for directional communication; the DTI can also be used for beamforming training between stations (both SLS and BRP phases) and to perform the BRP phase with the PCP/AP. Since the BRP phase follows the SLS one, a reliable frame exchange is ensured and a station may transmit BRP packets along with other packets. The channel access is extremely flexible, thanks to three core characteristics:

– The DTI is made up of contention-free Service Periods (SPs) for exclusive communication between a dedicated pair of nodes and Contention Based Access Periods (CBAPs) where stations compete for access. SPs and CBAPs can be in any number and combination, and their scheduling is advertised by the PCP/AP through beacons. This hybrid medium access allows to accomodate very diverse traffic patterns and application requirements.
– Allocations can be defined as pseudostatic, which means that they recur in subsequent BIs. This option is useful for periodic and predictable traffic patterns, as it limits the related signaling and management message flow.
– A dynamic channel time allocation mechanism allows stations to reserve channel time in almost real-time over both SPs and CBAPs. Stations can be polled by the PCP/AP and ask for channel time, which will be granted back to back. The dynamic mechanism also includes the possibility of truncating and extending SPs, to exploit unused channel time and finalize the ongoing communication without additional delay and scheduling, respectively.

3.2   802.11ay

With its Draft 1.0 published in November 2017, the 802.11ay amendment defines new PHY and MAC layers that enhance standard 802.11ad, with maximum achievable throughput of 100 Gbps and extended transmission distances of 300–500 m [12]. Backward compatibility and coexistence with 802.11ad are also ensured. The most relevant novelties of 802.11ay are the use of channel grouping mechanisms and of MIMO links, features that together yield improved channel access and beamforming training with respect to 802.11ad.

In 802.11ay there are up to 6 primary channels available, each with a bandwidth of 2.16 GHz, and they can be used in groups of 2, 3 or 4 through channel bonding and channel aggregation techniques. Unlike 802.11ad, 802.11ay supports MIMO, enabling multiplexing gain thanks to the use of multiple antenna elements that can be driven by different RF chains. In particular, 802.11ay supports Single-User (SU) MIMO and downlink Multi-User (MU) MIMO with transmissions to up to eight stations. There can be up to eight spatial streams per station, and the number of streams supported by a MIMO link depends on the environment, the antenna's directivity and whether the antenna polarization is exploited. MIMO communication adds multiplexing gain to the beamforming gain obtained by using antenna arrays. In this way, diversity in the spatial domain is fully exploited, bolstering the communication robustness, and leading to very high Signal-to-Noise Ratio (SNR) links almost immune to fading.

4   mmWaves in Smart Factories: The Work-Cell Case

mmWaves unveil new possibilities with respect to sub-6-GHz frequency bands. Industrial automation includes a myriad environments, which span different network sizes, topologies, and modes of connectivity; we focus on a work-cell scenario to provide an example of the potential of mmWaves in Industry 4.0.

4.1   Need of Ultra Reliable and Low Latency Communication

A work-cell is a cluster of equipment and workers that perform a specific task. Multiple work-cells may be grouped together to collectively manufacture a product, but they can be considered as autonomous and self-contained entities that perform separate production steps and have their own resources. This facilitates changes in internal processes, because it is possible to reconfigure only a subset of work-cells. A work-cell usually has a size in the order of tens of meters and includes 10–100 devices. Figure 2 shows a simplified illustrative work-cell.

Typically, every manufacturing step involves many sensors and actuators controlled by robot controllers, which are coordinated by some supervision intelligence. Most of the connections are still wired, which makes them often stressed by repeated movement, heat, corrosion, etc. Shielded cables are expensive and replacing them yields unproductive downtime. This, coupled with the desire of having reconfigurable work-cells as well as agile and mobile robotics, pushed interest in the use of wireless within a work-cell.

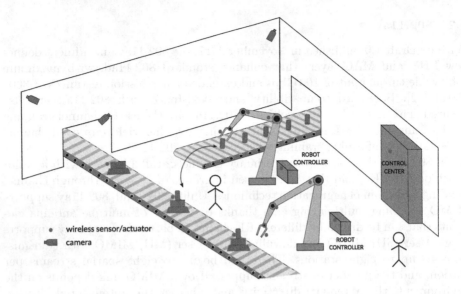

wireless sensor/actuator
camera

Fig. 2. Simplified example of a work-cell.

Achieving ultra low latency and high reliability in the work-cell communication enables *smart* robots and machines, able to operate alongside human workers or collaborating together towards a common goal. This is in fact hindered by "blind" machines, unable to detect nearby humans or objects and react accordingly, e.g., by changing their movements, slowing down their operating rate, or even shutting down completely. Such adaptive behavior is however necessary to protect human safety and achieve seamless cooperation within the work-cell. Humans can be provided with wearable sensors that send information about their presence to the robot controllers. Also the use of Vision Guided Robots (VGRs) is extremely helpful. A vision system all over the work-cell (e.g., on walls and ceilings), and possibly cameras embedded in the machines, enable a continuous monitoring of the environment. This information is used by the radio controllers for path planning and inverse kinematics decisions, i.e., to infer the movements needed by the robot to reach the desired position and orientation of its end-effectors, and to compute the corresponding joint angles. Such decisions are clearly affected by the presence of obstacles, and communication reliability and timeliness are essential to guarantee a successful performance. Notice also that, in the case of robots working together, the supervision intelligence needs to collect information from all the robot controllers to ensure smooth cooperation. Although VGRs already exist, their adoption is still limited to wired connections and hampered by the high monetary cost.

Another application that requires ultra reliable communication is represented by Safety Instrumented Systems (SISs), which are the systems responsible for monitoring the work-cell operating conditions and promptly triggering alarms whenever a risk condition occurs, to avoid accidents like fires, explosions, damages to equipment and, above all, human injuries. SISs are very time critical and need to report multiple simultaneous events in real time. Reliability is of utmost importance because human lives depend on its performance.

4.2 Potential of mmWaves in the Work-Cell Environment

Some distinctive aspects of communication at EHF could be decisive in achieving ultra low latency and reliability in the communication within the work-cell.

Channels in 802.11ad and 802.11ay have a bandwidth of 2.16 GHz, and the channel aggregation and bonding mechanisms provided in 802.11ay further increase the available bandwidth, allowing to use up to 4 channels jointly. The resulting bandwidth has the potential to yield peak data rates up to 100 Gbps in 802.11ay. This considerably helps the transmission of high-resolution videos and real-time motion capture, enhancing the performance of VGRs. Moreover, thanks to the small wavelength, the form factor of 60 GHz systems is approximately 140 times smaller compared to that of 5 GHz systems, so that compact radios can be easily deployed in robot arms, wheels, rotating engines, spindles, etc. [4].

A key advantage of mmWaves is that directional transmission severely mitigates the interference issues that choke the sub-6-GHz bands, enhancing throughput and timeliness. MmWave networks may operate in a noise-limited rather than interference-limited regime [13]; this, for example, helps collaborative robots to communicate simultaneously, and SISs to handle alarms from several components. A major concern for mmWave communication is the intrinsic high signal attenuation, exacerbated by the harsh propagation environment. Within the work-cell, it may in fact be difficult to establish a Line-of-Sight (LoS) link, due to the presence of numerous obstacles, metallic objects and machines, concrete walls, etc. Nonetheless, industrial environments mainly exhibit metallic scatterers, which have been shown to result in better mean channel capacity compared to wooden scatterers, because metallic structures result in more specular reflections [14]. Moreover, recent studies prove the suitability of mmWaves as PHY in industrial wireless networks [15]. Despite the impairments due to multipath, shadowing, non-LoS propagation, and moving devices, mmWave links can achieve reliable communication at a distance of tens of meters for a single hop, with performance of up to two orders of magnitude better compared to conventional sub-6-GHz wireless links in indoor industrial environments [15]. Notice also that the use of MIMO links (as introduced in the 802.11ay standard) helps exploiting the multipath propagation and could mitigate the propagation impairments of mmWaves in the work-cell and improve the communication robustness.

Finally, a distinctive feature of the 802.11ad/ay standards that is not directly related to mmWaves is the hybrid MAC, which can efficiently accommodate different traffic patterns and heterogeneous requirements. For example, the communication regime of a collaborative robot may change nearby a human worker: the reporting rate should increase to accurately monitor the obstacle position, while the movement speed should slow down, resulting in decreased feedback from the robot controllers to the actuators. SP allocations grant the use of dedicated resources and are particularly suitable for periodic reporting with QoS demands, like images sent by the VGRs in "normal" monitoring conditions, in the absence of obstacles. Directional communication enables spatial sharing, so that, e.g., multiple robot controllers could transmit with negligible cross interference. On the other hand, CBAPs may be preferable in case of less stringent QoS requirements because channel resources are available to more stations. CBAPs are distributed and robust, but the contention-based access may introduce delays in the message delivery, and the directional communication could alter the carrier sensing, erroneously showing the channel as idle. Finally, the dynamic allocation of channel time may prompt fast reaction to unexpected latency critical messages and accomodate bursty downstream traffic, since it allows quasi-real-time channel use; for example it could be extremely helpful for SISs.

4.3 Potential Areas of Research

The use of mmWaves in industrial scenarios requires additional research to investigate some issues prior to deployment, because the high potential described previously could be affected by an ill-designed implementation.

Directional Communication. Directionality reduces interference and increases spatial sharing, but, on the other hand, makes link maintenance and establishment tasks complex especially under device mobility, as misalignment of antenna beams leads to link disruption. Real-world measurements of the industrial propagation environment are necessary to build accurate signal propagation models [16] to be used as guidelines for the development of efficient beamforming training mechanisms. The network performance is significantly affected by beamforming training choices, like the number of sectors used, the beam widths, the way and order to try different sectors [9]. A careful planning of the SLS and BRP phases is also necessary: while the BRP introduces overhead and delays in the communication setup, it also enables more efficient directional communication with higher throughput, and this tradeoff impacts on latency and reliability.

Mobility. Another major focus should be the design of low latency beamsteering algorithms for fast link re-establishment to support seamless data provisioning even in case of device mobility. As shown in [17], the delay overhead of the beamforming training in 802.11ad is too burdensome for high mobility scenarios. A viable solution is to exchange the mmWave training information out-of-band, deploying a network operating in a heterogeneous manner [17]. Another strategy consists in beam tracking algorithms to "follow" a moving device and update the corresponding information on the sector to use [10]. Beam tracking induces less overhead than the full sector sweep of the SLS phase and allows to update the sector information adaptively, based on the mobility speed. However, the development of lightweight beam tracking algorithms is yet to be explored.

Power Consumption. The power consumption of mmWave communication may be high due to the use of large bandwidth and multiple antennas. A critical power drain for MIMO systems is the Analog-to-Digital Converter (ADC), and ongoing research tries to reduce the sampling rate and the quantization resolution of ADCs [18]. However, realizing low-power devices is not in itself sufficient, because the power consumption is also affected by network topology, channel access and routing protocols, and channel conditions. Energy efficiency thus needs to be explicitly included as a target in the design of processing algorithms and communication protocols. Notice that the 802.11ad and 802.11ay standards include a low-power single-carrier PHY for energy critical devices, and rules to prioritize their communication with respect to the other nodes.

Channel Access. To accomodate the heterogeneous traffic within the work-cell, it is necessary to design scheduling algorithms that fully exploit the high flexibility of the MAC layer of 802.11ad and 802.11ay. Each traffic pattern should be matched to the most appropriate type of allocation based on its characteristics and QoS demands. To this purpose, it is necessary to understand the performance achievable in the CBAP allocations depending on how much time is devoted to contention-free SPs [19], and, on the other hand, understand how to schedule SPs within a BI [20]. Another path that has not been explored is how to exploit the dynamic allocation mechanism of 802.11ad/ay.

5 Conclusions

Several emerging applications of Industry 4.0, like real-time error correction, VGRs, and intelligent logistics, have demanding reliability, timeliness and data rate requirements that current wireless technologies may be unable to satisfy. In this sense, mmWave communication may play a key role, thanks to the very large available bandwidth, the high achievable data rates, the compact radios, and the use of directional transmissions that mitigate interference.

The potential of mmWaves in industrial automation is still to be explored, and further investigation is needed prior to a successful deployment in smart industries. A main challenge is the development of beamforming training and beam tracking algorithms that are energy-efficient, with minimal latency overhead, and robust to the harsh industrial propagation environment. Moreover, it is necessary to design a transmission scheduler that fully exploits the hybrid channel access of 802.11ad/ay to optimally accomodate the QoS requirements.

A resilient and reliable smart factory will likely be accomplished by integrating diverse technologies, taking advantage of all of them with the possibility of switching across them in a flexible and context-aware fashion.

References

1. Rao, S.K., Prasad, R.: Impact of 5G technologies on industry 4.0. Wirel. Pers. Commun. **100**(1), 145–159 (2018)
2. Candell, R., Kashef, M.: Industrial wireless: problem space, success considerations, technologies, and future direction. In: 2017 Resilience Week (RWS), pp. 133–139. IEEE, September 2017
3. Schulz, P., Matthe, M., Klessig, H., Simsek, M., Fettweis, G.: Latency critical IoT applications in 5G: perspective on the design of radio interface and network architecture. IEEE Commun. Mag **55**(2), 70–78 (2017)

4. Athanasiou, G., Weeraddana, P.C., Fischione, C., Orten, P.: Communication infrastructures in industrial automation: the case of 60 GHz millimeterWave communications. In: IEEE 18th Conference on Emerging Technologies & Factory Automation (ETFA), pp. 1–6, September 2013

5. Wang, Q., Jiang, J.: Comparative examination on architecture and protocol of industrial wireless sensor network standards. IEEE Commun. Surv. Tutor. **18**(3), 2197–2219 (2016)

6. Christin, D., Mogre, P.S., Hollick, M.: Survey on wireless sensor network technologies for industrial automation: the security and quality of service perspectives. Future Internet **2**(2), 96–125 (2010)

7. Petersen, S., Carlsen, S.: WirelessHART versus ISA100.11a: the format war hits the factory floor. IEEE Ind. Electron. Mag. **5**(4), 23–34 (2011)

8. Nitsche, T., Cordeiro, C., Flores, A.B., Knightly, E.W., Perahia, E., Widmer, J.C.: IEEE 802.11ad: directional 60 GHz communication for multi-Gigabit-per-second Wi-Fi. IEEE Commun. Mag. **52**(12), 132–141 (2014)

9. Kutty, S., Sen, D.: Beamforming for millimeter wave communications: an inclusive survey. IEEE Commun. Surv. Tutor. **18**(2), 949–973 (2016)

10. Satchidanandan, B., Yau, S., Kumar, P., Aziz, A., Ekbal, A., Kundargi, N.: TrackMAC: an IEEE 802.11ad-compatible beam tracking-based MAC protocol for 5G millimeter-wave local area networks. In: International Conference on Communication Systems & Networks (COMSNETS), pp. 185–182. IEEE, January 2018

11. IEEE 802.11 WG: IEEE 802.11ad, amendment 3: enhancements for very high throughput in the 60 GHz band, December 2012

12. Ghasempour, Y., da Silva, C.R.C.M., Cordeiro, C., Knightly, E.W.: IEEE 802.11ay: next-generation 60 GHz communication for 100 Gb/s Wi-Fi. IEEE Commun. Mag. **55**(12), 186–192 (2017)

13. Shokri-Ghadikolaei, H., Fischione, C., Popovski, P., Zorzi, M.: Design aspects of short-range millimeter-wave networks: a MAC layer perspective. IEEE Netw. **30**(3), 88–96 (2016)

14. Cheffena, M.: Industrial wireless communications over the millimeter wave spectrum: opportunities and challenges. IEEE Commun. Mag. **54**(9), 66–72 (2016)

15. Saponara, S., Giannetti, F., Neri, B., Anastasi, G.: Exploiting mm-wave communications to boost the performance of industrial wireless networks. IEEE Trans. Ind. Inform. **13**(3), 1460–1470 (2017)

16. Rappaport, T.S., MacCartney, G.R., Samimi, M.K., Sun, S.: Wideband millimeter-wave propagation measurements and channel models for future wireless communication system design. IEEE Trans. Commun. **63**(9), 3029–3056 (2015)

17. Mavromatis, I., Tassi, A., Piechocki, R.J., Nix, A.: MmWave system for future ITS: a MAC-layer approach for V2X beam steering. In: IEEE 86th Vehicular Technology Conference (VTC-Fall), pp. 1–6. IEEE, September 2017

18. Alkhateeb, A., Mo, J., Gonzalez-Prelcic, N., Heath, R.W.: MIMO precoding and combining solutions for millimeter-wave systems. IEEE Commun. Mag. **52**(12), 122–131 (2014)

19. Hemanth, C., Venkatesh, T.: Performance analysis of contention-based access periods and service periods of 802.11ad hybrid medium access control. IET Netw. **3**(3), 193–203 (2013)

20. Khorov, E., Ivanov, A., Lyakhov, A., Zankin, V.: Mathematical model for scheduling in IEEE 802.11ad networks. In: Wireless and Mobile Networking Conference (WMNC), pp. 153–160. IEEE, July 2016

5G Radio Resource Management Approach for Internet of Things Communications

Ahlem Saddoud, Wael Doghri[✉], Emna Charfi, and Lamia Chaari Fourati

LAB (LR16CNRS01), Digital Research Center of Sfax,
Technopark, B.P 3021, Sfax, Tunisia
wael.doghri@yahoo.fr

Abstract. Internet of Things (IoT) communications have significant impact on our social life due to the exponential growth of many objects and devices creating a fully interconnected world. Due to the high performance requirements of 5G IoT applications, enhancements are needed to support the weighty uplink (UL) traffic produced by Machine-to-Machine (M-M) and Human-to-Human (H-H) communications. In this paper, we present a radio resource management (RRM) approach based on Quality of Service (QoS) requirements of the UL IoT flows. The proposed scheme provides best scenarios that aim to provide a tradeoff between the two types of traffic by guaranteeing the network performance, maximizing the bandwidth utilisation rate and avoiding flow starvation.

Keywords: Internet of Things · LTE-A · 5G
Radio resource management · Resource optimisation · QoS

1 Introduction

Nowadays, wireless technologies have significant impact on our social life due to the exponential growth of smart phones, tablets and many similar devices that create a fully interconnected society. It is a real revolution of the Internet of Things (IoT) [1] with the diversity of applications expanded in all areas of our life (electricity, health, transportation, industrial, etc. ...) and it will involve an enormous number of communicating and autonomous devices. Face to wireless technologies evolution, 5G networks is the suitable solution to bear the IoT services. Indeed, the 5G LTE-A (Long Term Evolution-Advanced) enhancements are defined to reach emerging features and trends such as device-to-device (D-D) and machine-to-machine (M-M) communications [2,3], cloud radio access network (CRAN) [4,5], reduced latency, enhanced indoor coverage, low energy consumption and massive MIMO [6].

Several key issues and challenges should be addressed in this context for the purpose to satisfy QoS provisionning. One of the 5G key issues is the network functions including radio resource management (RRM) for IoT communications.

© Springer Nature Switzerland AG 2018
N. Montavont and G. Z. Papadopoulos (Eds.): ADHOC-NOW 2018, LNCS 11104, pp. 77–89, 2018.
https://doi.org/10.1007/978-3-030-00247-3_7

The existing RRM solutions need to be reviewed with the expansion of IoT communications in wireless systems to put a good use of the technology.

Zheng et al. [7] reviewed some radio resource allocation and scheduling schemes for M-M communications. They proposed two radio resources allocation approaches in an M-M and H-H co-existence scenario. Based on orthogonal radio resource allocation, the first approach provided low spectral efficiency. The latter was improved by the second approach that is based on shared radio resource allocation between H-H/H-M users. Wang et al. [8] designed an analytical model to optimize uplink resource utilization for multi-user D2D communication. To achieve this goal, they proposed a non-orthogonal resource sharing strategies that maximize throughput with guaranteed QoS for cellular users. Some other works, such as [9–11], focused on the impact of periodicity of M-M communications since M-M users M-M repetitively access the networks to transmit collected data. Zhang et al. [9] proposed a tree structure with the aim to characterize the conditions of multiplexing users with different periods onto a single channel. Then, they proposed a persistent resource allocation algorithm that allocates resources to users in a recursive manner based on the tree. Madueno et al. [10] focused on the periodicity to propose a contention-free allocation approach based on a periodically occurring pool of available resources. The key of this approach is how to dimension the pool of M-M dedicated resources to promise the desired reliability of the report delivery within the deadline. Next, Song et al. [11] proposed a network integrated multi-period polling service approach for resource allocation. Using this scheme, all M-M devices having different report period consecutively use the same available resources without random access period.

We propose a RRM approach for multi-traffic communications in 5G system. Our main contributions can be summarized as follows:

(i) A RRM scheme is proposed to satisfy both M-M and H-H traffic in the context of 5G LTE-A networks.
(ii) The proposed scheme presents a shared allocation stategy between H-H and M-M flows providing demands tradeoff for the two types of traffic.
(iii) The resource allocation scheme can satisfy QoS requirements by maximizing the bandwidth utilisation rate and avoiding problem starvation for H-H flows.

The rest of this paper is organized as follows. In the next section, a detailed description of the proposed system model is provided. Performance analysis and simulation scenarios are presented and discussed in Sect. 3. Finally, the conclusion and future works are drawn in Sect. 4.

2   System Model

In LTE standard, the radio access technology is based on Orthogonal Frequency Division Multiple Access (OFDMA) and Single-Carrier Frequency Division Multiple Access (SC-FDMA) in downlink and uplink, respectively. Both technologies use the same radio frame structure (Fig. 1) which makes full use of channel subdivision. Basically, channels are divided into radio resources that are composed of two domains frequency and time. In the frequency domain, the channel bandwidth ranges from 1 to 20 MHz. The total available bandwidth which includes 1.4, 3, 5, 10, 15 and 20 MHz is divided into sub-channels of 12 sub-carriers of 15 kHz, totaling 180 kHz. The minimum allocation unit of radio resources is called Resource Block (RB). A single RB consists of 180 KHz in the frequency domain and 1ms in the time domain. Indeed, in the time domain, radio resources are divided into Transmission Time Intervals (TTI), also called sub-frame, with duration of 1 ms. One frame is formed by 10 TTI. Each TTI consists of two 0.5 ms slots, and each slot comprises seven symbols. A LTE-A network within the 5G environment is considered as a model, it is known as 5G LTE-A. We focus on a single-cell with one eNB at the center and a set of mobile user equipement as it is shown in Fig. 2. There are two types of user traffic: M-M and H-H. Assuming that the available bandwidth in the eNB is denoted by BW and it consists of a number of resource blocks denoted by RBs which is shared between M-M and H-H users.

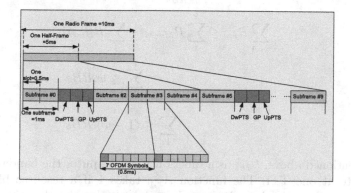

Fig. 1. TDD frame structure

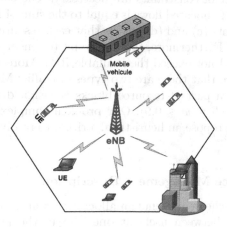

Fig. 2. Network model

2.1 Problem Formulation

Our proposed RRM scheme can be considered as a resource allocation problem. Let $RBs = \{1,\ldots,R\}$ the set of available resource blocks. Our optimization problem is formulated as it follows:

$$\max U_{IoT} = \sum_{x=1}^{z} \sum_{y \in RBs} R_{x,y} A_{x,y} \tag{a}$$

$$z \leq h + k \tag{b}$$

$$s.c. \quad A_{x,y} \in \{0,1\}; \forall x \in \{1,z\}; y \in RBs \tag{c}$$

$$\sum_{x=1}^{z} A_{x,y} \leq 1; \forall y \in RBs \tag{d}$$

$$\sum_{y \in RBs} R_{x,y} A_{x,y} \leq RBs \tag{e}$$

$$\sum_{x=1}^{z} R_{x,y} \leq \sum_{1}^{k} R_{M-M} + \sum_{1}^{h} R_{H-H} \tag{f}$$

$$\sum_{1}^{k} \leq w.RBs \tag{g}$$

$$\sum_{1}^{h} \leq (1 - w).RBs \tag{h}$$

As it is mentioned above, U_{IoT} is a function that computes the bandwidth utilization rate at one TTI. The function $A_{x,y}$ takes 1 if a resource block y is allocated for a flow x and 0 otherwise. In order to solve the objective function given by Eq. (a), a set of constraints are necessary. The constraint (b) ensures that the upper limit of allocated flows is equal to the sum of M-M and H-H flows $(h + k)$. The constraints (c) and (d) ensure that each resource block can only be allocated to one flow. Furthermore, the constraint (e) ensures that the allocated resource blocks should not exceed the available RBs. Moreover, the constraints (f), (g) and (h) ensure that there are two types of traffic; M-M and H-H, where for each traffic type, a part of resource blocks is assigned with respect to the random variable w ($0.5 \leq w \leq 0.9$). Our problem complexity is considered as NP-Hard [12], so we propose an heuristic algorithm to resolve the problem given by (a).

2.2 Radio Reource Management Description

The proposed RRM scheme presents an allocation strategy of available resource blocks (in the eNB) between users at one TTI in the purpose to maximize the bandwidth utilisation rate. It is based on differents steps and conditions described below. We start with the initialisation step which consists of choosing randomly the amount of resource blocks assigned for both M-M and H-H

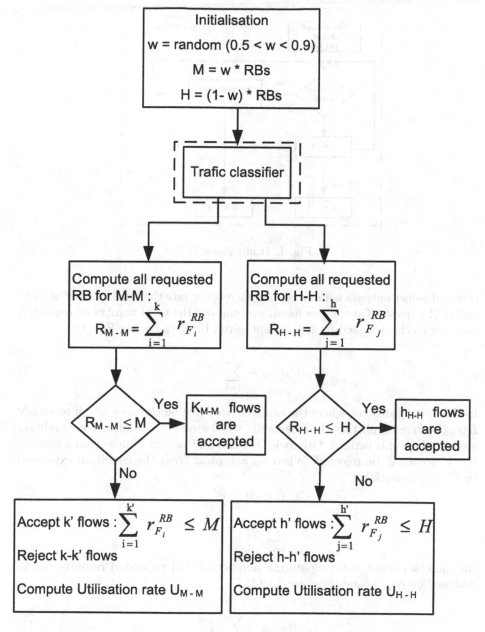

Fig. 3. Flowchart of the proposed RRM scheme

flows. In this step, we denote M and H the total number of resource blocks designed respectively for M-M and H-H traffic. In order to give priority for M-M flows, we give ramdom w between 0.5 and 0.9. A Traffic Classifier is proposed to distinguish between M-M and H-H requests as it is depicted in Fig. 4. The

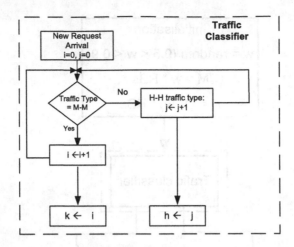

Fig. 4. Traffic classifier

traffic classifier outputs k and h represents respectively the total number of M-M and H-H requests. On the one hand, we compute the total number of requested resource blocks designed by R_{M-M} and given by the folowing Eq. (1):

$$R_{M-M} = \sum_{i=1}^{k} r_{F_i}^{RB} \tag{1}$$

In the best conditions, where the available resource blocks are enough to satisfy R_{M-M} requests, all the M-M demands will be accepted and so the condition given by Eq. (2) is verified. Otherwise, we can only accept k' flows and a number $k - k'$ flows will be rejected. When we accept k' flows the condition expressed by Eq. (3) is checked.

$$R_{M-M} \leq M \tag{2}$$

$$\sum_{i=1}^{k'} r_{F_i}^{RB} \leq M \tag{3}$$

On the other hand, we compute the number of H-H requested resource blocks designed by R_{H-H} and given by Eq. (4).

$$R_{H-H} = \sum_{j=1}^{h} r_{F_j}^{RB} \tag{4}$$

Having the number of H-H demands, two cases can be taken. The first one is occured when the amount of available resource blocks is sufficient and all demands are satisfied (Eq. (5)).

$$R_{H-H} \leq H \tag{5}$$

The second case will be considered only if h' flows are accepted (Eq. (6)) and thus $h - h'$ flows will be rejected.

$$\sum_{j=1}^{h'} r_{F_j}^{RB} \leq H \tag{6}$$

The proposed RRM scheme is summarized by a flowchart depicted by Fig. 3. The last step will be the computation of the bandwidth utilisation rate U_{IoT} given by the following equations:

$$U_{IoT} = U_{M-M} + U_{H-H} \tag{7}$$

$$= \frac{1}{M} \sum_{i=1}^{k'} r_{F_i}^{RB} + \frac{1}{H} \sum_{j=1}^{h'} r_{F_j}^{RB} \tag{8}$$

3 Performance Analysis and Simulation

In this section, a performance evaluation of our proposed RRM scheme is presented. An analytical study is carried out in the target to validate our proposal. The simulations are performed using MATLAB tools.

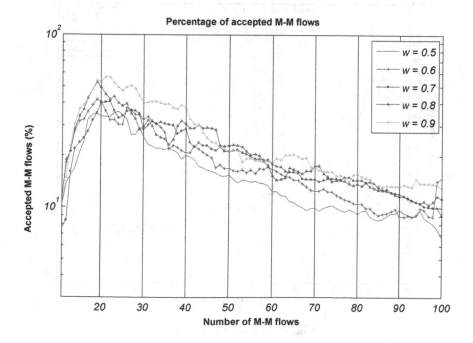

Fig. 5. Percentage of accepted M-M flows

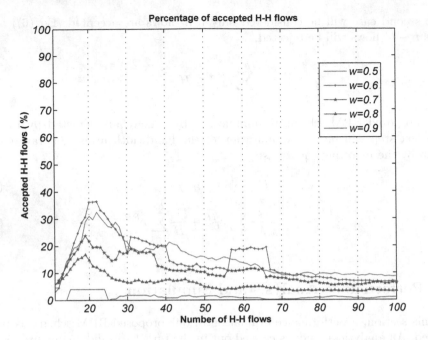

Fig. 6. Accepted H-H flows

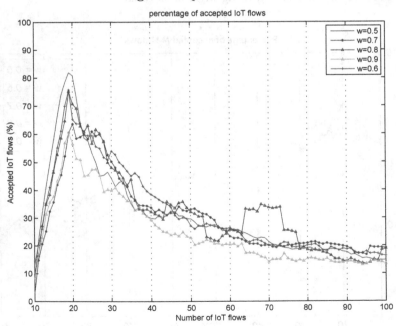

Fig. 7. Accepted IoT flows

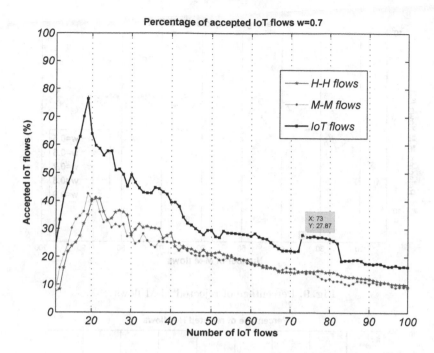

Fig. 8. Accepted IoT flows for w = 0.7

The available bandwidth is set 10 MHz or 50 RBs shared among all users in the cell. The studied model is evaluated based on the following performance metrics: percentage of accepted flows, percentage of rejected flows and the bandwidth utilisation rate. Figure 5 illustrates the percentage of accepted M-M flows by varying w from 0.5 to 0.9. In fact, when the value of w increases, M-M flows have more chances to be accepted than H-H flows as it is illustrated in Figs. 6 and 7. The best percentage of accepted M-M flows is reached when $w = 0.9$ and the worst one is reached when $w = 0.5$. Thus, the best value of w that ensures QoS requirements is 0.7 where we aim to provide a tradeoff between the two types of traffic (Fig. 8).

In addition, we compute the percentage of rejected M-M flows (Fig. 9), the percentage of rejected H-H flows (Fig. 10) and the percentage of IoT flows (Fig. 11). It is clear from Figs. 11 and 12 that the best scenario ensuring less percentage of rejected flows is set when $w = 0.7$. Furthermore, the proposed RRM avoids the starvation problem by guaranteeing traffic tradeoff.

The important challenge of the proposed RRM is to maximize the bandwidth utilization rate. It is proved by Fig. 13 where the total bandwidth frequency allocated for IoT flows (M-M and H-H) is almost used (10 MHz). Thus the overall performance of the proposed scheme is improved and the QoS requirements are satisfied.

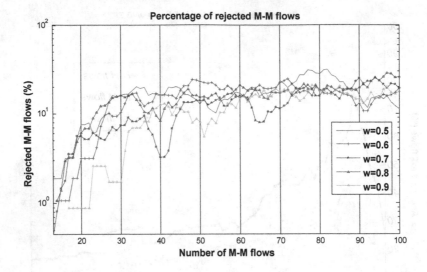

Fig. 9. Percentage of rejected M-M flows

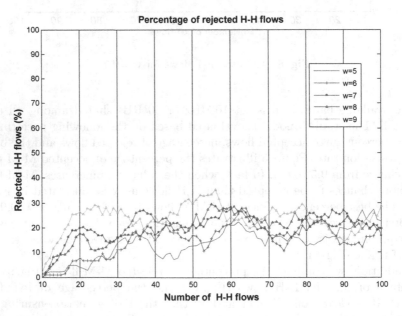

Fig. 10. Rejected H-H flows

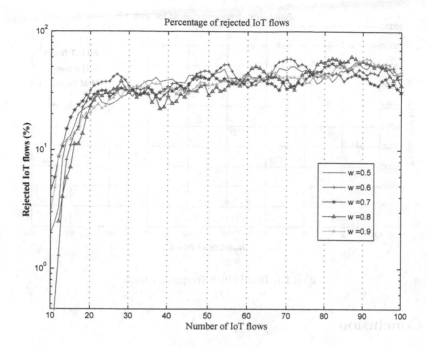

Fig. 11. Rejected IoT flows

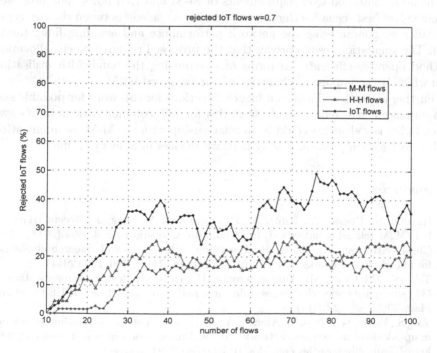

Fig. 12. Rejected IoT flows for w = 0.7

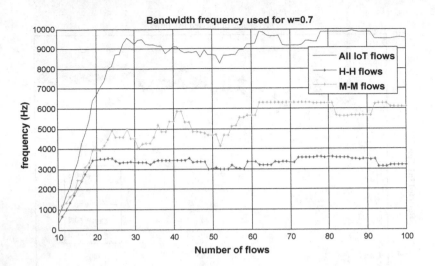

Fig. 13. Bandwidth frequency used

4   Conclusion

In this paper, we propose a radio resource management scheme for IoT communications based on QoS requirements of M-M and H-H flows. The proposed scheme gives best scenarios that aim to provide a tradeoff between the two types of trafics by guaranteeing the network performance and avoiding flow starvation. The simulation results proves that the proposed resource blocks allocation method operates efficiently in terms of maximizing the bandwidth utilisation rate which is the important challenge of our proposed RRM.

Further research will focus on future directions for this work for possible system enhancements, requirements scenarios for IoT communications in 5G systems. Other key elements could be in relationship with the M-M communication such as congestion problem among network devices in a heavy traffic.

References

1. Hussain, S., Prasad, A., Kunz, A., Papageorgiou, A., Song, J.: Recent trends in IoT/M2M related standards. J. Inf. Commun. Converg. Eng. **4**, S6n (2014)
2. Chin, W.H., Fan, Z., Haines, R.: Emerging technologies and research challenges for 5G wireless networks. IEEE Wirel. Commun. **21**(2), 106–112 (2014)
3. Tehrani, M., Uysal, M., Yanikomeroglu, H.: Device-to-device communication in 5G cellular networks: challenges, solutions, and future directions. IEEE Commun. Mag. **52**(5), 86–92 (2014)
4. Yan, S., Wang, W., Zhao, Z., Ahmed, A.: Investigation of cell association techniques in uplink cloud radio access networks. Trans. Emerg. Telecommun. Technol. (2014). http://onlinelibrary.wiley.com/doi/10.1002/ett.2894/abstract

5. Tony Q.S., Quek, M.P., Osvaldo, S., Wei, Y.: Cloud Radio Access Networks: Principles, Technologies, and Applications, 498 p. Cambridge University Press, Cambridge (2017)
6. Marzetta, T.L. Larsson, E.G., Yang, H., Ngo, H.Q.: Fundamentals of Massive MIMO. Cambridge University Press (2016). https://books.google.tn/
7. Zheng, K., Hu, F., Wang, W., Xiang, W., Dohler, M.: Radio resource allocation in LTE-advanced cellular networks with M2M communications. IEEE Commun. Mag. **50**(7), 184–192 (2012)
8. Wang, J., Zhu, D., Zhao, C., Li, J., Lei, M.: Resource sharing of underlaying device-to-device and uplink cellular communications. IEEE Commun. Lett. **17**, 1148–1151 (2013)
9. Zhang, Y.: Tree-based resource allocation for periodic cellular M2M communications. IEEE Wirel. Commun. Lett. **3**(6), 621–624 (2014)
10. Madueno, G.C., Stefanovic, C., Popovski, P.: Reliable reporting for massive M2M communications with periodic resource pooling. IEEE Wirel. Commun. Lett. **3**(4), 429–432 (2014)
11. Song, Q., Lagrange, X., Nuaymi, L.: An efficient M2M-oriented network-integrated multiple-period polling service in LTE network. In: Vehicular Technology Conference (VTC Fall), pp. 1–6. IEEE (2015)
12. Lee, S.-B., Pefkianakis, I., Meyerson, A., Xu, S., Lu, S.: Proportional fair frequency-domain packet scheduling for 3GPP LTE uplink. In: IEEE INFOCOM (2009)

Dynamic Joint Resource Allocation and Femtocell Selection for 5G HetNet

Amal Bouaziz[1], Ahlem Saddoud[1(✉)], Lamia Chaari Fourati[1], and Hakima Chaouchi[2]

[1] LAB (LR16CNRS01), Digital Research Center of Sfax, Technopark, B.P 3021, Sfax, Tunisia
ahlemsaddoud@gmail.com

[2] CNRS, SAMOVAR, Telecom Sud Paris, Institut Telecom, Paris-Saclay University, Paris, France

Abstract. Due to the growth explosion of Machine-to-Machine (M2M) and Human-to-Human (H2H) communications traffic, the majority of the mobile network operators (MNOs) recently start the deployment of heterogeneous network (HetNet) including femtocells. HetNet is a promising solution for next generation networks to meet the increasing of data rate demand. Whereas, femtocell selection scheme plays a critical role in improving the benefit of this technology. In this paper, we have developed and then evaluated a Dynamic Joint Resource Allocation and Femtocell selection for 5G HetNet (J5G-RAS). Besides, our work aims to enhance the resource utilization by dividing the resources of each station in static and dynamic resources. Significant simulation results, show the improvements of the system model performances in terms of resource utilization ratio, dropped request probability, and total average throughput of the system.

Keywords: HetNet · 5G · Dynamic allocation
Femtocell selection · M2M communications

1 Introduction

The conventional cellular networks are known with a star-shaped topology. A point of central control characterizes this structure, which is the base station (BS). This topology guarantees easily the quality of service (QoS). Otherwise, this structure might handicap bandwidth utilization efficiency where a massive number of users will proceed through the core network at the same time. Hence, it is better for cellular topology to be heterogeneous using different sort of connections and recent technologies such as small cells. This trend technology might help on overcoming the issues of next generation networks such as 5 generation (5G). Following 4G [1,2], 5G [3,4] is the next generation of cellular networking technology. It aims to not only stand faster and more reliable mobile communication but also to supply larger coverage for the devices and better support for

© Springer Nature Switzerland AG 2018
N. Montavont and G. Z. Papadopoulos (Eds.): ADHOC-NOW 2018, LNCS 11104, pp. 90–101, 2018.
https://doi.org/10.1007/978-3-030-00247-3_8

simultaneous communications. It is hard to define the accurate features of 5G. Nevertheless, relative to rapid growth of traffic, it is predicted that 5G will reach 100 times higher of user data rate, 1000 times higher mobile data volume and 10 times longer battery life [5]. Previous communication systems of cellular mobile were designed to handle human beings' requirement, which is indispensable to a human-centralized communication system. Whereas, 5G is desired to consider the thing-centralized system, which means machine-to-machine (M2M) communications [6] or device-to-device (D2D) [7]. It is expected that the 5G, as well as the entire next generation cellular network will support not only the traditional services but also a huge variety of M2M services [8]. In [9], the authors have called attention to the impact of massive M2M communications. In fact, they have analyzed the arising issues caused by high traffic of M2M devices, and have defined some network access mechanisms as probable congestion that can reduce the system performance. For M2M communications case, the access mechanisms in Long Term Evolution (LTE) and 5G are investigated in some other works. For example, [10,11] have modeled and analyzed the performance of the access procedure to the network. However, they have not highlighted the congestion problem at the BS, as well as the impact of blocking between the access mechanism and the BS. Both of the bottlenecks have been taken into consideration in massive access case through a measurement-based approach [12]. In [13] the authors have proposed a device-centric scheme for resource allocation for D2D users. These users are randomly distributed in the macrocell. In order to reduce load and time consumption in the process of resource allocation on BS side, concerned D2D pairs might allocated the resource to themselves. However, the authors have not considered the mode selection scheme. In order to increase system capacity, to expand wireless coverage area and to minimize the cost of evolved Node B (eNB) deployment, relay nodes and small cells have been specified to cover on the existing macro cell, and then create a heterogeneous network (HetNets) [14]. HetNet signifies that small cells such as microcell, picocell, femtocell and personalcell are located in a macrocell, knowing that small cells assume the same capabilities of a standard eNB. Those small cells have the ability to mitigate macrocell traffic overload by sharing out the mobile traffic. Moreover, they can improve the system capacity in global network since they reuse the frequency bandwidth allocated to the macrocell [15]. Recently, several studies, which joint resource allocation and user association, have been developed for HetNets. Aiming to improve the spectral efficiency and to reach traffic load balancing, Siddique et al. have proposed in [16] a channel-access with aware user association scheme. In [17], the authors have proposed a new user association method with constrained backhaul and dual connectivity. Some recent works, such as [18] and [19], have introduced the joint optimization of sub-channel allocation and user association in multicell networks. In [18], the sub-channel allocation and user association problem have been solved independently. Authors in [19] have considered a joint of user association, BS transmission power and resource allocation. A new propagation algorithm have been proposed for optimal joint downlink sub-channel assignment, user allocation and power control. However, these methods are sensitive to the cells topology and users' distribution. Nowadays, about 70% of mobile data are generated indoors. Thanks to its flexibility of deployment, femtocell has the capacity to efficiently resolve pertinent issues of indoor communications. Thus, deploying femtocells in a macro cellular network allows sharing the load of the BS between macrocell and femtocell. Hence, system performance is improved. Both types of cells can cooperate by using same or different frequencies [20]. In this paper, we have proposed a Dynamic Joint Resource Allocation and Femtocell selection for 5G HetNet (J5G-RAS). It allows the selection of the suitable femtocell by computing an utility function and presents an allocation strategy between H2H and M2M traffics. Our solution maximizes the total resource utilization in the system and ensures a balanced load between the eNB and the different Home eNB (HeNB) by jointly selecting the adequate femtocell for each user and optimally allocating the resources.

The rest of the paper is set out as follows. In Sect. 2, we present the system model by describing the architecture, our proposed joint resource allocation and femtocell selection scheme and the problem formulation. Performances analysis are depicted in Sect. 3. Finally, we form a conclusion and future work in Sect. 4.

2   System Model

In this work, we consider the downlink transmission (DL) of a single macrocell base station eNB architecture as shown in Fig. 1. The geographical region is completely overlaid by single eNB M located at (0,0) with 46 dBm transmission power, containing 12 femtocells F_i, with $i \in \{1, \ldots, 12\}$ that are uniformly located at (x_i, y_i) with a transmission power of 20 dBm. We take into account a minimum distance between two neighboring femtocells to efficiently distribute them based on the area overlaid. Two types of users are randomly distributed in this architecture: Human-to-Human (H2H) users $l \in \{1, \ldots, L\}$ where L is the total number of H2H flows in the system and M2M users $k \in \{1, \ldots, K\}$ where K is the total number of M2M flows in the system. The number of the accessing user follows the Poisson point process with a density of λ. We assume that the totality of the bandwidth is partitioned into orthogonal sub-channels. Therefore, the channel subdivision is fully used. Basically, in LTE-A standard, channels are a set of radio resource which consist of both frequency domain and time domain. In addition, the PHY frame are composed of 10 Transmission Time Intervals (TTI) sub-frames (a TTI is two slots of 0.5 ms each). In one sub-frame, the total number of Resource Blocks (RBs) that may be sent is depending on the channel bandwidth of frequency carrier. For example, 1.4 MHz of channel bandwidth provides 6 RBs since the total of sub-carriers are of 180 KHz. However, when the channel bandwidth raises to 20 MHz, sub-frame exhibits 100 RBs. The RBs exhibited by sub-frame per different channel bandwidths in LTE-A are depicted in Table 1.

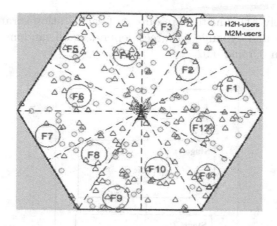

Fig. 1. System Model Scheme.

Table 1. Number of RBs given under different channel bandwidths

Channel bandwidth (MHz)	1.4	3	5	10	15	20
Number of RBs	6		15	25	50	75	100

2.1 Proposed J5G-RAS

The proposed solution is summarized by the flowchart shown in Fig. 2. After the initialization, J5G-RAS starts with the traffic classifier by distinguishing between H2H and M2M requests. Then, the femtocell selection stage is launched. For M2M requests, the system calculates the utility function of the users from each Home eNB (HeNB) (i.e. HeNB is the base station of the femtocell). According to the results of the utility function, the appropriate femtocell is selected to serve the user in consideration. The next stage concerns the resource allocation model. In fact, in the traditional allocation model, the resources of the different stations are fully shared between different traffics existing in the network since the users request is under cover area. This leads to a large delay that disagreed the QoS. However, J5G-RAS proposes a new dynamic model of resource allocation. In this model, the resources of each station, eNB or HeNB, are divided into static and dynamic resources. The static resources are used preferably if they are available and sufficient to supply service to users. However, when the system traffic is large, the dynamic resources will be allocated by the control center according to the type of the users. Let's note that:

$$RG_{Fi} = \alpha RS_{Fi} + (1 - \alpha)RD_{Fi}, \tag{1}$$

and

$$RG_M = \beta RS_M + (1 - \beta)RD_M, \tag{2}$$

where RG_{Fi} (respectively RG_M), RS_{Fi} (respectively RS_M) and RD_{Fi} (respectively RD_M) is the global resource, the static resource and the dynamic resource of a F_i (respectively M). The total resources of each station is randomly divided in static resources and dynamic resources depending on random values α and β which are between 0.5 and 0.9.

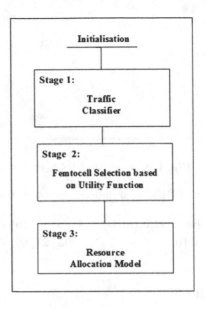

Fig. 2. J5G-RAS system model

2.2 Problem Formulation

In this section, we present the problem formulation of the J5G-RAS scheme. As a centralized station selection scheme is proposed, we consider the existence of a centralized entity that has the responsibility to find the suitable F_i to a given user. We also consider that the channel gain variations of radio propagation is perfectly known. Besides, the selection should be made in a manner that overall load balance is guaranteed into the network. For example, the contention for the resources in the eNB is high because of the high load, while in HeNB, the available resources could not be fully utilized because of the low load. Therefore, we define a parameter which is the HeNB load status aiming to have an effective F_i selection scheme. Moreover, our proposed scheme focuses on the idea that a station is selected only when if it owns enough resources to serve either M2M or H2H users. In order to do so, we introduce a utility function that takes into consideration the above constraints. This function $U_{k,i}$ where k refers to the user, is defined as a linear combination of three factors:

$$U_{k,i} = \gamma C_{k,i} + \mu R_{k,i} + \eta \frac{1}{PL_{k,i}}, \tag{3}$$

where the parameters γ, μ and η are the weights of the defined factors knowing that:

$$\gamma + \mu + \eta = 1. \tag{4}$$

$C_{k,i}$ is the charge factor of F_i for a user k estimated at a TTI. In fact, it defines the ratio of the number of available radio resources at the HeNB to the total capacity of this station. While, $R_{k,i}$ is the rate factor of a F_i for a user k. It is defined as the instantaneous rate factor offered by each F_i to a user k divided by the mean data rate provided by the nearby F_i during one TTI. $PL_{k,i}$ is the pathloss between the F_i and a user k. To estimate the PL in macrocell and femtocell, we assume ITU UMa model and UMi model defined in [21]. The PL for the case of an outdoor user in an urban area, is given by:

$$PL_{macro}(dB) = 15.3 + 37.6log10(D), \tag{5}$$

however, for an indoor user the PL can be expressed as follows:

$$PL_{macro}(dB) = 15.3 + 37.6log10(D) + Low, \tag{6}$$

where D is the distance between the transmitter to the receiver in meters and Low is the penetration loss of the wall in dB.

The path loss between a HeNB and an indoor user is calculated by the following equation:

$$PL_{Femto}(dB) = 20log10(\frac{4\pi f_c}{C}) + (10\alpha log10(D)) + 0.7D + qLiw. \tag{7}$$

whereas, for the case of an outdoor user, the PL will be:

$$PL_{Femto}(dB) = 20log10(\frac{4\pi f_c}{C}) + (10\alpha log10(D)) + 0.7D + qLiw + Low. \tag{8}$$

where f_c is the frequency in Hz, C is the speed of light in meters per second, α is the path loss exponent, q is the number of separating walls and Liw is the penetration loss of separating walls. This combination between the three factors $C_{k,i}$, $R_{k,i}$ and $PL_{k,i}$ provides a better F_i selection because the performance requirements of both user and network are taken into consideration. Once the utility function $U_{k,i}$ is computed by a user k for all the F_i, k selects the F_i which maximizes this utility function. Consequently, the selected F_i realizes the highest benefit for the user k as it ensures the available radio resources in order to satisfy the required throughput. The selection scheme of the adequate F_i in our HetNet is depicted in the Table 2. After the stage of the selection scheme, the J5G-RAS goes to verify the availability of the required resources according to the proposed resource allocation algorithm detailed in the flowchart shown in Fig. 3. This algorithm aims to prioritize M2M requests over H2H ones:

– If it is an M2M request, the system must check the availability of the RS_{Fi} of the selected F_i. If it is not available, it checks the availability of the RD_{Fi}. In the case of unavailability of the RG_{Fi} of the F_i in question, the system makes use of the RS_M then RD_M of the macrocell M. The system will abort the request when resources are fully allocated.

– If it is a H2H request, the system must check the availability of the RS_M of the macrocell M. If not, it checks the availability of its RS_M. In the case of unavailability of the global resource RG_{Fi}, we define an SNR threshold denoted δ. Then, J5G-RAS computes the received $SNR_{h,i}$ of the user h on each F_i. If $SNR_{h,i} \geq \delta$, the system makes use of the dynamic resources RD_{Fi} of the appropriate F_i. Otherwise, the request will be rejected.

Table 2. Proposed algorithm of the F_i selection scheme

Algorithm. Utility function for F_i selection scheme in HetNet
1. {Initialisation}
2. In TTI,
for each k,i **do**
a. calculate $C_{k,i}$ of each user k for each F_i
b. calculate $R_{k,i}$ of each user k for each F_i
c. calculate the inverse of $PL_{k,i}$ of each user k for F_i
d. calculate $U_{k,i}$ of each user k for each F_i
e. select the station I which supply the highest Utility $U_{k,i}$: $I = \arg(max_i \{U_{k,i}\})$
f. select the Femtocell I which provides this maximum
end for

Each user is selecting the appropriate HeNB or eNB according to our J5G-RAS. Our objective is to maximize the resource utilization within the system. To do so, we define the function RU as the rate of the allocated resources to the global resources. The overall rate of resource utilization in the system is thus expressed by:

$$max RU = \frac{1}{RG}(\sum_{i=1}^{12}\sum_{n=1}^{N}(RF_n) + \sum_{j=1}^{J}(RM_j)). \tag{9}$$

s.t:

$$\sum_{i=1}^{12}(RS_{Fi} + RD_{Fi}) + (RS_{Fi} + RD_{Fi}) = RG, \tag{10}$$

$$\sum_{i=1}^{12}(N \times RF_N) + (J \times RM_j) \leq RG \tag{11}$$

$$N + J \leq K + L \tag{12}$$

where RG is the global resources in the system and RF_n (respectively RM_j) is the rate of the allocated resources within a F_i (respectively M). N (respectively J) is the number of served user in each F_i (respectively M) where $n \in \{1,\ldots,N\}$ (respectively $j \in \{1,\ldots,J\}$). A set of constraints are required to solve the objective function given by Eq. (9). The constraint (10) ensures that the sum of all

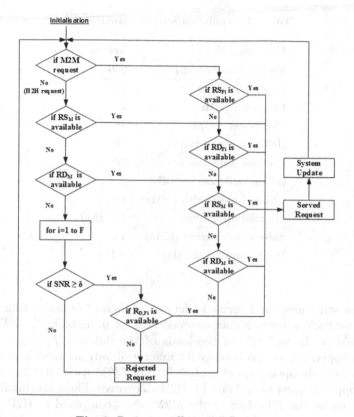

Fig. 3. Resource allocation flowchart

static and dynamic resources for all femtocell and for the macrocell must be equal to the global resources of the system with respect to the random variables α and β ($0.5 \leq \alpha, \beta \leq 0.9$). However the constraints (11) and (12) ensure that all allocated resources in both femtocells and macrocell must not exceed the global resources in the system and the total served users have not to exceed the total users in the system.

3 Performance Analysis

This section focuses on the evaluation of the effectiveness of our J5G-RAS in terms of dropped request probability, fairness, total average throughput and resource utilization rate. Matlab platform is used to analyze the performances of the J5G-RAS. Now, we have to notice that the values for the simulation setting parameters used in this model have been based on [22]. Table 3 gives an overview of the simulation parameters with the input values. Fig. 4 shows the dropped request probability in our system vs. the number of users in each type (H2H and M2M). When the users number increases, the dropped request probability increases too. Therefore, the quality of service (QoS) requirements are not

Table 3. Simulation setting parameters

Parameters	Values
Macrocell radius (m)	250
Femtocell radius (m)	20
Frequency (GHz)	2
eNB power (dBm)	46
HeNB power (dBm)	20
Outdoor walls loss low (dB)	20
Indoor walls loss liw (dB)	5
Channel bandwidth (MHz)	10
Modulation scheme	16 QAM
Sub-carrier spacing (KHz)	15
White noise (dBm/Hz)	−174

satisfied for some users and access is denied to them. We notice that classical macrocell network achieves higher dropped request probability than J5G-RAS, which considers the variation of the loads of the different F_i. Figure 4 shows that the dropped request probability for macrocell-only scenario is almost 60% higher than the dropped request probability for M2M users and 25% than the ones of dropped request probability for H2H. Moreover, Fig. 4 also highlights the priority given by the J5G-RAS to the M2M users compared to H2H users for the different values of α and β. The minimal dropped request probability case for M2M users is when $\alpha = 0.9$ and $\beta = 0.9$ because H2H users are denied to be served by the static resources of femtocells. In fact, it is the worst scenario for H2H users access. However, the best scenario for H2H users is when $\alpha = 0.5$ since they shared the half of each F_i resources. It highlights the degree of the satisfaction fairness for different users in the system with regards to users utility function. Figure 5 shows the enhancement of fairness among different type of users after the deployment of the femtocells, and particularly in the case of

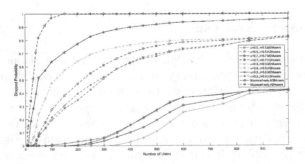

Fig. 4. Dropped request probability per number of users for different values of α and β.

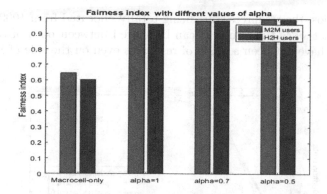

Fig. 5. Fairness index per type of request with different values α.

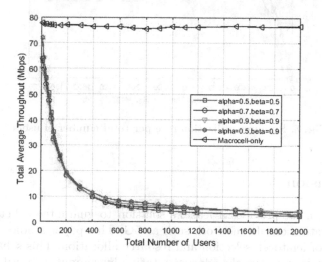

Fig. 6. Total average throughput per number of total users

$\alpha = 0.5$. This occurs since the resources of HeNB are 50% shared between M2M and H2H flows to satisfy the throughput requirements of all users in the system. We can notice that the fairness index metric exceeds 90% with the different values of α which approve that our defined utility function answers the satisfaction among all users in the system. In view of the above parameters, the cell throughput is estimated under the different scenarios. Each user throughput is evaluated via the Shannon capacity. Figure 6 presents how the total average throughput is affected by the total number of users in the system. In the case of macrocell-only scenario, the total average throughput is about 78 Mbps. As shown from this graph, the total average throughput is less than 74 Mbps and decreases as the number of user increases. Figure 7 depicts the rate of the resource utilization in the system as the number of total users. For the scenario of macrocell-only, the resources are almost fully allocated from 170 users. However, under the rest of the scenarios, the resources start being totally allocated from 1000 users. We can notice that since the resources can be shared between both of traffic type, there almost have not been a waste of resources even on the side of HeNB.

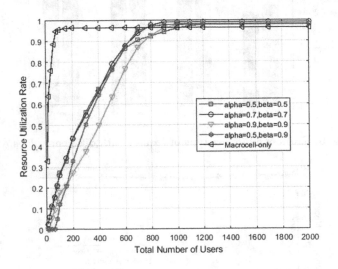

Fig. 7. Resource utilization rate per total number of users

4   Conclusion

HetNet deployment provides a feasible solution to guarantee a better overlay in next generation cellular network such as 5G. This paper studies an optimal joint scheme of femtocell selection and resource allocation. This solution allows the different users to select the adequate station by computing a utility function with taking into account the load of the different cells. The proposed J5G-RAS maximizes the total resource utilization in the system and ensures a balanced load between the eNB and the different HeNB by jointly selecting the cell for each user and optimally allocating the resources. Simulation results verify the effectiveness of our proposed model in terms of dropped request probability, fairness, total average throughput and resource utilization rate. This work might be expanded to a multi macrocell network and addressed to the QoS requirements.

References

1. TR 36.806: Evolved Universal Terrestrial Radio Access (E-UTRA): Relay Architectures for E-UTRA (LTE-Advanced),(Release 9), v9.0.0
2. TR 36.912: Feasibility Study for Further Advancements for E-UTRA (LTE-Advanced), (Release 14), v14.0.0
3. Agiwal, M., Roy, A., Saxena, N.: Next generation 5G wireless networks: a comprehensive survey. IEEE Commun. Surv. Tutor. **18**(3), 1617–1655 (2016)

4. Panwar, N., Sharma, S., Singh, A.K.: A survey on 5G: the next generation of mobile communication. Phys. Commun. **18**, 64–84 (2016)
5. Li, Q.C., Niu, H., Papathanassiou, A.T., Wu, G.: 5G network capacity: key elements and technologies. IEEE Veh. Technol. Mag. **9**(1), 71–78 (2014)
6. Verma, P.K., et al.: Machine-to-Machine (M2M) communications: a survey. J. Netw. Comput. Appl. **66**, 83–105 (2016)
7. Tehrani, M.N., Uysal, M., Yanikomeroglu, H.: Device-to-device communication in 5G cellular networks: challenges, solutions, and future directions. IEEE Commun. Mag. **52**(5), 86–92 (2014)
8. Castagno, P., Mancuso, V., Sereno, M., Ajmone Marsan, M.: A simple model of MTC in smart factories (2018)
9. Biral, A., Centenaro, M., Zanella, A., Vangelista, L., Zorzi, M.: The challenges of M2M massive access in wireless cellular networks. Digit. Commun. Netw. **1**(1), 1–19 (2015)
10. Madueno, G.C., Nielsen, J.J., Kim, D.M., Pratas, N.K., Stefanovic, C., Popovski, P.: Assessment of LTE wireless access for monitoring of energy distribution in the smart grid. IEEE J. Sel. Areas Commun. **34**(3), 675–688 (2016)
11. Cherkaoui, S., Keskes, I., Rivano, H., Stanica, R.: LTE-a random access channel capacity evaluation for M2M communications. In: Wireless Days (WD), pp. 1–6. IEEE, March 2016
12. Castagno, P., Mancuso, V., Sereno, M., Marsan, M.A.: Why your smartphone doesn't work in very crowded environments. In: 2017 IEEE 18th International Symposium on a World of Wireless, Mobile and Multimedia Networks (WoWMoM), pp. 1–9. IEEE, June 2017
13. Mishra, P.K., Pandey, S., Udgata, S.K., Biswash, S.K.: Device-centric resource allocation scheme for 5G networks. Phys. Commun. **26**, 175–184 (2018)
14. Ghosh, A., et al.: Heterogeneous cellular networks: from theory to practice. IEEE Commun. Mag. **50**(6) (2012)
15. Kwon, Y.M., Shin, J., Kim, J.S., Oh, S.M., Chung, M.Y., Park, A.S.: Development of system level simulator for evaluating performance of moving personal cell network. In: Proceedings of the 8th International Conference on Ubiquitous Information Management and Communication, p. 19. ACM (2014)
16. Siddique, U., Tabassum, H., Hossain, E., Kim, D.I.: Channel-access-aware user association with interference coordination in two-tier downlink cellular networks. IEEE Trans. Veh. Technol. **65**(7), 5579–5594 (2016)
17. Wu, Z., Xie, W., Yang, F., Bi, Q.: User association in heterogeneous network with dual connectivity and constrained backhaul. China Commun. **13**(2), 11–20 (2016)
18. Li, Y., Sheng, M., Sun, Y., Shi, Y.: Joint optimization of BS operation, user association, subcarrier assignment, and power allocation for energy-efficient HetNets. IEEE J. Sel. Areas Commun. **34**(12), 3339–3353 (2016)
19. Chen, Y., Li, J., Chen, W., Lin, Z., Vucetic, B.: Joint user association and resource allocation in the downlink of heterogeneous networks. IEEE Trans. Veh. Technol. **65**(7), 5701–5706 (2016)
20. Ye, F., Dai, J., Li, Y.: Game algorithm for resource allocation based on intelligent gradient in HetNet. Symmetry **9**(3), 34 (2017)
21. TR 36.942: Evolved Universal Terrestrial Radio Access (E-UTRA); Radio Frequency (RF) System Scenarios, (Release 11), v11.0.0
22. Simsek, M., Akbudak, T., Zhao, B., Czylwik, A.: An LTE-femtocell dynamic system level simulator. In: 2010 International ITG Workshop on Smart Antennas (WSA), pp. 66–71. IEEE, February 2010

Demo and Posters

Benchmarking Smartphone Performances for Cooperative Disaster Alert Diffusion

Farouk Mezghani[✉] and Nathalie Mitton

Inria, Lille, France
{farouk.mezghani,nathalie.mitton}@inria.fr

Abstract. When a disaster strikes, communication infrastructure such as cellular network may get destroyed, which makes rescue operations more challenging. Short range-based opportunistic communications using daily mobile devices such as smartphones present a promising solution to support infrastructure failure. In a previous work, we have proposed COPE, a cooperative opportunistic alert diffusion solution useful for trapped survivors during disasters to ease and speed up their rescue and assistance. It targets to maintain mobile devices alive as long as possible for a maximum network coverage until reaching proximate rescuers. COPE leverage mobile devices that come with multiple network technologies and aims to perform a systematic network interface selection. We have implemented a proof-of-concept of COPE for android smartphones using two network technologies: Bluetooth and Wi-Fi. This work presents a benchmark analysis of performances of smartphones based on COPE. Testing experiments have been carried out to measure the performance of smartphones in terms of energy consumption, clock synchronization and transmission range. We believe that such experimental results can support technological choices for rescue operations but also for many other applications relying on smartphone performances.

1 Introduction

Opportunistic communications have attracted considerable attention as a possible alternative to support infrastructure failure during disaster scenarios [5,6]. Indeed, mobile devices used daily by everyone such as smartphones can be useful to offer direct communications helpful to ease rescue operations during disasters such as to report location position of trapped survivors after earthquake.

Several research works have proposed solutions for disaster recovery leveraging mobile devices. However, these latter have left behind two important features: (i) multi-network assortment and (ii) various energy levels. These works have considered mobile devices that come with only one network technology while nowadays, mobile devices such as smartphones are equipped with multiple network technologies (e.g. Wi-Fi, Bluetooth and cellular) and users have no idea which is the best. Moreover, they do not consider mobile devices that come with various initial energy levels which obviously has an impact on the disaster recovery solution.

© Springer Nature Switzerland AG 2018
N. Montavont and G. Z. Papadopoulos (Eds.): ADHOC-NOW 2018, LNCS 11104, pp. 105–111, 2018.
https://doi.org/10.1007/978-3-030-00247-3_9

Unlike existing works, in a previous work, we have proposed a cooperative opportunistic alert diffusion solution named COPE useful for survivors during disasters to report their location, thus, to speed up their rescue operation [4]. COPE leverages multiple network technologies and considers mobile devices that come with various initial energy levels. It aims to maintain a maximum network coverage by keeping mobile devices alive for as long as possible. We have implemented a proof-of-concept of COPE for android smartphones considering Bluetooth and Wi-Fi technologies [3]. An overview of COPE solution is presented in the next section.

The contribution of this paper lies in a benchmark analysis of performances of smartphones considering COPE. We have conducted testing experiments and we provide results showing the performance of smartphones in terms of energy consumption, clock synchronization and transmission range. These results can also serve to support technological choices for rescue operations but also for many other applications relying on smartphone performances.

2   Background: The COPE Mechanism

Figure 1 illustrates a multi-technology communication view of COPE considering mobile devices equipped each with three network technologies (n_1, n_2 and n_3) corresponding for instance to those available nowadays in smartphones (Bluetooth, Wi-Fi, Cellular). This work classifies the available network technologies according to their energy consumption (E) and transmission range (TR) as follows: $TR_{n_3} > TR_{n_2} > TR_{n_1}$ and $EC_{n_3} > EC_{n_2} > EC_{n_1}$.

e.g. Bluetooth provides the shortest transmission range, thus consuming the lowest energy amount. This work relies on the assumption that network technologies can be sorted from the lowest to the higher energy-consuming and that there is a direct correlation between energy consumption and network performances (especially in terms of range). One of the goals of this paper is to validate or invalidate this assumption.

Nodes exchange periodic beacon messages to form cliques based on the less power network technology n_1 (i.e. cliques C_i, i = 1..5). Inside each clique, a cooperative communication is performed based on the n_2 network technology. Indeed, inside each clique, nodes alternately diffuse the alert message and discover neighbors using the network technology n_2. Time is divided into equal time-slots τ and each node determines its wake-up schedule based on the clique information (IDs and energy levels of nodes belonging to the same clique). The wake-up order is determined based on the node ID in comparison to those of nodes belonging to the same clique (i.e. node with the lowest ID occupies the first period during the time-slot). During its wake-up, each node activates its network interface n_2 for neighboring discovery and alert diffusion, otherwise, it switches to the power save mode.

If a node i discovers other proximate nodes j from the n_2 network perspective (nodes i and j are neighbors with n_2 technology), together, they form a zone that includes their respective cliques (the zone is a clique at an upper level). For

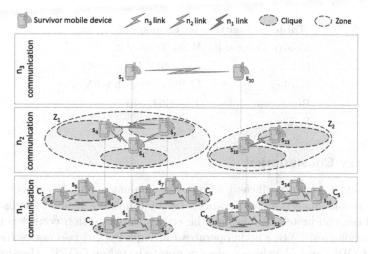

Fig. 1. Multi-technology communication overview

instance, as shown in Fig. 1-Layer n_2 communication, nodes s_{10} and s_{13} discover each other based on the n_2 network interface. Then, they exchange information (i.e. nodes IDs and energy levels) about their corresponding cliques C_4 and C_5 and then form a zone Z_2 that includes their corresponding cliques C_4 and C_5. Afterwards, they diffuse the zone information (nodes belonging to the zone and their energy levels) to their cliques through the active interface n_1.

Inside each zone, a cooperative diffusion can be performed from the n_3 communication perspective based on an alternative alert diffusion. Each node computes its wake-up schedule from the n_3 communication perspective by referring to its energy level and ID and those of nodes inside the same zone.

The network topology is dynamic due to leaving and joining nodes. This latter can be detected through the periodic messages exchanged between nodes belonging to the same clique/zone. When the topology changes, nodes exchange their 1-hop neighbors and update their cliques information and re-computes their wake-up schedules.

3   Smartphone Performance

We have conducted different experiments featuring six smartphones Wiko Tommy 2 and exploiting two network technologies Bluetooth and Wi-Fi. The main specifications of used smartphones are shown in Table 1. Testing scenarios target to measure and evaluate the performances of the smartphones using COPE application and considering the energy consumption, clock synchronization and transmission range metrics.

Table 1. Smartphones main specifications

Smartphone model	Wiko Tommy 2
OS	Android 7.1 (Nougat)
Battery	Li-Po 2500 mAh 9.5 Wh
Bluetooth	4.1, A2DP, LE
WiFi	Wi-Fi Direct

3.1 Energy Consumption

COPE should be energy efficient in order to maintain mobile devices alive as long as possible since rescue operations might take long time. Testing scenarios have been conducted to measure the energy consumption considering three network topologies; (i) one node operates individually, (ii) two nodes cooperate based on COPE, and (iii) three nodes cooperate based on COPE. Measurements have been carried out by only running COPE application (i.e. no other applications running in parallel) and the smartphone screen is turned off. Figure 2 illustrates the energy consumption over five minutes from the WiFi and Bluetooth perspective considering the three network topologies. Results show that when a node operates individually, it consumes more energy than in the other topologies where nodes are cooperating. Moreover, as we increase the number of nodes within the group, the energy consumption is reduced since nodes will be in a sleep mode for a longer period from the WiFi perspective. Therefore, cooperative scheme can help to reduce the energy consumption and thus to keep mobile devices alive for a longer time.

We would like to emphasize that these experiments validate that Bluetooth consumes less energy than WiFi in the context of applications requiring an exchange of small data (e.g. short text message). In the context of COPE that only needs to send short SOS messages, this confirms our assumptions.

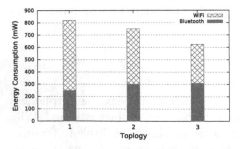

Fig. 2. Energy consumption

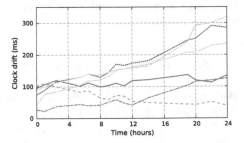

Fig. 3. Clock drift of six smartphones

3.2   Clock Drift

COPE assumes that mobile nodes are already synchronized since smartphones get the local time from the network providers with millisecond accuracy before disasters occur. In the following, we study the clock drift of the smartphones to check weather an additional synchronization is required during the post-disaster period. We have carried out a first simple experiment to check weather smartphones belonging to different network operators are synchronized. Results have shown that smartphones are a few milliseconds apart. Next, we have conducted an experiment to test the clock drift featuring the six smartphones. We initially synchronized all the mobile phones through Internet via a NTP (Network Time Protocol) time server. Afterwards, we prevent the automatic synchronization and we measure the clock drift referring to the NTP time server.

Figure 3 shows the clock drift of the different smartphones during a period of 24 h. Results show that mobile phones desynchronize by up to 0.3 s during 1 day which is not significant drift and does not impact the COPE scheme. Therefore, since the time-slot τ is at second level, COPE does not require an additional synchronization. We would like to emphasize that we have repeated the experiment considering various scenarios: smartphone display ON/OFF, smartphone in charge/not in charge and by running applications in parallel. We have obtained similar clock drift results. Smartphones synchronize their clock time with the cellular infrastructure. When disconnected from the cellular network, clock drift is not significant while difficult to predict. Indeed, results show that smartphones present different desynchronization behaviors even though we use the same mobile device model (i.e. Wiko Tommry 2).

3.3   Transmission Range

We have carried out experiments to test the transmission ranges of Bluetooth and WiFi-Direct. Testing the quality of the link and the transmission speed are not in the scope of this work. Indeed, we consider the necessity of exchanging short text messages that can be useful for alerting or asking for assistance. Thus, in our testing scenarios, we simply try to exchange some short messages of few bytes between smartphones and we keep increasing the distance between mobile nodes until the link interruption. We have carried out various testing scenarios considering: windy and humid weathers; calm and dry weathers; outdoor line of sight (see yellow lines on Fig. 4); indoor with obstacles (1 to 2 walls); between two buildings with a distance of about 80 m (see red line on Fig. 4).

Table 2 presents the transmission range of the Bluetooth and Wi-Fi Direct for outdoor and indoor scenarios. These results show the importance of the new version of Bluetooth offering an important transmission range comparing to the previous versions. Several research works consider the transmission range of Bluetooth of around 10 m while the new version of Bluetooth (Bluetooth Low Energy BLE) offers more important transmission ranges compared to what is expected even in theory. Moreover, experiments validate the assumptions considered in COPE solution that WiFi offers a higher transmission range than Bluetooth.

Fig. 4. Transmission range testing area (Color figure online)

Table 2. Bluetooth and Wi-Fi Direct transmission range

	Bluetooth	Wi-Fi Direct
Indoor	~35 m	≥100 m
Outdoor	~50 m	≥100 m

4 Related Works

Some research works have studied the performance of smartphones mainly in terms of energy consumption. Work in [2] have evaluated the energy consumption of wireless technologies (Bluetooth, WiFi, and 3G) that can be useful to reduce energy consumption for collaborative downloading. Authors in [1] evaluated the energy consumption based of smartphones based on its different components (e.g. CPU, displays). For data communication, most of these studies target to evaluate the performances of smartphones based on simple data exchange without referring to a specific application. In this work, we provide an evaluation of smartphone based on energy consumption and transmission range useful as reference for applications based on a short data communication. Additionally, we give an evaluation of clock synchronization between a group of smartphones.

5 Conclusion

This work investigates the smartphones behavior for opportunistic alert diffusion during disaster scenarios. It gives a benchmark analysis of performances of smartphones and provides additional experimental results on performances of COPE. Experiments have been conducted and results show that COPE can reduce energy consumption comparing to the individual alert diffusion. Moreover, testing experiments have been conducted showing results of clock synchronization and transmission ranges of Bluetooth and Wi-Fi that can facilitate deep study of advances for rescue operations and also for many other applications relying on smartphone performances. Adding another form of network technology (e.g. on the fly cellular network) to the proof-of-concept implementation and evaluating it in terms of energy consumption is a subject of our ongoing work.

References

1. Carroll, A., Heiser, G., et al.: An analysis of power consumption in a smartphone. In: USENIX Annual Technical Conference, vol. 14, p. 21 (2010)
2. Kalic, G., Bojic, I., Kusek, M.: Energy consumption in android phones when using wireless communication technologies. In: MIPRO, 2012 Proceedings of the 35th International Convention, pp. 754–759 (2012)
3. Mezghani, F., Bardol, V., Mitton, N., Laporte, J.L.: An android application for opportunistic alert diffusion in disaster scenario. In: IEEE PIMRC 2017 (2017)
4. Mezghani, F., Mitton, N.: Alternative opportunistic alert diffusion to support infrastructure failure during disasters. Sensors 17(10), 2370 (2017)
5. Nishiyama, H., Ito, M., Kato, N.: Relay-by-smartphone: realizing multihop device-to-device communications. IEEE Commun. Mag. 52(4), 56–65 (2014)
6. Trifunovic, S., Kouyoumdjieva, S.T., Distl, B., Pajevic, L., Karlsson, G., Plattner, B.: A decade of research in opportunistic networks: challenges, relevance, and future directions. IEEE Commun. Mag. 55(1), 168–173 (2017)

An Evaluation Tool for Physical Attacks

Hélène Le Bouder[1]([✉]), Gaël Thomas[3], Ronan Lashermes[4], Yanis Linge[5],
and Bruno Robisson[2], and Assia Tria[2]

[1] IMT-Atlantique, SRCD, Cesson-Sévigné, France
helene.le-bouder@imt-atlantique.fr
[2] EMSE, Centre de Microélectronique de Provence, Gardanne, France
[3] DGA Maîtrise de l'Information, Bruz, France
[4] INRIA, High Security Laboratory, Rennes, France
[5] STMicroelectronics, Rousset, France

Abstract. The security issues of devices, used in the Internet of Things
(IoT) for example, can be considered in two contexts. On the one hand,
these algorithms can be proven secure mathematically. On the other
hand, physical attacks can weaken the implementation. In this work, we
want to compare these attacks between them. A tool to evaluate and
compare different physical attacks, by separating the theoretical attack
path and the experimental parts of the attacks, is presented.

1 Introduction

When talking about the security of a device, numerous tools allow the developers to prove the security of algorithms and the software design. Unfortunately, physical attacks introduce another dimension: the interaction of the implemented algorithm with the physical environment. Physical attacks are a real threat, even for algorithms proved secure mathematically. They are divided in two families: the Side Channel Analysis (SCA) and the Fault Injection Attacks (FIA).

SCA are based on observations of the circuit behaviour during the computation. The first attacks were the Simple, the Differential and the Correlation, Power Analysis (SPA, DPA and CPA) [1–3]. SCA exploit the fact that some physical values of a circuit depend on intermediary values of the computation. This is the so-called leakage of information of the circuit. Leakage examples are timing [4], power consumption [5] and electromagnetic emissions (EM) [6].

FIA consist in disturbing the circuit behaviour in order to alter the correct progress of the algorithm [7,8]. Faults are injected into the device using various means such as laser [9], clock glitches [10], spikes on the power supply or electromagnetic perturbations [11].

Motivation and Contribution: The question that naturally arises is: how to evaluate and compare all physical attacks? Several works have been proposed to describe them with a common framework [12–14]. However, these works only cover SCA. In [15,16], the authors propose to write various SCA as DPA, a

© Springer Nature Switzerland AG 2018
N. Montavont and G. Z. Papadopoulos (Eds.): ADHOC-NOW 2018, LNCS 11104, pp. 112–119, 2018.
https://doi.org/10.1007/978-3-030-00247-3_10

lot of work has been done to compare distinguishers as in [17]. Likewise, there are frameworks for FIA [18–20]. In [21], Standaert *et al.* underline the interface between theory and practice for SCA, our work enlarges this vision for both families. The improvement of our paper is to unify the evaluation for the two families (SCA and FIA). A new tool evaluates the theoretical attacks separately form the real practical attacks.

2   Description of the Attacks in Three Steps

Physical attacks are decomposed in the following 3-step process. The target noted K is the goal of the attack, its domain of definition is noted $\mathbb{K}$.

Step 1: Campaign. An experiment $\mathcal{E}$ is a pair (O_S, O_R) (S for Stimuli and R for Reaction) of **observables**, taken during the execution of an algorithm. A set of n experiments is called a campaign. The observables could be data as plaintext, ciphertext, faulty ciphertext; or physical measurements as EM traces, power traces, signal provided by a micro-probe, computation time *etc.* The **attack path** is an exploitable relation $\mathcal{R}$ between the observables and the target K.

$$O_R = \mathcal{R}(O_S, K). \tag{1}$$

This relation is composed of **physical functions** f and algorithm functions. The physical functions f cannot always be described with a mathematical expression since they are often non deterministic. There is often only one physical function.

Step 2: Predictions. In the attack path $\mathcal{R}$ there are two unknowns: the target K and the physical functions f. The attacker make **guesses** k on the target K. The good guess is noted $\hat{k}$. A divide and conquer approach is generally chosen. The domain of definition of the target, $\mathbb{K}$, should be short enough so that all guesses can be tested. As already pointed out, physical functions do not always have a mathematical expression. But they can be approximated by mathematical functions called **models** or by a phase of characterization called **template** as in [22]. In FIA, models are called error functions and leakage functions in SCA. Several models m can be tested for one physical function f. Commonly, one or a small set of models is used. Finally, **predictions** are built with the attack path for each guess k on the secret, where the physical functions are replaced by models.

$$P_{m,k} = \mathcal{R}_m(O_S, k) \tag{2}$$

Step 3: Confrontation. For each hypothesis k and a model m, $P_{m,k}$ is confronted to the observables O_R with a distinguisher. A **distinguisher** is a statistical tool which is able to find the correct guess on the target. The distinguisher highlights links between physical function f and mathematical model m, they are based on different statistical criteria. $P_{m,k}$ and O_R can be considered as random variables. The distinguisher returns the guess k_d, if $k_d = \hat{k}$ the attack succeeds.

3 The Evaluate and Compare Tool

Generally different distinguishers are compared on a same device; or different campaigns with a same distinguisher; or different models with a same distinguisher. This paper presents a different approach. First, in a theoretical study, the models are evaluated independently from the physical functions; *i.e* $\mathcal{R}_m$ in Eq. (2) is studied. Then the adequacy of the models with respect to the physical functions is evaluated.

Evaluation of the Theoretical Attack. The set of predictions has a cardinal p. One has to remark that it is possible that $p \neq card\,(\mathbb{K})$. Indeed two guesses can have the same prediction during an attack. Let Θ_m be an oracle associated with a model m as illustrated in Fig. 1(a). The oracle Θ_m returns $P_{m,\hat{k}}$ the prediction which corresponds to the good guess $\hat{k}$ under model m for an chosen observable O_s. The required number of queries (on average) to Θ_m in order to retrieve the target K is noted q. It is a measure of how efficient is the theoretical attack path R_m. An oracle can combine sets of models.

Evaluation of the Attack in Practice. This section deals with the link between observables O_R and the good prediction $P_{m,\hat{k}}$. More precisely the two codomains, for the attack path $\mathcal{R}$ and for $\mathcal{R}_m$ are compared. Additionally there is not necessarily a bijection between the codomains (the prediction $P_{m,\hat{k}}$ and the observables O_R), as it has already been shown in [12,16,21].

A contingency table is filled with the results of n experiments. All the possible values of $P_{m,\hat{k}}$ are noted P_i, $i \in [\![1,p]\!]$ and the possible values of O_R are noted O_j, $j \in [\![1,o]\!]$. For each experiment $\mathcal{E} = (O_S, O_R)$, the reaction O_R is stored and $P_{m,\hat{k}}$ is computed. Then in the contingency table, shown in Table 1, the value at the corresponding row i (prediction is equal to P_i) and the column j (reaction is equal to O_j) is incremented. At the end, the value $a_{i,j}$ is the number of times the attacker computed the prediction P_i in conjunction with the measurement of the reaction O_j, *i.e.* the number of experiments with $P_{m,\hat{k}} = P_i$ and $O_R = O_j$.

Up to normalization by a factor n, this contingency table can be understood as the joint distribution of $P_{m,k}$ and O_R. Given an experiment (O_S, O_R), the correct prediction $P_{m,\hat{k}}(O_S)$ is given by $\Theta_m(O_S)$ and does not depend on O_R. Denote by $\hat{\imath}$, the row index corresponding to $P_{m,\hat{k}}$, so that $P_{m,\hat{k}} = P_{\hat{\imath}}$; and by $\hat{\jmath}$, the column index corresponding to the observed $O_R = O_{\hat{\jmath}}$. The probability of guessing the correct prediction $P_{m,\hat{k}}$ with O_R is:

$$\mathcal{P}\left(P_{m,\hat{k}}|O_R\right) = \frac{a_{\hat{\imath},\hat{\jmath}}}{A_{\hat{\jmath}}}, \quad \text{where } A_{\hat{\jmath}} = \sum_{i=1}^{p} a_{i,\hat{\jmath}}. \tag{3}$$

A new oracle Θ (Fig. 1(b)) is introduced. Given an observable O_S, it returns a (guessed) prediction $P_{m,k}$ with probability given by $\mathcal{P}\left(P_{m,k}|O_R\right)$, and with $O_R = \mathcal{R}(O_S, \hat{k})$. The probability (3) is then the probability of the oracle returning the correct prediction $P_{m,\hat{k}}$. This probability $\mathcal{P}$ is called the **matching probability** of O_S. The average number q' of queries to Θ required to gather q correct guesses is evaluated. The oracle Θ_m allows to evaluate the quality of an attack path $\mathcal{R}_m$ with the model m. A smaller q means a better adequacy between the attack path and the model. $\mathcal{P}$ represents the quality of the measures O_R with respect to the predictions $P_{m,\hat{k}}$. Finally this probability and the oracle are combined to globally evaluate the experimental attack with respect to the models thanks to q'.

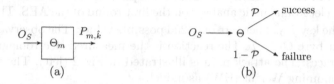

Fig. 1. (a) Oracle Θ_m. (b) Oracle with matching probability $\mathcal{P}$.

Table 1. Contingency table of the measured O_R and the predicted values $P_{m,\hat{k}}$.

	$O_R = O_1$	$O_R = O_2$	$\cdots$	$O_R = O_o$	Total
$P_{m,\hat{k}} = P_1$	$a_{1,1}$	$a_{1,2}$	$\cdots$	$a_{1,o}$	$\sum_{j=1}^{o} a_{1,j}$
$\vdots$	$\vdots$	$\vdots$	$\cdots$	$\vdots$	$\vdots$
$P_{m,\hat{k}} = P_p$	$a_{p,1}$	$a_{p,2}$	$\cdots$	$a_{p,o}$	$\sum_{j=1}^{o} a_{p,j}$
Total	$A_1 = \sum_{i=1}^{p} a_{i,1}$	$A_2 = \sum_{i=1}^{p} a_{i,2}$	$\cdots$	$A_o = \sum_{i=1}^{p} a_{i,o}$	n

4   Practical Examples

Targeted Algorithm: Advanced Encryption Standard (AES). The AES is a standard established by the NIST [23]. It is a block cipher. The encryption first consists in mapping the plaintext T of 128 bits into a two-dimensional array of bytes, called the State. Then, after a preliminary XOR between the input and the key, AES_{128} executes 10 times a round function that operates on the State. The operations used during these rounds are: **SubBytes** composed of non-linear transformations: 16 s-boxes noted SB; **ShiftRows** (SR), a byte shifting operation on each row of the State; **MixColumns** (MC), a linear matrix multiplication working on each column of the State; and a byte-wise xor $\oplus$ between the State and K_r, $r \in [\![0, 10]\!]$, the derived key used at round r.

Targeted Device. In this paper, the target is the cipher key of an AES_{128}. It is implemented on an ARM-based STM32F100RB micro-controller embedding a Cortex-M3 core and running in our case at 24MHz. The board used is the STM32VLDICOVERY. This chip does not embed any countermeasures against physical attack but it is a popular choice for IoT applications.

4.1   Differential Power Analysis

Experimental Protocol. An electromagnetic emissions analysis bench is composed of an EM probe from Langer (RF-R0,3-3) to capture the leakage, a preamplifier from Langer (PA 303) and an oscilloscope to measure it. The oscilloscope is a DSOS404A from Keysight. It achieves 10-bit resolution with a 20 Giga samples per second and 4 GHz bandwidth. Finally, a control computer is used to orchestrate the measurements and perform the analysis.

Description of the Attack. The first attack presented is the classic DPA/CPA attack [3] by electromagnetic analysis on the first round of the AES. The target is a byte $\hat{k}$ of the key K_0. There are only 256 possible values. The observable stimuli is a plaintext byte $O_S = T$. The reaction is the measured electromagnetic field, $O_R = $ EM traces. The attack path is illustrated in Fig. 2 (left). The theoretical path uses Hamming Weight (HW) as model.

$$\mathcal{R}(T, \hat{k}) = f(SB(T \oplus \hat{k}), \text{ with } f \text{ the physical function.}$$
$$\mathcal{R}_m(T, k) = HW(SB(T \oplus k)) = P_{m,k}.$$

The distinguisher can be a difference of mean, a correlation, a mutual information, a principal component or a linear discriminant. **Evaluation of the attack.** The oracle Θ_m returns a Hamming weight. On average, $q = 4$ queries to Θ_m are required to retrieve a key byte. Then the oracle Θ is called. It returns a guessed Hamming weight. With the measures O_R collected in this experiment, an average of $q' = 17.8$ calls to Θ are required to have $q = 4$ correct guesses.

4.2   Differential Fault Analysis

Experimental Protocol. The fault injection bench used electromagnetic pulses. These electromagnetic pulses are sent to the target thank to the inductive coupling of an EM probe with the target metal layers. Our bench is able to inject a pulse of ≈ 3 ns at the minimum and to repeat this pulse in order to achieve multi-faults if wanted.

Description of the Attacks. The second attack presented is an attack of type DFA. Our bench can produce faults at the end of the round 9. We wanted to realize the attack of Giraud [8]. The target is a byte $\hat{k}$ of the key K_{10}. There are only 256 possible values. The stimuli is a ciphertext byte $O_S = C$. The reaction is a faulty ciphertext byte $O_R = C^{*}$[1]. The attack path is illustrated in Fig. 2 (right). The theoretical attack path uses a single-bit fault model, i.e 8 possible models: $\oplus 2^i$ with $i \in [\![0, 7]\!]$, are considered together[2].

$$\mathcal{R}(C, \hat{k}) = SB\left(f\left(SB^{-1}\left(C \oplus \hat{k}\right)\right)\right) \oplus \hat{k}, \text{ with } f \text{ the fault injection process.}$$
$$\mathcal{R}_m(C, k) = SB\left(\left(SB^{-1}(C \oplus k)\right) \oplus 2^i\right) \oplus k.$$

---

[1] In this paper a faulty variable is denoted by an asterisk *.
[2] The function SR shift bytes, so it is omitted for the simplicity of the equation.

In the case of the Giraud's attack, the distinguisher could be a sieve [7] or a counter [8]. Unfortunately with our experimental protocol we cannot obtain single-bit faults, therefore the Non-Uniform Error Value Analysis (NUEVA) attack from [24] is chosen. The main idea in this attack comes from the fact that fault injection are never random. The stimuli is a pair of a ciphertext byte and a faulty ciphertext byte $O_S = (C, C^*)$. The reaction is the error observed, $O_R = e$. The attack path ans theoretical attack path are:

$$\mathcal{R}\left((C, C^*), \hat{k}\right) = f\left(SB^{-1}\left(C \oplus \hat{k}\right), SB^{-1}\left(C^* \oplus \hat{k}\right)\right),$$
$$\mathcal{R}_m\left((C, C^*), k\right) = SB^{-1}\left(C \oplus k\right) \oplus SB^{-1}\left(C^* \oplus k\right).$$

The model is $\oplus e$ (256 models). The distinguisher is an entropy. The goal is to detect if the distribution of the errors is uniform or not.

Evaluation of the Attacks. In the case of Giraud attack, the oracle Θ_m is build with 8 models, so it returns 8 guess values. In average, $q = 2.4$ queries are necessary to retrieve one byte (result given in [8]). This model is very good but very hard to realize in practice with our fault injection bench. In the case of NUEVA, the oracle Θ_m returns an error. In theory, an infinity of queries $(q = \infty)$ are necessary to evaluate if a distribution is uniform or not. Θ returns a guessed error. A faulty value can always be represented with a $\oplus$, so the matching probability is always equal to 1. So $q' = q = \infty$, and this model seems very bad. But in practice with our fault injection bench, 2500 faults are required in average.

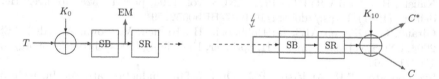

Fig. 2. Attack path of DPA (left) and DFA (right).

5   Conclusion

A new technique to evaluate physical attacks has been presented. The main idea is to evaluate the attack at different levels and not only on the final result. In a first time, only the models are studied, looking at the average number q of queries to an oracle that always returns the correct prediction. A smaller q means a better theoretical attack path. Then in a second time, only the predictions and the reactions are confronted, before using a distinguisher. Another oracle is introduced that returns a prediction but, contrary to the previous oracle, may return an incorrect one. The distribution of the returned predictions depends on the measures collected. The average number q' of queries to the new oracle to have q correct predictions evaluates the quality of the model with respect to the measures. At the end of this two-step evaluation, different distinguishers can be tested and a success rate can be computed. In case of failure, the advantage of our tool is to underline what part of an attack is weak.

References

1. Mangard, S.: A simple power-analysis (SPA) attack on implementations of the AES key expansion. In: Lee, P.J., Lim, C.H. (eds.) ICISC 2002. LNCS, vol. 2587, pp. 343–358. Springer, Heidelberg (2003). https://doi.org/10.1007/3-540-36552-4_24
2. Kocher, P., Jaffe, J., Jun, B.: Differential power analysis. In: Wiener, M. (ed.) CRYPTO 1999. LNCS, vol. 1666, pp. 388–397. Springer, Heidelberg (1999). https://doi.org/10.1007/3-540-48405-1_25
3. Brier, E., Clavier, C., Olivier, F.: Correlation power analysis with a leakage model. In: Joye, M., Quisquater, J.-J. (eds.) CHES 2004. LNCS, vol. 3156, pp. 16–29. Springer, Heidelberg (2004). https://doi.org/10.1007/978-3-540-28632-5_2
4. Kocher, P.C.: Timing attacks on implementations of Diffie-Hellman, RSA, DSS, and other systems. In: Koblitz, N. (ed.) CRYPTO 1996. LNCS, vol. 1109, pp. 104–113. Springer, Heidelberg (1996). https://doi.org/10.1007/3-540-68697-5_9
5. Mangard, S., Oswald, E., Popp, T.: Power Analysis Attacks: Revealing the Secrets of Smart Cards, vol. 31. Springer, Berlin (2008). https://doi.org/10.1007/978-0-387-38162-6
6. Quisquater, J.-J., Samyde, D.: Electromagnetic analysis (EMA): measures and counter-measures for smart cards. In: Attali, I., Jensen, T. (eds.) E-smart 2001. LNCS, vol. 2140, pp. 200–210. Springer, Heidelberg (2001). https://doi.org/10.1007/3-540-45418-7_17
7. Biham, E., Shamir, A.: Differential fault analysis of secret key cryptosystems. In: Kaliski, B.S. (ed.) CRYPTO 1997. LNCS, vol. 1294, pp. 513–525. Springer, Heidelberg (1997). https://doi.org/10.1007/BFb0052259
8. Giraud, C.: DFA on AES. In: Dobbertin, H., Rijmen, V., Sowa, A. (eds.) AES 2004. LNCS, vol. 3373, pp. 27–41. Springer, Heidelberg (2005). https://doi.org/10.1007/11506447_4
9. Skorobogatov, S.P., Anderson, R.J.: Optical fault induction attacks. In: Kaliski, B.S., Koç, K., Paar, C. (eds.) CHES 2002. LNCS, vol. 2523, pp. 2–12. Springer, Heidelberg (2003). https://doi.org/10.1007/3-540-36400-5_2
10. Zussa, L., Dutertre, J.M., Clédière, J., Tria, A.: Power supply glitch induced faults on FPGA: an in-depth analysis of the injection mechanism. In: IOLTS (2013)
11. Moro, N., Dehbaoui, A., Heydemann, K., Robisson, B., Encrenaz, E.: Electromagnetic fault injection: towards a fault model on a 32-bit microcontroller. In: FDTC. IEEE (2013)
12. Micali, S., Reyzin, L.: Physically observable cryptography. In: Naor, M. (ed.) TCC 2004. LNCS, vol. 2951, pp. 278–296. Springer, Heidelberg (2004). https://doi.org/10.1007/978-3-540-24638-1_16
13. Standaert, F.-X., Koeune, F., Schindler, W.: How to compare profiled side-channel attacks? In: Abdalla, M., Pointcheval, D., Fouque, P.-A., Vergnaud, D. (eds.) ACNS 2009. LNCS, vol. 5536, pp. 485–498. Springer, Heidelberg (2009). https://doi.org/10.1007/978-3-642-01957-9_30

14. Elaabid, M.A., Guilley, S.: Practical improvements of profiled side-channel attacks on a hardware crypto-accelerator. In: Bernstein, D.J., Lange, T. (eds.) AFRICACRYPT 2010. LNCS, vol. 6055, pp. 243–260. Springer, Heidelberg (2010). https://doi.org/10.1007/978-3-642-12678-9_15
15. Mangard, S., Oswald, E., Standaert, F.X.: One for all - all for one: unifying standard differential power analysis attacks. IET Inf. Secur. **5**(2), 100–110 (2011)
16. Whitnall, C., Oswald, E., Standaert, F.-X.: The myth of generic DPA...and the magic of learning. In: Benaloh, J. (ed.) CT-RSA 2014. LNCS, vol. 8366, pp. 183–205. Springer, Cham (2014). https://doi.org/10.1007/978-3-319-04852-9_10
17. Maghrebi, H., Rioul, O., Guilley, S., Danger, J.-L.: Comparison between side-channel analysis distinguishers. In: Chim, T.W., Yuen, T.H. (eds.) ICICS 2012. LNCS, vol. 7618, pp. 331–340. Springer, Heidelberg (2012). https://doi.org/10.1007/978-3-642-34129-8_30
18. Verbauwhede, I., Karaklajic, D., Schmidt, J.M.: The fault attack jungle - a classification model to guide you. In: FDTC (2011)
19. Moradi, A., Shalmani, M.T.M., Salmasizadeh, M.: A generalized method of differential fault attack against AES cryptosystem. In: Goubin, L., Matsui, M. (eds.) CHES 2006. LNCS, vol. 4249, pp. 91–100. Springer, Heidelberg (2006). https://doi.org/10.1007/11894063_8
20. Sakiyama, K., Li, Y., Iwamoto, M., Ohta, K.: Information-theoretic approach to optimal differential fault analysis. IEEE Trans. Inf. Forensics Secur. **7**(1), 109–120 (2012)
21. Standaert, F.-X., Malkin, T.G., Yung, M.: A unified framework for the analysis of side-channel key recovery attacks. In: Joux, A. (ed.) EUROCRYPT 2009. LNCS, vol. 5479, pp. 443–461. Springer, Heidelberg (2009). https://doi.org/10.1007/978-3-642-01001-9_26
22. Chari, S., Rao, J.R., Rohatgi, P.: Template attacks. In: Kaliski, B.S., Koç, K., Paar, C. (eds.) CHES 2002. LNCS, vol. 2523, pp. 13–28. Springer, Heidelberg (2003). https://doi.org/10.1007/3-540-36400-5_3
23. NIST: Specification for the Advanced Encryption Standard. FIPS PUB 197 (2001)
24. Lashermes, R., Reymond, G., Dutertre, J.M., Fournier, J., Robisson, B., Tria, A.: A DFA on AES based on the entropy of error distributions. In: FDTC (2012)

Demo: Do Not Trust Your Neighbors! A Small IoT Platform Illustrating a Man-in-the-Middle Attack

Renzo E. Navas[✉], Hélène Le Bouder, Nora Cuppens, Frédéric Cuppens, and Georgios Z. Papadopoulos

IMT Atlantique, UBL, Cesson-Sévigné, France
{renzo.navas,helene.le-bouder,nora.cuppens,frederic.cuppens,
georgios.papadopoulos}@imt-atlantique.fr

Abstract. This demonstration defines a small IoT wireless network that uses TI CC2538-OpenMote as hardware platform and state-of-the-art IETF network standards such as 6LoWPAN, RPL, and CoAP implemented by ContikiOS. The IoT nodes are controlled from outside the IoT network using end-to-end connectivity provided by IPv6-CoAP messages. We implement a man-in-the-middle attack that disrupts the normal behavior of the system. Our attack leverages on the inherent hierarchical routing topology of RPL-based IoT networks. The demonstration aims at highlighting the need for end-to-end source-authentication and authorization enforcement of information even inside a trusted IoT network. We also provide some insights on how these services can be offered in a IoT-friendly way.

Keywords: IoT · MITM attack · IPv6 · CoAP · RPL · e2e security

1 Introduction and Motivation

Internet of Things (IoT) lack-of-security awareness has been rising in recent years [4]. Mass-media publications label as "IoT" a wide and heterogeneous set of devices: smart-watches, thermostats, surveillance cameras, toasters, refrigerators, light-bulbs, etc. Most of them have more in common with a powerful desktop computer rather than with a 5-dollar system-on-chip. On this paper IoT represents constrained devices as defined on RFC7228 [2]. These devices can not run Linux systems or legacy Internet and security protocols: special solutions suited for their constraints must be used.

For this demonstration we set up an IoT platform reachable by IPv6 from external networks. The platform allows controlling a robot arm from an android tablet using CoAP messages. The defined IoT platform has a compromised node inside, that after behaving as expected for a certain amount of time, executes a Man-In-The-Middle (MITM) attack. The demonstration aims at highlighting the consequences of unrestrictedly trusting nodes of an IoT network, and the need

© Springer Nature Switzerland AG 2018
N. Montavont and G. Z. Papadopoulos (Eds.): ADHOC-NOW 2018, LNCS 11104, pp. 120–125, 2018.
https://doi.org/10.1007/978-3-030-00247-3_11

for end-to-end security. Risk of insider attacks is real from the very moment we use devices manufactured or programmed by a party we do not fully trust (i.e. *all*), a mitigation will be running full open-hardware and software solutions.

The rest of the paper is organized as follows: Sect. 2 presents the platform. Section 3 explains the attack: hypothesis, planning, implementation and execution. Section 4 comments on the feasibility of the attack on real-world settings and on possible solutions. Finally, Sect. 5 offers a brief conclusion.

2 The Platform

The platform tries to illustrate three concepts associated with the IoT: **heterogeneity**, **connectivity** and **interoperability**. Heterogeneous devices: android devices, WiFi access points, powerful PCs, and constrained IoT nodes; and heterogeneous networks: WiFi, Ethernet, USB-SLIP, IEEE 802.15.4. Connectivity end-to-end is assured by IPv6. Application-layer interoperability is guaranteed by the Constrained Application Protocol (CoAP), the equivalent of HTTP for IoT. A diagram of the platform can be seen on Fig. 1.

The use case involves an Android device that sends IPv6-CoAP packets to an IoT node who controls a robot-arm which serves beverages. The IPv6 packet travels through 4 different layer-2 technologies, but layer-3 (and up) remains unmodified end-to-end. Inside the IoT network the packet is routed by intermediate IoT nodes, leveraging on the RPL routing protocol, until it finally arrives to the destination node which drives the arm according to the CoAP message.

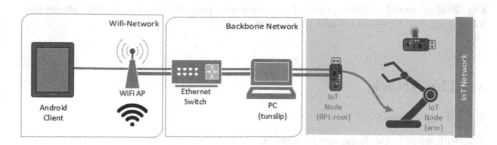

Fig. 1. Diagram of the platform. An heterogeneous platform for end-to-end IPv6-CoAP interoperability with an IoT-node. The green arrow represents the IPv6 message.

The hardware and software components used are the following:

- Android Client: Galaxy Tab A 10.1 (2016). SW: Samsung stock android 7.1.
- WiFi AP + Switch: Router Linksys E900. SW: Custom Firmware tomato-E900-NVRAM64K-1.28.RT-N5x-MIPSR2-140-Max (Needed to add custom IPv6 routing table rules).
- PC Lenovo ThinkPad T460 Intel i7-6600U CPU @ 2.60 GHz (x86_64). SW: Ubuntu 17.10 64-bits and binary *tunslip*.

– IoT Nodes: OpenMote-CC2538 Rev.A1 board (SoC: TI CC2538SF53, 256 KB Flash, 32 KB RAM). SW: ContikiOS 2.7.
– Robot Arm: RobotGeek Snapper Arduino Robotic Arm[1], five 13 kg-cm servomotors (16 Vpowered). And controller by an Ardhuino-uno-based device.

A real world picture of the platform can be seen on Fig. 2.

Fig. 2. Real world platform: the IoT-driven water-pouring robot arm. We can see the robot arm, two OpenMotes and the Android tablet.

3   The Attack

3.1   Hypothesis

The following hypothesis are needed to execute our attack:

Internal IoT Attacker: We assume an internal attacker, one of the IoT nodes has been compromised or has always been malicious but on a latent state.

Routing Tree-Like Topology: The attack relies on RPL (IPv6 Routing Protocol for Low-Power and Lossy Networks) routing tree-like hierarchy. The goal is for the compromised node to be conveniently placed on the RPL topology, so it becomes a legitimate router of most of the packets on the network. This can be achieved by exploiting well-known RPL vulnerabilities [5] (e.g. rank attack, version number attack). *Note*: For single-hop networks this attack is not possible as is: the malicious node will have to illegitimately intercept and forward packets.

---

[1]   https://www.robotgeek.com/robotgeek-snapper-robotic-arm

3.2   Plan

The following are the ordered steps needed to execute the attack:

1. **Insider IoT-node compromise.** IoT-node has been malicious from the beginning of its life-cycle. A modified version of ContikiOS was flashed on one of the nodes, the node behaves as a regular node until the malicious-mode is activated. The content of the custom code is explained on Subsect. 3.3. This kind of insider attack is a realistic threat: normally enterprises and users buy, configure, and use IoT nodes with pre-loaded closed-source firmware.
2. **Malicious-mode activation.** Activation is done by an external agent sending an HTTP request to a specific resource of the compromised node. The node is reachable by IPv6. Automatic activation is realistic also e.g. the compromised node activates itself after 72 h of use, or the 24th. Nov. 2020.
4. **RPL-attack.** The malicious node modifies the RPL-topology to be placed close to the root and legitimately route most of the packets. For simplicity of the implementation, the RPL root node is the compromised node, so no RPL attack was needed. An extension of the demonstration would be performing a RPL-attack.
5. **MITM: In-transit CoAP message modification.** Once the compromised node is placed on a privileged position on the routing hierarchy, it targets IP packets for a fixed destination inside the IoT network. In this demonstration, legitimate CoAP messages that control the robot arm are targeted, and its content is modified. Once in this position on the IoT network several attacks could be performed e.g. Black-hole attack (disrupting routing of the packets), information leakage (e.g. sending a copy of the IoT internal messages to an outsider); Layer-2 security does not prevent any of these attacks, as the compromised node is an insider.

The attack schema can be seen on Fig. 3. To activate the malicious node a Samsung Galaxy S8 cellphone with Android 7.1 is used, but any IPv6 capable device with an HTTP client could have been used.

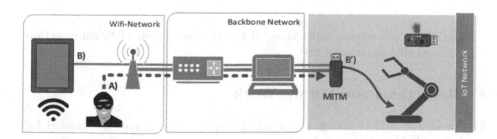

Fig. 3. Attack schema. In *A* the message to activate the malicious mode of the compromised node (MITM). In *B* a legitimate message for the IoT-arm, modified by MITM and routed in *B'*

3.3   Implementation Details and Execution

The most relevant part of the code modifications to present is the ContikiOS modification to target and modify specific IPv6 packets. This modification is done inserting code on line 1187 of the Contiki 2.7 file contiki/core/net/uip6.c [3] , this is inside the function uip_process(uint8_t flag) which does the IPv6 packet processing, and the node is about to forward a IPv6 packet with the line goto send. Before sending the packet, it checks if the malicious state is activated, if so it targets a specific IPv6 destination address and the UDP-CoAP port, then it modifies the CoAP message content, and recalculate the UDP checksum. On Fig. 4 a debug console of the malicious node modifying a message in transit is shown.

```
[*****************************     ^O^     *****************************]
                We are now an Evil Node, waiting for Specific
                CoAP messsage to moddify it in transit
[*****************************     ^---^     ****************************]

Attack_is_on, is this the message we want?: 1

        [**************    We attack!!  ^O^   **************]

        UDP before checksum: 0xdc26
        We modify the message in transit, need to recalculate checksum
        UDP we set to zero checksum: 0x0000
        UDP after checksum: 0xdc3a
Buff:
   0000   60 01 c7 26 00 13 11 3f aa aa 00 00 00 00 00 00   `..&...?.........
   0010   00 00 00 00 00 00 00 01 aa aa 00 00 00 00 00 00   ................
   0020   02 12 4b 00 04 30 53 e5 9d 99 16 33 00 13 3a dc   ..K..0S....3..:.
   0030   40 02 54 61 b3 61 72 6d 02 6f 5a                  @.Ta.arm.oZ
        [*****************    END Attack    *****************]
```

Fig. 4. Inside the compromised node while preforming the attack.

The reader can view a short video of the demonstration platform in action on [1], or on this alternative url[2].

4   Reflections and Future Work

The presented MITM attack is possible because the information intended for the IoT node is not protected end to end. To prevent this attack, at minimum source-authentication (integrity) of the information is needed, this enables to detect messages modified by a third party. Even if the attack on this demonstration seems trivial, it exemplifies what can happen in more complex Cloud-IoT

---

[2] Demo video: https://youtu.be/Zhrk5-IGKKE.

architectures where a false sense of security can be given: we can have strong cryptographic HTTPS-TLS protection from the cloud to an IoT gateway, but inside the IoT we rely on whatever security is offered at Layer 2 (IEEE 802.15.4, Sigfox, LoRaWAN Network Session Key); on such setting this insider IoT attack is still possible.

Security services need to be guaranteed end-to-end. This can be achieved at three different layers of abstraction on the TCP/IP model. *IPsec* at the Internet layer; Datagram Transport Layer Security (*DTLS*) or *TLS* at the Transport layer; And finally, at the Application layer where most current IoT-oriented standardization efforts are being made e.g. Object Security for Constrained RESTful Environments (*OSCORE*) or CBOR Object Signing and Encryption (*COSE*) [6]. Our current research efforts focus on application layer security, also called *object security*, and particularly COSE. We believe solutions at this layer offer the best flexibility (per-message security services), level of abstraction (agnostic to underlying layers), and good message overhead. A comprehensive solution will involve key-establishment protocols, an authorization-framework, a time-synchronization protocol, etc. all these services could leverage from COSE.

5 Conclusion

This demonstration platform illustrates some benefits and challenges of the IoT: connectivity, application-layer interoperability, and weak -or inexistent- security. We focus on IoT-insider attacks, IoT platforms and protocols should be designed with the principle of least privilege in mind: *do not trust your neighbors!* or rather, trust them only with what they need to be trusted. Fine-grained or capability-based authorization is possible for IoT, and the layered nature of protocols also helps. An IoT neighbor node that routes packets for others should only be able to do that, and in an authenticated way. To avoid the unknown evil men-in-the-middle to succeed **security services should be guaranteed end-to-end**. Object security solutions, by means of its flexibility and lower layers independence, seems to be the most suitable tool that can provide it for the future of the heterogeneous IoT.

References

1. Demo video: IoT man-in-the-middle attack (2018). http://www.industry-of-the-future.org/asset/demo/
2. Bormann, C., Ersue, M., Keränen, A.: Terminology for constrained-node networks. RFC 7228, May 2014. https://doi.org/10.17487/RFC7228
3. ContikiOS: The contiki 2.7 github repository (2018). https://github.com/contiki-os/contiki/blob/release-2-7/core/net/uip6.c#L1187
4. Granjal, J., et al.: Security for the internet of things: a survey of existing protocols and open research issues. IEEE Commun. Surv. Tutor. **17**(3), 1294–1312 (2015)
5. Kamble, A., Malemath, V.S., Patil, D.: Security attacks and secure routing protocols in RPL-based internet of things: survey. In: ICEI 2017 (2017)
6. Schaad, J.: CBOR Object Signing and Encryption (COSE). RFC 8152, Jul 2017. https://doi.org/10.17487/RFC8152

A Fuzzy Based Energy Aware Unequal Clustering for Wireless Sensor Networks

Sabrine Khriji[1,2(✉)], Dhouha El Houssaini[1,3], Ines Kammoun[2], and Olfa Kanoun[1]

[1] Chemnitz University of Technology, Measurement and Sensor Technology, Chemnitz, Germany
sabrine.kheriji@etit.tu-chemnitz.de, kanoun@ieee.org
[2] LETI Laboratory, National School of Engineers of Sfax, University of Sfax, Sfax, Tunisia
[3] Centre for Research on Microelectronics and Nanotechnology, Technopark of Sousse, University of Sousse, Sousse, Tunisia

Abstract. One of the most important issues in wireless sensor networks is energy autonomy. Thereby wireless communication leads to excessive demands of energy. In this paper, a fuzzy based energy aware unequal clustering algorithm is presented. The network is partitioned into certain number of rings. An energy analysis model is proposed to measure the optimal radius of each cluster. This enables to vary the size of clusters from one ring to another, which ensures the load balance of the network. Then, a fuzzy logic system is employed to select suitable cluster head. The fuzzy set relies only on three parameters; residual energy, number of neighboring nodes and centrality of node among its neighbors. The proposed algorithm outperforms other clustering approaches, like LEACH, DUCF and MCFL in terms of energy efficiency and network lifetime.

Keywords: Wireless sensor networks · Unequal clustering
Multi-hop communication · Optimal cluster radius · Fuzzy logic

1 Introduction

Wireless Sensor Networks (WSNs) is an interesting axis of research in the last decade for its wide range of applications such as industry, automation, smart buildings and smart agriculture [1]. Wireless communication can lead in general to excessive demands of energy. As a result, different communication strategies for energy consumption reduction are proposed to improve the efficiency of the network [2]. Many studies have shown that hierarchical routing protocols based on clustering schemes can reduce significantly the energy consumption [3].

A Low-Energy Adaptive Clustering Hierarchy [4] (LEACH) is the first hierarchical based protocol for WSN. Nodes create clusters and the cluster heads (CHs) act as routers communicating directly with the base station (BS) which will save energy during data transmission. A DUCF [5] algorithm is a distributed load balancing unequal clustering based on fuzzy approach. In this algorithm,

© Springer Nature Switzerland AG 2018
N. Montavont and G. Z. Papadopoulos (Eds.): ADHOC-NOW 2018, LNCS 11104, pp. 126–131, 2018.
https://doi.org/10.1007/978-3-030-00247-3_12

the smaller cluster size is assigned to CH nearer to BS since it acts as a router for other distant CHs. DUCF ensures load balancing among the clusters by varying the cluster size of its CH nodes. A multi-clustering algorithm based on fuzzy logic (MCFL) [6] reduces the number of CH selections which enables to reduce the number of sent messages while guaranteeing energy efficiency.

According to these related works, the calculation of the optimal radius of each cluster is not considered. However, having the appropriate radius can lead to load balancing. This paper is addressed for investigation of clustering and network organization of WSNs for low energy consumption. It focuses on an energy aware unequal clustering algorithm, which is characterized with a circular partitioning network model. The aim of this proposal is to balance the energy consumption among clusters by forming adequate sized clusters to solve the hotspot problem created by multi hop communication and increase the overall network lifetime. To determine the radius of each cluster, an energy analysis model is used, which enables to vary the size of clusters from one ring to another. Thus, the energy of the network is balanced. To select the CHs, the proposed clustering algorithm is based on fuzzy logic which uses three parameters; node residual energy, node density and node centrality.

In Sect. 2, a detailed description of the proposed data routing algorithm is performed including mainly the system model, assumptions, work contributions and the main characteristics. In Sect. 3, the proposed algorithm is compared with existing algorithms.

2   Proposed Fuzzy Based Unequal Clustering

Four our proposal, the network area is assumed as a circle with the BS in the center. It is partitioned into a certain number of rings with a specific radius. The choice of a circular partitioning scheme is based on the comparison performed in [7], which prove that circular network model have better accuracy in the energy consumption analysis than the rectangular one. In [7], authors prove also that the use of rectangular network is inaccurate for the varied dimension compared to circular partitioning scheme. All sensor nodes are randomly distributed with a uniform distribution of a density λ. All nodes are stationary with an unequal initial energy level. Each data packet will be transmitted from one cluster head to another in different rings.

The radio model used is based on the model introduced in [4,5,8,9]. To transmit an l bit message to a receiver over a distance d, the energy consumed by the transmitter $E_{Tx}(l, d)$ and by the receiver $E_{Rx}(l)$ are:

$$E_{Tx}(l, d) = \begin{cases} l \times E_{elect} + l \times \varepsilon_{fs} \times d^2 & \text{if } d < d_0 \\ l \times E_{elect} + l \times \varepsilon_{amp} \times d^4 & \text{if } d \geqslant d_0 \end{cases} \tag{1}$$

$$E_{Rx}(l) = lE_{elect} \tag{2}$$

E_{elect} presents the energy required for one-bit long time span to run the transmitter's or receiver's circuitry. The parameters ε_{fs} and ε_{amp} are defined, respectively, the energy consumption factor for free space and multi path radio models. d_0 is a threshold distance.

The proposed routing is divided into two phases; an off-line phase and cluster formation phase. The first phase introduces an energy analysis to compute the optimal cluster radius for different rings, while the second phase consists on cluster building and CH selection.

2.1 Off-Line Phase

Firstly, we assume that the nodes are aware of their position and the ring where they are located. After network deployment, the optimal radius of each cluster will be determined. Assuming that both sensor nodes and CHs are uniformly distributed in the area. The network area with radius R is partitioned into L rings. $R = L \times \delta$, with δ is the width of a ring. Due to multi-hop communication, distance used by single-hop schemes is relatively short. We assume, that the distance between all sensor nodes is less than the critical distance d_0, so the total energy of the whole network is expressed as in Eq. 3:

$$
\begin{aligned}
E_{Clusterk} = & lE_{Rx}\left(\frac{N_k}{m_k} - 1\right) + lE_{DA}\frac{N_k}{m_k} \\
& + l\frac{\sum_{i=k+1}^{L} m_i}{m_k}(E_{Rx} + E_{Tx} + \varepsilon_{fs}E[d_{CHk,CH(k-1)}^2]) \\
& + l(E_{Tx} + \varepsilon_{fs}E[d_{CHk,CH(k-1)}^2])
\end{aligned}
\tag{3}
$$

The total energy spent by all nodes in a ring is

$$
E_{Totalk} = m_k E_{Clusterk}
\tag{4}
$$

The optimal radius of cluster in a ring k is therefore described in Eq. 5

$$
R_{(CH_k)opt} = \delta\sqrt{\frac{2k-1}{m_k}} \quad k = 2, \ldots, L
\tag{5}
$$

2.2 Cluster Formation Phase

All nodes within same ring have same radius of cluster. This radius differs from one ring to another. After finishing the off-line phase, each node broadcasts a discovery neighboring message within the cluster radius to create its routing table containing list of neighbors, residual energy and current position.

Each node may calculate independently its chance to be a CH based on three parameters; residual energy, density and centrality which are extending the network lifetime. Node density presents the number of neighbor nodes in a tentative CH's neighbor nodes set. The centrality represents how central the node is among its neighbors. For the three parameters, a trapezoidal membership function is used for describing "Low" and "high" functions, while the "medium" function has a triangular membership function (see Fig. 1).

Node will transmit its input parameters to its fuzzy deduction engine which will calculate its chance to be a CH. A message enclosing node's chance is

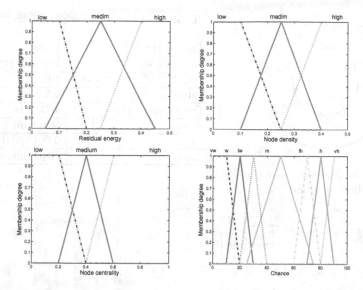

Fig. 1. Membership function for: residual energy, node density, node centrality, and chance to be a CH

exchanged between nodes within the same cluster. Then, the node will compare its chance to the chance of its neighbors within the same cluster. The node having the highest chance will select itself as a CH and transmit an announcement message to its node members informing them with its status. The nodes receiving this message will transmit a join message to the respective CH. If the node is not a final CH and has received more than one final CH message, it will select the final CH with the high cost to join it. If a node finished the clustering process and has not yet received any final CH message, it announces itself as a final CH.

After the selection of CH, each node transmits its data packet to its adequate CH. Only CHs from the first ring will transmit their aggregated packet directly to BS. Other CHs will transmit their packets to CH from previous ring, which plays the role of a relay node.

3   Performance Evaluation

To evaluate the performance of the proposed routing algorithm different metrics are respected which are the total remaining energy of the network, the number of first dead node in each round (FND), the half of dead nodes (HND) and last dead node (LND) are used to achieve this comparison. The simulations are performed using Matlab where 100 nodes are randomly deployed. The BS is located at center of the field as seen in Fig. 2. All detailed configuration is illustrated in Table 1. Simulations (Figs. 3a and b) show that the proposed algorithm outperforms LEACH, DUCF and MCFL in terms of FND, HND and LND metrics. Considering the FND metric, the proposed algorithm is more efficient than

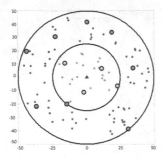

Fig. 2. Node dispersion and clustering for the first round

Table 1. Configuration parameters

Parameter	Value
Network size	100 m × 100 m
Number of sensor nodes	100
Initial energy	0.5 J
Data packet size	4000 bits
E_{elect}	50 nJ/bit
ε_{fs}	0.0013 pJ/bit/m^4
ε_{amp}	10 pJ/bit/m^2

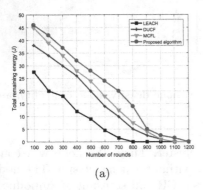

(a)

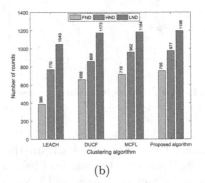

(b)

Fig. 3. (a) Total remaining energy of the methods in each round, (b) Number of nodes dead over rounds

LEACH by 49%, DUCF by 13% and MCFL by 5%. According to HND metric, the proposed algorithm is more efficient than LEACH about 21%, DUCF about 12% and MCFL about 2%. For the LND metric, FEAUC is more efficient than LEACH about 12%, DUCF about 2% and MCFL about 1%. The obtained results (Fig. 3a and b) show that the energy consumption of LEACH is maximum and the network lifetime is minimum because in each round, each node in the network has to compute the threshold and generates a random number, which consumes many CPU cycles. Cluster head selection ensures that nodes with high residual energy and maximum number of neighboring nodes decrease the overall energy consumption of network. Further, LEACH algorithm does not use unequal clustering which generates "hot spots" and reduces the number of data packets received at base station. Varying the cluster size of CH nodes, DUCF ensures good results in term of energy consumption and also network lifetime. Reducing the number of cluster head selection and reducing the repeated sending of messages, MCFL increases the network lifetime.

4 Conclusion

In this paper an unequal size clustering algorithm is proposed. The algorithm enables to balance the energy consumption among all sensor nodes which will increase the network lifetime. The proposed solution is split into two phases, off-line phase and cluster formation phase. The first phase is performed to compute the optimal radius of each cluster. The second phase uses fuzzy logic based on residual energy, number of neighboring nodes and centrality of node among its neighbors. Simulation results show that the proposed algorithm provides a better performance compared to LEACH, DUCF and MCFL clustering algorithms. It outperforms the others and realizes acceptable results in terms of energy management and network lifetime.

In future works, a new strategy based on the use of relay node will be employed during the CH selection which will be responsible for data packet transfer.

References

1. Khriji, S., El Houssaini, D., Jmal, M.W., Viehweger, C., Abid, M., Kanoun, O.: Precision irrigation based on wireless sensor network. IET Sci. Meas. Technol. **8**(3), 98–106 (2014)
2. Leite, J.R.E., Ursini, E.L., Martins, P.S.: Simulation of AdHoc networks including clustering and mobility. In: Puliafito, A., Bruneo, D., Distefano, S., Longo, F. (eds.) ADHOC-NOW 2017. LNCS, vol. 10517, pp. 199–209. Springer, Cham (2017). https://doi.org/10.1007/978-3-319-67910-5_16
3. Ogundile, O.O., Alfa, A.S.: A survey on an energy-efficient and energy-balanced routing protocol for wireless sensor networks. Sensors **17**(5), 1084 (2017)
4. Heinzelman, W.R., Chandrakasan, A., Balakrishnan, H.: Energy-efficient communication protocol for wireless microsensor networks. In: Proceedings of the 33rd Annual Hawaii International Conference on System Sciences, p. 10. IEEE (2000)
5. Baranidharan, B., Santhi, B.: DUCF: distributed load balancing unequal clustering in wireless sensor networks using fuzzy approach. Appl. Soft Comput. **40**, 495–506 (2016)
6. Mirzaie, M., Mazinani, S.M.: MCFL: an energy efficient multi-clustering algorithm using fuzzy logic in wireless sensor network. Wirel. Netw. **24**(6), 2251–2266 (2018)
7. Suharjono, A., Hendrantoro, G., et al.: A new area partitioning strategy for unequal clustering of wireless sensor networks. In: 2012 International Conference on Advanced Computer Science and Information Systems (ICACSIS), pp. 71–75. IEEE (2012)
8. Bagci, H., Yazici, A.: An energy aware fuzzy approach to unequal clustering in wireless sensor networks. Appl. Soft Comput. **13**(4), 1741–1749 (2013)
9. Kim, J.M., Park, S.H., Han, Y.J., Chung, T.M.: CHEF: cluster head election mechanism using fuzzy logic in wireless sensor networks. In: 2008 10th International Conference on Advanced Communication Technology, ICACT 2008, vol. 1, pp. 654–659. IEEE (2008)

The Trade-Offs of Cell Over-Provisioning in IEEE 802.15.4 TSCH Networks

Xenofon Fafoutis[1,2] and Georgios Z. Papadopoulos[3(✉)]

[1] Department of Electrical and Electronic Engineering,
University of Bristol, Woodland Road, Bristol BS8 1UB, UK
xenofon.fafoutis@bristol.ac.uk
[2] DTU Compute, Technical University of Denmark,
Richard Petersens Plads, 2800 Kongens Lyngby, Denmark
xefa@dtu.dk
[3] IMT Atlantique, IRISA, UBL, Cesson-Sévigné, France
georgios.papadopoulos@imt-atlantique.fr

Abstract. Wireless industrial applications require high level of Quality of Service (QoS) such as low-delay and jitter performances, low-power operations as well as end-to-end reliability close to 100%. However, considering the large number of wireless networks operating in 2.4 GHz, the radio technologies are more prone to the external interference, which eventually may negatively affect the reliability, the delay and the goodput performance due to collisions and retransmissions. To tackle the previously detailed issues, Time-Slotted Channel Hopping (TSCH) Medium Access Control (MAC) protocol emerged with IEEE 802.15.4-2015 as an alternative to the industrial standards such as WirelessHART and ISA100.11a. TSCH is based on frequency hopping to avoid the interference, while the medium access is based on a scheduler (i.e., slotframe) that repeats periodically to avoid the collisions. Yet, the majority of the proposed TSCH schedulers are based on traditional collision detection and retransmission in the following slotframe, which essentially increases the end-to-end delay performance. In this poster, we consider allocating consecutive timeslots for a single data transmission, to allow thus, to retransmit the data packet within the slotframe in case of losses. We study the potential trade-offs, reliability and delay versus energy consumption, when considering the over-allocation approach.

Keywords: Internet of Things · IEEE 802.15.4
Time-Slotted Channel Hopping · 6TiSCH · Industrial networks
Scheduling · Over-allocation

1 Introduction

Industrial automation networks require end-to-end reliability above 99.9% and guaranteed worst case delay [7]. In 2016, IEEE 802.15.4-2015 standard [1] was

---

X. Fafoutis—Work done prior to joining DTU Compute.

© Springer Nature Switzerland AG 2018
N. Montavont and G. Z. Papadopoulos (Eds.): ADHOC-NOW 2018, LNCS 11104, pp. 132–137, 2018.
https://doi.org/10.1007/978-3-030-00247-3_13

published to provide Quality of Service guarantees. Among the Medium Access Control (MAC) protocols defined in the standard, Time-Slotted Channel Hopping (TSCH) is the scheme that is especially designed for the Internet of Things (IoT). A TSCH-based schedule is a matrix that consists of timeslots and channel offsets, where each square (i.e., cell) is an transmission opportunity.

TSCH has attracted significant attention from the industrial and research community as it may provide low-power and low-delay operation, as well as reliable and predictable wireless communication. Indeed, TSCH has been implemented in several IoT-based Operating Systems (OSs)[1,2] and it has been already employed in number of real-world use cases, e.g. [3]. Furthermore, 6TiSCH Working Group (WG) was established in 2013 at the Internet Engineering Task Force (IETF) to enable IPv6 over the TSCH mode of IEEE 802.15.4[3].

A number of TSCH-based schedulers have been proposed to improve the network performance, i.e., minimize the latency or to reduce the energy consumption [8]. Indeed, to further improve reliability, some works consider cell over-provisioning [5], when it is observed that the reliability between a pair of nodes drops a certain threshold, then the schedule may over-allocate extra cells to transmit the frames [10]. In that case, over-provisioning allows to improve the network reliability, and bound the end-to-end delay by allocating more cells to each radio link, but has a negative impact on both the energy efficiency and the network capacity.

In this work, we study the impact of introducing cell over-provisioning, i.e., multiple consecutive opportunities to transmit a single data packet. To that aim, we study a TSCH-based wireless network over various link qualities, to identify the minimum required number of cells per use-case. Our simulation results show that there is trade-off between the number of allocated slots and performance metrics, such as network reliability, delay and energy consumption. Since, the number of allocated cells in a static TSCH schedule affects the networks performance: under low link qualities, multiple retransmissions are necessary to transmit per data packet, which eventually impacts the energy consumption.

2 Background and Motivation

2.1 IEEE 802.15.4-TSCH

TSCH is based on Time Division Multiple Access (TDMA) and Frequency Hopping Spread Spectrum (FHSS) schemes. Indeed, it forms a schedule that is a matrix of **timeslots** (χ axis) and **channel offsets** (ψ axis) to achieve high level of reliability by mitigating, through channel hopping, the impact of the external interference. The standard comes with 101 timeslots, which is one slotframe, and 16 channel offsets, thus, the maximum throughput is 1616 transmissions. In Fig. 1, a TSCH instant is illustrated. Similarly to TDMA, in TSCH the time

---

[1] https://github.com/contiki-ng/contiki-ng/wiki.
[2] https://openwsn.atlassian.net/wiki/spaces/OW/overview.
[3] https://datatracker.ietf.org/wg/6tisch/about/.

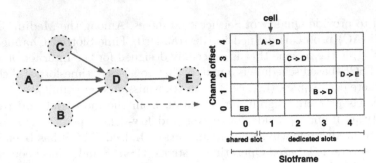

Fig. 1. An example of TSCH scheduling for node D. A → D stands for '*A transmits to D*'. EB cells are used for broadcast and advertisement frames.

is slotted into timeslots of equal length, typically 10 ms. At each timeslot, a node may transmit a frame and receive an acknowledgement. To achieve such communication, nodes' clocks should be constantly synchronized. A group of timeslots consists a slotframe that repeats perpetually. Each timeslot curries an Absolute Sequence Number (ASN), an integer value that counts the number of timeslots since the beginning of the TSCH network. Finally, the channel offset is translated into a physical radio channel through a Frequency Hopping Spread Spectrum (FHSS) algorithm.

2.2 Related Work

In 6TiSCH WG, the 6TiSCH Experimental Scheduling Function (SFX) [2] considers an over-provisioning algorithm to estimate the number of cells to be allocated. However, the term "over-provisioning" in SFX means to allocate additional cells for extra traffic, and not as conditional retransmission in consecutive timeslots of the same data packet.

In [5], the authors propose Adaptive Static Scheduling to allow, in a fully distributed manner, each pair of nodes to control their active timeslots in order to improve the energy efficiency of TSCH networks. A static scheduler is build at compilation time with excessive timeslot overallocation; yet, the nodes can dynamically activate or deactivate their *a priori* allocated timeslots, according to the traffic requirements. However, the authors did not consider the cost of blind over-provisioning in terms of delay performance.

In [10], the authors investigate the radio channel blacklisting issues. They consider an over-provisioning scheme to allocate additional timeslots per link to bound the end-to-end delay and to improve the network reliability in the case of losses. However, they did not study the impact of over-provisioning in terms of energy consumption.

In this work, we investigate the cost of cell over-provisioning depending on the link quality. Indeed, we highlight the potential trade-offs between network reliability and latency versus energy consumption.

3   Performance Evaluation

To evaluate the impact of the cells over-allocation in a TSCH networks, we employ an open-source numerical TSCH Simulator [4]. This tools simulates star-based TSCH networks with arbitrary TSCH schedules. For each radio link, the simulator allows to configure parameters, such as the maximum number of retransmissions per frame, the queue size, and the link-layer packet reception probability. The simulator supports both contention-free (dedicated) timeslots and contention-based (shared) slots. In this study, we employ the contention-free timeslots only. The simulation parameters are provided in Table 1. For evaluating the energy consumption, we use the measurements on the GINA mote [6], presented in [9].

Table 1. Simulation parameters

Parameter	Value
Frame size	100 slots
Duration of simulation	100 frames
Max. retransmissions	8
Max. queue size	8
No. of sender nodes	4
Traffic rate	2–4 ppf
Packet reception rate (PRR)	0.5–0.9
Energy efficiency exponent	1.2

The TSCH Simulator provides results on Packet Delivery Rates (PDR), energy consumption, and energy efficiency defined as the energy required per successfully delivered packet. The latency is evaluated analytically as follows. We denote as k the level of overallocation. Each transmission is modeled as a independent Bernoulli trial with the same probability of success, p (*i.e.* PRR), for each trial. For simplicity, we assume infinite retransmissions. The probability that a packet will be successfully delivered after i failed attempts is given by:

$$q_i = (1 - p)^i p. \tag{1}$$

Focusing on the worst case scenario, we consider the N-th node and assume that the packet is generated at beginning of the frame. If the transmission occurs on the i-th attempt, the delay is given by the following equation:

$$d_i = kN \left\lfloor \frac{i}{k} \right\rfloor + i \bmod k + k(N - 1). \tag{2}$$

where $k(N - 1)$ corresponds to the delay due to timeslots allocated to the other $N - 1$ nodes in the first slotframe, $kN \left\lfloor \frac{i}{k} \right\rfloor$ corresponds to the delay of whole

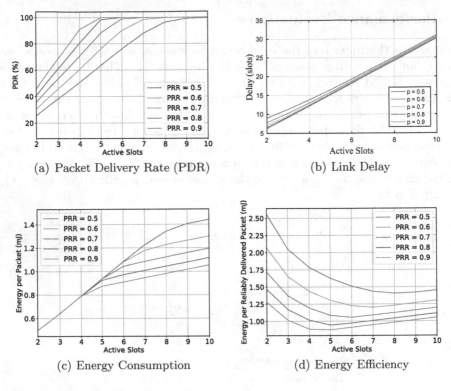

(a) Packet Delivery Rate (PDR)   (b) Link Delay

(c) Energy Consumption   (d) Energy Efficiency

Fig. 2. TSCH Performance for various link qualities.

slotframes (when $i \geq k$), and $i \bmod k$ corresponds to the delay due to failed attempts in the last slotframe. The average delay is calculated as the probability-based weighted sum of d_i, and it is given by:

$$D = \sum_{i=0}^{\infty} q_i d_i. \tag{3}$$

Figure 2 plots the reliability (PDR), delay and average energy consumed per packet of the TSCH network, respectively, for various numbers of active slots per sender per frame.

As it can be observed from the graphs, a trend shift strongly depends on PRR. Indeed, the lower is the PRR value the more active timeslots are necessary to achieve 100% of network reliability (i.e., Fig. 2(a)), which in turn affects the delay performance due to retransmissions (i.e., Fig. 2(b)) and increases the energy consumption, see Fig. 2(c). Furthermore, in Fig. 2(d), we plot the energy per reliably delivered packets, which is a metric that combines reliability and energy consumption. It is observed that increasing the level of cell over-provisioning, has a positive effect on PDR, yet has a negative effect on both delay, due to the other nodes' overprovisioned cells, and energy consumption, due to the increased amount of idle listening. It is also observed that there is an optimization point for the energy per reliably delivered bit, demonstrating a trade-off between reliability and energy consumption.

4 Conclusions

TSCH employs frequency hopping to combat the potential external interference, however it is still insufficient. Therefore, to further improve the network reliability, TSCH schedules rely on overallocation to allow multiple retransmissions within the slotframe. The level of cell overallocation in TSCH-based schedules, however, affects the network performance. Indeed, we observe a strong trade-off between reliability and delay versus energy consumption. In this poster, we investigate the costs of allocating additional timeslots per data packet.

References

1. IEEE Standard for Low-Rate Wireless Personal Area Networks (LR-WPANs). IEEE Std 802.15.4-2015 (Revision of IEEE Std 802.15.4-2011), April 2016
2. Dujovne, D., Grieco, L., Palattella, M., Accettura, N.: 6TiSCH Experimental Scheduling Function (SFX). Draft, IETF, March 2018
3. Elsts, A., Oikonomou, G., Fafoutis, X., Piechocki, R.: Internet of Things for smart homes: lessons learned from the SPHERE case study. In: Global Internet of Things Summit (GIoTS), pp. 1–6, June 2017. https://doi.org/10.1109/GIOTS.2017.8016226
4. Elsts, A., Fafoutis, X., Pope, J., Oikonomou, G., Piechocki, R., Craddock, I.: Scheduling high-rate unpredictable traffic in IEEE 802.15.4 TSCH networks. In: 13th International Conference on Distributed Computing in Sensor Systems (DCOSS) (2017)
5. Fafoutis, X., Elsts, A., Oikonomou, G., Piechocki, R., Craddock, I.: Adaptive static scheduling in IEEE 802.15.4 TSCH networks. In: Proceedings of the 4th IEEE World Forum on Internet of Things (WF-IoT) (2018)
6. Mehta, A.M., Pister, K.S.J.: WARPWING: a complete open source control platform for miniature robots. In: 2010 IEEE/RSJ International Conference on Intelligent Robots and Systems, pp. 5169–5174, October 2010. https://doi.org/10.1109/IROS.2010.5649382
7. Papadopoulos, G.Z., Matsui, T., Thubert, P., Texier, G., Watteyne, T., Montavont, N.: Leapfrog collaboration: toward determinism and predictability in industrial-IoT applications. In: Proceedings of the IEEE International Conference on Communications (ICC) (2017)
8. Hermeto, R.T., Gallais, A., Theoleyre, F.: Scheduling for IEEE802. 15.4-TSCH and slow channel hopping MAC in low power industrial wireless networks: a survey. Comput. Commun. 114, 84–105 (2017)
9. Vilajosana, X., Wang, Q., Chraim, F., Watteyne, T., Chang, T., Pister, K.S.J.: A realistic energy consumption model for TSCH networks. IEEE Sens. J. 14(2), 482–489 (2014). https://doi.org/10.1109/JSEN.2013.2285411
10. Zorbas, D., Kotsiou, V., Theoleyre, F., Papadopoulos, G.Z., Douligeris, C.: LOST: localized blacklisting aware scheduling algorithm for IEEE 802.15.4-TSCH networks. In: Proceedings of the 10th Wireless Days Conference (WD) (2018)

Wireless Network for In-Car Communication

Cristian Alderete, Guillaume Le Gall$^{(\boxtimes)}$, Alexandre Marquet,
Georgios Z. Papadopoulos, and Nicolas Montavont

IMT Atlantique, IRISA, UBL, Cesson-Sévigné, France
{cristian.alderete,guillaume.legall,alexandre.marquet,
georgios.papadopoulos,nicolas.montavont}@imt-atlantique.fr

Abstract. In this demo, we present a framework to retrieve data from an electric vehicle platform and publish it through an embedded wireless network. We developed driver programs to read the car's data (such as speed, battery level, etc.), and we built a IEEE802.15.4-TSCH network with a (CoAP) server to make it available to other devices. We also developed a dashboard, including a CoAP client, and multiple displays, to show the relevant information in real time to the driver.

Keywords: Electric vehicle · IoT · In-car networking
IEEE 802.15.4-TSCH · 6TiSCH · CoAP

1 Introduction

It has been about two decades since automotive manufacturers have moved away from point to point links for in-car communications. Indeed, they switched to using embedded buses such as Controller Area Network (CAN) to provide the on-board devices with a communication network. This was a first step towards cost, weight and complexity reduction in communication systems. With the emergence of Wireless Sensor Network (WSN) technologies, research effort is being made to introduce them for in-car communications [2,4].

In order to evaluate the usability of such a communication technology, we developed a proof-of-concept of a car network backbone, based on the Open-Source Vehicle (OSV) electric car platform [7]. Our goal is to retrieve the relevant data from the main devices of the vehicle and make it available to a low power and highly reliable wireless network. To this extent, we use state-of-the-art Internet of Thing (IoT)-based protocols. Finally, we display this data to the driver via a dashboard.

Considering that Medium Access Control (MAC) scheduling is one of the keys to a reliable wireless network [5], our effort will be centered around using the IEEE 802.15.4-TSCH MAC layer for our communicating devices.

© Springer Nature Switzerland AG 2018
N. Montavont and G. Z. Papadopoulos (Eds.): ADHOC-NOW 2018, LNCS 11104, pp. 138–144, 2018.
https://doi.org/10.1007/978-3-030-00247-3_14

2   Architecture and Protocols

2.1   The Open-Source Vehicle Electric Car

Platform. This demonstration is based on the Tabby Evo OSV, from Open Motors. We chose this platform due to its simplicity and because it offers a ground for add-ons, enhancements and concept demonstrations. As a vehicle platform, it only captures the essence of an actual car: it has no car body, nor any indicator and, in particular, no dashboard.

Our work is mainly focused on the OSV powertrain. This comprises every system involved in generating power and transforming it into mechanical forces, such as: the Lithium-Ion battery, the Battery Management System (BMS), the Engine Controller (EC) – or inverter – and the electric 3-phase AC engine. The EC and the BMS are the main devices that guarantee the safe and reliable operation of the powertrain.

The BMS handles the measurement of battery parameters, such as cells voltages, current, temperature, and calculates the State of Charge (SOC). Then, from all this information, it enables or disables the on-board charger and EC. This way, it ensures that the battery cells remain in their safety window (*i.e.*, their allowed voltage and temperature range).

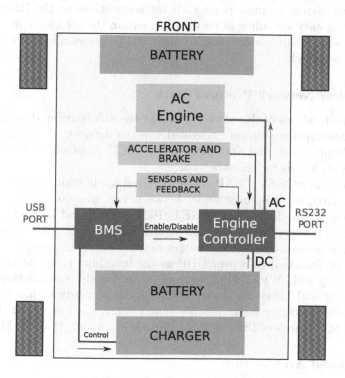

Fig. 1. OSV powertrain functional overview.

The EC's purpose is to generate the 3-phase AC current to run the engine and control its magnitude and frequency through a feedback loop.

These two core components hold important data about the vehicle, and are capable of exposing them to other devices, as depicted in Fig. 1.

Available Data. On the OSV platform, most of the relevant data can be retrieved from the BMS and EC. Some of it should be exposed to the driver in real time (*e.g.*, speed, battery SOC), while the rest of it can be displayed on-demand (*e.g.*, for maintenance). Table 2 shows the selected data for this demonstration. Even though this information is generated within the OSV, the original platform lacks displays to show it.

Both the BMS and EC expose their available data through a custom ad-hoc protocol built on top of a Universal Asynchronous Receiver-Transmitter (UART) connection. Each component implements its own protocol and data format. The BMS protocol is a simple enable/disable data flow model: the data stream starts when the reader device sends an "enable" command, and stops when a "disable" command is sent. This has the disadvantage of being forced to request the entire set of variables when just a few are needed. On the other hand, the EC implements a request/response communication protocol, meaning that each variable is requested separately with a specific command.

The stock system requires point to point connections to the BMS and EC which prevents easy spreading of information within the vehicle. This is why we build an in-vehicle wireless network: to make the powertrain's data available to the rest of the vehicle.

2.2   Wireless Network Protocol Stack

One of the motivations of this work is to break the link between data generation and data consumption with an embedded wireless network. Exposing the data through a Representational State Transfer (REST) Application Programming Interface (API) allows for enhanced usage.

In the context of WSN, CoAP is the preferred application-layer protocol [8]. It provides a request/response model between two endpoints, using a subset of HTTP request methods such as GET, PUT, POST and DELETE [3]. Furthermore, CoAP offers extensions such as OBSERVE which allows the client to subscribe to resources on a server and get notified upon changes.

The CoAP standard runs over UDP as the transport layer. At the network layer, we deploy a 6LoWPAN IPv6 network [6], and enable the Routing Protocol for Low-Power and Lossy Networks (RPL) [9], to be ready to handle possible future use cases involving more than one hop. Finally, the Time-Slotted Channel Hopping (TSCH) mode of IEEE 802.15.4-2015 is employed [1] at the MAC layer.

2.3   Proposed Architecture

Figure 2 illustrates the functional diagram of the proposed architecture. In this scenario, we distinguish two main blocks that communicate through a

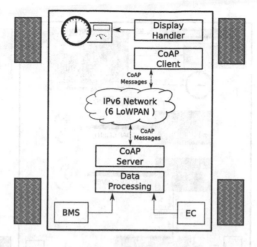

Fig. 2. Data flow from BMS and EC to the dashboard.

wireless network: the transmitter and the receiver. On the transmitter side, the information from the powertrain is retrieved, processed and then stored in the CoAP server. On the receiver side, the client requests information using GET or OBSERVE CoAP methods, and forwards it to the display handler.

3 Demonstration

3.1 Hardware

As an implementation of the ideas presented so far, we develop the full architecture shown in Fig. 3, which shows the hardware as well as the involved protocols. As a display handler, we use an Arduino UNO board, since it can natively handle UART and Inter-Integrated Circuit (I2C) protocols, as well as Pulse-Width Modulation (PWM) signals, which are needed by the different displays we use. For data collection and processing, we use an Arduino USB-HOST shield on Arduino UNO because a micro-controller board that supports USB hosting is required to communicate with the BMS. For the wireless communication, we employ two OpenMote CC2538 transceivers. These low power modules, running the Contiki Operating System, use IEEE 802.15.4 and support the protocol stack proposed in Sect. 2.2. Additionally, they provide serial ports that are used to communicate with the Arduino boards. Finally, note that voltage shifters are needed to avoid voltage level mismatches when interconnecting the chosen hardware. More details on hardware role and connections can be found in Table 1.

3.2 Resource Management

In order to address the trade-off between data freshness and network usage, we take advantage of the OBSERVE CoAP feature. This allows the server to immediately notify the client when resources are updated instead of having periodic

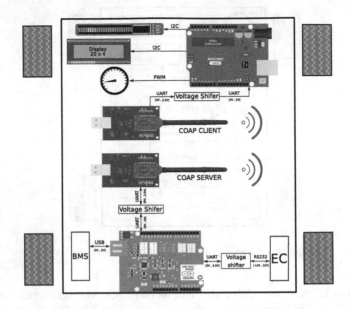

Fig. 3. Proposed architecture for this demonstration.

Table 1. Hardware used in the demonstration.

Device	Ports used	Main task
Arduino UNO + SHIELD	UART1/UART2/USB-host	Interface
Arduino UNO	UART1/UART2/PWM/I2C	Display handler
Openmote CC2538 REV-B	UART	Server
Openmote CC2538 REV-A1	UART	Client
LCD display	I2C	Display Km, °C, V
Servo-motor	PWM	Display Km/h
Bar led display	UART	Display SoC

Table 2. Resources management.

Resource	Origin	Request type	Server update strategy
Speed	EC	OBSERVE	Conditioned by charging
SoC	BMS	OBSERVE	Conditioned by speed and charging
Distance	EC	OBSERVE	Conditioned by speed
Charging	BMS	OBSERVE	Conditioned by speed
Temperature	BMS	OBSERVE	Periodically
Cells voltages	BMS	GET	Periodically

requests, thus reducing the network stress. Also, using this feature we can focus on optimizing when and how to update the server, knowing that the observing client will be automatically notified.

For this purpose, we implement an updating policy in the server, based on key relationships between the resources. For example, the CoAP server waits for the car to move to update the traveled distance, or similarly it does not update the speed if the vehicle is charging. Furthermore, we establish minimum thresholds to guarantee that the updated value has a relevant difference with the previous one before notifying clients. For demonstration purposes, we also implement the GET method to request the cells voltages. Table 2 sums up the monitored resources.

4   Conclusion

In this demo, we presented a prototype of a car network backbone using state-of-the-art WSN technologies, on top of an electric car platform. We retrieved some data from the core devices of the powertrain, and exposed them with a standard API. We also made a dashboard, which consumes this data.

We believe that the concepts brought by the RPL and CoAP protocols can lead to more flexible design for in-car communications. Wireless links also provide the benefits of cost and weight reduction. In the future, even though WSN will probably not become the default technology used for car network backbones, they could be complementary to a wired solution, mainly for monitoring or non-critical applications.

Furthermore, our set-up is a starting point to evaluate the performances of in-car wireless networks and how the IEEE 802.15.4-TSCH scheduler and RPL can be enhanced for such networks.

References

1. IEEE Standard for Low-Rate Wireless Networks. IEEE Std 802.15.4-2015 (Revision of IEEE Std 802.15.4-2011) pp. 1–709, April 2016. https://doi.org/10.1109/IEEESTD.2016.7460875
2. Bi, Z., et al.: Adopting WirelessHART for in-vehicle-networking. In: 2015 IEEE 17th International Conference on High Performance Computing and Communications, pp. 1027–1030, August 2015. https://doi.org/10.1109/HPCC-CSS-ICESS.2015.244
3. Fielding, R., Reschke, J.: Hypertext transfer protocol (http/1.1): semantics and content. RFC 7231, RFC Editor, June 2014. http://www.rfc-editor.org/rfc/rfc7231.txt
4. Huang, J., et al.: In-vehicle networking: protocols, challenges, and solutions. IEEE Netw., 1–7 (2018). https://doi.org/10.1109/MNET.2018.1700448
5. Koutsiamanis, R.A., Papadopoulos, G.Z., Fafoutis, X., Fiore, J.M.D., Thubert, P., Montavont, N.: From best-effort to deterministic packet delivery for wireless industrial IoT networks. IEEE Trans. Ind. Inform. (2018). https://doi.org/10.1109/TII.2018.2856884

6. Montenegro, G., et al.: Transmission of IPv6 Packets over IEEE 802.15.4 Networks. RFC 4944, RFC Editor, September 2007. http://www.rfc-editor.org/rfc/rfc4944.txt
7. Open Motors: TABBY EVO open source hardware platform for electrical vehicle. https://www.openmotors.co/osv-platform/. Accessed 30 Apr 2018
8. Shelby, Z., Hartke, K., Bormann, C.: The Constrained Application Protocol (CoAP). RFC 7252, RFC Editor, June 2014. http://www.rfc-editor.org/rfc/rfc7252.txt
9. Winter, T., et al.: RPL: IPv6 Routing Protocol for Low-Power and Lossy Networks. RFC 6550, RFC Editor, March 2012. http://www.rfc-editor.org/rfc/rfc6550.txt

Low Power Wide Area Networks

Enhanced Dynamic Duty Cycle
in LoRaWAN Network

Norhane Benkahla[1]($\boxtimes$), Hajer Tounsi[1], Ye-Qiong Song[2], and Mounir Frikha[1]

[1] Higher School of Communication Tunis, Aryanah, Tunisia
{norhane.benkahla,hajer.tounsi,mounir.frikha}@supcom.tn
[2] LORIA, University of Lorraine, Nancy, France
ye-qiong.song@loria.fr

Abstract. LoRa's long-range and low-power features have made it an attractive candidate for IoT devices in various fields. In this work, we present an enhanced LoRaWAN protocol. LoRaWAN MAC protocol is characterized by the restrictive use of the channel, limited by the regulatory authorities to a 1% duty cycle per cycle (i.e., 36 s per hour) per node. This regulation penalizes the nodes which require a channel access time greater than the limited duty cycle to occasionally transmit a large amount of data such as video surveillance or access control information in applications like smart school surveillance. However, some other nodes like environment sensors sharing a same LoRaWAN server may send very small amounts of information (e.g. temperature, humidity, ...) and under-use the authorized activity time of 1% duty cycle. Hence the idea of implementing an activity time sharing mechanism among nodes that allows devices to borrow additional activity time from a device or set of devices that have completed the transmission of their packets and do not need the remaining time of the corresponding duty cycle. Our work extends and improves the activity time sharing mechanism initially proposed in [1]. Instead of FIFO sharing-time allocation based on a global activity time, which may lead to the starvation of the nodes that are others than that in the head of FIFO line, we propose a new time allocation algorithm based on the classification of the different requests according to their needs in terms of their QoS requirements. It allows to satisfy a larger number of nodes requiring extra time, with less control overheads while ensuring fairness. Our time-sharing algorithm has been implemented and tested on the wasp-mote chip of libelium, showing the performance improvement and its practical usability.

Keywords: IoT · LPWAN · LoRa · Duty cycle · QoS

1 Introduction

IoT devices are used in a wide variety of intelligent systems: smart cities, smart transport, smart industry applications, security and emergencies, e-Health applications, etc. [2]. The deployment of these IoT devices is limited by challenges

© Springer Nature Switzerland AG 2018
N. Montavont and G. Z. Papadopoulos (Eds.): ADHOC-NOW 2018, LNCS 11104, pp. 147–162, 2018.
https://doi.org/10.1007/978-3-030-00247-3_15

such as range, cost, autonomy, etc. The use of traditional long-range and high-speed (3G, 4G) technologies for IoT is constrained by the relatively high cost and high energy consumption. Low power wireless technologies such as low energy Bluetooth or ZigBee are limited in their short range and are not suitable for applications requiring deployment in rural or isolated environments. In order to reduce the complexity and obtain longer range at low cost, the concept of extended networks low-power, low-bandwidth and long range (LPWAN) [3,4] is proposed. This type of networks is suitable for equipment that requires several years of autonomy and does not require high throughput. It is therefore promising for the Internet of Things. Among several LPWAN technologies, Semtech's LoRa is an interesting one, which can reach a range of 5 km in the urban area and 15 km in the rural area exploiting license-free sub-GHz frequency bands [5]. The flexibility of LoRa's long-range transmission is in expense of a low throughput and a limited channel activity time. In fact, the ETSI regulations impose to each node a maximum use of duty cycle of 1% per cycle, that means 36 s per hour. If this duty cycle limitation does not bother traditional low data rate IoT applications, it may exclude important applications where some sensors occasionally need more than 36 s per one hour cycle to transmit their urgent data following burst events detection, exceeding the per cycle authorized channel activity time. To introduce more flexibility while still keeping the total duty cycle limitation of an application composed of n sensor nodes, in [1], Pham has first introduced the idea to allow some throughput demanding nodes to occasionally exceed their 1% limitation (a kind of "last chance" solution) while still keeping the global duty cycle of the application under $n \times 1\%$. The basic mechanism, called activity time sharing, consists in broadcasting a "global activity time" G_{AT} informing each node the total remaining available time of the current cycle. A node needing more time will be allowed to use additional time until this G_{AT}. This approach provides indeed more flexibility to better manage the QoS issues, as demonstrated in [1]. It arises however some additional issues. One is the risk to starve the flowing nodes, especially if we assume that devices share 100% of their local activity time or the LoRa gateway allows the use of the maximum G_{AT} (i.e., $\alpha = 100\%$ where α is the G_{AT} ratio allowed for usage). Another issue is related to the way to broadcast G_{AT}, which introduces overheads and needs a synchronized radio wake-up mechanism.

In this paper, we leverage those limitations. We extend and improve the activity time sharing mechanism proposed in [1]. Instead of FIFO sharing-time allocation which may lead to the starvation of the nodes other than that in the head of FIFO line, we propose to define three classes of nodes (classical, donor and requester) and a new time allocation algorithm based on the classification of the different requests according to their needs in terms of QoS. It allows to satisfy a larger number of nodes requiring extra time, with less control overheads while ensuring fairness and without impacting other nodes' due time.

The rest of the paper is organized as follows. In Sect. 2, we present the LoRa/LoRaWAN technology. In Sect. 3, we review and discuss the principle of the time activity sharing mechanism presented in [1]. In Sect. 4, we present our solution and proposed improvements to solve the above-mentioned issues by describing the new activity time sharing mechanism and the time allocation algorithm according to a classification strategy that depends on a QoS criterion. Our implementation and our experimentation scenario will be discussed in Sect. 5 by showing how the mechanism is adapted to the devices and the server. We conclude in Sect. 6.

2 LoRa Network Overview

In this section, we present the LoRa/ LoRaWAN technology. Even if the terms LoRa and LoRaWAN are used interchangeably but they refer to two different concepts in the network. In fact LoRa corresponds to the PHYSICAL layer and precisely to the modulation technique used and LoRaWAN defines the LoRa MAC layer.

2.1 LoRa Modulation: Physical Layer

LoRa technology is a proprietary physical modulation designed and patented by Semtech Corporation. It is based on Chirp-Spread Spectrum (CSS) modulation [8] with Integrated Forward Error Correction. LoRa operates in the lower ISM bands (EU: 868 MHz and 433 MHz, USA: 915 MHz and 433 MHz). It offers different configurations (data rates, transmission range, energy consumption and resilience to noise) according to the selection of four parameters which are Carrier Frequency (CF), Bandwidth (BW), Coding Rate (CR) and Spreading Factor (SF). Each LoRa symbol is composed of 2^{SF} chirps [7], where SF represents the corresponding spreading factor in the range of 6 to 12. SF6 means a shortest range, SF12 will be the longest. Each step up in spreading factor doubles the time on air to transmit the same amount of data. The use of a larger SF decreases the bit rate and increases the time on Air (ToA) which induces greater power consumption. In fact, in the case of a 125 kHz bandwidth and a coding rate 4/5, the bit rate is equal to 250 bps for SF12 and it is equal to 5470 bps for SF7 [9]. With LoRa, transmissions on the same carrier frequency but with different spreading factors are orthogonal, so there is no interference.

2.2 LoRaWan: LoRa Mac Layer

Unlike the proprietary LoRa protocol, LoRaWAN is an open protocol defined by LoRa Alliance. A LoRaWAN network is based on star-of-stars topology and is composed of three elements.

- End devices: nodes that send uplink (UL) traffic and receives Downlink (DL) traffic through LoRa gateways. The communication between end-devices and gateways is based on LoRa modulation.
- LoRa gateways dispatch the LoRaWAN frames received from end devices via IP connections (using Ethernet, 3G, 4G or Wi-Fi, etc.) to a network server.

– A network server decodes the packets, analyzes information mined by end
devices and generate the packets that should be sent to end devices.

LoRaWAN end devices implement three classes: a basic LoRaWAN named
Class A and optional features (class B, class C) [13].

LoRaWAN operates in ISM bands (863–870 MHz band in Europe) which are
subject to regulations on radio emissions, thus radios are required to adopt either
a Listen-Before-Talk (LBT) policy or a duty cycled transmission to limit the rate
at which the end devices can actually generate messages. The current LoRaWAN
specification exclusively uses duty-cycled limited transmissions to comply with
the ETSI regulations [9]. In fact, each device is limited to an aggregated transmit
duty cycle of 1% that means 36 s per hour.

LoRaWAN defines three MAC message types in [13] which are: the join message for connecting a device with a network server, the confirmed message which
have to receive an ACK from a network server, and the unconfirmed message
without ACK. A MAC payload length varies between 59 and 250 Bytes depending on the modulation rate [9].

3   Related Work on LoRa Performance Enhancement

In order to optimize the performance of a LoRa network and the quality of
service, we identified three complementary approaches: (1) parameter selection,
(2) data compression, (3) activity time sharing.

3.1   LoRa Parameter Selection

As explained in previous section, for satisfying a desired performance level, one
can choose his configuration by combining the various parameters CR (4/5,
4/6, 4/7 and 4/8), BW (125 kHz, 250 kHz and 500 kHz), SF (from 7 to 12) and
TP (2 dBm to 17 dBm), resulting in total 1152 combinations. In [10] the authors
studied the impact of LoRa parameter settings (bandwith, coding rate, spreading
factor, transmission power, etc.) on energy consumption and communication reliability. They proposed a mechanism to automatically select LoRa transmission
parameters that satisfy the performance requirements. This solution is optimal
for a given application scenario, but it is not convenient when traffic dynamically
changes.

3.2   Data Compression

The authors in [11] were interested in data compression in order to reduce the
size of the data sent and thus minimize the transmission time and optimize
the energy consumption. A swapped huffman tree coding has been applied to
transmit the necessary data with a compression ratio of 52.3%. Data compression
has been used in various LoRa sensors in the industry [12] in order to reduce
energy consumption and thus reduce the data transmission time that will provide

better optimization of the LoRa network. The two studies mentioned above were interested in optimizing energy consumption without worrying about the regulatory constraints relating to the channel occupancy time.

3.3 Activity Time Sharing Mechanism

[1], proposes a mechanism for sharing the channel occupancy time in order to improve the overall performance of the network. We give more details on this mechanism, to which we are interested in our work. [1] proposed an activity time sharing mechanism in a long-range unlicensed LoRa network to face the problem of activity time limitation in the case of video surveillance applications. The proposed mechanism supposes that all devices that will participate in the sharing mechanism register with the LoRa gateway and announce their local remaining activity time (initially can be the total authorized activity time or just a fraction). Thus, the gateway computes the global activity time allowed for usage which can be an addition of the allowed time of each device *"Global Time"* (1) or just a fraction of it. After it informs it to all devices which will share it. This step is performed each cycle (every hour).

As long as this global activity time allows, a node Di that exhausts its duty cycle (allocated activity time) and needs additional time to send its data borrows the remaining time from the global time. A global view of the total remaining activity time is maintained by the LoRa Gateway (LR-BS) on reception of packets and sent back to devices at the appropriate moments.

$$GlobalTime = n \times 36\,s \tag{1}$$

In [1], the author did not evaluate nor propose a mechanism for selecting devices that will benefit the shared extra time. Indeed, he limited himself to serving the first applicant. Moreover, [1] assumes that all the nodes participating in the sharing mechanism must be on standby to be able to receive from the gateway the updated information of the global activity time and the list of nodes involved in the loan. Otherwise they must wake-up periodically to receive this update. This would not correspond to the behavior of class A nodes but rather to class B nodes. We believe that the activity time sharing mechanism proposed in [1] improves the quality of service but lacks an additional time allocation mechanism by a priority classification or a strategy that satisfies a larger number of requesting devices taking into account the range of a device and its battery level in the management of the allocation of additional time. In the next section, we will describe our solution to those above-mentioned issues.

4 Synopsis and Detailed Description of the Proposed Algorithm

The main idea of our mechanism is to provide devices, that do not use all their maximal allowed activity time, with the ability to share their remaining transmission time to devices that need to exceed the 1% duty cycle restriction in order to provide a better global quality of service. Unlike [1], we will consider two modes of LoRa "Sleep mode" and "Standby mode".

We suppose that the number of packets that each device has to send is known at the beginning of the transmission, so, each device can calculate the needed time on air per cycle instead of using "Last packet flag" as in [1]. The use of this flag in [1] is to indicate that the device will finish its transmission during the cycle. The management of this remaining time will be in the server which doesn't need to broadcast the information of the remaining global activity time as in [1] since if a node decides to share its remaining activity time then it will no longer need to use it. We also allow all the devices to benefit from the dynamicity of duty cycle when the remaining time is sufficient. We propose that each node informs the server of its role in the sharing mechanism during the OTAA (Over The Air Activation) registration process [13]. We define 3 node's roles:

- "Classical" devices: those who will neither give nor receive any additional activity time. So, they don't participate in the sharing mechanism.
- "Donor" devices: those that do not consume all their activity time during 1 h cycle, so they will give their remaining time to the devices that will need it.
- "Requester" devices: they are the devices whose local activity time is not sufficient to transmit their data in a cycle of 1 h. They try to benefit from the offer of the potential donors.

4.1 Registration Phase

At each cycle, during the registration phase, each node specifies in the "join request" message its role according to the size of the data to be sent during this cycle and therefore the transmission time that it needs. The estimation of the time on air is calculated according to the Semtech formula (6) [14], where T_{sym} is the time taken to send 2^{SF} chips at the chip rate and is calculated using (2). (3) defines a preamble duration where $n_{preamble}$ is the number of programmed preamble symbols. The number of symbols that make up the packet payload and header is given by (4) where PL is the payload size in bytes, CR is 16 if the CR is enabled and zero otherwise, H is 20 when the header is enabled and zero otherwise and DE is two when the low data rate optimization is enabled and zero otherwise. The payload duration is then the symbol period multiplied by the number of payload symbols which is defined in (5). Finally, the time on air is simply the sum of the preamble and payload duration (6).

Figure 1 illustrates the treatment done by a device to register with the server and be part of the sharing mechanism. In case of the device is a "Donor" (estimated transmission time < duty cycle), it will also indicate the remaining time it is willing to lend (7). Otherwise, if it is a "Requester" (estimated transmission time > duty cycle), it specifies the needed time to borrow before starting transmission (7). We propose to encode the information of the role of the equipment and the calculated time (for the loan or the donation) respectively in the fields RFU and FOpts of the MHDR field [13].

$$T_{sym} = \frac{2^{SF}}{BW} \tag{2}$$

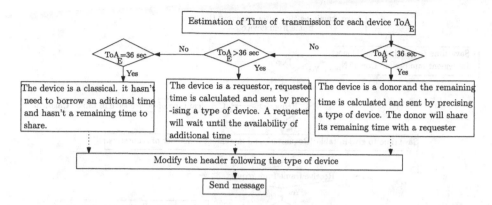

Fig. 1. Device's state registration

$$T_{preamble} = (n_{preamble} + 4, 25) \times T_{sym} \qquad (3)$$

$$PayloadSymbNb = 8 + max \left(ceil \left(\frac{8PL - 4SF + 28 + 16 - 20H}{4(SF - 2DE)} \right) (CR + 4), 0 \right) \qquad (4)$$

$$T_{payload} = payloadSymbNb \times T_{sym} \qquad (5)$$

$$ToA_E = Tpreamble + Tpayload \qquad (6)$$

$$(Requested/Given)time = LimitToA - ToA_E \qquad (7)$$

When the server receives the registration message, it saves the received information according to the type of each device in the corresponding table and assigns a priority to the node according to some criteria (battery level, range, etc.).

4.2   Description of the Activity Sharing Mechanism

After the registration phase, each node starts to send its data according to the LoRaWAN protocol. The node continues to send information about its participation in the activity sharing mechanism. Therefore, it can possibly change its offer or request dynamically. Also this allows a node that did not participate in the sharing mechanism during the join phase to do so during the transmission of its data. Upon receipt of the registration phase or a data frame from a given node, the server verifies the received information and takes the necessary actions depending on the role of the equipment. So if it is a donor node then the server just checks that the information is stored in the appropriate table otherwise it adds it. If it is a requesting node, then the server checks according to the priority given to it, if it could benefit from additional time then the server grants the requested time, otherwise the server ignores its request. Different criteria can be considered to choose the highest priority requesting node to be satisfied. In our work, we are interested in two approaches. The first one consists of serving first

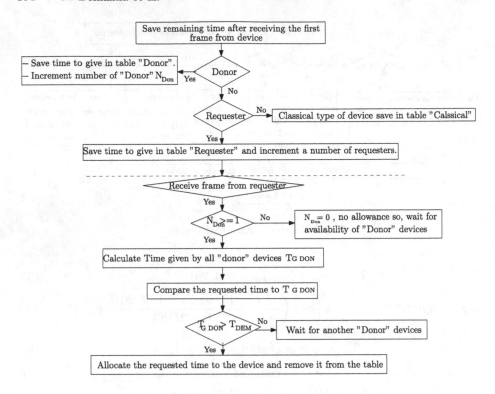

Fig. 2. Server processing

the lowest demand in order to satisfy the maximum number of demands. The second approach is to first satisfy the nodes with the lowest battery to avoid that battery runs out before the end of transmission of their messages in case of equality of the battery level, then we choose the farthest node whose transmission is the most unfavorable. The distance of each device is calculated according to (8).

$$distance(m) = 10^{(RSSIm-ReceivedRSSI)/20} \qquad (8)$$

Figure 2 shows the treatment done by the server upon the reception of a frame. Once the request received from a given node can be satisfied (the time offered by the donors is sufficient) then the server updates the remaining activity time of the donors, grants the borrowed time to the requester by sending to it an update message confirming the allocation of the additional activity time. The update message will be sent only for responding to the demands of the requesters. The update message (ACK0 to say "unauthorized borrowing" and ACK1 to say "allocation of additional time is done") must be sent during the two reception windows (class A). After additional time's allocation, the server removes the requester from the appropriate table. In case of both windows are not open, the server will wait for the next opening of both windows reception.

5 Implementation and Discussion of Scenarios

To evaluate our proposed mechanism, we have implemented it on waspmote SX1272 devices (wasp-mote SX1272 LoRa clients cards and a wasp-mote SX1272 LoRa gateway) [15,16]. We have integrated a flag in the ACK frame so that the requesters know if their requests have been accepted or not yet. We have tested several scenarios that will be presented and analyzed in the next subsections.

Table 1. LoRa modes for 250 bytes

LoRa mode	BW(kHz)	CR	SF	250 bytes
1	125	4/5	12	8295.41 ms
2	250	4/5	12	4509.69 ms
3	125	4/5	10	2312.50 ms
4	500	4/5	12	2254.84 ms
5	250	4/5	10	1147.90 ms
6	500	4/5	11	1050.30 ms
7	250	4/5	9	625.15 ms
8	500	4/5	9	312.57 ms
9	500	4/5	8	176.76 ms
10	500	4/5	7	99.90 ms

Table 2. LoRa modes for 100 bytes

LoRa mode	BW(kHz)	CR	SF	100 bytes
1	125	4/5	12	4104.18 ms
2	250	4/5	12	2052.09 ms
3	125	4/5	10	1067.00 ms
4	500	4/5	12	1026.04 ms
5	250	4/5	10	533.50 ms
6	500	4/5	11	504.46 ms
7	250	4/5	9	287.23 ms
8	500	4/5	9	143.61 ms
9	500	4/5	8	79.48 ms
10	500	4/5	7	44.86 ms

We consider an environment of smart school and smart bus scenario, where children take school buses to get school and to get home from school. The parents need to ensure the security of their children by checking the time of arrival at school or at home. A monitoring system allows a mobile application to notify parents during the get in and get out of their children from the bus. Children are identified by checking their cards and their information are sent to a server through a LoRa network.

5.1 Test Scenario Without Activity Time Sharing

We consider a first simple scenario with two devices to verify our implementation. The first (D_1) is dedicated for capturing image. An image of 2000 bytes should be sent in 8 packets because of the constraint of the maximum payload length of LoRa packet which is 250 Bytes. The second device (D_2) is a simple temperature sensor which sends 100 bytes' message containing Temperature, date and time. Each device is limited by a maximum transmission time "Limit-ToA $= 36$ s/cycle". The devices use LoRa mode 1, that means they use BW $= 125$ kHz and SF $= 12$. This choice is made because SF12 is the default one in some devices such as the waspmote ones and also because it is the most suitable for long range and in presence of obstacles which is the case of urban areas [17]. Indeed, our tests done in our school where the device was on the 1st floor and the gateway on the 2nd floor, at a distance of about 43 m using a

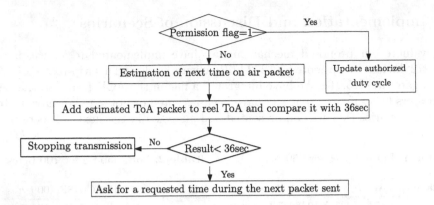

Fig. 3. The ACK response in the node

transmission power of 14 dB have confirmed that SF7 and SF8 are not adequate for great distances inside a school. The same test was done using the SF12 under the same conditions, the transmission of all packets was successful.

Tables 1 and 2 present the time on air respectively of a 250 Bytes and 100 bytes according to several parameters. The scenario is shown in Fig. 4. Table 3 shows the time of transmission consumed after the transmission of each packet for D_1. The time on air of the packet sent by D_2 is $\delta_1 = 2052.09$ ms. These time on air values are the same in all tests. After receiving the join accept, the cycle begins for all the clients in the network. Sending the fifth packet, the device D_1 realizes that it has consumed all its allowed activity time (36 s) so it reached the limit-ToA, the transmission of its following packets is stopped and it enters in a sleep mode until the next cycle when it will have 36 s again to finish its transmission. The same thing will happen for the data that should be sent during the second cycle. The image can only be decoded if all its packets are totally received which could be very late. Unlike the first device, the second client D_2 sends its packet and waits for an ACK, after that it enters in a sleep mode because it has finished its transmission during the first cycle.

Table 3. ToA for each packet sent by D_1

ζ_1 (ms)	ζ_2 (ms)	ζ_3 (ms)	ζ_4 (ms)	ζ_5 (ms)	ζ_6 (ms)	ζ_7 (ms)	ζ_8 (ms)
8295.41	16590.82	24886.23	33181.64	41477.05	49772.46	58067.87	66363.28

5.2 Test Scenarios with Dynamic Activity Time Sharing

In the two following scenarios (1 and 2) we suppose that there is no registration phase in the join procedure. We treat two cases: first when the donor is available before any request and second when the requester's demands are sent to the server but there are not yet available donors.

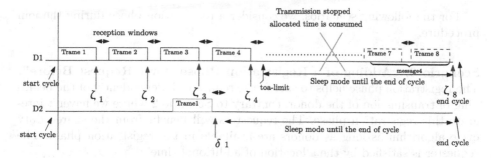

Fig. 4. LoRaWAN behavioral scenario

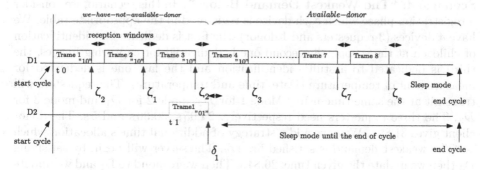

Fig. 5. Scenario with dynamic duty cycle

Scenario 1: "Donor Available Before the Transmission Time Limit of the Requester". We will test the same previous scenario using activity time sharing without a registration phase. D_1 begins the transmission of its image at t_0 and D_2 begins transmitting its 100 bytes at t_1. The scenario is shown in Fig. 5. The client D_1 informs the server that it is requesting a time of 30.37 s in its first frame and D_2 informs the server that is a donor of 33.94 s.

As soon as the first requester frame is received, the server starts updating its donor table to satisfy the requester. D_1 receives a favorable response to its request after sending its 4th packet at ζ_2 because at this time D_2 is registered in the donor's table. As a result, D_1 has an additional time to complete its transmission through the activity sharing time mechanism.

Scenario 2: "Donor Not Available Before the Transmission Time Limit of the Requester". We take the same scenario in Fig. 5, but a donor client will not be available before that requester client reaches a limit-ToA, D_2 will begin its transmission after that D_1 consumes its authorized duty cycle. As a result, the transmission of D_1 will be interrupted because the server could not answer the request of D_1 (there is no available donors at this time). D_1 can not benefit from the dynamic duty cycle for a non-availability of donors before achieving its limit-ToA.

For the following scenarios, we consider a registration phase during the join procedure.

Scenario 3: "Adding of a Registration Phase: First Request Before". The registration phase helps to satisfy the requester independently of the beginning of transmission of the donor, contrary to Scenario 2 where we haven't integrate this registration phase. The requesters will benefit from the shared duty cycle algorithm as long as donors are available in the registration phase. The requester is satisfied by the allocation of additional time.

Scenario 4: "The Weakest Demand Before". In this scenario, we consider a registration phase which each device is registered in the appropriate table. We have 4 devices (3 requesters and 1 donor), the first is dedicated for identification of children at the school, the second one is dedicated for capturing images, the third is dedicated to a stuff's identification and the last one is dedicated for measurement of temperature (Date, time and temperature). The requesters will transmit at the same time using: Mode 1 for D_2, mode 2 for D_1 and mode 3 for D_3. The three requesters need respectively: 24.95 s, 30.36 s and 5 s. The donor client gives 31.89 s. We have add a strategy of additional time's allocation which is "The weakest demand is satisfied firstly". The server will begin by satisfying D_3 then we update the given time: 26.84 s. Then we respond to D_1 and we update the given time: 1.89 s. Arriving to D_2, the server realizes that the given time can not satisfy a D_2's demand. The goal of this strategy is to satisfy a maximum number of requesters, for example, if we have begin with the bigger demand, we will satisfy only D_2. The number of the satisfied requesters will decrease.

Scenario 5: "The Lowest Battery Level Before". We resume the same Scenario 4 but with a priority's strategy. D_1, D_2 and D_3 send their registration message as requesters. By receiving the requests for the equipment D_1, D_2 and D_3 during the registration phase, the server sets a priority for each of them according to the level of their batteries and their distance. So, the highest priority is given to the device with the lowest battery level and in case of equality the farthest one (the longest distance). The server will save the information (type of device, requested/given time, distance and the battery level) of each device. If there is a device with the same battery level and distance, we will firstly satisfy the smallest request in order to maximize the number of satisfied clients. The results of the attribution of additional time for Scenario 5 for each device are shown in Fig. 7.

The devices begin the transmission of their first frames, the server will satisfy the requester having a highest priority then will pass to the requester whose priority is less. In our experimentation, D_1 and D_3 have the same battery level and the same distance, so the server will attribute the highest priority to D_3 because it has the lower request. After serving D_3, the server satisfies D_1. When the remaining given time is updated, the server verifies it and realizes that

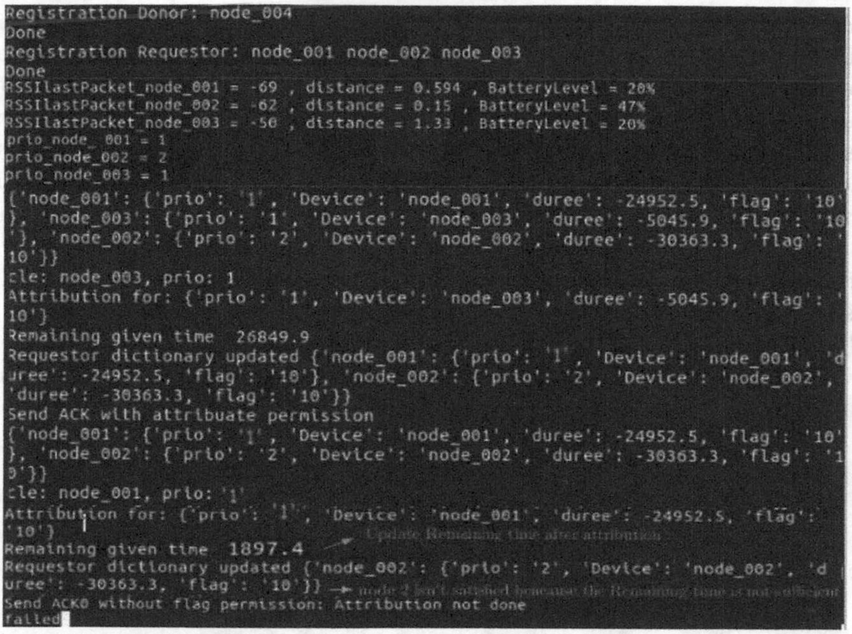

```
Registration Donor: node_004
Done
Registration Requestor: node_001 node_002 node_003
Done
RSSIlastPacket_node_001 = -69 , distance = 0.594 , BatteryLevel = 28%
RSSIlastPacket_node_002 = -62 , distance = 0.15 , BatteryLevel = 47%
RSSIlastPacket_node_003 = -50 , distance = 1.33 , BatteryLevel = 20%
prio_node_001 = 1
prio_node_002 = 2
prio_node_003 = 1
{'node_001': {'prio': '1', 'Device': 'node_001', 'duree': -24952.5, 'flag': '10'
}, 'node_003': {'prio': '1', 'Device': 'node_003', 'duree': -5045.9, 'flag': '10
'}, 'node_002': {'prio': '2', 'Device': 'node_002', 'duree': -30363.3, 'flag': '
10'}}
cle: node_003, prio: 1
Attribution for: {'prio': '1', 'Device': 'node_003', 'duree': -5045.9, 'flag': '
10'}
Remaining given time  26849.9
Requestor dictionary updated {'node_001': {'prio': '1', 'Device': 'node_001', 'd
uree': -24952.5, 'flag': '10'}, 'node_002': {'prio': '2', 'Device': 'node_002',
'duree': -30363.3, 'flag': '10'}}
Send ACK with attribuate permission
{'node_001': {'prio': '1', 'Device': 'node_001', 'duree': -24952.5, 'flag': '10'
}, 'node_002': {'prio': '2', 'Device': 'node_002', 'duree': -30363.3, 'flag': '1
0'}}
cle: node_001, prio: '1'
Attribution for: {'prio': '1', 'Device': 'node_001', 'duree': -24952.5, 'flag':
'10'}
Remaining given time  1897.4
Requestor dictionary updated {'node_002': {'prio': '2', 'Device': 'node_002', 'd
uree': -30363.3, 'flag': '10'}}
Send ACK0 without flag permission: Attribution not done
failed
```

Fig. 6. Implementation result of Scenario 5 in the server

it's not sufficient compared to the client's demand. D_2 sends its frames but its transmission will be stopped when the limit-ToA is achieved, it will not benefit from the sharing duty cycle.

5.3 Synthesis

In Fig. 7 we present the number of devices that have finished their transmission in each scenario for both methods (with and without time activity sharing). We can see that our approach maximizes the number of satisfied clients. For Scenario 1 and 2, we can benefit from the sharing mechanism if the available donors are present before a requester reaches its limited authorized time. In the opposite case we will have a basic behavior of the clients where a requester's transmission stops at 36 s. Regarding scenarios 3, 4 and 5, thanks to the configuration phase, we ensure the sharing of duty cycle even if a donor arrives after finishing the transmission of a requester. This means that the sharing do not depend anymore on the beginning of donor's transmission but on its availability in the network during the one-hour cycle (If a donor exists in a network regardless of its t_{start}, the requester can always benefit from the given time provided that it is sufficient to meet the demand of the requesting client). As can be seen, our approach satisfies a larger number of devices by using a additional time management strategy.

As conclusion, our algorithm, in addition to a dynamic duty cycle, allows the devices which have a low battery level (their batteries may be exhausted) and are distant from the LoRa Gateway to benefit from the duty cycle before the others devices. It means we start by the emergency cases (exhausted battery level). This proposition is a combination of the default algorithm, an enhanced duty cycle and a management mechanism of additional time in order to maximize the number of satisfied clients starting with the highest priority. The mechanism occurs normally in the case where the additional time is not enough to make a sharing mechanism, but when the conditions are good and the request can be satisfied the mechanism follows a sharing algorithm with selection of clients. In both cases each donor client register its remaining time in the server in order to allow the requester to benefit from an additional time when this remaining time is sufficient.

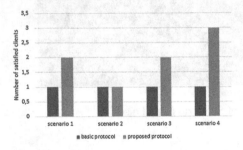

Fig. 7. Number of satisfied clients   **Fig. 8.** Join request processing time

Table 4. Join request packet size and processing time

	Join request payload	Join request processing time
Basic LoRaWAN	18 bytes	1.48 s
Proposal	24 bytes	1.646 s

As can be seen in Table 4 and Fig. 8, the payload length of the join request message is bounded by an increase of 6 bytes. The join request processing time (basic join request + registration phase) is increased by about 0.166 s on average in the proposed approach. This overhead is the same when coded in data frames and is kept scalable for practical use. Also our mechanism did not introduce new messages but was based on the LoRa messages (join, confirmed message).

6 Conclusions

In this paper, we proposed a new algorithm allowing dynamic time sharing among LoRaWAN nodes for allowing flexible node duty cycles while still respecting the total duty cycle limitation of 1% in average. We have improved the previous result in [1] based on the remaining activity time of each device, where the server will allow a client requiring additional time to finish its transmission by borrowing additional time from the unused time left by other clients, thus by adding an allocation management mechanism according on the QoS requirement of each client. This solves the problem of clients that want to exceed their limit-ToA for urgent applications for example. With this algorithm, we can maximize the number of satisfied requesters needing to occasionally exceed their duty cycle limitation. Our solution has been implemented and thoroughly tested. According to the experimental results, we have shown that the proposed sharing mechanism with an appropriate priority-based requester selection improves the overall quality of service. Also our mechanism includes both the sharing in a static mode (registration phase) and in a dynamic situation during the node transmission. Due to the limited available nodes in our lab, our study was limited to a few devices for validating the prove of our concept in real. In our future work, the scalability will be further conducted with a high number of devices. For further enhance the performance, different approaches must be combined. So we also plan to investigate the dynamic LoRa parameter selection and especially the adaptive data rate (ADR) and its combination with the activity time sharing approach.

References

1. Pham, C.: QoS for long-range wireless sensors under duty-cycle regulation with shared activity time usage. TOSN **12**, 1–33 (2016)
2. Atzori, L., Iera, A., Morabito, G.: The Internet of Things: a survey. Comput. Netw. **54**, 2787–2805 (2010)
3. Link Labs: A Comprehensive Look at Low Power, Wide Area Networks For Internet of Things Engineers and Decision Makers (2016)
4. Xiong, X., Zheng, K., Xu, R., Xiang, W., Chatzimisios, P.: Low power wide area machine-to-machine networks: key techniques and prototype. IEEE Commun. Mag. **53**(9), 64–71 (2015)
5. Sinha, R.S., Wei, Y., Hwang, S.-H.: A survey on LPWA technology: LoRa and NB-IoT. ICT Express **3**, 14–21 (2017)
6. LoRa & LoRaWAN Primer. https://www.leverege.com/research-papers/lora-lorawan-primer
7. Sikken, B.: Project DecodingLoRa (2016)
8. Springer, A., Gugler, W., Huemer, M., Reind, L., Ruppel, C., Weigel, R.: Spread spectrum communications using chirp signals. In: Proceedings of the IEEE/AFCEA, Munich, Germany, pp. 166–170, 19 May 2000
9. LoRa Alliance Technical committee LoRawan regional parameters, Revision 1.0, July 2016

10. Bor, M., Roedig, U.: LoRa transmission parameter selection. In: 13th International Conference DCOSS, Ottawa, ON, Canada, June 2017
11. Jang, Y.S., Usman, M.R., Usman, M.A., Shin, S.Y.: Swapped Huffman tree coding application for low power wide area network (LPWAN). In: International Conference ICSGTEIS, October 2016
12. nkeWatteco: LoRaWANTM Press'O. V2.0. Updated 04 Sept 2016
13. Sornin, N., Luis, M., Eirich, T., Kramp, T., Hersent, O.: LoRa specification 1.0 LoRa alliance standard specification, January 2015
14. Semtech corporation SX1272/3/6/7/8: LoRa modem an1200.13, Revision 1, July 2017
15. Libelium comunicaciones Distribuidas S.L.: Waspmote LoRa 868 MHz 915 MHz SX1272 networking guide, Revision 4.2, November 2015
16. Libelium Comunicaciones Distribuidas S.L.: Waspmote data frame programming guide. version 7.2, October 2017
17. Blenn, N., Kuipers, F.: LoRaWAN in the Wild: Measurements from The Things Network. ArXiv2017, June 2017

Specificities of the LoRa™ Physical Layer for the Development of New Ad Hoc MAC Layers

Nicolas Gonzalez[1,2](✉), Adrien Van Den Bossche[2], and Thierry Val[2]

[1] Snootlab SAS, 10 Boulevard d'Arcole, 31000 Toulouse, France
ngonzalez@snootlab.com
[2] Institut de Recherche en Informatique de Toulouse, Université de Toulouse,
UT2J, Blagnac, France
{nicolas.gonzalez,vandenbo,val}@irit.fr

Abstract. The Internet of Things and particularly energy constraint object revealed these last years some radio frequencies technologies which allow to realize wireless transmissions at long range and with low energy. This change of paradigm makes tip over the problems of multi-hop networks to multi-channel MAC networks. The LoRa™ technology arises from this sphere of influence by using the spread spectrum to reach the expected performances. This physical layer is very original compared with the physical layers used for a long time with the IEEE 802.15.4 standard. This article highlights the specificities of the LoRa™ physical layer to design new MAC layers for the ad hoc Internet of Things.

1 Introduction

The Internet of Things (IoT) is a growing field. This is a relatively large area of application where many scientific, technological and societal issues arise. Technologically, IoT can be addressed by the data side or by the network side. Regarding the network part, we distinguish the collection network, wireless and energy constrained, from the rest of the backbone constraints and challenges are not the same. It is considered that the wireless part of the IoT (Device-Layer of the IoT [1]) inherits ad hoc mobile networks (MANET) and wireless sensor networks (WSN) from the proximity of constraints and latches [2]. However, recent technological advances in narrow-band (NB) and ultra-narrow-band (UNB) technologies are opening up new possibilities, such as radio range, topologies, and multi-channel access. These possibilities make it possible to consider new collection network, especially at the MAC level. This is for example the case with LoRa™ technology, the acronym for "Long Range" which is a NB wireless transmission technology for long range and energy efficient transmissions for the node sensors. Thanks to its various parameters, LoRa™ makes it possible to imagine new medium access controls. This article proposes to list the different technical levers that the LoRa™ radio physical layer offers and to study the performances

© Springer Nature Switzerland AG 2018
N. Montavont and G. Z. Papadopoulos (Eds.): ADHOC-NOW 2018, LNCS 11104, pp. 163–174, 2018.
https://doi.org/10.1007/978-3-030-00247-3_16

outside any MAC consideration. This study shows the beginnings of the development of new MAC layers for the Internet of Things.

This article is structured as follows: after this introduction, we present in more detail the problematic of the transition from multi-hop to multi-channel. Next, we present a detailed analysis of the LoRa™ technology and the different levers that it allows to activate, particularly in terms of the isolation of logical channels, followed by a state of the art of the techniques for using these methods. Then we present an experimental study evaluating, on a real test bench, the logical isolation capacity offered by LoRa™. In a final part, we present ways to improve MAC mechanisms in LoRa™, before concluding the article.

2   Problem: From Multi-hop to Multi-channel

For many years, in the dynamics of the IEEE 802.15.4 standard, a major difficulty in scaling up the number of nodes is at the routing level. The very limited resources in terms of datarate, computational performances and energy of the nodes of this type of network do not make it possible to search and find routes efficiently on a large number of nodes of the global network. The IEEE 802.15.4 standard, heavily used in recent years, mainly uses physical layers that have a fairly high throughput for a sensor network (250 kbit/s) but whose range is limited (200 to 300 m in *outdoor* and 30 m in *indoor*).

The use of physical layers like LoRa™ makes it possible to greatly increase the radio range, which has the effect of changing the type of topology, protocol architecture and therefore globally, paradigm [3]. It is interesting to note that for the usual applications of the Internet of Things, with an equal node density, for a LoRa™ network, the density of the links increases and the distance in number of jumps decreases, compared to a network 802.15.4. The Fig. 1 makes it possible to represent this change of scale at the level of the radiofrequency cells. This last point makes it possible to release the constraints on the layer 3 and on the multi-hops routing algorithms. However, this constraint is transferred to the MAC layer because with the increasing density, a larger number of nodes must share the medium on the same local geographical area. This disadvantage is accentuated by a longer transmission time, which collapses the capacity of the medium.

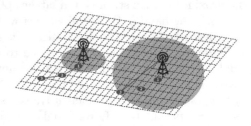

Fig. 1. From multi-hop to multi-channel

It is necessary, at the MAC level, to take advantage of the possibility of instantiating several channels in order to distribute the nodes on all the available channels and to find suitable temporal performances, thus making it possible to scale up.

3   Analysis of the Levers Offered by LoRa™

LoRa™ is a narrow-band wireless transmission technology, which gives it a high degree of robustness (high receiver sensitivity, long range). The trade-off that needs to be made is at fairly low throughput. There is also a limitation of the emission duty cycle (*duty cycle*) related to the fact that the LoRa™ modulation is intended for ISM bands (*Industry, Scientific and Medical*) which are unlicensed bands. These bands are said to be unlicensed because they can be used by any user without a license, which favors the uncoordinated deployment of varied and generally incompatible networks. This is an essential detail in our reflection because the use of these bands can be very strong and they can be very polluted and electromagnetically congested.

LoRa™ technology is based on CSS (*Chirp Spread Spectrum*) which is a particular spread spectrum technique. The goal of the CSS techniques is to spread the spectrum on different frequencies and on different instant of the time by adding both a strong redundancy and a correlation in the signal in order to greatly increase the robustness thus limiting the multipath phenomenon. This modulation is obtained by coding the information using orthogonal codes, quantified by the Spreading Factor (SF). In the next section, the different parameters of the LoRa™ physical layer are presented.

3.1   LoRa™ Physical Layer Settings

Spreading Factor. In order to increase the reliability of the transmission and thus make it possible to send messages at long range, the LoRa™ modulation uses a strong redundancy of information. For this, each bit of the message is coded by a symbol composed of several bits. In this way, it is much more difficult to confuse a '1' or a '0' received. This increases the signal-to-noise ratio, which makes it possible to reach objects in harsh environments or at longer distances. The SF simply corresponds to the number of "bits" per symbol. The Table 1 shows the different spreading factors currently available in LoRa™ tranceivers. A Chirp is a frequency sweep used by CSS to represent a bit at the physical level. The number of Chirp/symbol represents the number of symbols at the physical level to represent a bit of information. This metric gives us the number of symbols used to represent a bit of information, so this is the coding efficiency at the physical level. For each SF, there are two codes, one for the '0' symbol and one for the '1' symbol. Note that the more the SF increases, the longer the code length is and therefore the lower the useful bit rate is. When we increase the SF by 1, we multiply the length of the code by 2 and thus we divide the data rate by 2. According to the Friis formula (1), one can deduce that a gain of 6 dB on the link budget makes it possible to double the transmission range. For example, moving from a SF 7 to a SF 12, improves the coding gain of +12.5 dB. This gain makes it possible to have a transmission distance multiplied by four. The Friis model is a simple model that is not adapted to a Smart City environment but we use it here to just give an idea of the impact of the spreading factor.

Table 1. Range of spreading factors from datasheet [4]

SpreadingFactor	6	7	8	9	10	11	12
Chirps/symbol	64	128	256	512	1024	2048	4096
LoRa™ Demodulator SNR	−5 dB	−7.5 dB	−10 dB	−12.5 dB	−15 dB	−17.5 dB	−20 dB

$$Pr = Pt + Gt + Gr - 32.45 - 20 \times \log(freq) - 20 \times \log(rang) \qquad (1)$$

Pt : Emission power

Pr : Reception power

Gt : Gain of the reception antenna

Gr : Gain of the emitter antenna

freq : Emission frequency in MHz

rang : Range in km

An important property of the SF is that the codes used are orthogonal to each other from a mathematical point of view. That is, from a theoretical point of view, a message coded with a certain SF can not influence a message with another SF present at the same time on the same medium, in the same place. We are in the presence of several logical channels, even if they are on the same frequencies. Of course, the LoRa™ modulation requires that the receiver and the transmitter are parameterized with the same SF to be able to communicate together. It is very interesting to note that in the current LoRa™ radios, there is a technological difference between an end-device and a gateway. A gateway is able to receive messages with different Spreading Factors without having to reconfigure its radio. This property allows it to have a privileged place in the network, however, it is still bound to the same legislation as the End-Devices.

Coding Rate. The LoRa™ modulation natively uses cyclic redundancy codes, of the Hamming code type, which make it possible to check the integrity of the message received. This check is performed after receiving a message to the correct SF. The tranceiver automatically recalculates the cyclic code and depending on the result decides whether or not to validate the received message. In the header of the physical layer, there is a field that indicates the coding rate of the message. This allows a receiver to receive messages with different coding rates. On the other hand, the coding rate does not make it possible to create new channels unlike the SF! The array Table 2 shows the different possible coding rate values in a LoRa™ tranceiver.

Table 2. Set of coding rate from datasheeet [4]

Cyclic coding rate	4/5	4/6	4/7	4/8
Overhead ratio	1.25	1.50	1.75	2

Bandwidth. Bandwidth (BW) is the bandwidth used during a transmission. It is expressed in Hertz. For the modulation LoRa™, it is possible to send a chirp per second and per Hertz of bandwidth. That is, if you select a bandwidth of 500 kHz, you will be able to send 500000 chirps per second. Depending on the SF and the Coding Rate that we have chosen, we will be able to determine the maximum possible data rate. According to [5], the division of the value of BW by two makes it possible to gain 3 dB of additional sensitivity. According to the formula Friis (1), a 125 kHz emission instead of 500 kHz allows to gain 6 dB and thus to double the transmission range in free field.

3.2   LoRa™ Logical Channels

In our problem of densification of nodes in radio range, it is necessary to make the best use of the available parameters in order to create a multitude of subsets of communication channels that do not interfere with each other. Here in after, we briefly present the frequency and time division techniques that have already been used. In a second step, we will present the creation of channels by coding using the SF.

Channels by Frequency Division. It is currently possible to use LoRa™ directly in the 433 MHz, 868 MHz and 2.4 GHz bands due to the availability of associated transceivers on the market. For example, the SX1276, the SX1272 and the RN2483A. Take for example the 868 MHz band in Europe that is used by the LoRaWAN protocol. LoRaWAN is a MAC and network protocol based on a LoRa™ physical layer. This band ranges from 868.0 MHz to 868.6 MHz with a radiated power limit of +14 dBm, a duty cycle of less than 1% and no limit on bandwidth [6]. Therefore, it is possible to divide this 600 kHz band into several frequency channels. This is what was decided for the LoRaWAN protocol with the use of three main channels at 868.10 MHz, 868.30 MHz and 868.50 MHz center frequencies. On these bands, it was chosen to use a bandwidth of 125 kHz, which leaves a width of 75 kHz between the channels. We see that it is possible to go much further in the cutting of this band, using channels with different bandwidths for example.

Channels by Time Division. As with other radio technologies, it is possible to set up a time multiplexing of transmissions. The specificity, however, is that currently, LoRa™ is used on the so-called 'ISM' bands and that the limitation of these unlicensed bands obliges an emitter to respect the duty cycle limitation at 1% maximum. This imposes a cumulative total issue time of 36 s maximum over a rolling hour. The limitation on the transmission time is 3.6 s and 1.8 s between two transmissions. With a relatively standard setting (SF7, 125 kbps) a frame of 30 bytes lasts 70 ms on the medium. With the legal limitation, it is possible to send 514 messages per hour. This limitation on the duty cycle is not applicable if the MAC layer implements a Listen Before Talk (LBT) mechanism, i.e. an analysis of the free or busy medium before sending. The effect of LBT is similar to that of Clear Channel Assessment (CCA) used in CSMA/CA type MAC protocols but not based on an energy threshold.

Channels by Coding. Coding multiplexing is the most original and interesting for the LoRa™ physical layer. Indeed, the use of SF will allow to create a third dimension of channels. As the codes used by the different Spreading Factors are orthogonal, it is possible to perform simultaneous transmissions on the same medium air while avoiding collisions. It is conceivable to think that, as there are 7 spreading factors (from 6 to 12), the number of channels available by time and/or frequency multiplexing is multiplied by 7. It should be noted that the SF 6 is a bit special because it requires the use of the implicit mode which is a payload transmission mode of fixed size. However the choice of a SF is not insignificant! The first remark is the emission time that evolves at power 2 according to the SF. At the same time, the robustness of the signal is improving! We will therefore be able in a given frequency channel to create several channels depending on the state of the link. A transmitter that is very far from the receiver or in adverse conditions will be able to change SF to pass on a more robust channel, and better radio range.

Synthesis. The use of LoRa™, in unlicensed bands today, allows via different techniques to make many logical channels. It must be remembered that despite all the use of unlicensed bands imposes a limitation of the duty cycle which is in no way solved by multi-channel MAC techniques. The coding channels are very original and interesting in the LoRa™ technology because they allow very different channels in terms of range and robustness. This diversity of channel parameters could be used to setup the physical layer according to the range between two nodes.

An important parameter for MAC layer development is the impact of synchronization on performance. Indeed, the logical tightness between the channels must not be dependent on the temporal phase shifts between the channels because it is a very difficult problem to solve.

4   Related Works

The most deployed MAC layer based on a LoRa™ physical layer is LoRaWAN. This MAC layer already uses datarate adaptation mechanisms, by changing SF and transmission power, in order to optimize communications [7]. It is the device (connected sensor) and not the central base station, which can choose to automatically adapt its parameters or ask the network to determine them. LoRaWAN therefore already uses a SF pluralism mechanism but only for the purpose of optimizing static devices. This is not enough because the goal for LoRaWAN is to optimize the objects independently and not to distribute them intelligently in channels.

The joint optimization strategy of the transmission power and SF is justified by [9] because changing SF is much less optimal from an energy point of view than increasing the transmission power. The strategy to optimize the robustness of the links is to increase the transmission power to a point where it is more optimal to change the SF and reduce the transmission power.

In addition to this justification [9] shows that the optimization of energy can only be done by a strict spatial re-use by using the orthogonality property of the spreading factors.

According to [10] routing algorithms like RPL are difficult to use in a LPWAN context on unlicensed bands. The strict legislation in terms of number of messages does not leave much space for algorithms requiring frames dedicated to the operation of the network. It is necessary to design new MAC layers that counterbalance these routing issues.

In order to design these MAC layers, it is important to carry out a rigorous theoretical and practical study of the isolation between the spreading factors and the influence on the properties of an associated MAC layer. Several articles have treated the theory as [11], we propose to complete this study by experiments in real environment.

5   Performance Analysis of Logical Isolation Between Spreading Factors

5.1   Experience with Time Phase Collisions

Experimental Protocol. In order to prove the hypotheses advanced, we set up an experiment with 4 nodes, two transmitters and two receivers of End-Device type (Adafruit Feather [13] with HopeRF RFM95 transceiver [14]). We seek to study the impact of a simultaneous emission of two nodes on the same frequency band but with different spreading factors. The choice to use four nodes makes it possible to group them in pairs with the same parameters, one node in transmission and the other in reception. By analyzing the received frames and what they contain, we can deduce the frame error rate (FER) and compare it with the same rate without simultaneous emissions. The synchronization of the nodes is very important to finely control the phase shifts between the two transmitting nodes. Thanks to this synchronization, we can select a large frame and a small frame to analyze if the rate varies according to the crush zone of the packet. In order to achieve this synchronization, we connected the two transmitters by two wires and two Boolean signals. Figure 3 shows the wiring of this synchronization. One node is master and the other slave, the master waits

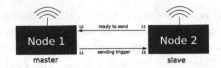

Fig. 2. Synchronization of transmitters by wire

for the first signal of the slave which indicates to him that he is ready to emit. Once the master is ready to transmit and has received the signal from the slave, it sends a signal to the slave to tell him to start transmitting the frame (Fig. 2).

When the SF is increased by 1, the size of the packet is approximately doubled. We chose to use one package with a SF of 9 and another of 7. The packet sizes are respectively 250 ms and 70 ms. These sizes make it possible to take the longest packet as a reference and to crush it (disrupt it or collide it) by shifts by the second. This experiment was carried out in these realistic conditions that is to say that the two transmitters were side by side in one side and the two receivers on the other side. The two couples are separated from a distance of 200 m with a building in between. The distance of 200 m seems weak but given the indoor conditions of the nodes, we noticed by the practice, that we were in limit of reach for the link to SF7 which is the least robust. We have observed in practice and it is explained in [8] that in the near field there are orthogonality problems between SF. We decided not to do the measurements in this topology which is not representative of reality.

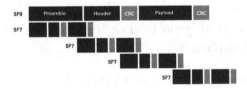

Fig. 3. Simultaneous transmission of frames at the same frequency but with different spreading factors

Results. The experiment consists of sending 500 frames for a fixed time offset between the frame at SF 9 and that at 7. We decided to send 500 packets in order to have a correct estimate of the frame error rate. We have selected these values for the time offset so as to test crashes (overlaps or collisions) on different parts of the packet. This proves that this overwriting property is valid on all parts of the packet (Table 3).

Analyse. The frame error rate is very low and uniform whatever the area of the packet, this allows us to demonstrate that it is possible to send several frames simultaneously at the same frequency, with the same parameters but with a different SF. This physical isolation makes it possible to assert that it is

Table 3. Estimate of FER on an emission of 500 frames per measurement point.

Delay	2 frames ok	SF9 frame ok	SF7 frame ok	FER
0 ms	494	0	6	0.012
77 ms	489	0	11	0.022
154 ms	475	0	25	0.05
231 ms	490	0	10	0.02

possible to create physical channels on the same frequency that have different characteristics in terms of reliability and throughput. This physical isolation is not dependent on a time synchronization between the different channels and is not dependent on the content of the frame.

5.2 Collision Matrix on All Spreading Factors

Experimental Protocol. After proving that for a given pair of spreading factors (7 and 9), there is a real tightness at the physical channel level, it is necessary to generalize this property. For this, we place ourselves in the same experimental conditions, with two transmitters synchronized by logic signals, and two non-synchronized receivers. We will build a collision matrix. For this we parameterize a transmitter/receiver pair with a SF1 SF and the other pair with SF2. Then under these conditions, we re-test all possible time offsets.

Results. Table 4 is an example of a result for a delay of 10 ms between the two transmitters. The numbers are very similar regardless of the delay, so showing only one sample is enough.

Table 4. Spreading factor matrix for 10 ms delay

sf1	7	7	7	7	8	8	8	8	9	9	9	9	10	10	10	10
sf2	7	8	9	10	7	8	9	10	7	8	9	10	7	8	9	10
ok	0	500	488	497	497	0	484	500	489	489	37	489	487	491	495	8
1 ok	49	0	12	3	3	18	16	0	11	11	6	11	13	9	5	16
error	205	0	0	0	0	449	0	0	0	0	456	0	0	0	0	474
nok	246	0	0	0	0	33	0	0	0	0	1	0	0	0	0	2

Analyse. For the diagonal of the matrix of the array Table 4, when the two emitters use the same SF, we notice that there are many collisions. We can not conclude that there is a tightness when two transmitters speak simultaneously with the same SF. When the two nodes emit with different SFs, the number of collisions is limited. It can happen, with a rate of 2.2%, that one of the two messages is not received by the receiver.

6 Towards New Ad Hoc MAC Layers for the Internet of Things

The results presented in this paper show that the LoRa™ physical layer proposes several levers that make it possible to envisage new MAC protocols that benefit from the characteristics of this mode of transmission. In view of what has been described above, we propose a new concept of 3-dimensional MAC layer, using the three frequency, time and code multiplexing, illustrated by the Fig. 4.

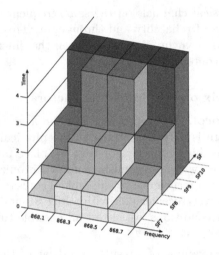

Fig. 4. Channel multiplexing on the time, frequencies and by code

The first two multiplexes (frequency, time) are relatively conventional, they are used by most technologies. Frequentially, the selected band, for example the 868 MHz ISM band, can be subdivided into frequency channels with a fixed (as in LoRaWAN) or variable bandwidth, in order to better use the properties of the LoRa™ modulation. In this case, higher bandwidths will allow links with higher throughput for short-range communications. On the second (temporal) multiplexing, we have seen in the experiments that the othogonality of the links does not depend a priori on a strict synchronization. However, it is necessary to synchronize the nodes constrained in energy; the Listen Before Talk technique can help limit temporal collisions. On these two first multiplexings, we are finally in a standard case of multi-channel MAC where it is possible to apply the algorithms of this domain (with or without an appointment, with or without a dedicated channel, etc.). What the LoRa™ technology allows to add, is that for a given channel {frequency, temporal}, a communication can be realized via a SF whose value will have an impact on the robustness and the range of the link. In addition, SF being orthogonal, several links between several objects can be made at the same time on the same channel {frequency, temporal}. The object can, for example, start with a low value of SF and attempt a communication with the target gateway. If he can not reach his recipient, after several tries, he can increment his SF and retry to connect. Once the connection is established, the gateway can record the parameters of the transmission in order to respond to the transmitter with the same parameters. The transmission will be more and more robust until you succeed. In this way, a node will be able to adapt its transmission technique to the quality of the link and/or its distance. The Fig. 4 represents this type of 3-dimensional multi-channel MAC. The different colors represent the SF used by a sending node. During the initialization phase of a node and dynamically during its lifetime, the node is colored according to the state of the link between it and the gateway. If the link is degraded, the node will change its settings and change color to a darker color.

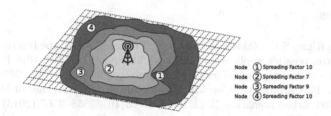

Fig. 5. Topology of a multi spreading factor MAC (Color figure online)

In the Fig. 5 one observes an example of topology of a MAC multi SF. It is interesting to see that depending on the zone in which it is, the node will have a different SF setting. The node number 4 is very far, it uses a high SF like the node number 1. By cons this node number 1 is much closer in terms of distance. It must surely be in a difficult environment (deep indoor, behind an obstacle between him and the gateway for example...). These solutions are made possible by the fact that a gateway has the possibility of receiving several SF without having to change configuration. This is generally not the case for End Devices, which, for ad-hoc communications between objects, requires to think of another strategy. These few solutions are to be developed later, but have been made possible by the metrology phase that we have just presented.

7 Conclusion

The LoRa™ technology may seem very close to the usual modulations of the IEEE 802.15.4 historical standard, but because of its intrinsic parameters and its context of use, it must lead to rethink the MAC and network layers to much higher topologies star or mesh with two hops. The context of the Internet of Things and LoRa™ defines transmissions in a very dense environment as transmission distances are high. This paper permit to define the main mecanisms which can be exploited in order to answer the problem of distribution of nodes in well disjoined channels.

This preliminary work opens the way for many perspectives, such as to propose an original and efficient MAC layer for IoT. In order to overcome the constraints related to the duty cycle imposed by the standardization, it lacks a final tool to define concerning the detection of occupancy of the channel as that used in the well-known CSMA/CA. LoRa™ uses a type of modulation that allows transmissions above the noise level. The RSSI measure is no longer a valid indicator of channel occupancy. The LoRa™ tranceivers integrate a so-called CAD (Channel Activity Detection) mechanism which makes it possible to detect a coherent preamble, the preamble of a message with the same SF. We are currently working to propose a MAC called CSMA/CAD without temporal constraint linked to a duty cycle.

References

1. Khan, R., Khan, S.U., Zaheer, R., Khan, S.: Future internet: the Internet of Things architecture, possible applications and key challenges. In: 2012 10th International Conference on Frontiers of Information Technology, Islamabad, pp. 257–260 (2012)
2. Bellavista, P., Cardone, G., Corradi, A., Foschini, L.: Convergence of MANET and WSN in IoT urban scenarios. IEEE Sens. J. **13**(10), 3558–3567 (2013)
3. Pham, C.: QoS for long-range wireless sensors under duty-cycle regulations with shared activity time usage. ACM Trans. Sens. Netw. **12**, 33 (2016)
4. Semtech: Datasheet of Semtech sx1276 LoRa™ tranceiver. http://www.semtech.com/images/datasheet/sx1276_77_78_79.pdf
5. Augustin, A., Yi, J., Clausen, T., Townsley, W.M.: A study of LoRa™: long range & low power networks for the Internet of Things. Sensors **16**, 1466 (2016)
6. CEPT ECC: ERC Recommendation 70–03, Relating to the use of Short Range Devices (SRD), 19 May 2017
7. LoRa™ Alliance: LoRaWAN Specification V1.1 (2017)
8. Croce, D., Gucciardo, M., Mangione, S., Santaromita, G., Tinnirello, I.: Impact of LoRa imperfect orthogonality: analysis of link-level performance. IEEE Commun. Lett. **22**(4), 796–799 (2018)
9. Ochoa, M.N., Guizar, A., Maman, M., Duda, A.: Evaluating LoRa energy efficiency for adaptive networks: from star to mesh topologies. In: IEEE 13th International Conference on Wireless and Mobile Computing, Networking and Communications (WiMob) (2017)
10. Sartori, B, Bezunartea, M., Thielemans, S., Braeken, A., Steenhaut, K.: Enabling RPL multihop communications based on LoRa. In: IEEE 13th International Conference on Wireless and Mobile Computing, Networking and Communications (WiMob) (2017)
11. Lim, J.T., Han, Y.: Spreading factor allocation for massive connectivity in LoRa systems. IEEE Commun. Lett. **22**(4), 800–803 (2018)
12. Cheong, P.S., Bergs, J., Hawinkel, C., Famaey, J.: Comparison of LoRaWAN classes and their power consumption. In: IEEE Symposium on Communications and Vehicular Technology (SCVT) (2017)
13. Adafruit: Feather Hardware. https://www.adafruit.com/feather
14. HopeRF: The HopeRF RFM95 Transceiver User Manual

A Comparative Evaluation
of the Performance of the Multi-hop
IoB-DTN Routing Protocol

Yosra Zguira[1,2](✉), Hervé Rivano[1](✉), and Aref Meddeb[2](✉)

[1] University of Lyon, INSA Lyon, Inria, CITI, 69621 Villeurbanne, France
yosra.zguira@insa-lyon.fr, herve.rivano@inria.fr
[2] NOCCS Laboratory Higher Institute of Computer Science and Communication
Technologies, ISITCom, University of Sousse, Sahloul, 4054 Sousse, Tunisia

Abstract. Following the trend of the Internet of Thing, public transport systems are seen as an efficient bearer of mobile devices to generate and collect data in urban environments. Bicycle sharing system is one part of the city's larger transport system. In this article, we study the "Internet of Bikes" IoB-DTN protocol which applies the Delay Tolerant Network (DTN) paradigm to the Internet of Things (IoT) applications running on urban bike sharing system based sensor network. We evaluate the performances of the protocol with respect to the transmission power. Performances are measured in terms of delivery rate, delivery delay, throughput and energy cost. We also compare the multi-hop IoB-DTN protocol to a low-power wide-area network (LPWAN) technology. LPWAN have been designed to provide cost-effective wide area connectivity for small throughput IoT applications: multiyear lifetime and multikilometer range for battery-operated mobile devices. This work aims at providing network designers and managers insights on the most relevant technology for their urban applications that could run on bike sharing systems. To the best of our knowledge, this work is the first to provide a detailed performance comparison between multi-hop and long range DTN-like protocol being applied to mobile network IoT devices running a data collection applications in an urban environment.

1 Introduction

The self-service bicycles, also known as bicycle-sharing systems, have been introduced as part of the urban transportation system in many cities of the world. They allow people to borrow a bicycle from bike station A and return it at bike station B with a very small price. As of June 2014, public bicycle sharing systems were available in 50 countries on 5 continents, including 712 cities and having approximately 806,200 bicycles at 37,500 stations [1]. The present paper focuses on the use of IoT on real networks and in particular on connected bikes. We are interested in opportunistic communications based on converge cast algorithm. We consider a smart bike sharing system to collect and transfer the data from

© Springer Nature Switzerland AG 2018
N. Montavont and G. Z. Papadopoulos (Eds.): ADHOC-NOW 2018, LNCS 11104, pp. 175–187, 2018.
https://doi.org/10.1007/978-3-030-00247-3_17

bikes to a set of sinks. In our preceding work [2], we proposed the "Internet of Bikes" IoB-DTN protocol which applies the DTN paradigm to the IoT applications running on urban bike sharing system based sensor network. The Delay Tolerant Networking approach is designed for intermittent connections resulting in a lack of instantaneous end-to-end paths between mobile devices [3]. In this type of network, routing is performed over time to send data by employing long-term storage at the intermediate nodes. Thus, the intermediate node stores the receiving data, carries it while a contact is not available and forwards when the connection occurs. Therefore, data will be relayed hop by hop until reaching its destination.

In this article, we give a more detailed performance evaluation of IoB-DTN protocol. First, we evaluate the performance of the protocol by ranging the transmission power. Performance is measured in terms of delivery rate, delivery delay, throughput and protocol cost resulting in the number of packets transmitted and received in the network. Then, we compare the performance of the multi-hop IoB-DTN protocol with a low-power wide-area network (LPWAN) technology. The performance metrics used for the comparison are the energy consumption and the throughput. The low power wide area networks represent a novel communication paradigm in the evolution of the wireless communication technologies [4]. They have been designed to provide cost-effective wide area connectivity for the IoT applications: multiyear lifetime and multikilometer range for battery-operated mobile devices. The battery lifetimes can possibly operate up to ten years and the operating range is from over 10 km in rural areas up to 1–2 km in urban environments. LPWANs consume low power and use a low data rate for data transmission. They are typically seen as cellular networks by connecting end devices (ED) directly to base stations (BS) which relay data packets between the EDs and an application server. An ED communicates only to a BS forming a star-topology network that brings huge energy saving advantages. LPWAN technologies include unlicensed band technologies (e.g. Sigfox, LoRa/LoRaWAN, and Weightless), advanced cellular technologies (e.g. LTEM and NB-IoT) and recent reforms to IEEE standards (e.g. IEEE 802.11ah, IEEE 802.15.4g, and IEEE 802.15.4k). In this paper, we compare IoB-DTN protocol to LoRa/LoRaWAN[1] technology which is based on chirp spread spectrum modulation. The use of this modulation provides enhanced performances in terms of range, significantly increasing the robustness of the signal and the sensitivity of the receiver while maintaining low power consumption.

Our contributions can be summarized as follows:

- A performance evaluation of IoB-DTN protocol for different transmission power of sensors. The optimal value is conducted in terms of the performance metrics mentioned before.
- A performance comparison between the multi-hop IoB-DTN protocol and the long range LoRa technology.
- Results are discussed to identify the best technology to adapt in IoT data collection applications running on urban bike sharing system.

---

[1] LoRa: https://www.lora-alliance.org/.

The rest of the article is organized as follows. The following section discusses the related work. The description of our scenario is presented in Sect. 3. The simulation environment is described in Sect. 4. The performance evaluations of IoB-DTN protocol as well as the analysis of our results are discussed in Sects. 5 and 6 respectively. Finally, Sect. 7 concludes the paper.

2   Related Work

In the literature, several researchers have focused on communication based public transport networks. For example, the DakNet [5] provides low-cost digital communication to remote villages in India and Cambodia. Buses are used in DakNet to transfer data between Internet access points and Internet kiosks in villages. The KioskNet [6] uses buses and cars as "mechanical backhaul" devices to transfer data between remote villages and Internet gateway. Zhao et al. [7] present a vehicle assisted data delivery (VADD) protocol for vehicular ad hoc networks. The VADD is based on the carry and forward paradigm where vehicles are used as data carriers and the path to the destination is determined based on the ad hoc connectivity of the vehicles.

Bikes are considered also as an urban transport system to sense, collect and forward data. The BikeNet project [8] corresponds to the earliest working mobile sensing and sparse radio network connectivity system for cyclists. In BikeNet, the sensors are embedded into a cyclist's bike to collect quantitative data about the cyclist's journeys. The data gathered is forwarded by the cellular data channel of the cyclist's mobile phone. Nakamura et al. [9] propose the design of a web framework for a ubiquitous sensor network (u-framework). In the experimental field trial, they used bikes equipped with small and high-precision NO2 sensors to gather and share information on air pollution in Tokyo, Japan.

Over the past few years, many works focused on applying DTN paradigm to the Internet of Things. Wirtz et al. [10] discuss the notion of a "Challenged IoT" under intermittent Internet connectivity. They discuss the need to enable interaction between smart objects and mobile users in the Internet of Things. They propose Direct Interaction with Smart Challenged Objects (DISCO), enabling objects to define their interaction patterns and interface. Al-Turjman et al. [11] propose DIRSN, an optimized delay-tolerant framework for integrated RFID-sensor networks (RSNs) in the IoT. Their framework provides an optimized architecture for integrated RSNs besides to a delay-tolerant routing scheme. In [12], the authors propose an enhanced architecture to interconnect standard-based machine-to-machine (M2M) platform to opportunistic networks in order to collect data from sensor devices.

Many researches focused also on applying DTN with IoT and more precisely in the field of delay-tolerant WSN that focus on routing algorithms. Most of these proposals do not use standard protocols, but they are dedicated to targeted sensors or applications, e.g. underwater sensor networks. In [2], we introduced the "Internet of Bikes" IoB-DTN protocol which applies the DTN paradigm to the IoT applications running on urban bike sharing system based sensor network.

It is designed for being applied to mobile network IoT devices running a data collection application. It is a multi-hop protocol where data are forwarded via bike-to-bike communication.

In this article we aim at providing an evaluation of IoB-DTN protocol by varying the transmission power of the sensors and a comparison of IoB-DTN with a low-power wide-area network (LPWAN) technology. Several LPWAN technologies have been deployed in previous years. There are many forms of LPWA networks and they all have a different market approach and technology stack. Among them, we quote Sigfox, LoRaWAN, Weightless. The Sigfox[2] technology was developed in 2010 by the start-up Sigfox in Toulouse, France. It applies a technique of the ultra-narrowband IoT communications designed to support IoT deployments over long range communications. It operates in the 869 MHz (in Europe) and 915 MHz (in North America) bands. LoRa was developed by the start-up Cycleo in 2009 in Grenoble, France and was purchased by Semtech (USA) in 2012. In 2015, LoRa was standardized by LoRa-Alliance and was deployed in 42 countries. It is based on chirp spread spectrum modulation which uses the same low power characteristics as FSK modulation but greatly increases the communication range. The LoRa physical layer operates on the 433 (in Asia), 868 (in Europe) or 915 (in North America) MHz ISM bands. Three open standards for LPWAN were developed by the Weightless Special Interest Group: Weightless-W, Weightless-N and Weightless-P[3]. Weightless-W is based on narrow-band FDMA channels with Time Division Duplex between uplink and downlink. It is designed to operate in TV whitespaces (470–790 MHz). Weightless-N is based on the ultra-narrow-band technology and it provides only uplink communication. Weightless-P provides ultra-high performance LPWAN connectivity.

3   Scenario Description

We consider an ad-hoc network of bikes. Each bike has embedded sensors, a 802.11p communication device, periodically generates a data packet and stores it in its buffer. All bike stations are equipped with base stations which are connected to the Internet. Each bicycle station has a 802.11p interface and acts as a fixed sink. In IoB-DTN protocol, a packet is relayed until it reaches one of the sinks. IoB-DTN is based on the DTN paradigm which is designed for low connectivity that results in the absence of instantaneous end to end path. Due to the intermittent connection between bikes, the store-carry-forward mechanism is applied. The data are stored in the buffers of the intermediate nodes and sent at a later time to the final destination or to another intermediate nodes. The IoB-DTN protocol is inspired by flooding protocols which diffuse multiple copies of the packet in the network in order to maximize its probability to reach the destination. In particular, it is a lightweight version of Binary Spray and Wait routing protocol which limits the number of copies sprayed in the network to

---

[2] Sigfox: https://www.sigfox.com/en.
[3] Weightless: https://www.weightless.org/.

minimize the resource consumption. In Binary Spray and Wait protocol, the source node starts with N copies of the packet, and whenever it encounters a neighbor node, it sends half of copies to it and keeps the other half for itself. If it has only one copy of the packet, it switches to direct transmission to the destination node.

In IoB-DTN protocol, each node generates a packet P at each reading period. The packet is then stored, with the corresponding number of copies N, if the buffer management policy provides a slot. When the duty cycle is over, each node verifies if there is base stations in its neighborhood. If it exists, it sends all the data packets stored in its buffer and then it receives the acknowledgements (ACKs) from the corresponding sinks. If there is only neighbouring nodes, it forwards only the packets that have more than one copy. In the packet reception phase, each node calculates the new number of copies N' that it should keep, it stores the received packet if there is a slot in the buffer and it sends an ACK to the source node. When a node receives an ACK, it verifies the sender type. If it is a base station, it deletes the packet from its buffer. If not, it updates the number of copies of the corresponding packet.

Note that the copies of a data packet stored in a buffer are virtual. We are incrementing a counter and each packet occupies only one slot of the buffer. The buffer management policy is a major parameter of IoB-DTN. When the buffer is not full, it provides the next slot. If it is full, it must decide which packet should be kept and which packet should be discarded. In our previous work [2], we have proposed and simulated four buffer management policies. From the results obtained, GPP (Generated Packet Priority) policy which protects the self production gives the best results in terms of loss rate and delivery delay. In GPP policy, when the buffer is full and a new packet is generated, it replaces the oldest received packet. If there are only generated packets stored in the buffer, it replaces the oldest one. In this strategy, all received packets are discarded. In this paper, we consider the GPP policy and the number of copies is set to 8 in all our simulations.

4   Simulation Environment

This section describes the simulation settings used for our scenarios. The urban environment we used to evaluate our proposal is the city of Lyon, France. The bike sharing system in Lyon is called Vélo'v[4]. The system, launched in May 2005, provides over 3000 bicycles available from over 350 stations situated around the cities of Lyon and Villeurbanne. The bicycles can be taken from any station by citizens and returned to any other station. The platform "Data Grand Lyon"[5] provides open data including the description of the Vélo'v system. These data are integrated with the map of Lyon from OpenStreetMap[6]. The fusion of these two data is then imported to SUMO, an open source road traffic simulator [13].

---

[4] Vélo'v: https://velov.grandlyon.com.
[5] Data Grand Lyon: https://data.grandlyon.com.
[6] Openstreetmap: https://www.openstreetmap.org.

Fig. 1. Considered area of Lyon

Table 1. Simulation parameters

	Buffer size	Duty cycle (s)
Case 1	250	50
Case 2	250	150
Case 3	500	50
Case 4	500	150

SUMO simulates a realistic mobility of the bikes on the streets of the map. The Veins framework[7] connects SUMO to the event-based network simulator OMNeT++[8] and provides realistic radio propagation and models of 802.11p. For our simulations, we assume 49 bicycle stations deployed in the city center of Lyon as depicted in Fig. 1 as well as 51 bikes moving between those bike stations. The simulation time is 30 min. We simulate 10 scenarios with different paths of the bikes in each scenario. We simulate four sets of parameters as shown in Table 1 by varying the buffer size and the duty cycle. The latter corresponds to the period defined in seconds to send all data packets stored in the buffer.

5   Performance Evaluation of IoB by Ranging the Transmission Power

In this section, we evaluate the impact of IoB-DTN protocol on the energy. The transmission power used in our simulations in [2] was 10 mW, which gives a communication range ⌄350 m. In the present paper, we focus on the performance evaluation of IoB by assessing four values of the transmission power: 1 mW, 5 mW, 10 mW and 20 mW. We present the average results of the ten simulated scenarios.

Figure 2 shows the average distances obtained for each transmission power and for each case. We notice that by increasing the value of the transmission power, the communication range of nodes increases respectively.

The average delivery rate obtained is depicted in Fig. 3. As expected the delivery rate increases by enhancing the transmission power. In this case, the communication range of bikes increases so they encounter more neighbors nodes and more base stations which allows to have a higher delivery rate.

---

[7] Veins: http://veins.car2x.org/.

[8] OMNeT++: https://omnetpp.org.

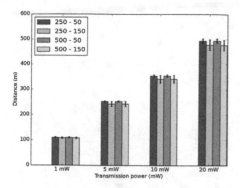

Fig. 2. Average distances

Fig. 3. Average delivery rate

Figure 4 shows the average delivery delays of the received packets. We notice that the impact of the transmission power on the delivery delay is negligible compared to the duty cycle and the size of the buffer. It shows that the connectivity is more impacted by the dynamics of the network than the transmission range. The size of the buffer increases the average delay partly because it prevents more packets to be discarded. The transmission range impacts the throughput of the network as depicted in Fig. 5. The impact of the duty cycle and the buffer size is still very important since the whole buffer is sent at each duty cycle.

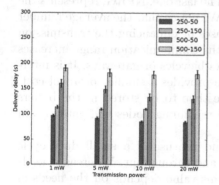

Fig. 4. Average delivery delay

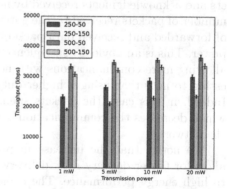

Fig. 5. Average throughput

We evaluated the average protocol cost of IoB-DTN protocol in terms of the number of transmitted and received packets in all the considered scenarios. The results illustrated in Fig. 6 present all the communications between bike to bike and bike to bike station. In our setting, each bike finishing its trip forwards all the data packets stored in its buffer to the final bike station that we assume having a very high throughput and we do not consider it in energy consumption

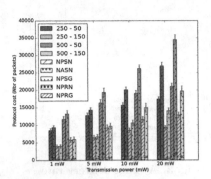

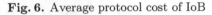

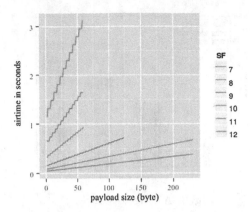

Fig. 6. Average protocol cost of IoB

Fig. 7. Airtime for different SF and payloads [14]

assessments. For each case, we can see two columns: the first column represents all the data packets forwarded and the second one depicts all the received data packets. On one hand, the first column contains three fields: NPSN, NASN and NPSG. First, NPSN represents the number of packets sent to nodes. Secondly, NASN is the number of acknowledgments sent to nodes. Finally, NPSG represents the number of packets sent to gateways. On the other hand, the second has two fields: NPRN and NPRG. The first one corresponds to the number of packets and acknowledgments received by nodes. The last one, NPRG, represents the number of packets received by the gateways. We notice that the average number of forwarded and received data packets increases by enhancing the transmission power. This is an obvious consequence since the communication range increases allowing more communications with neighbors bicycles or gateways. It is interesting to note that using a higher duty cycle provides a smaller protocol cost. Indeed, in this case, the packets spend more time to be stored in the buffers which decreases the communication with the remaining nodes and gateways in the network.

We notice that the increase in power and the use of a small duty cycle allow for better delivery rate, delivery delay and throughput. Whereas it leads to high energy performance. The choice of this value depends on the needs of the designers of the network. In the next section, we consider IoB-DTN with 10 mW as transmission power since it gives the compromise between the evaluated metrics.

6   Performance Evaluation of IoB and IoB Long-Range

In this section, we wish to compare the performance between the multi-hop IoB-DTN protocol and a long range technology. We consider IoB-DTN protocol with a radio propagation that gives us around 1 km as communication range as denoted IoB-LR. In IoB-LR, each node periodically generates data packets, stores them in its buffer and when the duty cycle is over and whenever a base station comes in range it sends all the data stored in its buffer. Therefore, there is only bike to bike station communication.

Since there is not a simulation model for long range technology in OMNeT++ network simulator, we assume that IoB-LR follows the behavior of the LoRa Semtech SX1272 chipset [15]. As in IoB-DTN protocol, the nodes and gateways have a 802.11p communication device, in our theoretical results we consider the parameters offered by the Qualcomm AR6004 chipset [16], presented in Table 2.

Table 2. Parameters used

	IoB	IoB-LR
Tx	237 mA	26 mA
Rx	66 mA	12 mA
Packet duration	213 μs	250–50: 0.2 s
		250–150: 0.6 s
		500–50: 0.1 s
		500–150: 0.3 s
ACK duration	213 μs	0.05 s
Packet size	160 Byte	250–50: 92 Byte
		250–150: 260 Byte
		500–50: 20 Byte
		500–150: 175 Byte

From Table 2, we remark that the packet duration of the long range technology varies according to the four cases simulated. For example, considering the scenario: 250 as buffer size and 50 s as duty cycle, the 250 packets stored in the buffer have to be forwarded during the 50 s time frame of the duty cycle. Thus, each packet needs to have a maximum airtime of 0.2 s. To determine the corresponding packet size of IoB-LR for each case, we refer the reader to Fig. 7. It represents the airtime in seconds (time to transmit a packet) for different spreading factors (SF) and payloads presented by an operational LoRaWAN namely The Things Network [14]. The bandwidth used is 125 KHz and the coding rate (CR), which reports to Forward Error Correction, is $\frac{4}{5}$.

Table 3 describes the values of the payload sizes obtained for different spreading factors for each case. The spreading factor denotes the number of chirps used to encode a bit and it varies from SF7 to SF12.

Higher chirp rate allows a better reconstruction of the received signal, whereas it delays the time to send a bit. In our simulations, we consider the payload size of IoB-LR using the spreading factor SF7 since it offers the highest values of payload size.

In our results, we evaluate the energy consumption and the throughput for IoB and IoB-LR. To evaluate the average energy consumption, we calculated the average transmission cost per bike and the average consumption background per

Table 3. Different payload size (PS) with different SF of IoB-LR

	Airtime (s)	PS (Byte) SF 7	PS (Byte) SF 8	PS (Byte) SF 9	PS (Byte) SF 10	PS (Byte) SF 11	PS (Byte) SF 12
250–50	0.2	92	40	x	x	x	x
250–150	0.6	260	220	100	28	x	x
500–50	0.1	20	x	x	x	x	x
500–150	0.3	175	80	25	x	x	x

bike. Figure 8 shows the average transmission cost per bike. It is measured in mAh and computed as follows:

$$TC = [NPS * Tx * DP] + [NAR * (Tx + Rx) * DA] + \underbrace{[NPR * Rx * DP]}_{\text{for IoB}} \quad (1)$$

TC is the transmit cost expressed in mAh. NPS corresponds to the number of sent packets. Tx and Rx represents the transmit and the receive consumption respectively. DP and DA are the packet and the ACK duration in seconds. NAR corresponds to the number of received ACK and NPR is the number of received packets from nodes.

We notice that IoB-LR has a higher forwarding cost because bikes send all the data packets only to the gateways. On the other hand, IoB offers a smaller forwarding cost thanks to the bike to bike communication that decreases the transmission cost in the network. In order to respect the duty cycle of radio devices regulated in Europe by section 7.2.3 of the ETSI EN300.220 standard, we consider the maximum theoretical duty cycle allowed which is 10% using the sub-bands (869.4–869.65 MHz) [17]. The duty cycle indicates the real period during which a resource is active. Therefore, we present, in Fig. 8, the average transmission cost for LoRa, respecting the maximum theoretical duty cycle 10%. In fact, from the four simulated cases, the third case that has a buffer size equal to 500 slots and a time to send all the stored packets equal to 50 s represents the real value of the maximum duty cycle allowed by the long range LoRa technology. To fill the $\frac{1}{10}$ of 500 slots in 50 s, the duty cycle is then 10%. By following the same concept, the duty cycle for the four simulated cases are: 20% for the first case 250–50, 60% for the second case 250–150 and 30% for the last case 500–150.

We note that similar to using the maximum real duty cycle of LoRa technology, IoB gives smaller transmission cost per bike thanks to the bike to bike communication.

Figure 9 shows the average consumption background per bicycle. It corresponds to the total consumption per bike and it is measured in mAh. It is computed as follows:

For IoB:

$$BC = \sum (Ta - Td) * Rx \quad (2)$$

For IoB-LR:

$$BC = \frac{Rx * BWT}{DC} * \sum (Ta - Td) \quad (3)$$

BC is the average background consumption calculated. Ta and Td represent the arrival and the departure time of the bike expressed in seconds. DC is the duty cycle defined in seconds to send all data packets stored in the buffer. It takes as value 50 s or 150 s depending on the simulated case. BWT corresponds to the beacon waiting period defined in seconds. This period is fixed to 10 s in all our simulations. We notice that IoB has higher results in terms of consumption background than IoB-LR since opportunistic communications require the nodes to be always listening for beacons to relay the data packets in the network. Whereas, in long range technology, the nodes enter in sleep mode and they wake up few seconds before starting the packets forwarding. In Fig. 9, we also present an optimal average consumption background per bicycle for IoB. In this case, it behaves like IoB-LR. We consider that each bike, having a full buffer, enters in sleep mode. It wakes up a few moments before the packets transmission. From the results obtained in Figs. 8 and 9, we can remark that IoB-LR offers lower energy consumption than the multi-hop IoB protocol.

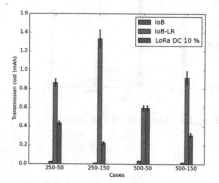

Fig. 8. Average transmission cost per bike

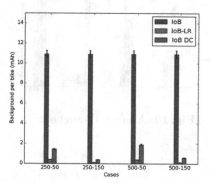

Fig. 9. Average consumption background per bike

Figure 10 shows the average throughput for IoB and IoB-LR. We note that, in all cases, IoB gives better results in terms of throughput by using a smaller duty cycle. While IoB-LR offers better throughput by adopting a higher duty cycle.

This is related to the size of the sent packets in each simulated case. The Fig. 10 shows also the throughput results for IoB-LR when respecting the maximum theoretical duty cycle allowed by LoRa technology. We remark that IoB has better throughput, in all scenarios, than the long range technology respecting the theoretical duty cycle.

In Fig. 10, we also present the average throughput results for IoB-LR when respecting the effective duty cycle. It represents the real duty cycle for the bikes in each simulation scenario. It is presented in Fig. 11 and it is measured as follows:

$$EDC = \frac{NPS * Rt}{\sum (Ta - Td)} \tag{4}$$

EDC is the effective duty cycle calculated. NPS represents the number of sent packets. Rt is the airtime defined in seconds. For example, by respecting the theoretical duty cycle for the first case simulated when having a buffer size equal to 250 slots and the period to send the packets in the buffer equal to 50 s, the duty cycle should be 20%. Whereas in reality, the effective duty cycle for this case is around 16%. It is then interesting to note that IoB protocol offers better throughput, in all cases, than the long range technology respecting the theoretical and the real duty cycle.

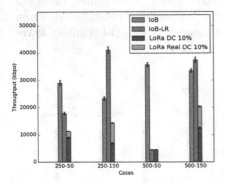

Fig. 10. Average throughput

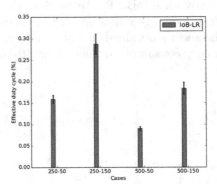

Fig. 11. Average effective duty cycle

7   Conclusions

In this paper, we provide two performance evaluations of IoB-DTN protocol. First, we give a performance evaluation by varying the transmission power values of sensors. This parameter is important since by increasing the sending power value the communication range of the device raises. In such case, it allows more communications with neighbors nodes and base stations which increases the delivery rate, the throughput and the energy consumption. It is worth to note that using a small duty cycle offers better delivery rate, delivery delay and throughput. Second, we provide a performance comparison of the multi-hop IoB-DTN protocol with a low-power wide-area network (LPWAN) technology, in particular LoRa/LoRaWAN. Our results show that by using a multi-hop topology, it offers better throughput while by applying a long range technology, where there is only bike to bike station communication, it gives better energy consumption.

References

1. Shaheen, S.A., Martin, E.W., Cohen, A.P., Chan, N.D., Pogodzinski, M.: Public bikesharing in North America during a period of rapid expansion: understanding business models, industry trends & user impacts. MTI report 12–29 (2014)
2. Zguira, Y., Rivano, H., Meddeb, A.: IoB-DTN: a lightweight DTN protocol for mobile IoT applications to smart bike sharing systems. In: WD 2018, 10th IFIP Wireless Days, Dubai, UAE, April 2018
3. Fall, K.: A delay-tolerant network architecture for challenged internets. In: Proceedings of the 2003 Conference on Applications, Technologies, Architectures, and Protocols for Computer Communications, pp. 27–34. ACM (2003)
4. Raza, U., Kulkarni, P., Sooriyabandara, M.: Low power wide area networks: an overview. IEEE Commun. Surv. Tutor. **19**(2), 855–873 (2017)
5. Pentland, A., Fletcher, R., Hasson, A.: DakNet: rethinking connectivity in developing nations. Computer **37**(1), 78–83 (2004)
6. Seth, A., Kroeker, D., Zaharia, M., Guo, S., Keshav, S.: Low-cost communication for rural internet kiosks using mechanical backhaul. In: Proceedings of the 12th Annual International Conference on Mobile Computing and Networking, pp. 334–345. ACM (2006)
7. Zhao, J., Cao, G.: VADD: vehicle-assisted data delivery in vehicular ad hoc networks. IEEE Trans. Veh. Technol. **57**(3), 1910–1922 (2008)
8. Eisenman, S.B., Miluzzo, E., Lane, N.D., Peterson, R.A., Ahn, G.S., Campbell, A.T.: BikeNet: a mobile sensing system for cyclist experience mapping. ACM Trans. Sens. Netw. (TOSN) **6**(1), 6 (2009)
9. Nakamura, T., et al.: Proposal of web framework for ubiquitous sensor network and its trial application using NO2 sensor mounted on bicycle. In: 2012 IEEE/IPSJ 12th International Symposium on Applications and the Internet (SAINT), pp. 83–90. IEEE (2012)
10. Wirtz, H., Rüth, J., Serror, M., Link, J.Á.B., Wehrle, K.: Opportunistic interaction in the challenged Internet of Things. In: Proceedings of the 9th ACM MobiCom Workshop on Challenged Networks, pp. 7–12. ACM (2014)
11. Al-Turjman, F.M., Al-Fagih, A.E., Alsalih, W.M., Hassanein, H.S.: A delay-tolerant framework for integrated RSNs in IoT. Comput. Commun. **36**(9), 998–1010 (2013)
12. Elmangoush, A., Corici, A., Catalan, M., Steinke, R., Magedanz, T., Oller, J.: Interconnecting standard M2M platforms to delay tolerant networks. In: 2014 International Conference on Future Internet of Things and Cloud (FiCloud), pp. 258–263. IEEE (2014)
13. Behrisch, M., Bieker, L., Erdmann, J., Krajzewicz, D.: Sumo-simulation of urban mobility: an overview. In: Proceedings of SIMUL 2011, The Third International Conference on Advances in System Simulation. ThinkMind (2011)
14. Blenn, N., Kuipers, F.: LoRaWAN in the wild: measurements from the things network. arXiv preprint arXiv:1706.03086 (2017)
15. Casals, L., Mir, B., Vidal, R., Gomez, C.: Modeling the energy performance of LoRaWAN. Sensors **17**(10), 2364 (2017)
16. Qualcomm Technologies: AR6004 Single Chip 2X2 802.11 A/B/G/N MIMO MAC/BB/Radio, Data Sheet, September 2016
17. https://www.thethingsnetwork.org/docs/lorawan/duty-cycle.html

Performance of Selection Combining Macro Diversity with Outage Probability Constraint in LPWAN

Qipeng Song[1,2]([⊠]), Xavier Lagrange[1,2], and Loutfi Nuaymi[1,2]

[1] IMT Atlantique, 35510 Cesson-Sevigne, France
qipeng.song@imt-atlantique.fr
[2] IRISA, 35576 Cesson-Sevigne, France

Abstract. In low power wide area networks (LPWAN), a packet transmitted by a device can be received and decoded by all surrounding base stations (BS). If at least one of the base stations decodes the packet, the latter is delivered to the system. This scheme is called selection combining (SC) macro diversity and has been studied in the literature. However, the existing research only cares about the average packet-loss probability over the entire networks. In this paper, we consider as the main performance indicator the outage probability, which better takes into account the real availability of the service in any part of the area: the outage probability. Given an outage probability constrain, we study the minimum required BS spatial density of SC macro diversity based LPWAN. The numerical results show that if both target packet loss rate and outage probability are 10%, the minimum BS spatial density required by SC macro diversity is at most half of that required by traditional BS attach method. The performance gain is more significant when the network load increases.

Keywords: Macro diversity · Selective combining · LPWAN

1 Introduction

Low Power Wide Area Network (LPWAN) is regarded as a promising solution to handle future machine type communication (MTC) traffic [12]. There are several technologies, but most representative ones (Sigfox and LoRaWAN) are based on Aloha because of its simplicity [10].

In cellular networks, a device always attaches to the Base Station(BS) for which the received power averaged over all fading realizations is the strongest and then transmits packets to its attached BS. This scheme is referred to as *Best BS attach* mode. However, a device in LPWAN works in a different way: it sends a packet in broadcast mode without BS attach procedure and benefits from *macro reception diversity*, which is defined as the capacity of several BS to receive the same packet (see Fig. 1). Each BS autonomously and independently decodes the packets and then sends the decoded packets to the core network. That is to

© Springer Nature Switzerland AG 2018
N. Montavont and G. Z. Papadopoulos (Eds.): ADHOC-NOW 2018, LNCS 11104, pp. 188–198, 2018.
https://doi.org/10.1007/978-3-030-00247-3_18

say, each BS is equipped with a packet decode function, and the backhaul link between BS and core network transmits only when a packet is received at the BS. The core network is in charge of duplicate received packets removal (e.g., by comparing the identity and message content conveyed in packets). A packet is successfully delivered if at least one BS decodes the packets. This scheme is referred to as *selection-combination-based macro diversity*, simply written as **SC macro diversity**. It is currently used by Sigfox and LoRaWAN [10].

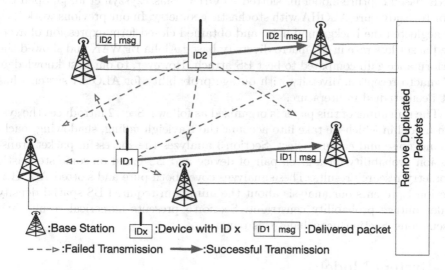

Fig. 1. Macro reception diversity scheme illustration

In the literature, the performance of ALOHA is usually evaluated with indicator (e.g. packet loss rate) that is averaged over the entire networks. This kind of indicator gives a global view about the quality of service in LPWAN networks but still have its limitations. For example, with a target network level packet loss rate such as 10%, it is very possible that devices in the neighborhood of BS never fail while devices at the border of BS coverage area have packet loss rate higher than 10%.

In this paper, we consider a performance indicator that better takes into account the real availability of the service in any part of the area: the *outage probability*. This indicator is defined as the probability that at any location a device has a link-level packet loss rate greater than a target value. For example, the statement that a LPWAN network has an outage probability of 10% with target packet loss rate 1%, means that at any location, the probability that a device has a packet loss rate higher than 1% is 10%. With outage probability, we can study the minimum BS spatial density if a LPWAN operator needs to guarantee a certain level of grade of service (i.e. outage probability). These studies can help LPWAN operators to deploy their network in an efficient way.

Combining techniques were studied to improve the performance of cellular networks in the 1990s. For example, the performance of SC macro diversity is studied for GSM networks with a remote antennas system by using hexagonal topology [7]. The packet loss rate and system capacity in ALOHA networks are usually analyzed with Stochastic geometry. The performance of SC macro diversity for BS with multiple receiver branches was studied in [9]. Stochastic geometry has served as a powerful tool to study the performance of LPWAN. In this field, Baccelli et al. [2] use Laplace transform for interference analysis for slotted ALOHA. Haenggi et al. [6] extensively study the outage probability in SINR-based capture model for slotted ALOHA. Błaszczyszyn et al. [3] open the door to study pure ALOHA with stochastic geometry. In our previous work [11], we neglected the background noise and obtained closed-form expression of average packet loss rate in SC macro diversity based Aloha LPWAN and showed the performance gain compared to best BS attach. However, to our best knowledge, SC macro reception diversity with outage probability for ALOHA systems has not been studied in literature.

The remaining of this paper is organized as follows: Sect. 2 introduces the system model in which we take into account the Rayleigh fading, shadowing, background noise and capture effect. Section 3 analyzes the successful packet transmission probability for a given pair of device and BS based on some stochastic geometry research results. These analyzes cover both pure and slotted ALOHA. Section 4 presents our analysis about the minimum required BS spatial density under outage probability constraint. Section 5 presents numerical results and discussions. Section 6 concludes this paper.

2   System Model

For any random variable (RV) X, let $f_X(x), F_X(x), \mathcal{L}_X[s], \phi_X(\omega)$ be its probability density function (PDF), cumulative distribution function (CDF), Laplace transform (LT) and characteristic function (CF), respectively.

2.1   Distribution of Nodes and Traffic Model

We consider a large wireless network over a two-dimension infinite plane. The locations of terminals form a stationary Poisson point process (PPP) $\Phi_m = \{x_i\}$ on the plane $\mathbb{R}^2$, where x_i refers to the coordinates of device with label i. The spatial density of Φ_m is λ_m. Similarly, the locations of base stations also form a stationary PPP $\Phi_b = \{y_j\}$ with spatial density λ_b.

2.2   Slotted ALOHA and Pure ALOHA

In the system model, we consider pure ALOHA (P-ALOHA) and slotted ALOHA (S-ALOHA). For slotted ALOHA, the time domain is equally divided into slots with duration T_{slot}. In each slot, each device independently decides to transmit a packet with probability p. The propagation delay is assumed to be much smaller than T_{slot}. Hence, there is a global slot synchronization over the whole network. In pure ALOHA, devices send packets without synchronization, but we still use parameter p. The packet generation process can be seen as an internal slotted system in each device with p the probability to transmit in a slot of duration T_{slot}. At a given time, the locations of terminals that are transmitting a packet form a thinned PPP with spatial density $p\lambda_m$. For slotted and pure ALOHA, we define the normalized load (per BS) as $L = p\lambda_m/\lambda_b$.

2.3 Propagation Model

The propagation model is based on Okumura-Hata with both shadow and Rayleigh fading. We assume that MTC devices transmit with identical power level denoted by P_t. The received power P_r of a packet at the BS is given by:

$$P_r = P_t K r_g{}^{-\gamma} H 10^{\sigma_{\text{dB}}\chi/10} = P_t K r_g{}^{-\gamma} H \exp\left(\sigma_{\text{dB}}\tfrac{\ln(10)}{10}\chi\right), \tag{1}$$

where K is a constant which depends on the antenna characteristics and the average channel attenuation, r_g refers to the Euclidean distance between the transmitter and the receiver, γ is the path-loss exponent, H is an exponentially distributed RV with mean 1, and χ is a standard normal variable. For the sake of simplification, we define $\sigma = \sigma_{\text{dB}} \ln(10)/10$. We assume that H and χ are both constant during a packet transmission, and mutually independent for different links.

Capture effect is taken into account to determine whether a BS could decode a received packet. Thus, the transmission success probability p_s for a transmit-receiver pair is defined as follows:

$$p_s = \mathbb{P}\left\{\text{SINR} = \frac{P_r}{I + \sigma_n^2} \geq \theta_T\right\}, \tag{2}$$

where I refers to the suffered cumulative interference during packet transmission, σ_n^2 is the background noise power.

2.4 Displacement Theorem

To facilitate the analysis, we use the displacement theorem, which is formulated as a lemma in [4, lemma 1].

Lemma 1. *For a homogeneous PPP $\Phi \subset \mathbb{R}^2$ with spatial density λ_b, if each point $r_g \in \Phi$ is transformed to $r \in \mathbb{R}^2$ such that $r = X^{-\frac{1}{\gamma}}r_g$, where $\{X\}$ are i.i.d., such that $\mathbb{E}\left[X^{-\frac{2}{\gamma}}\right] < +\infty$, the new point process $\Phi' \subset \mathbb{R}^2$ defined by the transformed points r is also a homogeneous PPP with density $\lambda_b' = \lambda_b \mathbb{E}\left[X^{\frac{2}{\gamma}}\right]$.*

We thus rewrite (1) as follows:

$$P_r = P_t K H r^{-\gamma}, \text{ with } r = P_t K \exp(-\chi/\gamma)r_g, \tag{3}$$

which indicates that the performance analysis in the initial PPP with shadowing is equivalent to that in a transformed PPP of intensity $\lambda_b' = \lambda_b \mathbb{E}\left[e^{\frac{2}{\gamma}\chi}\right] = \lambda_b e^{\frac{2\sigma^2}{\gamma^2}}$

without shadowing but with the modified distance r. The PDF of r, proved in [1], is given as follows:

$$f_r(r) = 2\pi\lambda_b' \exp(-\lambda_b'\pi r^2)r, r \in [0, +\infty], \qquad (4)$$

In the following, all distances are the modified ones in the transformed PPP.

3   Link-Level Transmission Success Probability

We first study the transmission success probability $p_s(r)$ for a given uplink between a device with label x_0 and a device with label y_0. The distance between x_0 and y_0 is denoted by r. For the considered device x_0, all the other interfering devices constitute a PPP $\Phi_m \backslash \{x_0\}$. Combining (1) and (2), we have:

$$p_s(r) = \mathbb{P}\left\{\frac{P_t K H r^{-\gamma}}{\sum_{x_j \in \Phi_m \backslash \{x_0\}} P_t K H_{x_j} r_{x_j}^{-\gamma} + \sigma_n^2} \geq \theta_T\right\}, \qquad (5)$$

Using Slivnyak's theorem [14] [Theorem 2.3.3], (5) can be further simplified:

$$p_s(r) = \mathbb{P}\left\{\frac{P_t K H r^{-\gamma}}{\sum_{x_j \in \Phi_m} P_t K H_{x_j} r_{x_j}^{-\gamma} + \sigma_n^2} \geq \theta_T\right\}. \qquad (6)$$

Let $I = \sum_{x_j \in \Phi_m} P_t K H_{x_j} r_{x_j}^{-\gamma}$, which is the cumulative interference suffered by x_0. As shown in [6], $p_s(r)$ can be expressed in terms of Laplace transform of cumulative interference $\mathcal{L}_I(s)$ at point $\theta_T r^\gamma$:

$$\begin{aligned}
p_s(r) &= \mathbb{P}\left\{H \geq (I + \frac{\sigma_n^2}{P_t K})\theta_T r^\gamma\right\} \\
&= \exp(-\frac{\sigma_n^2 \theta_T}{P_t K} r^\gamma)\left[\int_0^{+\infty} \exp(-y\theta_T r^\gamma) f_I(y) dy\right] \\
&= \exp(-\frac{\sigma_n^2 \theta_T}{P_t K} r^\gamma)\mathcal{L}_I\{\theta_T r^\gamma\},
\end{aligned} \qquad (7)$$

Now the problem is down to calculate the Laplace transform of cumulative interference suffered by the BS at the origin.

Interference I in (2) is constant during a packet transmission for S-ALOHA, but may vary with respect to time for P-ALOHA because other MTCs start or stop their transmissions during the packet transmission. With advanced transmission techniques (e.g., interleaving, robust channel coding, etc.), I is the average value within the considered packet transmission and the access is called Pure Aloha with average interference (Pa-ALOHA). For both access schemes, the Laplace transmission of I, proved in [3], is as follows:

$$\mathcal{L}_I(s) = \exp\left\{-p\lambda_m \pi A \exp\left(2\sigma^2/\gamma^2\right) s^{2/\gamma}\right\}, \qquad (8)$$

where A is defined as follows:

$$A = \begin{cases} \Gamma(1 - 2/\gamma)\,\Gamma(1 + 2/\gamma), & \text{for S-ALOHA} \\ \frac{2\gamma}{\gamma+2}\Gamma(1 - 2/\gamma)\,\Gamma(1 + 2/\gamma), & \text{for Pa-ALOHA} \end{cases}$$

where $\Gamma(\cdot)$ is the gamma function.

For P-ALOHA without advanced transmission techniques, I is the maximum interference value during the packet transmission and is called *maximum interference* (Pm-ALOHA). Its closed-form expression of LT does not exist [3]. In [11, Sec.III-B], we propose to approximate I_{y_j} by un upper bound that is the sum of interference levels at the start and end time of the considered packet transmission. With our proposed proposed upper bound, (8) is extended to cover the case of Pm-ALOHA with $A = 2\,\Gamma(1 - 2/\gamma)\,\Gamma(1 + 2/\gamma)$.

By combining (7) and (8), we can generalize the link-level success transmission probability $p_s(r)$ for all ALOHA cases (slotted and pure ALOHA):

$$p_s(r) = \exp(-\frac{\sigma_n^2\theta_T}{P_tK}r^\gamma)\exp(-p\lambda_m\pi A\theta_T^{\frac{2}{\gamma}}e^{\frac{2\sigma^2}{\gamma^2}}r^2)$$
$$= \exp\left(-\eta_T r^\gamma\right)\exp\left(-\epsilon_T r^2\right) \tag{9}$$

where σ_n^2 is the background noise power, θ_T is the capture ratio, P_t refers to the device transmit power, K is a positive constant related to propagation model and constant A is defined in (8). For the simplicity of notation, let $\eta_T = \frac{\sigma_n^2\theta_T}{P_tK}$, $\epsilon_T = p\lambda_m\pi A\theta_T^{\frac{2}{\gamma}}e^{\frac{2\sigma^2}{\gamma^2}}$.

4   Minimum Required BS Density

The transmission success probability $p_s(r)$ paves the way to study the minimum required spatial density $\lambda_{b,\min}$ for best BS attach and SC macro diversity.

4.1   Best BS Attach

Consider a device at the origin. If best BS attach method is applied, according to (9), the link level packet loss rate $p_{f,b}(r)$ is:

$$p_{f,b}(r) = 1 - \exp\left(-\eta_T r^\gamma\right)\exp(-\epsilon_T r^2), \tag{10}$$

where $\eta_T = \frac{\sigma_n^2\theta_T}{P_tK}$, $\epsilon_T = p\lambda_m\pi A\theta_T^{\frac{2}{\gamma}}e^{\frac{2\sigma^2}{\gamma^2}}$.

Let $P_{f,\max}$ be the target network loss rate and $P_{\text{outage},b}$ be the outage probability (the subscript b refers to the best BS attach method). Since the link level packet loss rate $p_{f,b}(r)$ is a function of r, thus, the proportion of devices that have higher packet loss rate than $P_{f,\max}$, namely the outage probability $P_{\text{outage},b}$, can be expressed as follows:

$$P_{\text{outage},b} = \int_0^{+\infty} \mathbb{1}_r[p_{f,b}(r) > P_{f,\max}]f(r)dr = \int_{r_c}^{+\infty} f(r)dr$$
$$= 1 - \int_0^{r_c} f(r)dr = \exp(-\lambda_b e^{\frac{2\sigma^2}{\gamma^2}}\pi r_c^2), \tag{11}$$

where $\mathbb{1}_r[\cdot]$ is a indicator function about r and its PDF is given in (4), r_c is the critical distance that can be numerically calculated from equation $p_{f,b} = P_{f,\max}$. The critical distance r_c is calculated by substituting $p_{f,b}(r_c) = P_{f,\max}$ into (10).

$$1 - \exp\left(-\eta_T r_c^\gamma\right)\exp(-\epsilon_T r_c^2) = P_{f,\max} \tag{12}$$

Although there is no closed-form expression for critical distance r_c, the latter can be easily numerically calculated by leveraging the fact that $p_{f,b}(r)$ is a mono-increasing function with respect to r.

With the obtained r_c and a given outage probability, the minimum BS spatial density $\lambda_{b,\min}$ can be obtained by inversing (11):

$$\lambda_{b,\min} = -\ln(P_{\text{outage},b})\frac{1}{\pi \exp(2\sigma^2/\gamma^2)r_c^2}, \tag{13}$$

where $\ln(\cdot)$ is the natural logarithm operator.

Without Background Noise. In an interference-limited LPWAN system, the background can be reasonably neglected. Closed-form expression r_c can be obtained from (12) by letting $\eta_T = 0$:

$$r_c = \left[\ln(1 - P_{f,\max})\middle/\left(-p\lambda_m \pi A\theta_T^{\frac{2}{\gamma}} e^{\frac{2\sigma^2}{\gamma^2}}\right)\right]^{1/2} \tag{14}$$

With substitution of (14) into (13), $\lambda_{b,\min}$ is as follows:

$$\lambda_{b,\min} = p\lambda_m \frac{\ln(P_{\text{outage},b})A\theta_T^{2/\gamma}}{\ln(1 - P_{f,\max})}. \tag{15}$$

4.2 SC Macro Reception Diversity

Different from best BS attach method, whose link-level packet loss rate only depends on the distance to the nearest BS, the performance of SC macro reception diversity depends on a distance vector $r_i, i = 0,1,2....$ Thus, we need to know the characteristics of such a vector. However, the distance to the nearest BS r_0 has the most impact to SC macro reception diversity. Thus, to reduce the complexity and keep the tractability, for a given device, its packet loss rate can be approximately expressed in terms of r_0 (instead of the distance vector to all surrounding BS $r_i, i = 1,2...$).

Let $p_{f,sc}(r_0)$ be link-level packet loss rate with respect to r_0. Recall that in case of SC macro reception diversity,

$$p_{f,sc}(r_0) \approx (1 - p_s(r_0))\mathbb{E}\left[\prod_{r_i \in \Phi_b}(1 - p_s(r_i))\right], \text{with } r_i \in [r_0, +\infty], \tag{16}$$

where r_i refers to the distance between the device and BS with label i. Note that r_i should be not less than r_0. The impact of BS other than the nearest one to the packet loss rate is thus reflected by term $\mathbb{E}\left[\prod_{r_i \in \Phi_b}(1 - p_s(r_i))\right]$.

Term $\mathbb{E}\left[\prod_{r_i \in \Phi_b}(1 - p_s(r_i))\right]$ in (16) is actually the Probability Generating FunctionaL (PGFL) of PPP Φ_b for BS, which states for some function $f(x)$ that:

$$\mathbb{E}\left[\prod_{x \in \Phi} f(x)\right] = \exp(-\lambda(\int_{\mathbb{R}^2}(1 - f(x))dx))$$

Thus, it can be simplified as follows:

$$\mathbb{E}\left[\prod_{r_i \in \Phi_b}(1 - p_s(r_i))\right] = \exp\left\{-\pi\lambda_b e^{\frac{2\sigma^2}{\gamma^2}}\int_{r_0^2}^{+\infty}\exp(-\eta_T r^{\frac{\gamma}{2}} - \epsilon_T r)dr\right\} \quad (17)$$

With substitution of (17) into (16), we have:

$$p_{f,sc}(r_0) = (1 - e^{-\eta_T r_0^\gamma - \epsilon_T r_0^2})\exp\left\{-\pi\lambda_b e^{\frac{2\sigma^2}{\gamma^2}}\int_{r_0^2}^{+\infty}\exp(-\eta_T r^{\frac{\gamma}{2}} - \epsilon_T r)dr\right\} \quad (18)$$

By letting $p_{f,sc}(r_0) = P_{f,\max}$ and substituting (13) into (18), the critical distance r_c can be numerically calculated due to the fact that $p_{f,sc}(r_0)$ is a mono-increasing function (even though its closed-form expression does not exist). Then we can use formula (13) to calculate the minimum BS spatial density, given an outage probability and target network packet loss rate.

5   Numerical Result

The system settings to get the numerical results are resumed in Table 1. Some explanations are given as follows: to evaluate the impact of the background noise to the system performance, we need to determine the values of P_t, K, σ_n^2. For one LPWAN device running on ISM band (e.g. with 868 MHz), from a regulatory point of view, the effective radiated power (ERP) may not exceed 14 dBm (or 25 mW) in any direction [13], we thus assume that the transmit power P_t is set as 14 dBm.

About noise power level, we use the same formula given in [5]: $\sigma_n^2 = -174 + $ NF $+ 10\log(B)$, where NF is the noise figure, usually set as 6 dB, B is the bandwidth occupied by the transmitted packet. The occupied transmission band is assumed to be 200 kHz (e.g. LoRaWAN). Thus, σ_n^2 is -115 dBm.

In terms of propagation path-loss model, Okumura-Hata model is applied. In urban area, the path-loss between one device with antenna height $h_d = 1.5$ m and a BS with height $h_{bs} = 50$ m is [8]: $Path\_Loss = -10\log_{10}(K) + \gamma 10\log_{10}(r) = 123.6 + 33.8\log(r)$, where $\log_{10}(\cdot)$ is 10-based logarithm operator, r is in unit of kilometer. Thus, the constant $10\log_{10}(K)$ is -123.6 dB.

We consider a LPWAN network with target network packet loss rate 10%. With a given outage probability requirement, we calculate the minimum required BS spatial density (per km^2) with respect to the network load (per slot). The latter varies from 0.05 to 0.3. The numerical results are shown in Fig. 2 (with outage probability 10%) and Fig. 3 (with outage probability 1%).

Table 1. Parameter values for numerical results

Parameter name	Parameter notation	Value
Transmit power	P_t	14 dBm
Noise figure	NF	6 dB
Occupied bandwidth	B	200 kHz
Target network packet loss rate	$P_{f,\,max}$	10%
Outage probability	P_{outage}	1%, 10%
Device height	h_d	1.5 m
BS antenna height	h_{bs}	50 m
Noise power	σ_n^2	−115 dBm

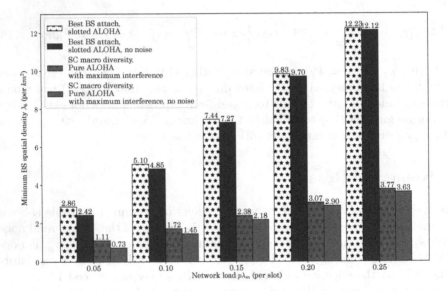

Fig. 2. Minimum BS spatial density with respect to network load. The target packet loss rate and outage probability threshold are both 10%.

From (15), we know that, if the background noise is neglected, there exists a linear relationship between network load (i.e. $p\lambda_m$) and minimum BS spatial density (i.e. λ_b) if target network packet loss rate and outage probability is given. This can be confirmed in Figs. 2 and 3. For slotted ALOHA based best Best BS attach with background noise, we unfortunately have no closed-form expression between minimum required BS density and network load. From these two figures, the relationship between minimum required BS density and network load can be assumed to be linear and we can use curve fitting techniques to get a closed form expression for the case with noise with high accuracy. In addition, It is not surprised that with background noise, the minimum required BS density is more larger.

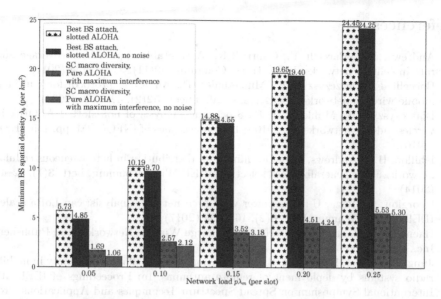

Fig. 3. Minimum BS spatial density with respect to network load. The target packet loss rate is 10% and outage probability threshold is 1%.

From these two figures, we observe that as network load increases, the increase of minimum BS spatial density in case of macro diversity is significantly smaller than that in case of best BS attach. One straightforward explanation is: to guarantee a certain level of outage probability, as the load increases, the network should be more dense and the distance between a considered device and its surrounding BS is closer. The chance that one packet is received by several surrounding BS is thus much higher in a dense network. Thus, macro diversity has more obvious effect.

6   Conclusion

In this paper, we study the performance of selection combining macro diversity in LPWAN with outage probability constraint. The outage probability is a performance indicator that better takes into account the real availability of the service in any part of the area. We compare the minimum required BS spatial density between best BS attach and SC macro diversity to confirm the interest of applying selection combining macro diversity. From numerical result, we observe that minimum required BS density and network load can be assumed to be linear if best BS attach method is applied and outage probability constraint is given. SC macro diversity is more resistant to such a constraint.

References

1. Andrews, J.G., Baccelli, F., Ganti, R.K.: A tractable approach to coverage and rate in cellular networks. IEEE Trans. Commun. **59**(11), 3122–3134 (2011)
2. Baccelli, F., Blaszczyszyn, B., Muhlethaler, P.: An Aloha protocol for multihop mobile wireless networks. IEEE Trans. Inf. Theor. **52**(2), 421–436 (2006)
3. Błaszczyszyn, B., Mühlethaler, P.: Stochastic analysis of non-slotted ALOHA in wireless ad-hoc networks. In: 2010 IEEE Proceedings of INFOCOM, pp. 1–9. IEEE (2010)
4. Dhillon, H.S., Andrews, J.G.: Downlink rate distribution in heterogeneous cellular networks under generalized cell selection. IEEE Wirel. Commun. Lett. **3**(1), 42–45 (2014)
5. Georgiou, O., Raza, U.: Low power wide area network analysis: can LoRa scale? IEEE Wirel. Commun. Lett. **6**(2), 162–165 (2017)
6. Haenggi, M., Ganti, R.K.: Interference in Large Wireless Networks. Now Publishers Inc., Breda (2009)
7. Jung, P., Steiner, B., Stilling, B.: Exploitation of intracell macrodiversity in mobile radio systems by deployment of remote antennas. In: Proceedings of IEEE 4th International Symposium on Spread Spectrum Techniques and Applications Proceedings, vol. 1, pp. 302–307. IEEE (1996)
8. Lagrange, X., Godelewski, P., Tabbane, S.: Réseaux GSM: des principesa la norme (2000)
9. Pena-Martin, J.P., Romero-Jerez, J.M., Tellez-Labao, C.: Performance of selection combining diversity in $\eta - \mu$ fading channels with integer values of μ. IEEE Trans. Veh. Technol. **64**(2), 834–839 (2015)
10. Raza, U., Kulkarni, P., Sooriyabandara, M.: Low power wide area networks: an overview. IEEE Commun. Surv. Tutor. **19**(2), 855–873 (2017)
11. Song, Q., Lagrange, X., Nuaymi, L.: Evaluation of macro diversity gain in long range ALOHA networks. IEEE Commun. Lett. **21**(11), 2472–2475 (2017)
12. Song, Q., Nuaymi, L., Lagrange, X.: Survey of radio resource management issues and proposals for energy-efficient cellular networks that will cover billions of machines. EURASIP J. Wirel. Commun. Netw. **2016**(1), 1–20 (2016)
13. Sornin, N., Luis, M., Eirich, T., Kramp, T.: LoRaWAN specification. Technical report V.1.0, LoRa Alliance, Jan 2015. https://www.lora-alliance.org/portals/0/specs/LoRaWAN%20Specification%201R0.pdf
14. Vaze, R.: Random Wireless Networks: An Information Theoretic Perspective. Cambridge University Press, Cambridge (2015). https://books.google.fr/books?id=PSfZrQEACAAJ

Authenticated Preambles for Denial of Service Mitigation in LPWANs

Ioana Suciu[1], Jose Carlos Pacho[1], Andrea Bartoli[1], and Xavier Vilajosana[1,2(✉)]

[1] Worldsensing S.L, Viriat 47, Barcelona, Catalonia, Spain
{isuciu,jcpacho,abartoli,xvilajosana}@worldsensing.com
[2] Universitat Oberta de Catalunya, Barcelona, Catalonia, Spain
xvilajosana@uoc.edu

Abstract. In this article we introduce authentication preambles as a mechanism to mitigate battery exhaustion attacks in LPWAN networks. We focus on the LoRaWAN technology as an exponent of industrial LPWANs. We analyze the impact of DoS attacks in Class B deployments and implement authentication preambles to limit attacker options when forcing nodes to overhear clàss B beacons. The article presents realistic results demonstrating significant energy savings (91% energy saving when a network is attacked) versus a 4% energy overhead of the mechanism in normally operating networks.

Keywords: DoS attack · LoRaWAN · Preamble · Authentication
Energy consumption

1 Introduction

In the context of the new market demands, such as smart cities, e-health, intelligent transportation, infrastructure monitoring and many other industrial applications, wireless sensor networks allow users to remotely access data and take decisions based on it. For example, an infrastructure monitoring application could trigger alarms when a maintenance cycle is needed, allowing for taking timely and appropriate actions.

Low Power Wide Area Networks (LPWANs), are wireless sensor networks communication technologies that provide low power operation and long range connectivity at the cost of reduced data rates and strict duty cycle regulations. Current technologies [6,7,17], operate in the sub-GHz bands in order to cover a communication range in the order of kilometers, have a single hop network topologies and an Aloha or CSMA-based MAC access. Moreover, a gateway is able to accommodate thousand of sensor nodes, allowing for low cost deployments and customizable applications and services. The sensor nodes hardware and software is built to be simple and minimalistic with the goal to ensure years of battery lifetime. The low energy consumption and the possibility of powering the nodes using energy harvesting, reduces even more the costs of batteries and maintenance. All these factors make LPWAN the technology with the lowest

© Springer Nature Switzerland AG 2018
N. Montavont and G. Z. Papadopoulos (Eds.): ADHOC-NOW 2018, LNCS 11104, pp. 199–210, 2018.
https://doi.org/10.1007/978-3-030-00247-3_19

energy consumption per provided service, but also makes them be vulnerable in front of attackers.

In [4] the main cyberattacks faced by the critical infrastructure owners and operators are introduced. Amongst others, those wireless devices are exposed to phishing, unpatched vulnerabilities and Denial of Service (DoS) attacks. Phishing opens the door to a wide range of possibilities: traffic capture, network flood, controlling of network parameters and other further possible exploitations. In mesh networks, wormhole attacks are used to create false route information and routing loops that increase the energy consumption of these networks [12].

The eventual vulnerabilities existent in the application or operating system allow an attacker to perform actions for which it's not authorized and it mainly leads to collection of information. For example, in the case of an energy management system, an attacker could get information about when and where power is used, that could further lead to knowing if and when anyone is in that property [2].

Both phishing and the exploit of vulnerabilities can lead to DoS. The DoS prevents a system from carrying its designated tasks. Jamming can be a way towards service disrupt [2]. Moreover, in LPWANs, because of the low data rate that leads to a long time on air of the messages, jamming is possible and effective [12].

In this paper, our attention is focused on the LoRa technology, one of the most used industrial LPWAN technology. Security issues have been analyzed for LoRa networks [11,12,19]; Still, the analysis made in the literature explores how these issues impact the traffic performance and the actual data privacy, while in this work we focused on the impact on energy consumption and network lifetime. We analyze the impact of a DoS attack on the network lifetime through real data collection using the Loadsensing sensor nodes developed by Worldsensing [8]. The novelty of this work consists in considering LoRaWAN class B in a scenario in which an attacker aims at draining the batteries of the sensor nodes in order to kill the network. Then we evaluate the efficiency of a possible solution based on authenticated preambles against this type of attack.

2   Security Mechanisms in LoRaWAN

LoRaWAN [17] is a promising technology for IoT. It's proprietary physical layer uses CSS modulation [18]. Orthogonal spreading factors (SF) allow for variable data rates ranging from 0.3 kbps to 27 kbps. SF can vary from 7 to 12, the least corresponding to the smallest datarate and highest communication range. LoRa enables the trade-off between throughput for coverage range and robustness while keeping a constant bandwidth. In Europe, the sensor nodes can send data on randomly chosen channels in the 868 MHz ISM band, subject to the allowed duty cycle [9,10]. A typical gateway can listen on 8 channels at once.

LoRaWAN follows a star topology: the end-devices or sensor nodes communicate directly with a LoRa gateway. There are three categories of end-devices [14]: Class A, Class B and Class C, but for all devices is mandatory to be able to support class A by default. A class A end-device supports bi-directional communication, in the sense that a DL transmission can be received only in the pre-defined reception windows that the device opens following it's UL data. Class A devices provide the lowest possible energy consumption: the end-device transmits messages using Aloha protocol restricted by a mandatory 1% duty cycle [9]. Normally, no acknowledgements are provided by the gateway, as these are expensive in terms of energy. The DL traffic is the mainly dedicated for MAC commands for making an end-device use a different datarate, channel or transmission power [14].

Class B end-devices have additional receive windows determined by the gateway's beaconing interval (1 s to 128 s). Class C devices allow continuous reception of data. Industrial solutions based on LoRaWAN use class A devices. Class B devices would allow for more feedback from the gateway.

Because of the Aloha-based protocol, collisions of signals can happen at the gateway. Collisions happen if two or more packets are sent on the same channel, with the same SF and they overlap in time. In case of collision, all of the collided packets are dropped. For two packets arriving at the gateway with the same SF at the same time, the gateway could decode one if it has a power greater than 6 dB above the other peak [16]. As for different SFs the rejection gain ranges from 16 to 36 dB, we can consider there is no inter-spreading factor interference.

In what concerns non-LoRa interferers, due to the redundancy associated with wideband spread-spectrum modulation, LoRa is resilient to the interference mechanism that appears as bursty short duration pulses [1]. According to [13], LoRa can tolerate a non LoRa interferer if this is less than 5 dB (19.5 dB) above desired signal for SF = 7 (12) for the case of an error coding scheme of 4/6. Being wide-band, a narrow band jamming signal would only add noise on a very small portion of this band and the LoRa signal would still be recoverable. Also, a jammer that floods the channel can easily be detected and dealt with. Moreover, it would need to transmit with high energy on a very wide band of the radio spectrum, which poses an important problem for a potential attacker.

LoRaWAN offers a good degree of protection against impersonation, as the end-device needs to be authenticated: a message authentication code (MAC) confirms that the message comes from an authorized sender. The LoRaWAN network and application layer use EUI64, while the device specific key, EUI128. AES CCM (128-bit) is used for encryption and authentication [14]. The network session key (NwkSKey) is used for checking the validity of messages (MIC-message integrity check). The application session key (AppSKey) is used for encryption and decryption of the payload.

Regarding replay attacks, LoRaWAN offers a mechanism to prevent them [12]: the MIC of a message, once validated by a gateway, prevents any further occurrences of the same sequence number. The lack of timestamp in LoRaWAN headers, makes it possible for a packet to be replayed at a later time as legitimate, only if the original message was jammed and no message with a higher sequence number has been received by the gateway. This attack could be used to hide the changes detected by the sensor nodes.

A more subtle type of attack that can be classified as a denial of service is represented by the exhaustion attacks: it exploits the communication protocol in order to drain the battery of the device. The lack of authentication at link or network layer can be exploited by injecting forged packets in the network. Also, another way would be by making a given sensor node continuously transmit and receive messages. In the former case, the malicious packet is often detected at the application layer and thus precious network resources are wasted processing the packet. In the latter case, an attacker sending useless messages can exhaust the node's resources, as these messages are completely received before being discarded. This type of attack is unpractical for the case of class A devices, as the only opportunity it has is after the uplink transmission, which happens normally every few hours. Class B devices have a higher listening rate and so are much more exposed to this type of attack, especially on devices that require high reactivity.

3   Preamble Authentication in LoRaWAN

3.1   Exhaustion Attacks in LoRaWAN

In the industrial context, sensor networks must be resilient and robust against any external disruption. We address the problem of exhaustion attacks, which is a type of Denial of Service (DoS) attack for battery powered devices. This type of attack exploits the communication protocol in order to drain the device battery, rendering it inoperative. We consider LoRaWAN class B end-devices, as class A devices have a reactivity limited to the transmission rate of the uplink messages, although the attack still applies. Class B allows for an efficient downlink communication at the expense of increased power draw due to periodic listening for beacons.

To carry out this attack, an attacker sniffs the medium for any downlink message addressed to the target end-device (for class A a node may listen for the uplink message to be able to attack the downlink windows afterwards). Then the attacker would synchronize with the listening window of the LoRaWAN device and send a single but very long packet on each listening window. Since the device needs to receive the whole packet in order to calculate the network level message authentication code (MAC) before discarding it, it would be forced to receive up to 255 bytes of payload message which could take up to 14 s depending on the SF in use.

3.2   Early Message Authentication

We propose a verification method at the PHY-layer that is extensible to any wireless protocol. The use of an authentication preamble (AP) is able to reject malicious packets sooner, saving energy and so guaranteeing network's long-term availability. Figure 1(a) shows the packet structure as used in LoRaWAN, while Fig. 1(b) shows the proposed packet structure that would lead to a sooner

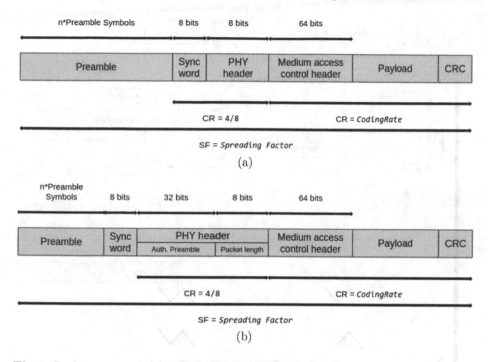

Fig. 1. Packet structure: (a) as defined by LoRaWAN; (b) new structure allowing early authentication of the packets received by an end-device.

verification of a message authenticity. This allows discarding the malicious packet after receiving the first 4 bytes after the synchronization word.

Normally, the message authentication code (MAC) is generated using the payload of the message it accompanies. As we want to be able to reject the packet sooner, we would not have the payload in order to compute the MAC. Therefore we must generate a MAC that is known at the start of the reception frame and that is different at each frame. We propose a token exchange scheme: the end-device uses a token that the gateway will use to authenticate at the physical layer all subsequent communication.

The end-device does not have to authenticate its messages to the gateway at the physical layer. This is because the gateway does not have energy constraints. In Fig. 2 we propose to use a frame counter as the token upon which the MAC will be generated. Given that each reception frame has a fixed duration, the gateway, once it has obtained the frame counter from the node, can easily predict the frame counter no matter how much time has passed. If the gateway knows the counter value ϕ for the frame f_i, to know the counter for a frame in the future f_m it simply needs to divide the elapsed time between f_i and f_m by the frame duration. The resulting value is then added to ϕ to obtain the frame counter for f_m.

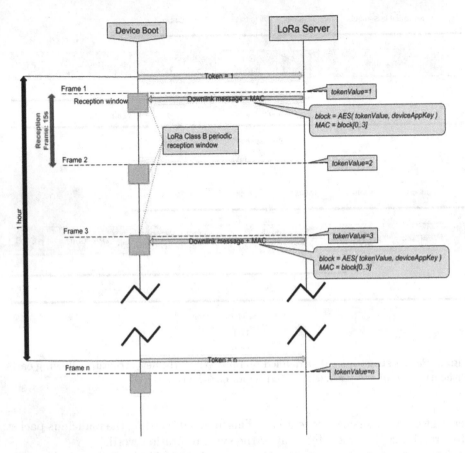

Fig. 2. Token exchange as a form of message authentication: the first token value is generated when the end-device is booted. The token value is then used to authenticate any packet coming from the LoRa server and through the gateway.

3.3 Securing the Token Exchange

The token is sent to the gateway once the end-device boots. This ensures that reception is available as soon as possible. To deal with possible desynchronization, the token is retransmitted periodically at a predefined interval. The token exchange must be coupled with a strong cipher algorithm such as AES. The application key is distributed during the device manufacturing and it is only known by the device itself and by the network server. A possible vulnerability arises when an adversary can capture the moment a device reboots because it will then know the exact token value. The token value can be initialized during manufacturing to a random value for each device, which would remove this vulnerability.

The message authentication code (MAC) is then calculated as follows:

1. The frame counter value k is computed

2. The value k is padded to up to 16 bytes. The 16 byte block is then encrypted using an AES algorithm with a shared key
3. The last 4 bytes of the resulting cipher text represents the MAC value.

The end-device follows the same procedure in order to determine the accepted MAC value for the current reception frame.

Regarding the suitability of our proposed approach in face of a brute force attack, which is an attacker trying to sniff and guess the next MAC value, the 64-bit token makes the search space close to intractable, even if using rainbow tables [15]. Also, a cipher-text attack would result difficult because when using either a cipher or a hash on the token, the entire result of the computation, usually a 16 bytes block, is not sent over the air, only 4 bytes of it, in the MAC field. The adversary does not then have a complete set of cipher-text to attack the cipher algorithm.

4   Evaluation

In this section we evaluate the efficiency of using authentication preambles in a realistic LoRaWAN setting. Figure 3 shows the behavior of an end device in both cases of using and not using authentication preamble. On the left side of the figure we can see that if the end device does not use AP it will stay in reception mode for all the packets sent by an attacker, without being able to discard them before their transmission is completed. On the right side of Fig. 3, an end device implementing AP is able to discard the attacker's packet, 4B after the synchronization word composing this message.

The experimental setup we used was composed of a Loadsensing sensor node [3], a LoRaWAN gateway and a sniffer that would synchronize with the node and it would send it packets, acting as if it was a legitimate gateway. The end device is implementing LoRaWAN class B and is set to wake up every 15 s to listen for DL messages coming from the LoRaWAN gateway. The predefined listening period for downlink packets from the gateway is 300 ms. The sensor node is configured to take samples at a very low rate (12 h–24 h), and thus most of the time is sleeping.

In a typical scenario, the DL messages from the gateway are very limited, so the end device would normally wake up, listen for 300 ms and go back to sleep, as there would be no packets to hear. This is why, in our setting, the attacker is the only one sending DL messages to the end device. The attacker would send every 15 s (the wake-up period of the end device) a packet with the payload set to the maximum allowed value (242B) [14]. Using SF12, this transmission takes 14 s. The goal of the attacker is to keep the node awake as much time as possible.

4.1   Energy Exhaustion Attack: End Device Does Not Implement AP

Figure 4 shows the end device current consumption versus time, for the case when AP is not implemented and the attacker sends packets with the maximum payload size.

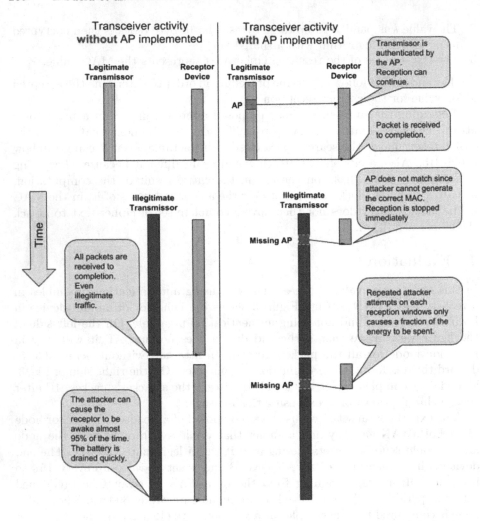

Fig. 3. The behavior of an end device subject to an energy exhaustion attack: (left) the end device does not implement AP; (right) end device implements AP.

We can observe the periodicity in node's activity: the node wakes up, starts receiving the packet and cannot discard it, it has to receive it completely before being able to see that it is not a legitimate packet. For obtaining this plot, we used the PowerScale tool [5], taking measurements for 1 min and repeating the tests 1000 times. There are 10 000 samples/s, so the whole test shows 600 000 samples. We can see in Fig. 4 that the packet reception lasts for approximately 14 s out of the 15 s configured as beaconing interval.

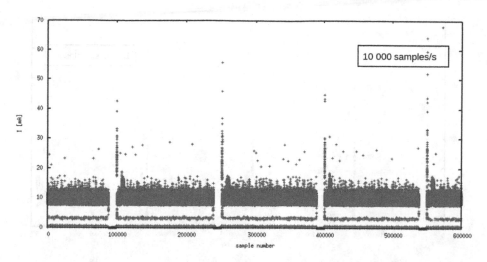

Fig. 4. End device current consumption versus time (sample number), for the case when AP is not implemented and the attacker sends packets with the maximum allowed payload size. Listening periodicity: 15 s; Packet duration: 14 s; Awake time: 14 s; Test duration: 1 min.

4.2   Energy Exhaustion Attack: End Device Implements AP

This setting is similar to the previous one, with the only difference that the end device implements the AP and it is expecting the gateway to send the correct message authentication code described in Sect. 3.3.

In Fig. 5 we can see that when using AP, the node wakes up every 15 s, but it is able to discard attacker's packet after checking for the existence of AP. As the attacker does not have any AP, or it is not able to generate the correct MAC, the end device is able to go back to sleep state. Every 15 s the node will wake up for approximatively 1 s.

4.3   Analysis of Energy Consumption

In this section we analyze the energy consumption of a node running in a typical Class B LoRaWAN network. The results have been extrapolated from real measurements conducted on a LoadSensing device [3]. The performed tests aimed at understanding what is the energy drained from the battery of a node in normal operation conditions and under a DoS attack, when implementing the preamble authentication. The parameters we used for the analysis are presented in Table 1.

We considered the real case of a Loadsensing end device using 4x Li-SOCl2 primary batteries of 5.8 Ah each. It sends a 20 B data message per day, transmission which takes about 5 s in the air. The used radio has a transmission energy consumption (at 7 dB) of 18 mA. Reception energy consumption is 11.5 mA.

The sensor node wakes up every 15 s to listen for DL data. In normal operation mode the listening duration is 300 ms, while in the case of an DoS attack,

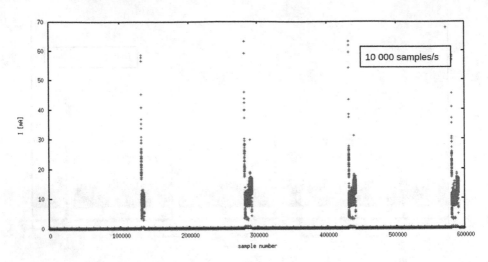

Fig. 5. End device current consumption versus time (sample number), for the case when AP is implemented and the attacker sends packets with the maximum allowed payload size. Listening periodicity: 15 s; Packet duration: 14 s; Awake time: 1 s; Test duration: 1 min.

Table 1. Technical parameters

Parameter	Value	Unit
Battery capacity	23.2	Ah
Sensor power draw	2.2	Ah/year
Sensors UL data	0.025	Ah/year
DL listening	1.983	Ah/year
AP beacon	0.17	Ah/year
Attack power drain (no AP)	94.024	Ah/year
Attack power drain (with AP)	6.354	Ah/year

if the node implements the AP, it can discard the packet after 0.9 s. If no AP is implemented, the node stays in reception mode for 14 s.

In Table 2 the expected battery duration of the device is presented, considering a normal network operation and when a DoS attack is performed. Preamble authentication is considered incurring an extra overhead of 4 B which causes extra energy consumption.

As observed, the impact of the preamble authentication technique on the energy consumption under normal operation conditions (no attack) is small, reducing the battery less than 4%.

These results confirm the fact that using the authentication preamble can reduce with 91% the effect of an exhaustion attack, this means increasing the battery lifetime from 0.24 years to 2.65 years.

Table 2. Expected battery lifetime summary considering normal operation and exhaustion attacks for nodes using an authentication preamble.

Operation mode	Authentication preamble	Battery duration
Normal operation	No	5.51 years
	Yes	5.3 years
DoS Attack	No	2.9 months
	Yes	2.65 years

The battery lifetime reduction due to the using of the authentication preamble under an exhaustion attack is 53.9% (this is the worst case scenario, when in each 15 s the node has to stay awake to check the preamble of the malicious message), compared with 95.6% when not using the preamble.

5   Conclusions

In this article we studied the suitability of authenticated preambles to cope with exhaustion attacks in LoRaWAN networks. We demonstrate that a short 4B preamble, can incur a small energy consumption overhead of less than 4% in operational networks while it prevents malicious attackers to significantly impact the operation of a network. This article presented results based on an industrial data logger platform used commercially for critical infrastructure control and monitoring.

Acknowledgements. This project has received funding from the European Union Horizon 2020 research and innovation programme under the Marie Sklodowska-Curie grant agreement No. 675891 (SCAVENGE project) and the grant agreement No. 700378 (CIPSEC). This work is also partially supported by the Spanish Ministry of Economy and the ERDF regional development fund under SINERGIA project (TEC2015-71303-R).

References

1. AN1200.22, LoRa Modulation Basics. https://www.semtech.com/uploads/documents/an1200.22.pdf. Accessed 15 July 2018
2. Energy and information sabotage: The threats facing our smart cities. https://www.zdnet.com/article/energy-and-information-sabotage-the-threats-facing-our-smart-cities/. Accessed 15 July 2018
3. Loadsensing. https://www.worldsensing.com/product/loadsensing/. Accessed 16 July 2018
4. Most common attack vector over Critical Infrastructures. http://www.cipsec.eu/content/most-common-attack-vector-over-critical-infrastructures. Accessed 15 July 2018
5. PowerScale with ACM technology. https://www.hitex.com/tools-components/test-tools/analyzer/energy-optimization/powerscale/. Accessed 16 July 2018

6. Sigfox Technology Overview. https://www.sigfox.com/en/sigfox-iot-technology-overview. Accessed 15 July 2018
7. Weightless. http://www.weightless.org/. Accessed 15 July 2018
8. Worldsensing. https://www.worldsensing.com/. Accessed 16 July 2018
9. ETSI EN 300 220–2 V3.1.1 (2007)
10. Adelantado, F., Vilajosana, X., Tuset-Peiro, P., Martinez, B., Melia-Segui, J., Watteyne, T.: Understanding the limits of LoRaWAN. IEEE Commun. Mag. **55**(9), 34–40 (2017). https://doi.org/10.1109/MCOM.2017.1600613
11. Singh, B., Kaur, B.: Comparative study of Internet of Things infrastructure and security, abstract from Global Wireless Submit 2016, Aarhus, Denmark (2016)
12. Aras, E., Small, N., Ramachandran, G.S., Delbruel, S., Joosen, W., Hughes, D.: Selective Jamming of LoRaWAN using Commodity Hardware (2017). arXiv:1712.02141v1 [cs.NI]
13. Staniec, K., Kowal, M.: LoRa performance under variable interference and heavy-multipath conditions. Wirel. Commun. Mob. Comput. **2018**, 9 (2018). Article ID 6931083
14. LoRa Alliance: LoRaWAN Specification (2017)
15. Oechslin, P.: Making a faster cryptanalytic time-memory trade-off. In: Boneh, D. (ed.) CRYPTO 2003. LNCS, vol. 2729, pp. 617–630. Springer, Heidelberg (2003). https://doi.org/10.1007/978-3-540-45146-4_36
16. Georgiou, O., Raza, U.: Low power wide area network analysis: can LoRa Scale? (2017). arXiv:iv:1610.0479 [cs.NI]
17. Semtech: What is LoRa? http://www.semtech.com/wireless-rf/internet-of-things/what-is-lora/. Accessed 31 Oct 2017
18. Semtech Wireless and Sensing: SX1272/3/6/7/8: LoRa Modem Designer's Guide-AN1200.13 (2013). https://www.semtech.com/uploads/documents/LoraDesignGuide_STD.pdf. Accessed 31 Oct 2017
19. Tomasin, S., Zulian, S., Vangelista, L.: Security analysis of LoRaWAN join procedure for internet of things networks. In: 2017 IEEE Wireless Communications and Networking Conference Workshops (WCNCW), pp. 1–6, March 2017. https://doi.org/10.1109/WCNCW.2017.7919091

Mobile Communications and Networks

Communication Architecture
for Unmanned Aerial Vehicle System

Lobna Krichen⊙, Mohamed Fourati⊙, and Lamia Chaari Fourati⁽✉⁾⊙

Laboratory of Smart Systems Technologies (LT2S),
Digital Research Center of Sfax (CRNS), Sfax University, Sfax, Tunisia
lobnaakrichen@gmail.com, fourati@tunet.tn, lamiachaari1@gmail.com

Abstract. During this last decade, Unmanned Aerial Vehicles (UAV)
are receiving more attention and are being useful in harvesting area and
for many applications and for different critical scenarios. In this paper, we
focalize our investigation on the military domain for land inspection. In
this context, this paper describes state of the art related to technologies
and communication systems that handle cooperation and traffic exchange
between Unmanned Aerial Vehicles and Ground Control Station (UGS).
Accordingly, we propose a holistic architecture that involves Multi-UAVs,
wireless sensor network, cellular network, terrestrial control node and
satellite for recovery to get more reliable solutions. Furthermore, this
paper details information flows between UAVs and UGS.

Keywords: Unmanned Aerial Vehicle · Ground Control Station
Communication system · Information flow · Wireless networks

1 Introduction

The beginning of the 21st century was marked by the development of a new
category of flying equipment: drones, commonly known as an unmanned aerial
vehicle (UAV) [1]. An UAV is an aircraft that doesnt require a human pilot
aboard. It can operate autonomously depending on its pre-programmed software or can be supervised and managed remotely from the ground, by a system
embedded on Ground Control Station (GCS). There is currently an increase
in the use of UAVs by civilian [3] for leisure [4], or by military [3,5]. Accordingly, many applications use UAVs, such as forest fire detection and monitoring
[6], meteorological services [3], aerial photography [3,7], mapping [8], package
delivery [9], filming [10], persons rescue and precision agriculture [11,12], etc.
Moreover, Facebook project use UAVs to bring the Internet to isolated areas
[13]. Furthermore, we can search for missing persons using UAVs [14], for that
UAVs have been taken on search and rescue task [15]. The most important use

Supported by the Tunisian program "Tunisian Federated Research Project" within
the framework of the project Supervision Sensitive de lieux Sensibles multi-capteurs:
Super-Sens.

© Springer Nature Switzerland AG 2018
N. Montavont and G. Z. Papadopoulos (Eds.): ADHOC-NOW 2018, LNCS 11104, pp. 213–225, 2018.
https://doi.org/10.1007/978-3-030-00247-3_20

of UAVs is in the military domain, due to its greater stealth, its reduced size and its real-time capacities for hostile areas and borders supervision [16]. Therefore, UAVs can be deployed easily to fight against terrorism without any human life loss in different scenarios. In this context, the real-time surveillance task will include several data collected during UAV flights such as telemetry and payload subsystem, as well as, commands that must be sent from the ground station to manage UAV and guarantee the success of the mission. This exchange of data between UAVs and GCS requires reliable, available, high-bandwidth and high-performance wireless communication channel to provide real-time communications and distributed data exchange. In this context, the rest of this paper is organized as follows. In Sect. 2, we present different works and studies related to UAVs. In Sect. 3, we present the standard architecture, we describe the different components of this system, the relationship between them, and we define the communication links established between the different components. Then, we discuss in Sect. 4 various communication models that could be used to handle communication between UAVs and the ground terminal. In Sect. 5, we focus on information flows between UAV and GCS, by specifying protocols and data frame structures. In Sect. 6, we examine various network technologies that could be a candidate for communication establishment for our holistic architecture. Section 7 includes some challenges of this system and our future directions to improve it. Finally, we conclude this paper.

2   Related Works

Recently, many research activities and projects were carried related to UAVs communication and their use. Accordingly, in this section, we present the most recent and cited surveys papers. In [2], the authors investigate on the characteristics and requirements of UAV networks for civil applications, Furthermore, they classify civil applications into four categories (Search and Rescue, Coverage, network, Delivery, transportation, and Construction). This taxonomy is based on mission goals, the on-board sensors and data rate required (depending on the type of data sent and the distance between two nodes). Furthermore, the authors compare existing communication technologies and their ability to ensure the needs of each application by identifying mission requirements and network needs, such as throughput, QoS, frequency etc.

In [17], the author proves that UAVs have been a great success in traffic surveillance, due to its features and functionalities. He mentioned various projects and researches carried out by universities and laboratories, such as, the Airborne Traffic Surveillance Systems (ATSS), a project realized by University of Florida (UFL), who aims to monitor remotely rural areas of the state of Florida, by using UAV equipped with a camera. Similarly, he described a research project which is done by Ohio State University (OSU) in the Department of Transportation Research Consortium. The purpose of this research is to highlight potential benefits of UAV applications in case of transportation surveillance and information collection on freeway conditions. In [18], the author focuses on the multi-UAV architecture. The communication between multiple UAVs, to ensure collaboration between them, is the most important challenge in the system. Use of ad hoc network between UAVs is a perfect solution. For that, the author introduced the concept of a network called FANET (Flying Ad-Hoc Network). In [19], the author compared FANET with the other ad hoc network, role and relationship between different modules. Then, by comparing different communication architecture (direct architecture, cellular-based architecture and UAANET architecture) by mentioning their strength, and their weakness, the authors assume that the most suitable architecture is UAANET (UAV Ad-hoc NETwork). The authors mentioned its characteristics, its advantages and the applications and projects working with it. Finally, there is a discussion about the routing protocols used in UAANET and security challenges that must be faced, and they propose suggestions to improve the security of UAANET routing protocols. In [20], the authors published a survey paper on important issues related to UAV communication networks. Firstly, they compare the characteristics of existing ad-hoc networks, which are, MANETs, VANETs and UAV networks. Then they classify UAV networks according to the topology (Infrastructure-based or ad hoc), the architecture (Star or Mesh), and if the UAVs act as servers or as clients, etc. Afterward, there is a discussion on existing routing protocols (which are classified as static, proactive, reactive and hybrid routing protocols), to choose the best suitable for UAV networks, by taking into consideration several issues like power consumption, the limited life of the UAV, and network dynamicity, etc.

As we see above, the existing surveys focused on the importance of UAVs deployment and communication links between UAVs. However, in our acknowledges there is no surveys or studies focused on the communication aspects between UAV and GCS. Accordingly, our main objective in this paper is to investigate deeply on different architectures providing reliable and secured communication between the UAV and the GCS.

3   Networking Architecture for UAVs Monitoring System

The surveillance task of hostile areas requires synchronization and collaboration between UAVs network and Wireless Sensors Network (WSN). Thus, we study a multi-systems communication architecture as illustrated in the first figure. According to our needs, the architecture will contain three networks:

- Flying Ad-Hoc network for the communication among UAVs.
- Terrestrial WSN which is a cooperating set of sensors deployed in a geographical area, on the ground level, to detect any phenomenon (like intensity, humidity, pressure temperature, etc.) and to collect data in an autonomous way.
- Mobile communication network that provides communication between a base station (BS) and UAV as well as the communication between BS and WSN cluster head. This network acts as a relay between GCS and UAV networks.

The architecture includes GCS, also known as the mission planning and control station (MPCS) [21], is the operational control center of the UAV system. The GCS allows the user to build a mission and monitor a flight to UAVs. It facilitates the supervision of UAV since it collects all the details about the aircraft status and display command, telemetry data and UAVs current situation for the supervisor on the screen.

There is a large variety of GCS that can suit for different purposes. For example, there is a GCS which size is similar to a room named the Global Hawks station. On the other hand, it can be a software application [22] which runs on a ground-based computer, there is already a variety of open source GCS available like Mission Planner (Windows, Mac OS X, Linux), APM Planner 2, MAVProxy etc. [23].

Moreover, there are autopilots (such as Ardupilot) which have his own Control Station software (Ardupilot Mega Planner) [24]. This surveillance system integrates six communications links (see Fig. 1)

- L1 is the communication link between UAV commonly based on IEEE 802.11.
- L2 corresponds to the communication between the BS and a UAV.
- L3 is the communication link between the sink or a WSN cluster head and the BS. It connects WSN with the GCS via the BS. It could be LTE or 5 G.
- L4 corresponds to the link between two WSN nodes. In general, this is based on IEEE 802.15.4 standard. It provides data gathering and forwarding to the sink.
- L5 corresponds to the links between BS.
- L6 corresponds to the link between GCS and the BS.

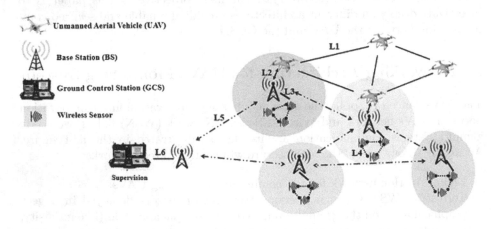

Fig. 1. Holistic architecture for land monitoring based on multi-UAVs.

To communicate with UAV, the information must be transmitted continuously from a UAV to a GCS, therefore a bidirectional link must be established between them to ensure real-time telemetry and to make adjustments and to send commands during flight. The down-link, from the UAV to the GCS, is dedicated to telemetry. It contains flight data collected by the drone, such as, for example, the geographical position, and, the video streaming captured by the camera during flight. On the up-link, from the GCS to UAV, controls commands are sent to interact with the UAV (e.g. changing the direction of the UAV). In this context, our study will focus on the communication between UAVs and the ground.

Due to the critical functions to be implemented, communication between UAV and GCS should operate in a protected spectrum. Furthermore, a backup link via satellite(see Fig. 2) should be implemented. The primary link is via the 5G, it is preferred for delay reasons. However, the backup link enhances robustness and reliability. Besides that, advanced security mechanism should be employed to avoid ghost control scenario in which the UAVs are monitored by unauthorized agents such as a terrorist.

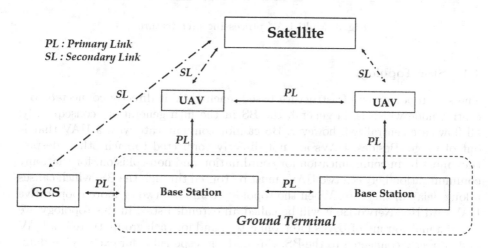

Fig. 2. Communication links between UAVs and Ground Control Station.

To achieve effective tasks management, a mission central processing unit should be implemented on the GCS controller, as well as a task manager, could be integrated into each UAV. The multi UAV processing architecture is illustrated in (see Fig. 3).

4 Network Topologies Including UAVs and GCS

There are different communication architectures to establish the connection between UAVs and ground terminals [20,25], we can split these architectures into two categories, star and mesh [26].

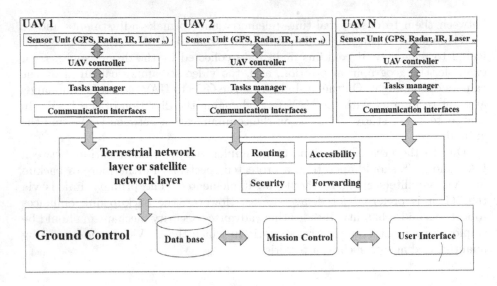

Fig. 3. Multi UAV processing architecture.

4.1 Star Topology

The star topology is infrastructure based, each UAV is directly connected to a central node which is, in general, the BS in the fifth generation, consequently, all flows are centralized, however, BS cannot communicate with a UAV that is out of range. Besides, UAVs are not directly connected to each other, despite they must be in communication for coordination and non-collision, for that, any communication between two UAVs must be routed through the BS, which causes a long delay in this case. When the topology combines two or more cooperative UAVs Ad Hoc Networks, it will be called an extended star. In this topology, we found a multi-group of UAVs interconnected, and for each group, there is a UAV node directly connected to the BS, this node is responsible for exchanging data. If two groups of UAVs want to exchange data, it is necessary to pass through the BS. Issues of the star topology are the high latency and the requirement of high bandwidth for the downlink. Also, if the BS is out of order, then the whole network will fail, which implies no communication between UAVs, without forgetting that a central node could be a vulnerability for the UAVs network.

4.2 Mesh Topology

Concerning mesh topology, there is no centralized communication to BS, each UAV can act as a relay and will have the ability to forward data between other UAVs without passing through the BS. This topology is Ad Hoc based, there is only one UAV, named backbone, in direct connection with BS, which plays the role of a gateway node between BS and other UAVs. It collects data from UAVs and send it to BS, and dispatching commands and information from GCS to UAVs at the same time. Then, there is a single link between the BS and all UAVs. Another topology similar to the extended star topology is the extended mesh, it contains multiple groups too, but the difference is that all groups can communicate and transmit data between each other without the need to pass through BS, and as mentioned previously, there is only one UAV gateway in direct communication with the BS. Compared to the star topology, mesh topology offers the advantage of keeping the communication between UAVs, directly or through one or more intermediate UAVs, even if the BS is out of order. Moreover, it provides the advantage of using less downlink bandwidth between UAVs and the BS.

5 Information Flows Between UAVs and GCS

As previously mentioned, there are an enormous amount of data sent between the UAV and the GCS. In this section, we will discuss its and distinguish diverse types and formats. This data can be partitioned into service data and sensed data.

5.1 Service Data and Sensed Data

Service data is the data exchanged between UAVs and GCS, which includes control COMMANDS, MISSION UPLOADS, STATUS REPORTS ETC to guide and manage UAV. Concerning data collected by the sensors on-board UAV during the flight, it is classified as sensed data which can be presented in different forms [27]. Firstly we highlight images and video, various images types can be captured by cameras (optical, thermal and so forth) from a different point of views. With a high speed and a reliable network, these images and videos will be transmitted in real time to the GCS and will be displayed to the supervisor to be able to detect a suspect. Additionally, there is others information dispatched by the UAV such as its speed, its battery level, the altitude, the current flight mode, etc. Furthermore, the UAV send its position captured by the GPS which is a module included in it.

5.2 Communication Protocols

Data exchanging between GCS and UAV are defined by different protocols such as the MAVLINK protocol (Micro Air Vehicle Link), which is the most standardized communication protocol employed in the communication data channel for UAVs, or the STANAG 4586 protocol. MAVLink is an open source protocol used for the exchanging of messages between the autopilot and the GCS [28,29], in fact, it acquires telemetry data from UAV and transmits control and navigation command to it. In [30], there is a list of the available MAVLINK Common Message Set carried out by most GCS and autopilots. MAVLink is a lightweight protocol tested on several UAV platforms and numerous GCS software application. It can support until 255 UAVs controlled by only one GCS. The minimum packet length in the MAVLink protocol is 8 bytes (contains acknowledgment without payload), and the maximum packet length is 263 bytes with a full payload. Figure 4 demonstrates the MAVLINK frame structure and the Table 1 give details of the MAVLink packet. On the other hand, STANAG 4586 is a NATO (North Atlantic Treaty Organization) standard which defines interfaces, architectures and message formats for UAVs and allows interoperability between them. Contrary to MAVLink, STANAG protocol is not an open source protocol [31].

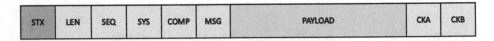

Fig. 4. MAVLINK frame structure.

The MAVLink packet details are given in Table 1.

Table 1. MAVLink packet detail.

Field	Value	Purpose
STX	0xFE	Indicates start of new packet
LEN	0 - 255	Indicates the length of the payload
SEQ	0 - 255	Enables packet loss detection
SYSID	1 - 255	Identifies the security systems
COMP	0 - 255	Allows multiple components on the same platform
MSG	0 - 255	Identifies the message being sent
PAYLOAD	0 255	Data of the message
CKA, CKB		CRC parameters

5.3   Securing MAVLink

Security is critical to any communication protocol to guarantee reliable and safe data transmission between many components. However, UAV carries secure information especially in the military mission, which causes dangerous problems if the data is sniffed by attackers. MAVLink protocol has security gaps, for that, many researchers were realized to solve and examine security problems of this protocol [32,33]. Hence, protecting UAV from unapproved access is essential in our future works which will be focused on improving and evolving the MAVLink protocol.

6   Communication Networks

In the previous sections, we focus on the communication architecture between UAV and GCS. we presented topologies that can be elaborated between them, then we mentioned data exchanged. According to the architecture presented in Fig. 1, many network technologies could be a candidate for the communication systems to establish a reliable link between them. Consequently, we highlight the most characteristics of the technologies in Table 2. Based on this table and in the existence of various technologies, we will classify them by the range and the data rate. Thus, for short distances communication, WIFI (802.11) or ZigBee can be employed, otherwise, for a cover over a large area, the cellular network, WiMAX, or the satellite communication will be selected. Furthermore, the requirement of throughput for videos and images is not the same for commands or for GPS data. Consequently, the network technology will be selected in accordance with the demand of the mission.

Table 2. Comparison between technologies for communication links

Technology	Theoretical rate	Range	Advantages	Limitations	Data traffic
Satellite [1, 34]	10 Mbps uplink 1 Gbps downlink	Up to the entire earth	Wide coverage Provides connection in all areas	Limited bandwidth High delays Low data rates High cost	Live and real-time operations
IEEE 802.11(a,g) IEEE 802.11(b) IEEE 802.11(n) IEEE 802.11(ac) Ref. [1, 35, 36]	54 Mbps 11 Mbps Up to 300 Mbps Up to 866.7 Mbps	30 m 75–100 m 75 m 35 m	High speed Cheap	Limited range Limited support for users	Control commands Telemetry Downlink sensor data
GSM GPRS UMTS LTE 5G Ref. [1, 37, 38]	Up to 9.6 kbps Up to 144 kbps 2 Mbps Up to 1 Gbps 10 Gbps and more	Depends on BS (1 km to several Kms)	Extended coverage Redundancy One infrastructure for multiple UAVs High bandwidth Mobility support	Expensive	Control commands Telemetry Downlink sensor data (Images, Videos)
WiMAX Ref. [37, 39]	70 Mbps	Up to 50 km	High throughput Low cost Vaste coverage Easy installation Mobility support	Interference issues	Control commands Telemetry Downlink sensor data (Images, Videos)
Zigbee Ref. [40]	250 Kbps	Up to 30 m	Low cost	Low data rate Short range	Control commands
Bluetooth IEEE 802.15 Ref. [1]	1 Mbps	Up to 30 m	Low cost	Low data rate Short range Low security	Data communication Inside UAV

7   Open Issues and Future Directions

The standard architecture established between GCS and UAVs was discussed in this paper. In fact, there are some challenges that make it inadequate, which are summarized as follows. Ubiquity: Users need to monitor UAVs and to access to the UAV system at any time from any device. Limited resources: the surveillance task requires a large volume of data to achieve it, whereas the UAV has a limited storage and a limited power. Therefore, they require an architecture that does not consume their resources. Real-time management: UAV task distribution, mission status monitoring, and flight path should be supplied in real-time. Moreover, UAVs requires real-time communication among each other, to indicate its location and status, for the purpose of realizing collaboration, and performing the mission successfully. Solid connection: UAVs requires continuous connection and a reliable communication link. However, connection network may be unavailable especially in the borders. Additionally, the link must assure the security of data and protect it from attacks. Scalability: Adding new component in the system must be secure, easy and uncomplicated. Hence, in an urgent case, which requires adding a new UAV, it must be attached to the mission directly in real time. Consequently, we notice that this architecture must have improvements to be more appropriate to our request. On the other hand, there are popular emerging concepts such as the Internet of Things (IoT) [41,42], the cloud [43,44] and the Software Defined Network (SDN) [45–47], which became employed in several applications, including UAVs network, due to its functionalities. In fact, the IoT is responsible for establishing and facilitating connectivity between things over the internet, the Cloud make the system flexible and accessible from anywhere in any time, additionally, it provides storage and computing over the internet for the data collected from devices, and finally, the SDN which is responsible for managing the heterogeneous environment by providing orchestration for the network. In this context, our future researches will be focused on these concepts which are more and more sophisticated in order to treat the limits and the challenges of UAVs network system.

8   Conclusion

UAVs are growing in importance and general interest for different domains such as the military domain. In this context, we studied the architecture of communication system for controlling hostile areas using UAVs and WSN. We explored various links established in the system and examined various architecture model and different technologies that can be used in the communication link between the flying vehicles and the ground terminal. We inspected some reliability problem, for that we propose a backup link via satellite, it will be the second link. This paper is focused not only on the communication link but also on the data exchanged between the components of the system mentioning the purpose of securing them. Finally, and as mentioned above, there are weaknesses in this communication system, that will be treated in our future works, which will be based on SDN and on IoT.

Acknowledgement. This work is supported by the Tunisian program "Tunisian Federated Research Project" within the framework of the project Supervision Sensitive de lieux Sensibles multi-capteurs: Super-Sens.

References

1. Jawhar, I., Mohamed, N., Al-Jaroodi, J., Agrawal, D.P., Zhang, S.: Communication and networking of UAV-based systems: classification and associated architectures. J. Netw. Comput. Appl. **5**(84), 93–108 (2017)
2. Hayat, S., Yanmaz, E., Muzaffar, R.: Survey on unmanned aerial vehicle networks for civil applications: a communications viewpoint. IEEE Commun. Surv. Tutor. **18**(4), 2624–2661 (2016)
3. Austin, R.: Unmanned Aircraft Systems: UAVS Design, Development and Deployment, vol. 54. Wiley, Hoboken (2011)
4. http://www.aeronewstv.com/en/lifestyle/sports-leisure/2161-when-using-leisure-drones.html . Accessed 01 Apr 2018
5. Coffey, T., Montgomery, J.A.: The emergence of mini UAVs for military applications. Def. Horiz. **22**, 1 (2002)
6. Casbeer, D.W., Beard, R.W., McLain, T.W., Li, S.M., Mehra, R.K.: Forest fire monitoring with multiple small UAVs. In: American Control Conference, pp. 3530–3535, IEEE, Portland (2005)
7. Eisenbeiss, H.: The autonomous mini helicopter: a powerful platform for mobile mapping. Int. Arch. Photogram. Remote Sens. Spat. Inf. Sci. **27**, 977–983 (2008)
8. Steffen, R., Frstner, W.: On visual real-time mapping for unmanned aerial vehicles. In 21st Congress of the International Society for Photogrammetry and Remote Sensing (ISPRS), Beijing, China, pp. 57–62, July 2008
9. Barr, A.: Amazon Testing Delivery by Drone, CEO Bezos Says, in USA Today. http://www.usatoday.com/story/tech/2013/12/01/amazon-bezos-drone-delivery/3799021/. Accessed 02 Apr 2018
10. Johnson, T.: FAA May Approve Use of Drones for Hollywood Film-Making, Variety, p. 1, 2 June 2014
11. Costa, F.G., Ueyama, J., Braun, T., Pessin, G., Osrio, F.S., Vargas, P.A.: The use of unmanned aerial vehicles and wireless sensor network in agricultural applications. In: International Conference on Geoscience and Remote Sensing Symposium (IGARSS), pp. 5045–5048. IEEE, Munich (2012)
12. Primicerio, J., et al.: A flexible unmanned aerial vehicle for precision agriculture. Precis. Agric. **13**(4), 517–523 (2012)
13. Dockrill, P.: Facebook is preparing its Internet-beaming drone for maiden launch, ScienceAlert. http://www.sciencealert.com/facebook-is-preparing-its-internet-beaming-drone-for-maiden-launch. Accessed 02 Apr 2018
14. Doherty, P., Rudol, P.: A UAV search and rescue scenario with human body detection and geolocalization. In: Orgun, M.A., Thornton, J. (eds.) AI 2007. LNCS (LNAI), vol. 4830, pp. 1–13. Springer, Heidelberg (2007). https://doi.org/10.1007/978-3-540-76928-6_1
15. Waharte, S., Trigoni, N.: Supporting search and rescue operations with UAVs. In: International Conference on Emerging Security Technologies (EST), pp. 142–147. IEEE, Canterbury (2010)
16. Berrahal, S., Kim, J.H., Rekhis, S., Boudriga, N., Wilkins, D., Acevedo, J.: Border surveillance monitoring using quadcopter UAV-aided wireless sensor networks. J. Commun. Softw. Syst. **12**(1), 67–82 (2016)
17. Puri, A.: A survey of unmanned aerial vehicles (UAV) for traffic surveillance, pp. 1–29. Department of Computer Science and Engineering, University of South Florida (2005)

18. Bekmezci, I., Sahingoz, O.K., Temel, Ş.: Flying ad-hoc networks (FANETs): a survey. Ad Hoc Netw. **11**(3), 1254–1270 (2013)
19. Maxa, J.A., Mahmoud, M.S.B., Larrieu, N.: Survey on UAANET routing protocols and network security challenges. Ad Hoc Sens. Wirel. Netw. (2017)
20. Gupta, L., Jain, R., Vaszkun, G.: Survey of important issues in UAV communication networks. IEEE Commun. Surv. Tutor. **18**(2), 1123–1152 (2016)
21. Fahlstrom, P., Gleason, T.: Introduction to UAV Systems. Willy, Hoboken (2012)
22. Zaheer, Z., Usmani, A., Khan, E., Qadeer, M.A.: Aerial surveillance system using UAV. In: Thirteenth International Conference on Wireless and Optical Communications Networks (WOCN), Telangana State, India, pp. 1–7. IEEE, July 2016
23. http://ardupilot.org/copter/docs/common-choosing-a-groundstation. htmlcomparison . Accessed 02 Apr 2018
24. Mission Planner: Ground control station for APM (ArduPilotMega). http:// planner.ardupilot.com/wiki/mission-planner-overview/. Accessed 02 Apr 2018
25. Li, J., Zhou, Y., Lamont, L.: Communication architectures and protocols for networking unmanned aerial vehicles. In: 2013 IEEE Globecom Workshops (GC Wkshps), Atlanta, GA, USA, pp. 1415–1420, December 2013
26. Frew, E.W., Brown, T.X.: Airborne communication networks for small unmanned aircraft systems. **96**(12) (2008)
27. Andre, T., et al.: Application-driven design of aerial communication networks. IEEE Commun. Mag. **52**(5), 129–137 (2014)
28. Santos, N., Raimundo, A., Peres, D., Sebastio, P., Souto, N.: Development of a software platform to control squads of unmanned vehicles in real-time. International Conference on Unmanned Aircraft Systems (ICUAS), Miami, USA, pp. 1–5. IEEE, June 2017
29. del Arco, J.C., Alejo, D., Arrue, B.C., Cobano, J.A., Heredia, G., Ollero, A.: Multi-UAV ground control station for gliding aircraft. In: 23th Mediterranean Conference on Control and Automation (MED), Torremolinos, Spain, pp. 36–43. IEEE, June 2015
30. http://mavlink.org/messages/common
31. Rodrigues, A.V., Carapau, R.S., Marques, M.M., Lobo, V.: Unmanned aerial vehicles: system architecture and protocols. Sci. Bull. "Mircea cel Batran" Naval Academy **20**(1), 140 (2017)
32. Butcher, N., Stewart, A., Biaz, S.: Securing the MAVLink communication protocol for unmanned aircraft systems. Appalachian State University, USA (2013)
33. Marty, J.A.: Vulnerability analysis of the MAVLink protocol for command and control of unmanned aircraft (no. Afit-eng-14-m-50). Air Force Institute of Technology Wright-Patterson Graduate School of Engineering and Management (2013)
34. Skinnemoen, H.: UAV satellite communications live mission-critical visual data. In: International Conference on Aerospace Electronics and Remote Sensing Technology (ICARES), Yogyakarta, Indonesia, pp. 12–19. IEEE, November 2014
35. Gabriel, C.: WiMAX: The Critical Wireless Standard 802.16 and Other Broadband Wireless Options. Blueprint WiFi Monthly Research Report. ARC Chart Ltd. (2003)
36. Ribeiro, C.: Bringing wireless access to the automobile: a comparison of Wi-Fi, WiMAX, MBWA, and 3G. In: 21st Computer Science Seminar, pp. 1–7, April 2005
37. Volko, T., Moucha, V., Lipovsk, P., Draganov, K.: Possibility of usage the latest GSM generations for the purpose of UAV communication. In: New Trends in Signal Processing (NTSP), pp. 1–4. IEEE, October 2016

38. Zhu, L., Yin, D., Yang, J., Shen, L.: Research of remote measurement and control technology of UAV based on mobile communication networks. In: IEEE International Conference on Information and Automation, Gothenburg, Sweden, pp. 2517–2522. IEEE, August 2015
39. Rahman, M.A.: Enabling drone communications with WiMAX Technology. In: The 5th International Conference on Information, Intelligence, Systems and Applications, IISA, Chania, Crete, Greece, pp. 323–328. IEEE, July 2014
40. Fourty, N., Val, T., Fraisse, P., Mercier, J.J.: Comparative analysis of new high data rate wireless communication technologies from Wi-Fi to WiMAX. In: International Conference on Autonomic and Autonomous Systems and Networking and Services, ICAS-ICNS, p. 66. IEEE (2005)
41. Rodrigues, M., Pigatto, D.F., Fontes, J.V., Pinto, A.S., Diguet, J.P., Branco, K.R.: UAV integration into IoIT: opportunities and challenges. In: ICAS 2017, vol. 95. ISO 690 (2017)
42. Kouba, A., Qureshi, B., Sriti, M.F., Javed, Y., Tovar, E.: A service-oriented cloud-based management system for the internet-of-drones. In: IEEE International Conference on Autonomous Robot Systems and Competitions (ICARSC), Coimbra, Portugal, pp. 329–335. IEEE (2017)
43. Mahmoud, S., Mohamed, N.: Broker architecture for collaborative UAVs cloud computing. In: 2015 International Conference on Collaboration Technologies and Systems (CTS), pp. 212–219. IEEE. ISO 690, June 2015
44. Luo, C., Nightingale, J., Asemota, E., Grecos, C.: A UAV cloud system for disaster sensing applications. In: 2015 IEEE 81st Vehicular Technology Conference (VTC Spring), pp. 1–5. IEEE, May 2015
45. Yuan, Z., Huang, X., Sun, L., Jin, J.: Software defined mobile sensor network for micro UAV swarm. In: International Conference on Control and Robotics Engineering (ICCRE), Singapore, pp. 1–4. IEEE, April 2016
46. Sharma, V., Song, F., You, I., Chao, H.C.: Efficient management and fast handovers in software defined wireless networks using UAVs. IEEE Netw. 31(6), 78–85 (2017). ISO 690
47. Barritt, B., Kichkaylo, T., Mandke, K., Zalcman, A., Lin, V.: Operating a UAV mesh internet backhaul network using temporospatial SDN. In: Aerospace Conference, Mountain Trail, USA, pp. 1–7. IEEE, March 2017

DACAR: Distributed & Adaptable Crosslayer Anticollision and Routing Protocol for RFID

Abdoul Aziz Mbacke[1,2(✉)], Nathalie Mitton[1], and Herve Rivano[2]

[1] Inria, Rocquencourt, France
{abdoulaziz.mbacke,nathalie.mitton}@inria.fr
[2] Univ Lyon, INSA Lyon, CITI, Villeurbanne, France

Abstract. In the midst of Internet of Things development, a first requirement was tracking and identification of those mentioned "things which could be done thanks to Radio Frequency Identification. However, since then, the development of RFID allowed a new range of applications among which is remote sensing of environmental values. While RFID can be seen as a more efficient solution than traditional Wireless Sensor Networks, two main issues remain: first *reading collisions* and second proficient *data gathering* solution. In this paper, we examine the implementation of two applications: for industrial IoT and for smart cities, respectively. Both applications, in regards to their requirements and configuration, challenge the operation of a RFID sensing solution combined with a dynamic wireless data gathering over multihops. They require the use of both mobile and fixed readers to cover the extent of deployment area and a quick retrieval of tag information. We propose a distributed crosslayer solution for improving the efficiency of the RFID system in terms of collision and throughput but also its proficiency in terms of tag information routing towards one or multiple sinks. Simulation results show that we can achieve high level of throughput while maintaining a low level of collision and a fairness of reader medium access above 95% in situations where readers can be fix and mobile, while tag information is routed with a data rate of ≈97% at worst and reliable delays for considered applications.

Keywords: RFID · IoT · Resource allocation · Routing · MAC layer

1 Introduction

Radio Frequency Identification (RFID) has for the longest time been used as a mean for identification and tracking of goods, animals and even humans. Indeed, thanks to its operating scheme, it allows a contactless and non direct line of sight recognition. Using a device called a *reader*, one can identify an object thanks to a small chip attached to it known as a *tag* that stores the relative

This work was partially supported by CPER DATA and IPL CityLab@Inria.

N. Montavont and G. Z. Papadopoulos (Eds.): ADHOC-NOW 2018, LNCS 11104, pp. 226–238, 2018.
https://doi.org/10.1007/978-3-030-00247-3_21

information. Different types of tags can be found and can be categorized as *(i)* active, if they embed an energy source, *(ii)*: passive, if they entirely rely on the received signal power from the reader to power themselves and communicate [10] or **semi active/passive tags**: they stand in between the two precedent ones. They carry a battery intended to power some of their attached components but still rely on the reader's energy to communicate. In the following of this paper, we will mainly target passive tags which are more compliant with IoT applications requirements. UHF RFID systems operating in the frequency band of 865–868 MHz or 902–928 MHz, according respectively to ETSI [8] or FCC regulations are considered a interesting complement for IoT applications and services thanks to the longer interrogation range. Multiple works have been conducted towards ambient energy harvesting and in particular [13] discuss harvesting energy in UHF RFID. Previously in [23], authors present how sensors could be attached to passive RFID tags in order to get both the original identification but also battery-free environmental sensing. A comparative study of sensing using the different RFID bands is done in [24]. Authors also present the case of wireless temperature and pressure sensors using passive battery-free RFID sensors for industrial applications.

In this paper, we venture into the use of RFID for two particular applications. The first one considers a large warehouse with tags attached to goods disposed in horizontally disposed shelves while readers, considered mobile, are attached to forklifts or hand-held by operators walking through alleys. Such an application assesses the use of RFID in supply chain management where the products could be foodstuffs such as dairy, meat or seafood products that need to be monitored in terms of humidity or temperature to prevent deterioration. The second application we consider is a smart city where passive tags are considered to be attached to vehicles, public city bikes and urban infrastructures. Targeting the vehicles and public city bikes allows the tracking of their position inside the city which, outside of the privacy issues not tackled here, can facilitate the work of law enforcement agencies, identify traffic stops for better management, scarcity of public bikes in given neighborhoods, etc. Urban infrastructures such as buildings, roads or bridges need to be monitored for different "vitals" like humidity, state of corrosion and pH-value to be able to address any defects as soon as possible before any more expensive fix or major catastrophe.

However, both of these applications share *(i)* **the density of readers' deployment** and *(i)* **their mobility** inside the given environment which affect the efficiency of readers' interrogation due to collisions. Next is the collection of information towards a base station which has to be done in regards of readers activity and available communication medium. Indeed, in these deployments where readers are scattered throughout the environment, they cannot all be equipped with a long range communication interface to join the decision center. Not only would that be more expensive in terms of cost but also more energy consuming [9]. As such, they have to rely on each other using their deployment topology and short range wireless communication interfaces to reach a sink responsible for uploading the data to the decision center. In order to reach the sink, a multi-hop routing algorithm must be set that integrates the readers activity (reading round) as well as the type of data being gathered in its scheduling to optimize global performance.

In [15], we presented a joint reading-gathering mechanisms for static multi-hop RFID reader networks. However, this proposal was not suitable for mobile deployments of readers where the topology is always evolving. Tag interrogation and data forwarding suffered from collisions and decreased the data rate. In this paper, we present DACAR for Distributed & Adaptable Crosslayer Anticollision and Routing protocol for RFID. A work on the compliance with mobile deployments which have different requirements in terms of scheduling and routing. The solution proposed here to overcome issues brought by mobility and to tackle the constraints of the applications introduced above features the following:

- **distributed and local**: same algorithm runs on all devices based on information gathered from neighbors;
- **fair**: medium access is regulated while ensuring no reader is prejudiced;
- **reliable**: data rate is highly successful with suitable latency for applications;
- **adaptable**: our solution can be adapted to most anti-collision protocols already available.

The main contributions of this work are: *(i)* a novel cross-layer scheduling and routing solution for RFID systems compliant with IoT applications and their requirements, *(ii)* its evaluation over two considered applications challenging the expressed concerns (density, mobility, data gathering and routing) and *(iii)* a discussion over future research directions regarding RFID sensing. This paper also provides the following insights: high performance can be obtained regarding the contention resolution with fairness levels close to 100% and quick coverage of all deployed tags in under 60 or 90 s depending on the application; in regards to the contention algorithm chosen, the successfully forwarded packet data ratio is above 96% and go as high as 99.5% which is on par with considered industrial and urban application requirements; the end-to-end delay needed to retrieve and deliver tag information from the furthest point to the sink is on average around 15 to 44 s, depending on the scenario, which once again can be considered reliable for the given applications.

The rest of this paper is organized as follows. Section 2 presents the issues and concerns addressed in this work. Section 3 introduces our proposed algorithm DACAR. The evaluation over given scenarios is done in Sect. 4. Section 5 presents related work. Section 6 discusses the possible future research directions and issues that need to be focused on before we conclude in Sect. 7.

2   Problem Statement

When applying RFID solutions to industrial or urban scenarios, several issues need to be resolved. They are either directly related to the technology itself or to the application requirements and constraints. We detail here these different concerns and introduce the different ways then can be coped with.

2.1 Density of Deployment

The evolution of IoT and the requisites of intended applications lead to larger deployment of nodes in restrictive spaces. In light of the wireless nature of the technology used, this causes radio collisions. Regarding RFID, this can be translated into different types of collisions, either tags or readers collisions. Tag collisions happen when multiple tags are laying within the interrogation range of a reader and upon reception of interrogation signal, attempt to answer all at the same time. The multiple answers collide and are not perceived by the reader. Reader collisions are the result of multiple readers interrogating the same tags simultaneously. Their interrogation signals overlay at the tags level. The tags are unable to dissociate the different signals and fail to answer to the interrogation resulting in missed tags. Both issues have been topics of research in the late years, regarding tag collisions, a survey is also available in [7] which classifies proposals in their main categories, solutions are now even embedded in commercial products and we will thus not tackle this issue in this paper. Reader collisions however, remain an important issue. Our solution being compliant with most anti-collision protocols in the literature, we will re-use most performing algorithms from the state-of-the-art.

2.2 Mobility

In regards to the applications presented in Sect. 1, we understand the need to have dynamic readers and not only static placed ones. In order to reach the furthest regions of the city or warehouse, having a mobile reader is more efficient than deploying even more readers which is not cost effective, produces more collisions due to density and consumes more energy. Just as density does, the mobility of readers also produces collisions, since in a non-controlled mobility setting, readers can meet at random spots producing collisions. In order to cope with both the density and mobility of readers, having distributed algorithms is more convenient. As such, using wireless communicating readers, instead of wired ones connected to a central server synchronizing all devices, allows them to roam freely in the deployment area. Being able to wander about, the relative density of readers based on their vicinity is always changing hence the need for the algorithms to be scalable.

2.3 Data Gathering

Upon scheduling the readers' interrogations, much more tag information is made available and needs to be forwarded in the most efficient way possible towards a base station for computing and decision making. While in traditional WSN, nodes may access to a long range communication interface (cellular, LPWAN technologies, etc.), in our paper, we focus on the previously mentioned wireless communication interface to both schedule reading activity and collect data. Since we opted for a distributed and scalable solution, readers based on their activity, relative position to the sink and neighbors perform their best effort to forward the data. Having a combined activity scheduling as well as a routing scheme allows the system to be more energy efficient and prevents from overlapping of interrogation and forwarding phases making the solution more proficient.

In the remaining of our manuscript, we assume readers have two distinct wireless interfaces. The first interface is the traditional RFID interrogation antenna. It is used by readers to communicate with tags and retrieve the stored information. The range of this interface is d_{CRT}. The second interface is the peer communication antenna. It is used by readers to send beacons used for activity scheduling as seen in [4, 11, 20, 22]. In our proposal, this interface is also used to forward tag information to the base station. The range of this interface is d_{Com}. In order for reader to be able to identify colliding neighbors, the value of d_{Com} has to be set to at least $d_{Com} = 2 \times d_{CRT}$ [1].

3   DACAR

The chosen topology and its initialization remains the same as in [15] and will briefly be explained before moving on to the improvements made to comply with dynamic deployments.

3.1   Background

Topology: In order to self-organize, readers discover their hop count to the sink. This position will then determine both their interrogation activity as well as their routing behavior. The chosen topology is a gradient where readers are organized around the sink based on the hop count needed to reach it.

Network Initialization: In order for each reader to estimate its hop count to the sink, a beacon propagation emanating from the sink is conducted. At first, the sink sends a beacon containing its ID and a $rank_{local} = 0$. This beacon is received by readers within range that compare their own $rank_{local}$, with the $rank_{RX}$ enclosed in the beacon. If $rank_{RX} < rank_{local} + 1$, the reader sets its $rank_{local}$ to $rank_{RX} + 1$ and stores the beacon source node as its direct parent $parent_{local}$. Otherwise, if $rank_{RX} >= rank_{local} + 1$, the reader discards the beacon as it originates from a node either with a greater or similar rank. Before forwarding the beacons with their own rank, readers draw a random backoff and wait it out to reduce collisions.

3.2   Proposal

In [15], readers were considered as static and the topology would not change. However, using mobile readers the topology is dynamic and the gradient needs to be maintained with readers relative positions. This work thus considers an additional gradient maintenance to keep $rank_{local}$ and $parent_{local}$ values up to date. Figure 1 illustrates the activity of 7 readers disposed around a sink. The network initialization has already been done and each reader display its respective $rank_{local}$ and $parent_{local}$. Since the highest rank in the network is $rank_G = 4$, readers can choose timeslots within [0–3] in regards to Algorithm 1. Dashed circles represent the wireless communication range of nodes d_{Com} while dotted circles portray the tag interrogation range d_{CRT}. Beacon exchanges regarding the scheduling are not depicted here to avoid clutter.

Gradient Maintenance: Whenever a reader has to forward data, it broadcast a beacon, answered by its neighbors with their own values. The reader then selects the neighbor with the lowest rank and sets it as its new parent $parent_{local}$ and updates its $rank_{local}$ as well. Since the network is dense, unconcerned neighbors receiving the beacon still update their $rank_{local}$ and $parent_{local}$. These values are then conserved with a timeout value in order to avoid too much overhead and unnecessary energy drain. As such, depending on the state of the timeout a reader will either update its values or conserve the ones already stored. This timeout value is set depending on the speed of the reader and its communication range. Depending on the anti-collision algorithm in use, readers will behave differently and the vicinity knowledge of each reader can be affected.

Interrogation Scheduling: As with most distributed TDMA anti-collision protocols, readers activity is organized in timeslots themselves gathered in rounds. The active timeslot, here called $slot_{local}$, is usually randomly chosen within a range before contention and tag interrogation. However, with our approach, instead of randomly selecting a timeslot $slot_{local}$ within $[0; round\_size[$, readers select their timeslot based on their ranks. The maximum rank value observed in the network is set as the new maximum value to choose from. As such, readers with an even (resp. odd) rank, i.e. $rank_{local}\%2 = 0$ (resp. $rank_{local}\%2 \neq 0$), will randomly chose an even (resp. odd) timeslot between $[0; round\_size[$. This has the advantage of decreasing the number of potential collisions since readers within two consecutive ranks will not interrogate tags at the same time whatsoever. Readers within the same rank are not only disposed within a concentric circle but can also choose different timeslot $slot_{local}$ values, lowering the probability of collisions. In Fig. 1b, during $t = 0$, readers F & G respectively ranked $rank_F = 2$ and $rank_G = 4$ choose slot 0 while reader C & D, ranked $rank_{C;D} = 2$ choose slot $t = 2$, as seen in Fig. 1d (i.e. Algorithm 1 11–2). On the other hand, readers A & B ranked $rank_{A;B} = 1$ choose slot $t = 1$, depicted in Fig. 1c, and reader E, $rank_E = 3$, chooses $t = 3$, as seen in Fig. 1e (i.e. Algorithm 1 13). Similar to almost all TDMA anti-collision schemes, 2 durations are defined: T_{Beacon}, time during which readers exchange beacons for scheduling their activity and T_{CRT}, time used by readers to communicate with tags within range.

Algorithm 1. Slot determination - run on each reader i

1: **if** $rank_{local}\%2 = 0$ **then**   ▷ Rank is an even value
2:     $slot_{local} = (int)\lfloor \frac{random[0;2*round\_size[}{2} \rfloor$
3: **else**   ▷ Rank is an odd value
        $slot_{local} = (int)\lfloor \frac{random[0;2*round\_size[}{2} \rfloor + 1$
4: **end if**

Tag Information Gathering: The data gathering leverages the new rank-based scheduling. Indeed, the time difference observed between even and odd ranked readers is used to perform data forwarding during periods of inactivity of readers. After interrogating tags in its range during slot n, a reader will forward the collected data towards its $parent_{local}$ during slot $n + 1$. Since the wireless communication channel is different from the tag interrogation channel, the data forwarding will not interfere with the interrogation activity (see Sect. 2.3). After contending during slot n, the following course of actions can happen:

- the reader needs to transmit data (its own reading or data to forward from its children): At slot $n + 1$, the reader forwards the data to its $parent_{local}$ during T_{CRT} and then waits for the next round (Algorithm 2 l1–3). If the tag information has not been fully transmitted, it will be continued on the next relay occasion. In order to avoid collisions during the forwarding process, readers draw a backoff before following an RTS/CTS mechanism [21] with their $parent_{local}$. This is the case in Fig. 1c, readers F & G which previously read during slot $t = 0$, now forward their data during $t = 1$. Same in Fig. 1d, with readers A & B which read during $t = 1$ and attempt to forward during $t = 2$, and E which received data from G during $t = 1$ and forwards it in $t = 2$ as well. However, B fails to forwards in $t = 2$, due to the RTS/CTS mechanism and avoid collisions with A. Next, in Fig. 1e (Algorithm 2 l7–10), C which read in $t = 2$, forwards data in $t = 3$;
- the reader has no tag information to send. It waits for the next round to perform the interrogation scheduling contention again (Algorithm 2 l6). This is the case of reader D in Fig. 1 which failed its contention with reader C during slot $t = 2$ and also did not receive data from any neighbors. It waits for the following round to contend again;
- the reader performed its interrogation contention in the last available slot of the current round and thus cannot forward its data on the next round. It must wait for the following round, performs the contention algorithm and according to the new $slot_{local}$ chosen, will forward the tag information if any (Algorithm 2 l4). In Fig. 1e, reader E interrogates tags in the last slot $t = 3$, and waits for the next round to forward its data.

Algorithm 2. Data forwarding

1: After contention at slot n
2: **if** Packet to send **then**
3:     **If** n ¡ round_size **then** Send data at slot $n + 1$
4:     **else** Waits for next frame **end**
5: **end if**
6: Waits for next frame
7: Upon reception of tag_info
8: **if** $parent_{RX}$ == node **then**   ▷ packet comes from children
9:     $pkt\_to\_fwd_{local}$++   ▷ Stores packet for forwarding
10: **end if**

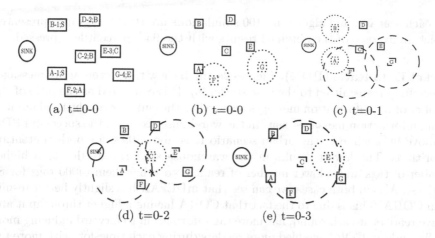

(a) t=0-0   (b) t=0-0   (c) t=0-1

(d) t=0-2   (e) t=0-3

Fig. 1. Tag interrogation and data forwarding

4   Performance Evaluation

In order to evaluate the performances of DACAR, we stage 2 application scenarios. We implemented DACAR using two anti-collision protocols CORA and mDEFAR [14] that both highly perform for dense and mobile deployments of readers compliant with the scenarios depicted. They perform similarly to results obtained in [14,16].

4.1   Simulation Scenarios

The first scenario stages an industrial IoT deployment in a warehouse of $100 \times 100\,\text{m}^2$. 4000 tags are disposed inside the area. They are organized in 20 horizontally disposed shelves of 200 tags each. In order to cover all tags and test the behavior of our algorithms in dense environments, we deployed 80 mobile readers moving between aisles at a speed ranging between [0.5–1.5] m/s. This allows the consideration of both readers attached to forklifts as hand-held ones. The only sink is centered in the area. The next scenario represents a city district of size $555 \times 555\,\text{m}^2$ with 3000 tags are randomly deployed, either mobile roaming freely in the area at a speed ranging in [21–36] km/h or static supposed on buildings. 570 readers are also considered either mobile at a speed ranging in [14–20] km/h or static disposed at street corners. Five sinks are deployed in the area to test the behavior of our algorithms with multiple base stations.

4.2   Results

Simulations were run on WSNet[1], an event-driven simulator for large scale wireless networks. T_{Beacon} and T_{CRT} are respectively set to 5 ms and 460 ms [1,4,8].

---

[1] http://wsnet.gforge.inria.fr/.

For each scenario and algorithm, 100 simulations are run. The graphs presented depict an average of the obtained results with the 95th percentile expressed.

Packet Data Ratio (PDR): Figures 2a and b show the percentage of messages successfully transmitted to the base station(s). It is computed as the ratio of the number of tag information messages received at the sink(s) over the total number of tag information messages sent. In the warehouse scenario, the successful PDR is above 96% while in the urban scenario it is above 99% for both contention algorithms. The lowest results in the warehouse scenario are due to a higher number of tags and a lower number of readers covering them (4000 tags for 80 readers). Also in both cases, we can see that mDEFAR has slightly better results than CORA. This is due to the fact that CORA having a higher throughput and active readers at each round, has more tag information to forward inducing more traffic. Indeed, CORA enabled more readers during each timeslot, with more tag information to forward to the sink. Several involved readers collide, which affects the PDR. However, with such levels of PDR, the results are quite reliable, since tags can be covered by several readers, as such even if the information is lost by one reader it will be picked up by another neighbor and forwarded to the sink(s). Once again, the mobility and density of deployment become an advantage for the considered applications.

Latency: The latency assesses the delay between a tag information being read and its reception by one of the base stations. In DACAR, since readers are organized in a gradient topology, the latency is given according to the relative rank of the source reader. In Fig. 2c, we can see the latency, in seconds, for all 4 ranks during simulations. We can see that, on average, the on-air time for a tag information to reach the sink is around 15 s whichever contention algorithm is chosen. This duration seems to be quite reliable for the application concerned. Indeed, in case a product inside the warehouse is considered defective according to presets, depending on its position, it will take less than 16 s for the system to be notified and the appropriate countermeasure to be taken. Figure 2d shows the results for our urban simulation. Due to the higher mobility of readers, results are slightly different. However, results remain reliable with on average 44 s for the furthest tag information to reach a sink. In case a urban infrastructure needs to be evacuated due to safety measures, it would take less than a minute for the system and authorities to be notified. Also, in case of a suspect vehicle being researched, within this given time, it will be located and notified to authorities. We can see that in both scenarios, mDEFAR has slightly better results than CORA, this is once again due to the fact that mDEFAR, with a lower throughput, has less tag information to forward inducing less congestion.

5   Related Work

RFID as an enabler for IoT has been a main topic of research in the later years. Indeed, RFID is now a mature technology that can be used in a range of IoT

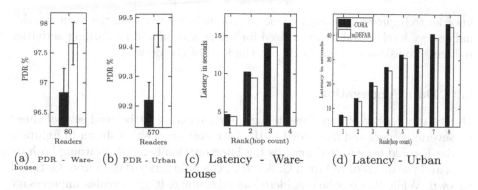

(a) PDR - Warehouse   (b) PDR - Urban   (c) Latency - Warehouse   (d) Latency - Urban

Fig. 2. Data gathering results

applications [6]. Indeed, multiple experiments have shown how RFID could be a better alternative for IoT applications thanks to its communication perquisites compared to traditional Wireless Sensor Networks (WSN) solutions. As such, several applications can be found with RFID being evaluated in challenging environments such as embedded in concrete [3], disposed in water [5], buried underground [2] or attached to metallic materials [18]. However, most of these works fail to discuss one of the concerns of using RFID which is collisions. As discussed in Sects. 2.1 and 2.2, in case of a dense deployment of RFID devices, collisions can negatively impact the performance of deployed systems. Multiple anti-collision proposals can be found throughout the literature. In [12], authors discuss the implementation of an RFID architecture with a base station and propose an anti-collision protocol. Their solution is based on differential backoff periods based on readers' energy levels. In [20], a central server schedules the readers. The ETSI [8] standard proposes the use of "Listen Before Talk" in which readers listen to the medium for a defined period of time to ensure it is idle before interrogating tags. In case the medium is occupied, the readers can switch to another channel and perform their listening. Several other proposals can be found as detailed in [17].

6 Discussions

6.1 Energy Consumption

Although DACAR balances the periods of inactivity of readers for a better efficiency, energy consumption still needs to be addressed. Indeed, the contention itself as well as the topology maintenance rely on the exchange of several beacons between devices. Implementing a timeout before the topology update process allows the reduction of the overhead, however, further investigations are required to guarantee a fully autonomous system and lengthen its lifetime. Carrying out an energy harvesting solution for readers based either on photo-voltaic panels or regenerative braking for mobile nodes could also be a factor to integrate in order to improve the energy efficiency. As such, readers with the highest residual energy levels could be prioritized for interrogation and forwarding activities reducing collisions and balancing out the load of the network.

6.2 Data Aggregation

Due to the density of deployment, tag information might be read several times by several readers and forwarded to the base station. Also as shown in Figure 1, reader E could have waited until its tag interrogation before forwarding both its data and the one received from G. As such, C would forward data from G, E and its own. While this can be considered an advantage, it also creates unnecessary congestion in the network. A solution would be to aggregate data and drop duplicate packets. This has been discussed in the literature for traditional WSN networks and could be applied to RFID as well. For instance, [19] investigates the energy efficiency of distributed compressed sensing in WSNs.

6.3 Metrics

In DACAR, the topology construction and maintenance are based solely on the number of hops between readers and their relative sink(s). While this metric could be considered as reliable for some applications where for instance the state of the radio medium is not fluctuating, several other metrics can be taken into account to offer a solution that could be validated in industrial and urban scenarios. Indeed, these environments are known to be unstable and noisy due to either confinement or multiple other sources of radiation in cities. As such, we believe that link quality between readers, latency, packet drop rate, energy levels between neighbors should also be considered to propose a more robust solution.

7 Conclusion

This paper presents DACAR, a complete RFID solution to enable IoT in industrial and urban applications. This work is conducted through the performance study of our solution under different scenarios and constraints. Analysis show that proficient interrogation can be conducted using the contention algorithm proposed and this is confirmed by the throughput, collisions, fairness and coverage delay results. On the other hand, data forwarding results are reliable and guarantee both steady knowledge of the network thanks to high packet data ratio and respectable delay to provide safe outcome for the considered applications. However, improvements are achievable in regards to the issues presented in Sect. 6 and will be addressed in future works. Experiments conducted in controlled environments or in an RFID test-bed are also considered.

References

1. Amadou, I., Mitton, N.: High adaptive MAC protocol for dense RFID reader-to-reader networks. In: Mitton, N., Kantarci, M.E., Gallais, A., Papavassiliou, S. (eds.) ADHOCNETS 2015. LNICST, vol. 155, pp. 82–93. Springer, Cham (2015). https://doi.org/10.1007/978-3-319-25067-0_7
2. Aroca, R.V., Hernandes, A.C., Magalhães, D.V., Becker, M., Vaz, C.M., Calbo, A.G.: Application of standard epc/gen2 uhf RFID tags as soil moisture sensors. In: Proceedings of Multidisciplinary Digital Publishing Institute, vol. 1 (2016)
3. Bartholmai, M., Johann, S., Kammermeier, M., Müller, M., Strangfeld, C.: Transmission characteristics of RFID sensor systems embedded in concrete. In: Proceedings of IEEE SENSORS (2016)
4. Bueno-Delgado, V., Ferrero, R., Gandino, F., Pavon-Marino, P., Rebaudengo, M.: A geometric distribution reader anti-collision protocol for RFID dense reader environments. IEEE T-ASE 10, 296–306 (2013)
5. Cassel, M., Dépret, T., Piégay, H.: Assessment of a new solution for tracking pebbles in rivers based on active RFID. Earth Surf. Process. Landf. 42, 1938–1951 (2017)
6. Da Xu, L., He, W., Li, S.: Internet of Things in industries: a survey. IEEE Trans. Ind. Inform. 10, 2233–2243 (2014)
7. Dheeraj, K.K., Kwan-Wu, C., Raad, R.: A survey and tutorial of RFID anti-collision protocols. IEEE Commun. Surv. Tutor. 12(3), 400–421 (2010)
8. ETSI: Radio frequency identification equipment operating in the band 865 MHz to 868 MHz with power levels up to 2 W and in the band 915 MHz to 921 MHz with power levels up to 4 W; harmonised standard covering the essential requirements of article 3.2 of the directive 2014/53/eu (2016)
9. Fedor, S., Collier, M.: On the problem of energy efficiency of multi-hop vs one-hop routing in wireless sensor networks. In: Proceedings of the International conference on AINA (2007)
10. Finkenzeller, K.: RFID Handbook: Fundamentals and Applications in Contactless Smart Cards and Identification, chap. 3. Wiley, Hoboken (2003)
11. Gandino, F., Ferrero, R., Montrucchio, B.: DCNS: an adaptable high throughput RFID reader-to-reader anticollision protocol. IEEE TPDS 24(5), 893–905 (2013)
12. Golsorkhtabaramiri, M., Hosseinzadeh, M., Reshadi, M., Rahmani, A.: A reader anti-collision protocol for RFID-enhanced wireless sensor networks. Wirel. Pers. Commun. 81, 893–905 (2015)
13. Kim, S., et al.: Ambient RF energy-harvesting technologies for self-sustainable standalone wireless sensor platforms. Proc. IEEE 102, 1649–1666 (2014)
14. Mbacke, A.A., Mitton, N., Rivano, H.: RFID reader anticollision protocols for dense and mobile deployments. Electronics 5(4), 84 (2016). MDPI Electronics Special Issue "RFID Systems and Applications"
15. Mbacké, A.A., Mitton, N., Rivano, H.: Data gathering solutions for dense RFID deployments. In: Proceedings of the IEEE UIC (2017)
16. Mbacké, A.A., Mitton, N., Rivano, H.: RFID anticollision in dense mobile environments. In: Proceedings of the IEEE WCNC. IEEE (2017)
17. Mbacke, A.A., Mitton, N., Rivano, H.: A survey of RFID readers anticollision protocols. IEEE J. RFID 2, 38–48 (2017)
18. Ramirez, R., Rojas-Nastrucci, E., Weller, T.: UHF RFID tags for on/off-metal applications fabricated using additive manufacturing. IEEE Antennas Wirel. Propag. Lett. (2017)

19. Razzaque, M.A., Dobson, S.: Energy-efficient sensing in wireless sensor networks using compressed sensing. MDPI Sens. **14**, 2822–2859 (2014)
20. Rezaie, H., Golsorkhtabaramiri, M.: A fair reader collision avoidance protocol for RFID dense reader environments. Wirel. Netw. **24**, 1953–1964 (2017)
21. IEEE Computer Society: IEEE standard for information technology, IEEE 802.11 standard (1999)
22. Waldrop, J., Engels, D.W.: Colorwave: an anticollision algorithm for the reader collision problem. In: ICC (2003)
23. Want, R.: Enabling ubiquitous sensing with RFID. IEEE Comput. **37**, 84–86 (2004)
24. Zalbide, I., D'Entremont, E., Jiménez, A., Solar, H., Beriain, A., Berenguer, R.: Battery-free wireless sensors for industrial applications based on UHF RFID technology. In: Proceedings of the IEEE SENSORS (2014)

Low Frequency Mobile Communications
in Underwater Networks

Abdel-Mehsen Ahmad[1], Michel Barbeau[2], Joaquin Garcia-Alfaro[3]([⊠]),
Jamil Kassem[1], Evangelos Kranakis[2], and Steven Porretta[2]

[1] School of Engineering, Lebanese International University, Bekaa, Lebanon
[2] School of Computer Science, Carleton University, Ottawa, ON K1S 5B6, Canada
[3] Telecom SudParis, CNRS Samovar, UMR 5157, Evry, France
jgalfaro@ieee.org

Abstract. We present a receiver for low frequency underwater acoustic communications addressing the Doppler shift that occurs during the transmission of frames at a very low data rate. The receiver handles constant or variable (linearly and nonlinearly) Doppler shift patterns. The waveform supported by the receiver is adapted to difficult underwater channel conditions, such as the ones present in long range under-ice Arctic communications. The bandwidth is extremely narrow (less than six Hz). Redundancy is very high (300%). Our main contributions are in an aspect of the receiver that handles arbitrary types of Doppler shifts. We use the idea of signal tracking function. It follows the progression of a carrier during the reception of a frame. Evaluation results are reported using our GNU Radio implementation.

1 Introduction

Underwater data communications and networking have applications in monitoring and surveillance of coastal waters [1], submarine activity sensors [2], autonomous undersea vehicles [3] and submerged airplane locator beacons [4]. We focus on low frequency mobile communications [5,6], i.e., in the range 0.3 to 3 kHz. Relative to higher frequencies, Stojanovic stressed that attenuation is lower [7]. Hence, there is potential for long distance contacts [8]. However, because of the narrow half-power bandwidth of low frequency and long distance operation, only extremely low data rates are possible. Furthermore, the relative mobility of a transmitter and a receiver affects the acoustic waves used for underwater communications. This is the Doppler effect. Contrasted with classical electromagnetic communications, it has a significant impact.

In this paper, we consider the Doppler shift that occurs during the reception of low-data rate frames in low frequency and long distance acoustic underwater communications. There are three cases: constant, linearly variable and nonlinearly variable Doppler shift. In background research [9,10], we concluded that in the case of transmitter-receiver collateral motions, in the zero to eight knot range, we have constant relative velocity and constant Doppler shift within zero

© Springer Nature Switzerland AG 2018
N. Montavont and G. Z. Papadopoulos (Eds.): ADHOC-NOW 2018, LNCS 11104, pp. 239–251, 2018.
https://doi.org/10.1007/978-3-030-00247-3_22

to eight Hz. For transverse motions, the Doppler effect is nonlinearly variable in time. For a transmitter carried by a meandering current and a vertically oscillating receiver, the Doppler effect is nonlinearly variable in time, up to 35 Hz. Regarding a transmitter in a diagonal oscillation, the Doppler shift is nonlinearly variable in time (up to 15 Hz), decreasing with elevation. Finally, when multiple receivers are in motion, they observe different shifts.

We propose a receiver that handles constant, linearly variable or nonlinearly variable Doppler shifts. The type of signal and data encoding produced by the protocol supported by the receiver are suitable for harsh conditions (e.g., long range and long distance Arctic communications). The bandwidth is extremely narrow. The signal occupies less than six Hz. Forward Error Correction (FEC) with 300% redundancy and probabilistic decoding are used. Our main contribution is in the receiver design. Decoding is done in three steps: energy search, synchronization and demodulation. The demodulator generates soft symbols. Each bit a superposition of zero or one, with a certain probability for each value. Considering the most probable values first, the decoder tries to obtain a valid frame (which passes error correction). If it does not work, other possibilities are tried. The number of attempts is controlled (by a parameter). This type of decoding was invented by Fano [11]. Classical decoding uses Viterbi, much faster and less complex, but it cannot tolerate high error rates as Fano. In the case of underwater communications, Fano is suitable because the data rates are very low. The computer is very fast relative to the channel speed and can spend a lot of time decoding and searching for signals. To handle arbitrary forms of Doppler shift, we introduce the concept of signal tracking function that models the evolution of a carrier during the reception of a frame.

Section 2 covers the channel model. A trajectory model that yields nonlinearly changing Doppler shift patterns is presented in Sect. 3. The detailed receiver design is discussed in Sect. 4. We elaborate our evaluation approach and review simulation results in Sect. 5. We conclude with Sect. 6.

2   Channel Model

This paper builds upon a Doppler shift analysis [9, 10] and a protocol design for communications with slow-rate data frames carried by low frequency underwater acoustic signals [12]. The protocol already handles constant or linearly variable Doppler shifts. It does not handle nonlinearly variable Doppler shift. The goal of the work presented in this paper is to extend the protocol in [12] to handle nonlinearly variable Doppler shifts.

Let $v(t)$ be the relative speed (m/s) between a transmitter and a receiver at time t. Let c be the signal propagation speed (m/s). At nominal frequency f_0 Hz, the Doppler effect causes a frequency shift defined is

$$f_\Delta(t) = f_0 \frac{v(t)}{c} \text{ Hz.} \tag{1}$$

Let $x(t)$, $y(t)$ and $w(t)$ denote the transmitted baseband signal, received signal, and additive white Gaussian noise. As a function of time, the level of the received signal is $y(t) = \alpha e^{-\sqrt{-1}\theta(t)}x(t) + w(t)$. Attenuation is represented by factor α. Doppler shift is modelled in the phase term $\theta(t) = 2\pi\left[f_0 + f_\Delta(t)\right]t$ rad. Constant Doppler shift means that the function f_Δ is constant during reception of a frame. The transmitter-receiver relative speed $(v(t))$ is constant, as a function of time. Linearly variable Doppler shift implies that during the reception of a frame the value f_Δ is variable, but can be modelled by a first degree polynomial. For the nonlinear case, f_Δ is an arbitrary function and cannot be modelled by a first degree polynomial.

3 Trajectory Model

We study and model trajectories, of underwater vehicles, producing nonlinearly variable Doppler shifts.

Consider two vehicles R_a, R_b moving along trajectories defined in the Euclidean space[1]

$$t \to \boldsymbol{A}(t) = (A_1(t), A_2(t), A_3(t)) \text{ and } t \to \boldsymbol{B}(t) = (B_1(t), B_2(t), B_3(t)) \quad (2)$$

such that at time t they occupy positions $\boldsymbol{A}(t), \boldsymbol{B}(t)$ while moving with constant speeds v_a, v_b, respectively (see Fig. 1).Each trajectory is a smooth, rectifiable, and non-crossing curve. Since the two vehicles move with constant speeds, by time t they must have covered a trajectory of length $v_a t, v_b t$, respectively, and therefore the following two equations are valid

$$v_a t = \int_0^t \|\boldsymbol{A}'(s)\|ds \text{ and } v_b t = \int_0^t \|\boldsymbol{B}'(s)\|ds, \quad (3)$$

where $\boldsymbol{A}'(s), \boldsymbol{B}'(s)$ denote the derivatives of $\boldsymbol{A}(s), \boldsymbol{B}(s)$, with respect to the variable s, and $\|\boldsymbol{A}'(t)\|, \|\boldsymbol{B}'(t)\|$ is the norm of these vectors in Euclidean space.

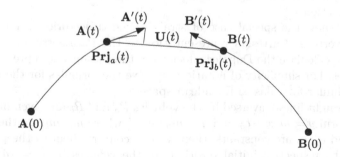

Fig. 1. Movement of the vehicles along their corresponding smooth, rectilinear trajectories $t \to \boldsymbol{A}(t)$ and $t \to \boldsymbol{B}(t)$.

---

[1] An analogous formulation using two instead of three cartesian coordinates is possible in the Euclidean plane.

From the fundamental theorem of calculus and Eq. (3), it follows that $v_a = \|A'(t)\|$ and $v_b = \|B'(t)\|$, for all $t \geq 0$.

We project $A'(t)$ and $B'(t)$ onto the vector $U(t) = B(t) - A(t)$ as depicted in Fig. 1, thus forming the corresponding projection vectors $Prj_a(t)$ and $Prj_b(t)$. They yield the following formula for the projection vector $Prj_a(t)$ of $A'(t)$ on the vector $U(t)$,

$$Prj_a(t) = \|A'(t)\| \cdot \frac{<A'(t), U(t)>}{\|A'(t)\| \cdot \|U(t)\|} \cdot \frac{U(t)}{\|U(t)\|} = \frac{<A'(t), U(t)>}{\|U(t)\|} \cdot \frac{U(t)}{\|U(t)\|}$$

where $<\cdot, \cdot>$ denotes the inner product of vectors. They yield a similar formula for the projection vector $Prj_b(t)$ of $B'(t)$ on the vector $U(t)$. Subtracting the projection vectors and using the fact that the inner product is bilinear we see that

$$Prj_a(t) - Prj_b(t) = \frac{<A'(t) - B'(t), U(t)>}{\|U(t)\|} \cdot \frac{U(t)}{\|U(t)\|}. \tag{4}$$

Using Formulas (4) and (1), we derive the Doppler effect resulting from the movement of the two vehicles in Theorem 1.

Theorem 1 (Doppler Effect). *For two vehicles R_a, R_b moving in Euclidean space with constant speeds v_a, v_b on their respective smooth, rectifiable trajectories $t \to A(t)$ and $t \to B(t)$ the change in frequency is*

$$\Delta f(t) = -\text{sign}\left(\|U(t)\|'\right) \cdot \frac{|<A'(t) - B'(t), U(t)>|}{\|U(t)\|} \cdot \frac{f_0}{c} \tag{5}$$

where $|\cdot|$ denotes the absolute value, and f_0 is the transmission frequency and c is the sound speed.

Note that the quantity $-\text{sign}\left(\|U(t)\|'\right)$ is positive when the projection vectors $Prj_a(t), Prj_b(t)$ are pointing towards each other and negative when they are in opposite directions.

We treat now the special case of straight line trajectories. First, we show how to convert the Cartesian representation to the Parametric one. Next, we show how to calculate the Doppler effect from the Parametric representation of straight lines. For simplicity of notation, we give the formulas for the Euclidean plane but similar formulas to Euclidean space.

If the straight lines traversed by the vehicles R_a and R_b are given in standard Cartesian form $y = m_a x + c_a$ and $y = m_b x + c_b$, where m_a, m_b are the slopes of the lines and c_a, c_b are constants, then we can convert them to the parametric form. Let the respective initial positions of the vehicles be $\bar{a} = (\bar{a}_1, \bar{a}_2)$ and $\bar{b} = (\bar{b}_1, \bar{b}_2)$. From the equations of the two lines we see that

$$\bar{a}_2 = m_a \bar{a}_1 + c_a \text{ and } \bar{b}_2 = m_b \bar{b}_1 + c_b. \tag{6}$$

Let $A(t), B(t)$ be the positions of the vehicles at time t on their respective line trajectories. Further, let $x_a(t), y_a(t)$ and $x_b(t), y_b(t)$ be the horizontal and vertical offsets from their starting positions positions at time t. Observe that since the vehicles are moving with constant speeds their positions satisfy

$$\boldsymbol{A}(t) = (\bar{a}_1 + x_a(t), \bar{a}_2 + y_a(t)) \text{ and } \boldsymbol{B}(t) = (\bar{b}_1 + x_b(t), \bar{b}_2 + y_b(t)), \quad (7)$$

where by assumption, $x_a(0) = y_a(0) = x_b(0) = y_b(0) = 0$. Since the vehicles are moving on straight lines, we have by definition that $y_a(t) = m_a x_a(t)$ and $y_b(t) = m_b x_b(t)$; further, since they are moving with constant speeds we conclude that $x_a^2(t) + y_a^2(t) = (v_a t)^2$. Combining these last two equations, we conclude that the corresponding offsets for vehicle R_a are $x_a(t) = v_a t/\sqrt{1 + m_a^2}$ and $y_a(t) = m_a v_a t/\sqrt{1 + m_a^2}$. Entirely similar formulas are valid for the vehicle R_b. It follows that the positions of the vehicles at time t are given by the formulas:

$$\boldsymbol{A}(t) = \boldsymbol{a}t + \bar{\boldsymbol{a}} \text{ and } \boldsymbol{B}(t) = \boldsymbol{b}t + \bar{\boldsymbol{b}} \quad (8)$$

where

$$\boldsymbol{a} = \left(\frac{v_a}{\sqrt{1 + m_a^2}}, \frac{m_a v_a}{\sqrt{1 + m_a^2}} \right) \text{ and } \boldsymbol{b} = \left(\frac{v_b}{\sqrt{1 + m_b^2}}, \frac{m_b v_b}{\sqrt{1 + m_b^2}} \right). \quad (9)$$

Consider two vehicles R_a and R_b moving along trajectories defined by the straight lines $t \to \boldsymbol{A}(t) := \boldsymbol{a}t + \bar{\boldsymbol{a}}$ and $t \to \boldsymbol{B}(t) := \boldsymbol{b}t + \bar{\boldsymbol{b}}$, where $\boldsymbol{a}, \boldsymbol{b}, \bar{\boldsymbol{a}}, \bar{\boldsymbol{b}}$ are constant vectors in the Euclidean plane. Thus, the initial positions of the vehicles are $\boldsymbol{A}(0) = \bar{\boldsymbol{a}}$ and $\boldsymbol{B}(0) = \bar{\boldsymbol{b}}$. Using elementary calculations and the notation established in this section, we can derive the following:

$$\boldsymbol{A}'(t) = \boldsymbol{a}, \boldsymbol{B}'(t) = \boldsymbol{b} \text{ and } \boldsymbol{U}(t) = (\boldsymbol{b} - \boldsymbol{a})t + \bar{\boldsymbol{b}} - \bar{\boldsymbol{a}} \quad (10)$$

$$\| \boldsymbol{U}(t) \| = \sqrt{\sum_{i=1}^{2}((b_i - a_i)t + (\bar{b}_i - \bar{a}_i))^2} \quad (11)$$

$$\| \boldsymbol{U}(t) \|' = \frac{\sum_{i=1}^{2}(b_i - a_i)}{\sqrt{\sum_{i=1}^{2}((b_i - a_i)t + (\bar{b}_i - \bar{a}_i))^2}} \quad (12)$$

Substituting these formulas into Eq. (5), we can determine the following formula for the change in frequency $f_\Delta(t)$ as measured by the Doppler effect in Theorem 1. We summarize this in the following:

Corollary 1.

$$f_\Delta(t) = -\text{sign}\left(\sum_{i=1}^{2}(b_i - a_i) \right) \cdot \frac{|<\boldsymbol{a} - \boldsymbol{b}, (\boldsymbol{b} - \boldsymbol{a})t + \bar{\boldsymbol{b}} - \bar{\boldsymbol{a}}>|}{\sqrt{\sum_{i=1}^{2}((b_i - a_i)t + (\bar{b}_i - \bar{a}_i))^2}} \cdot \frac{f_0}{c}, \quad (13)$$

where f_0 is the transmission frequency and c is the sound speed.

4   Receiver Design

Underwater communications use sound waves. Significant communication impairments include attenuation and numerous sources of noise [7]. For long range communications, attenuation is an important issue. It is due to conversion of acoustic energy into heat and geometrical spreading. Its importance grows with distance and frequency. Hence, for long distances, solely the use of low frequencies can be envisioned. Another important fact is the gradient of the attenuation versus frequency. It limits the operating bandwidth. The half-power bandwidth is commonly used to define cutoff frequencies and bandwidths of filters by using frequency response curves, using 3 dB points in the frequency response of a band-pass filter [13]. At low frequency (in the few kilohertz range) attenuation is low relative to higher frequencies (e.g., 20 kilohertz), but the gradient of the attenuation is high. Consequently, the half-power bandwidth is very narrow, i.e., just a few Hz. Solely narrow-band modulation is possible, i.e., a few Hz.

We revisit the receiver design in [12], addressing low frequency underwater acoustic communications. The sender design is exactly as originally defined in [12], which is based on ideas authored by Taylor and Walker [14], Franke and Taylor [15], Karn [16] and Fano [11]. The associated protocol is asynchronous frame-oriented. Each frame comprises 162 channel symbols, which encode 50 information bits. Convolutional FEC is used, with a constraint of 32 and a rate of 1/2 [11]. Convolutional encoding of the information bits yields 162 bits. They are interleaved with 162 synchronization bits s_i ($i = 1, \ldots, 162$). Every data bit is paired with a synchronization bit. Each pair makes a channel symbol. Modulation is four-tone Multiple Frequency-Shift Keying (MFSK) at 1.46 (375/256) baud. The complex modulation envelope frequencies are -2.2, -0.7, 0.7 and 2.2 Hz, corresponding to channel symbols 0, 1, 2 and 3. The transmission time of a frame is 111 s.

The new receiver has the capability to search for frames with possibly linearly or nonlinearly drifting carriers. Audio is captured by a hydrophone, digitized, band pass filtered and centred to zero Hz. Digitized audio processing is done according to a sliding window model. Each window represents 120 s of channel data. The next window slides in time for nine seconds. Each two-minute interval of channel data is represented as a series of discrete complex samples $x_0, x_1, \ldots, x_{N-1}$. In the sequel, N is set to 45,000 samples. Hence, the sampling rate f_s is $N/120 = 375$ samples per second (sps). Each channel symbol is represented by 256 samples. A frame consists of 256 samples per symbol times 162 channel symbols, i.e., 41,472 samples.

Each window of channel data is searched for the presence of 111-second frames. Windowed Discrete Fourier Transforms (DFTs) are calculated. Each DFT represents a time interval corresponding to the duration of two symbols, i.e., 512 samples. The size ν of each DFT is 512 bins. The DFTs are calculated from the beginning of a two-minute interval, in steps of half symbol (128 samples). The number of DFTs is: $n = \lfloor N/128 \rfloor - 3 = 348$ DFTs. The term "-3" is present because calculations of windowed DFTs stop before the third to last half-sample. At 375 sps and according to Nyquist criterion, the frequency range of each DFT is lower than $375/2$ Hz, i.e., including the negative frequencies within the range ± 187 Hz. From frequency-bin-to-frequency-bin, there is an offset Δf of $375/512 = 0.73$ Hz. Let m be equal to $\lfloor 187 \cdot \nu/f_s \rfloor = 255$. Every coefficient of the DFTs is denoted as $X_{i,j}$, with the window index i in the range $0, \ldots, n-1$ and frequency index j in the range $-m+1, \ldots, 0, \ldots, m-1$. Every DFT coefficient is defined as:

$$X_{i,j} = \sum_{t=0}^{\nu-1} x_{128i+t} \cdot w(t) \cdot e^{-\sqrt{-1} \cdot 2\pi jt/\nu} \tag{14}$$

where $w(t) = \sin\left(\frac{\pi}{512} \cdot t\right)$ is the windowing function. Equation (14) represents the relative amplitude and phase of frequency $\frac{j \cdot f_s \text{ sps}}{\nu \text{ samples}}$ Hz. In the frequency domain, every two-minute time interval is represented by the following matrix:

$$X = \begin{bmatrix} X_{0,-m+1} & \cdots & X_{0,0} & \cdots & X_{0,m-1} \\ \vdots & \cdots & \vdots & \cdots & \vdots \\ X_{n-1,-m+1} & \cdots & X_{n-1,0} & \cdots & X_{n-1,m-1} \end{bmatrix} \tag{15}$$

The frequency domain representation is used for a coarse signal search. The procedure looks for candidates in the frequency domain, i.e., columns in matrix (15), where there is a *local Signal-to-Noise Ratio (SNR) maximum*, see [12]. Using the corresponding frequencies as candidate carriers, refined signal paths are searched. A path is defined by a *signal tracking function* $f_\theta : \{0 \ldots n-1\} \mapsto \{-m+1 \ldots 0 \ldots m-1\}$, where θ is a parameter of f. Let Φ denote the set of all instances of such signal tracking functions (assume it is finite size, i.e., there is a finite number of functions and the domains of their parameters are finite).

Example 1. *Tracking of a signal not subject to the Doppler effect, i.e., its frequency is not drifting, is represented by a constant function $f(i) = c$, where i is the half-symbol index and c is the carrier frequency.*

Example 2. *Tracking of a signal subject to a Doppler effect such that the carrier frequency is drifting linearly, is represented by function $f_\delta(i) = c + \delta i$. The parameter δ represents the quantity of frequency drift per half symbol.*

Example 3. *Tracking of a signal subject to a Doppler effect such that the carrier frequency is drifting nonlinearly, is represented by an arbitrary function. The number of possibilities is $(2m-1)^n$, i.e., exponential. An approach for handling this case is further discussed in Sect. 5.*

For each candidate signal, defined by a signal tracking function f_θ, this step finds a coarse time offset, from the start of a two minute interval. Each candidate signal is examined. A complete frame can start anywhere from the beginning to a time delay corresponding to nine seconds (26 half symbols) into the interval. Let $W_{i,j} = |X_{i,j}|$ denote the magnitude spectrum at indices i and j. For signal tracking function f_θ, the timing offset τ is the value in the range $0, \ldots, 26$ that maximizes the sum:

$$\sum_{i=1+\tau}^{162} (2s_i - 1) \left[\frac{(W_{i,f_\theta(i)-4} + W_{i,f_\theta(i)+1}) - (W_{i,f_\theta(i)-4} + W_{i,f_\theta(i)+1})}{\sum_{k=-4,-1,1,4} |W_{i,f_\theta(i)+k}|} \right]$$

The summation measures the correlation of the spectrum power around frequency $f_\theta(i)$ with the synchronization bit-string s. The multiplicand $2s_i - 1$ maps the synchronization bit s_i, which is 0 or 1, to value -1 or 1. The term $W_{i,f_\theta(i)-4} + W_{i,f_\theta(i)+1}$ is the sum of the power at the frequencies of synchronization bit value 1, while the term $W_{i,f_\theta(i)-4} + W_{i,f_\theta(i)+1}$ is the sum of the power at the frequencies of synchronization bit value 0. The denominator represents the sum of all power around frequency $f_\theta(i)$. The power at synchronization bits is relativized to all the power at the candidate frequency.

For each signal tracking function f_θ, over a symbol interval of length T, the power is summed to obtain the energy ($f = -2.2, -0.7, 0.7, 2.2$):

$$r_{i,f} + \sqrt{-1}q_{i,f} = \sum_{t=iT+\tau}^{(i+1)T+\tau} x_t \cdot e^{-\sqrt{-1}2\pi[f_\theta(t)\cdot0.73+f]t} \tag{16}$$

Which is mapped to a magnitude $P_{i,f} = |r_{i,f} + \sqrt{-1}q_{i,f}|$. The four magnitudes $P_{i,f}$ are used to calculate soft symbols. A soft symbol represents a value and its quality. Receive quality metrics are associated with the symbols. This information is used in the decoding process. The most likely symbols are selected first. A de-interleaving procedure reorders the 162 data soft symbols. The resulting 162 soft symbols are passed to a FEC decoder. This part is exactly as originally defined in [12].

5   Evaluation

The exponential search space of the nonlinear case (Example 3) poses a practical problem of time complexity. We resolve this issue making assumptions about the mobility profiles of the vehicles. The Doppler effect is an issue relative to two vehicles, a transmitter and a receiver. In the underwater environment, assumptions can be made about their positions, trajectories and speeds. It is reasonable to assume self position and speed awareness [17]. It is also plausible to suppose that a peer is travelling along a sea route or a navigation channel. Assumptions can also be made regarding its speed [3]. Hence, a straight line model, as discussed in Sect. 3, can be used to make tractable the problem of searching nonlinearly drifting signals. The search space, i.e., the size of the signal tracking function set Φ, is limited to a number of plausible trajectories. The trajectory model of Eq. (6) is applied with assumptions with respect to the domains for the slopes of the lines (m_a, m_b), constants (c_a, c_b), positions of the vehicles $(\bar{a}, \bar{b})$ and speeds (v_a, v_b). Corollary 1 is applied. Assuming ranges of values for parameters in Eq. (6), the Doppler shift-handling aspect of the decoding search strategy is summarized in Fig. 2. Three embedded loops generate plausible mobility tuples (m_a, v_a, x, y) for vehicle a including a slope m_a in the interval $[m_{min}, m_{max}]$, a velocity v_a in $[v_{min}, v_{max}]$ and a position (x, y) in $[(x, y)_{min}, (x, y)_{max}]$. The corresponding signal tracking function f_θ is produced and used in the energy search (Eq. (16)) and demodulation. We simulated the following three cases for a transmitter and a receiver moving following the motion model presented in Sect. 3: (i) transmissions without any Doppler shifts (base case); (ii) transmissions with linear Doppler shifts; (iii) transmissions with nonlinear Doppler shifts. The data set used to evaluate the nonlinear case is pictured in Fig. 3. Each curve represents the frequency drift captured by one of the individual nonlinear test. It plots the carrier frequency (within 1496 Hz and 1502 Hz) as a function of time, from zero to 120 s. Speed varies from five to 10 km/h. Light color is 5 km/h and as you go darker it increases to 10 km/h. The 10 curves close together are due to variation in x ordinate. Trajectories in the Euclidean plane are pictured in Fig. 4. Each trace of hollow circles represents a transmitter trajectory, together with the start position (red star). Start coordinate x is varied from -800 m to one km in steps 100 m. Start coordinate y is always zero. The receiver (blue star) is fixed at the origin. The results of the evaluation are shown in Fig. 5. The plots show our estimates when there is no Doppler shift (base), linear Doppler shift and nonlinear Doppler shifts during reception of a frame. 300 packets were sent to obtain each data point. The base an linear cases data points were obtained using the original receiver in Ref [12]. The nonlinear case data points were obtained using the receiver described in this paper. According to our simulations, our protocol can operate from the -25 dB SNR range (assuming a 2.5 kHz noise bandwidth). Compared with the data obtained in other research [18], SNRs well above zero are required to obtain similar performance. For equivalent Packet Error Rate (PER) performance and equivalent noise conditions, our protocol can operate with weaker signals. Of course, our data rate is much lower (0.5 bps) and packets are very short (50 bits of data). Using curve fitting, a performance model is produced, see Table 1. The PER as a function of the SNR is modelled with function $f(x) = e^{-\beta(x+32)}$, were x is the SNR. Values for parameter β and 95% confidence bounds are provided.

Algorithm 1 The new operations of the protocol decoder

01: **for** $m_{min} < m_a < m_{max}$ // *slope search*

02:    **for** $v_{min} < v_a < v_{max}$ // *velocity search*

03:       **for** $(x,y)_{min} < (x,y) < (x,y)_{max}$ // *position search*

04:          find the best tuple (m_a, v_a, x, y)

05:          use the tuple to identify candidate signals w.r.t. energy & frequency search

06:          store candidate signals as f_θ

07:          use f_θ w.r.t. time & demodulation // *time resolution & signal demodulation*

08:       **end for**

09:    **end for**

10: **end for**

Fig. 2. Trajectory parameter enumeration of the decoding search strategy.

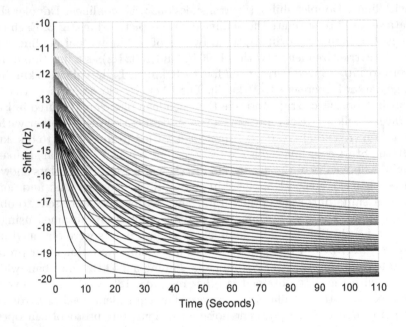

Fig. 3. Curves representing the frequency drift captured by one of the test cases.

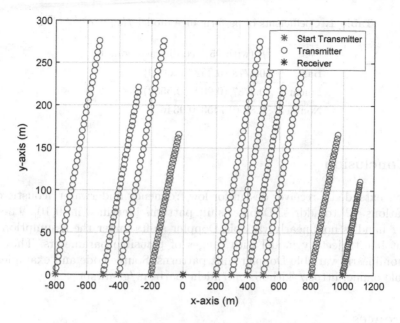

Fig. 4. Evaluated trajectories of transmitter and location of receiver. (Color figure online)

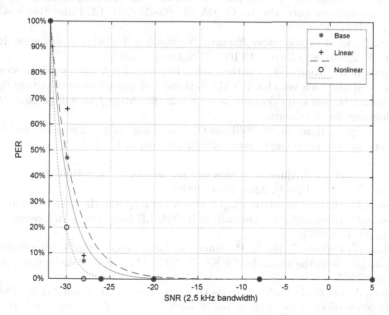

Fig. 5. PER versus SNR for the base case (no Doppler). (Color figure online)

Table 1. Coefficients of performance model $f(x) = e^{-\beta(x+32)}$.

Case	β (with 95% confidence bounds)
Base	0.4778 (0.3527, 0.6029)
Linear	0.3787 (0.2021, 0.5552)
Noninear	0.84 (0.7453, 0.9346)

6 Conclusion

We have extended a receiver design for low frequency underwater acoustic communications [12] to address Doppler shift patterns identified in [9,10]. The new receiver handles nonlinearly variable Doppler shifts under the assumption of a straight line trajectory model with ranges of plausible parameters. They produce nonlinearly variable Doppler shift patterns. Source code and examples are available online: https://github.com/michelbarbeau/gr-uwspr.

References

1. Otnes, R., Voldhaug, J.E., Haavik, S.: On communication requirements in underwater surveillance networks. In: OCEANS 2008-MTS/IEEE Kobe Techno-Ocean, pp. 1–7. IEEE (2008)
2. Otnes, R., et al.: Underwater Acoustic Networking Techniques. Springer, Heidelberg (2012). https://doi.org/10.1007/978-3-642-25224-2
3. Button, R.W., Kamp, J., Curtin, T.B., Dryden, J.: A survey of missions for unmanned undersea vehicles. RAND National Defense Research Institute (2009)
4. Wikipedia: Underwater locator beacon (2018). https://en.wikipedia.org/wiki/Underwater_locator_beacon
5. Decarpigny, J., Hamonic, B., Wilson, O.: The design of low frequency underwater acoustic projectors: present status and future trends. IEEE J. Ocean. Eng. **16**(1), 107–122 (1991)
6. Hixson, E.: A low-frequency underwater sound source for seismic exploration. J. Acoust. Soc. Am. **126**(4), 2234–2234 (2009)
7. Stojanovic, M.: On the relationship between capacity and distance in an underwater acoustic communication channel. SIGMOBILE Mob. Comput. Commun. Rev. **11**(4), 34–43 (2007)
8. Freitag, L., Partan, J., Koski, P., Singh, S.: Long range acoustic communications and navigation in the arctic. In: OCEANS 2015 - MTS/IEEE Washington, pp. 1–5, October 2015
9. Ahmad, A.-M., Barbeau, M., Garcia-Alfaro, J., Kassem, J., Kranakis, E., Porretta, S.: Doppler effect in the underwater acoustic ultra low frequency band. In: Zhou, Y., Kunz, T. (eds.) Ad Hoc Networks. LNICST, vol. 223, pp. 3–12. Springer, Cham (2018). https://doi.org/10.1007/978-3-319-74439-1_1
10. Ahmad, A.-M., Barbeau, M., Garcia-Alfaro, J., Kassem, J., Kranakis, E., Porretta, S.: Doppler effect in the acoustic ultra low frequency band for wireless underwater networks. Mob. Netw. Appl. (2018). https://doi.org/10.1007/s11036-018-1036-9

11. Fano, R.: A heuristic discussion of probabilistic decoding. IEEE Trans. Inf. Theory **9**(2), 64–74 (1963)
12. Barbeau, M.: Weak signal underwater communications in the ultra low frequency band. In: Proceedings of the 7th GNU Radio Conference, San Diego, CA, U.S.A., pp. 1–8 (2017). https://pubs.gnuradio.org/index.php/grcon/article/view/20/14
13. Wu, B.: A correction of the half-power bandwidth method for estimating damping. Arch. Appl. Mech. **85**, 315–320 (2015)
14. Taylor, J., Walker, B.: WSPRing around the world. QST **94**(10), 30–32 (2010)
15. Franke, S., Taylor, J.: WSPR (2017). Accessed 9 May 2017
16. Karn, P.: Convolutional decoders for amateur packet radio. In: ARRL Digital Communications Conference, pp. 45–50 (1995)
17. McCartney, B.S.: Underwater acoustic positioning systems: state of the art and applications in deep water. Int. Hydrograph. Rev. **LVIII**(1), 91–113 (1981)
18. Blouin, S., Barbeau, M.: An experimental baseline for underwater acoustic broadcasts. In: 2017 IEEE 86th Vehicular Technology Conference (VTC-Fall), pp. 1–5, September 2017

FPMIPv6-S: An Enhanced Mobility Protocol for 6LoWPAN-Based Wireless Mobile Sensor Networks

Abdelwahed Berguiga[1(✉)], Ahlem Harchay[1], Mohamed Kassab[2], and Habib Youssef[3]

[1] Jouf University, Sakakah, Saudi Arabia
{awberguiga,ahberguiga}@ju.edu.sa
[2] Monastir University, Monastir, Tunisia
mohamed.kassab@gmail.com
[3] Sousse University, Sousse, Tunisia
habib.youssef@fsm.rnu.tn

Abstract. In this paper, we propose an IP-based mobility management protocol named Fast handover Proxy Mobile IPv6 for Sensor networks (FPMIPv6-S). FPMIPv6-S provides network-based mobility support for 6LoWPAN WSN when a sensor node moves between two Personal Area Networks (PANs). It is an improved version of the Proxy Mobile IPv6 (PMIPv6) protocol proposed for mobility management in IPv6 networks. We compared via simulations FPMIPv6-S with other well-known mobility protocol namely Mobile IPv6. Performance results show that our proposed protocol achieves reduction of packet loss by as much 70% and improve the network throughput by over 25% compared to MIPv6. Further, we implemented our proposed protocol and MIPv6 with NS3 simulator and made extensive simulations runs to compare both protocols.

1 Introduction

Wireless sensor networks constitute a disruptive technology that is affecting our way of life dramatically. They are used in health, environmental control, agriculture, smart home, to cite few. Sensors are low cost tiny devices and when combined together can achieve marvelous things. For example, in the healthcare field, a patient can wear wireless sensors that monitor some of their vital signs (temperature, heart beat frequency, blood pressure sensors, etc.). A distant doctor can communicate with each of these sensors through the Internet to acquire the patient's condition parameters and enable to quickly detect abnormal situations.

The opportunities opened up by this technology have led some companies and standards such as Amtel, Cisco, Intel SAP, Sun Microsystems and others to found the "IP for Smart Objects (IPSO)" corporate alliance to promote the use of IP for Low-power and lossy devices. Accordingly, the IETF 6LoWPAN

© Springer Nature Switzerland AG 2018
N. Montavont and G. Z. Papadopoulos (Eds.): ADHOC-NOW 2018, LNCS 11104, pp. 252–263, 2018.
https://doi.org/10.1007/978-3-030-00247-3_23

working group is organized to define the problem of supporting "IPv6 over Low Power Wireless Area Networks" [1].

There are still some problems in applying IPv6 mobile standards to 6LoW-PAN WSN. Sensor devices are energy and resource constrained. Enabling mobility related IP protocols in these devices may lead to rapid depletion of battery resources due the control messages exchanged to synchronize with the new access router. Also, mobility management protocols proposed for IPv6-based networks such as MIPv6 are host-based, i.e., the mobile node plays an active role at the occurrence of any mobility event. This will lead to rapid depletion of battery resources.

Mobility management in IP-based wireless sensor networks is still an open issue. Many research efforts seek to develop solutions to guaranteed low hand-off latency, reduce the packet loss rate, resolve the binding requests scheduling problem, and improve energy efficiency. The proposed FPMIPv6-S protocol is integrated with the routing protocol for Low-power and Lossy networks RPL. This paper provides major extensions to our previous work presented in [2–4]. The major extensions consist of the following:

- A correct implementation of FPMIPv6-S, MIPv6, and IEEE802.15.4 within NS3 simulator, as opposed to reported works, which incorrectly rely on simulations of their protocols assuming IEEE802.11 in the link layer.
- We performed a thorough performance evaluation via simulations of FPMIPv6-S. Simulation results show that FPMIPv6-S offers a feasible implementation and deployment mobility management solution for IPv6 based sensor networks. Indeed, it presents several advantages, namely (1) it avoids software complexity of network entities, (2) it has much lower handoff and signaling cost thus minimizing power consumption, (3) it eliminates binding update message storms, and (4) it reduces packet loss rate. Performance results show that the proposed scheme can significantly reduce the packet loss rate by nearly 70%, and improve the network throughput by over 25%.

The remainder of this paper is organized as follows: Sect. 2 discusses related work and focuses on the classification criteria of existing mobility management protocols proposed for wireless sensor networks. Section 3 presents a detailed description of FPMIPv6-S. In Sect. 4, we provide performance results obtained with simulations. Section 5 concludes the paper and suggests some perspectives.

2   Related Work

Mobility can be defined as the ability of a device to access all services to which it has usually access regardless of its location. Changing the access network leads to change the link between two communicating nodes. When a node moves and changes its attachment point, a set of procedures should be performed before being able to send or receive data. These procedures include: (i) validate all conditions of changing the radio link, (ii) establish a connection with the new attachment point, (iii) acquiring a valid IP address.

This mobility can be classified into two classes; a micro-mobility and a macro-mobility. With the first class, mobility occurs in the same network domain that is the mobile node keeps the same network prefix, whereas with the macro-mobility, the mobile node changes network domain and thus the network prefix. Also, mobility can happen either on a single Mobile node, named as a *"terminal mobility"* or a set of MNs move together referred to as *"network mobility (or group mobility)"*.

2.1   Terminal Mobility

The IETF has proposed several mobility management protocols for IP networks to maintain connectivity of mobile nodes regardless of the type of handover. These protocols can be classified into two groups: the first is called *"host-based mobility solutions"*, and the second is the *"network-assisted mobility solutions"*.

Host-Based Mobility Management Schemes. Existing protocols for IP mobility management such as MIPv6 [5] and HMIPv6 [6] are not suitable for WSNs. Indeed, MIPv6 and HMIPv6 are host-based protocols where the mobile device exchanges several control messages to ensure the communication continuity during his movement from one location to another. Moreover, deploying these protocols in wireless mobile sensor networks require protocol stack modification of mobile devices.

Montavont et al. [7] stated that Mobile IPv6 can be a useful solution to achieve layer 3 mobility on 6LoWPAN by evaluating a light version of Mobile IPv6 over 6LoWPAN. In this work, authors proposed a new mechanism called MOBINET that relies on overhearing in the neighborhood of a mobile node. By detecting a change in the neighborhood, the mobile node sends router solicitation in order to resume the neighbor discovery mechanism. However, the overhearing process requires the reception of unnecessary packets, which increases network overhead and consequently energy consumption.

Shin et al. [8] proposed a 6LoPWAN mobility management architecture where a sensor node only moved within a personal area network (PAN). In this architecture, if a sensor node's position changed, then it had to register the new position's information with all the gateway nodes. However, authors discussed neither the IPv6 address configuration algorithm for all-IP WSN nor the routing scheme.

Network-Based Mobility Management Schemes. Islam et al. [9] have proposed a Sensor Proxy Mobile IPv6 (SPMIPv6) scheme, a network-based mobility scheme which follows the idea of PMIPv6 [10]. The protocol presents the network architecture and message formats, and its performance is evaluated including mobility handover cost and delay. The data results show that SPMIPv6 reduces the mobility handover cost significantly.

Petajajarvi et al. [11] propose a soft handover for WSNs based on 6LoW-PAN (SH-WSN6). The proposal allows mobile sensor nodes to be registered with several attachments points (gateways - APs) at the same time. The APs periodically broadcast router advertisement (RtrAdv) packets to announce their presence. These RtrAdv packets enable mobile node to decide for the best gateway. If a node receives a RtrAdv from an AP, it checks if it is already registered with it or not. If not, the node replies with a registration message.

2.2 Sensor Group Mobility

Many researchers have proposed Network Mobility Basic Support (NEMO-BS) protocol to address the management needs of the global mobility of an entire network named "mobile network". NEMO protocol has been standardized as a solution for supporting network mobility based on MIPv6. Within the Internet of Things, such scenario can be found in many applications, such as patient health status monitoring, military applications, etc.

The basic idea is to use a mobile router (MR) to perform the handoff process of the entire network behind this router. The IP devices on the mobile network, mobile network nodes (MNNs), are either fixed to the mobile network, named fixed mobile node (FMN), or visiting the mobile network, named visiting mobile node (VMN). Mobile network nodes are not aware of the network's mobility given that all traffic sent/received by the mobile network must be transited by the mobile router. Therefore, in NEMO, network complexity brought back to the mobile router since it acts as an aggregation point for mobility management and routing.

Only few studies have focused on NEMO to prove its suitability in WSNs. For example, in [12] Kim et al. have proposed a mobility support scheme for IP WSN based on Network Mobility protocol. In the scheme, mobile routers are proposed to achieve the mobility support. In order to minimize the signaling overhead, a compressed mobility header is added into the IPv6 payload. However, this header was not compatible with the layered design principles of the IPv6 protocol, as well as they do not consider neither the 6LoWPAN node mobility nor a unique addresses for each sensor node.

To address these problems, PMIPv6 can be considered as the most suitable protocol which can be integrated with NEMO, aiming at reducing the signaling overhead and handoff latency during mobility. Our scheme, FPMIPv6-S, follows a hybrid network and sensor group-based approaches.

3   Proposed FPMIPv6-S Mobility Scheme

3.1 FPMIPv6-S Protocol Architecture

In this section, we describe our proposed Fast handover scheme for Sensor Proxy Mobile IPv6.

The main objective of FPMIPv6-S is to reduce the handover latency of 6LoW-PAN MN while moving and changing the attachment point.

In our wireless mobile sensor network design, as shown in Fig. 1, we assume that we have five important entities:

- **Sensor Local Mobility Anchor (SLMA):** It is the root of the DAG (DODAG root) and it acts like a Home Agent in Mobile IP. SLMA is selected during network installation and configuration. The construction of the new DODAG begins at the SLMA that broadcast a DIO message to announce its DODAGID, its rank information, and the OF. SLMA is responsible to provide connectivity of the 6LoWPAN mobile nodes (descendants) to external networks. Herein, the term external networks may be other DAGs in the same or different RPL instance.
- **Sensor Mobile Access Gateway (SMAG):** Acts like an access gateway router. It performs the mobility-related signaling with SLMA on behalf of the MN. Packets sent/received to/from the MN are routed through a tunnel created between the SMAG that is currently serving the 6LoWPAN MN and the SLMA.
- **Access Point (AP):** Is a device that allows mobile nodes to connect to a wired network using IEEE 802.15.4 standard. An access point is connected to an SMAG and its main role is to detect MN's movements.
- **6LoWPAN MN:** It is a full-function device (FFD) that can move randomly from one place to another. The 6LoWPAN MN can be one single node or a set of sensor nodes attached to mobile node (vehicle, clothes, human body, etc.) that move together as a single unit. In such case, one of the sensor nodes in the group is selected to act as a *coordinator*. The coordinator has the responsibility to receive all data collected by other sensors and forward them to the access point. Also, only the coordinator needs to exchange control messages with the AP.
- **Corresponding Node (CN):** It is the end-user. The CN device receives collected data from 6LoWPAN MNs. All data gathered by the 6LoWPAN MN are sent towards the end-user via AP, SMAG, and SLMA.

3.2 Protocol Vocabulary

As discussed in Sect. 3.1, we have considered a wireless mobile network where 6LoWPAN MNs move randomly.

A number of control messages should be exchanged among FPMIPv6-S entities to perform the binding, handoff, and communication processes in the Sensor PMIPv6 domain.

Structure of Modified DIS Message. The DIS message is sent by a node to solicit DIO messages from neighboring nodes. We exploited one of the unused flag bits to indicate whether the DIS message carries or not a FPMIPv6-S message. This is the first bit which we refer to as the "S-bit". If the "S-bit" is set, then it is an SDIS message, i.e. a DIS carrying an FPMIPv6-S message, else (that is, $S = 0$), it indicates a regular DIS message. Note that the SDIS message MUST include 6LoWPAN MN identifier (coordinator ID).

Structure of Modified DAO Message. As with DIS message, if the "S-bit" is set, then it is an SDAO message, i.e. a DAO carrying an FPMIPv6-S message, else (that is, S = 0), it indicates a regular DAO message. The SDAO message includes, among others, the previous Access Point (p-AP) address.

3.3   FPMIPv6-S Procedural Rules

Figure 1 shows the time sequence diagram relative to the messages exchanged when a node moves from one SMAG to another within the same DODAG. We can distinguish 8 steps:

- **Step 1:** with native RPL, SMAGs broadcast periodically DIO messages to maintain network topology. A "Trickle Timers" [13] has been adopted to schedule the transmission of unsolicited DIO messages and therefore eliminate redundant control messages. The timer's duration is adaptive and increases exponentially with network stability. However, with wireless mobile sensor network, as the topology changes continuously, the timer mechanism is not efficient given that a node moves randomly and hence can change its parent periodically.
  Instead of waiting for the trickle timers expiration, we propose, as an alternative, that when a 6LoWPAN MN[1] enters in the covered area of a new AP, and if it is willing to select it as an appropriate parent, it sends an SDIS message.
- **Step 2 and 3:** On receiving the SDIS message from MN, the n-AP issues a DIO message immediately without waiting for timer expiration. The information conveyed in the DIO message includes: the DAGID, rank information, and objective function identified by Objective Code Point (OCP).
  Upon receiving a DIO message, describing how the network is pre-configured, the coordinator initiates immediately the exchange of the handoff information by sending the SDAO message to the n-AP.
- **Step 4 and 5:** The network update mechanism is started in the new PAN as soon as the new AP receives the SDAO message. However, based on its neighbor local table, n-AP can determine the previous SMAG (p-SMAG) address according to the p-AP address received on the SDAO message. Then, the n-AP initiates the exchange of the handoff information by sending the Handover Initiate (HI) message to the previous SMAG. When the serving SMAG receives the HI, it updates its routing table and replies by sending a Handover Acknowledgment message (HAck). The HAck message contains the SLMA address that is currently serving the MN.
- **Step 6:** Once the n-AP receives the HAck message, it sends an SDAO message to its parent the new SMAG (n-SMAG) to populate the new attached MN.
- **Step 7:** The n-SMAG sends an SBU message to the SLMA on behalf of the MN. The SBU message contains the default information like PBU message

---

[1] Herein, the term 6LoWPAN mobile node is the same as a MN, coordinator, and a body coordinator.

on PMIPv6 plus the MN ID. Upon receiving the SBU message by SLMA, it will first check if the MN already belongs to the DODAG. If it does, SLMA searches its binding table to find which SMAG is currently serving the MN. Then, SLMA updates the requesting 6LoWPAN MN in its Binding Cache Entry with the new SMAG. Otherwise, SLMA allocates an appropriate home network prefix and create a new Binding Cache Entry for the coordinator.

- **Step 8:** After successfully updating the MN, SLMA will reply with a SBA message to the n-SMAG. The SBA contains the SMAG address who's the CN is attached for delivery data packets, and HNP of the mobile node. The n-SMAG then sets up a bidirectional tunnel with SLMA for the routing of traffic to and from the 6LoWPAN MN. After that, n-SMAG sends, via n-AP, a RtrAdvFP message to 6LoWPAN MN to advertise MN-HNP as the hosted on-link prefix. RtrAdvFP is a new format message of Router Advertisement standard message. RtrAdvFP message contains the following parameters: $<Header, ICMPv6, CoordinatorID, HNP_1, HNP_2, \ldots, HNP_n>$, where HNP_i indicate the Home Network Prefix of the ith wireless sensor.

4 Performance Evaluation

4.1 Simulation Results

In this section, we detail the performance evaluation of the proposed solution FPMIPv6-S and compare it with the existing MIPv6 protocol. This study was performed by simulation using the NS-3 network simulator tool. We analyze the performance of the two protocols in terms of throughput, packet loss ratio, and end-to-end delay. First, we quickly describe the simulation set-up and the evaluation methodology, then we show the obtained results.

Simulation Setup. In order to figure out the performance of FPMIPv6-S, we performed extensive simulations comparing it with MIPv6. We assume that all sensors are mobile nodes except the APs, SMAGs, and SLMA. In our simulation scenarios, we varied the mobile sensors from 5 to 50 nodes. The nodes are assumed randomly scattered in a 200 m × 400 m sensing area. The experimental evaluation uses the *"Random Walk Mobility Model"*. The direction of 6LoWPAN MNs is chosen independently and randomly.

The scenarios consider a 6LoWPAN mobile node that travels across two SMAGs within the same proxy domain.

It should also be mentioned, that as opposed to many other researchers who adopted the 802.11 MAC layer standard in their simulations, in our NS-3 models, we have implemented the association/disassociation procedure defined by IEEE 802.15.4 standard.

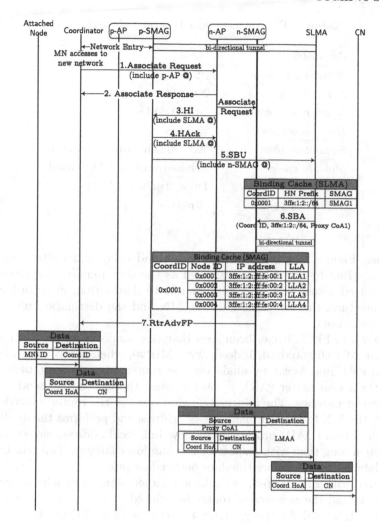

Fig. 1. FPMIPv6-S handover procedure

All simulations are performed 30 times with different random number seeds and the results are averaged over all the outcomes [14].

Table 1 summarizes the common simulation parameters used in all scenarios.

Simulation Discussions. In this study, we evaluate the proposed FPMIPv6-S approach with simulations. We used three QoS criteria to be used for the evaluation: (1) the network latency; (2) the packet loss rate; (3) and the throughput.

Network Latency. The main aim of a seamless handover is to minimize the interruption of packet transmissions during moving away from the parent AP

Table 1. Performance evaluation related parameters

Parameter	Value
Network simulator	NS-3
Network size	200 m × 400 m
Number of mobile nodes	5-to-50 nodes
Data packet size	35 bytes
Simulation time	300 s 30 simulations/scenario
Mobility model	Random walk mobility model
Sensor nodes velocity	1 m/s; 2 m/s; 3 m/s; 4 m/s
Number of packets	10 pkts/s

to another. Figures 2 and 3 show the end-to-end delay and packet loss ratio, respectively. End-to-end delay is regarded as the time required for a packet to be transmitted across a network from source to destination. From our simulation architecture, the source node is the MN and the destination node is the correspondent node.

As shown in Fig. 2, it can been seen that the handover with FPMIPv6-S is faster than MIPv6 standard. Indeed, with MIPv6, when a MN looses connection with its Home Agent by analysing the router advertisement periodically sent by the access router (AR), it must request the new AR to send a router advertisement message. The information contained in the router advertisement will allow the MN to create a new care-of address and performs the duplication address detection (DAD) process on its new link-local address. However, DAD takes quite a long time with respect to the handover latency. This will increase handoff latency and therefore the data packet loss rate.

However, with FPMIPv6-S, as explained earlier, signaling traffic between the mobile node and the new access router is reduced, which lead to a significant reduction of the handoff latency. Figure 4 shows the handoff delay. It can be seen that with the increase of network node number the handoff delay of MIPv6 and FPMIPv6-S also increase. This is mainly due to the fact that as the number of nodes increases, the signaling workload of the mobility agents increases as well. We can see that the handoff performance of FPMIPv6-S is better than MIPv6. However, when a mobile node moves between two access points, handoff delay increases with extra messages exchanging between mobile node and the access point in the visited network. Such messages play a major part of the overall handoff delay. To attain seamless mobility, handoff latency and packet loss need to be reduced. Our approach aims at reducing the handoff latency and minimizing the signaling overhead in the network by restricting handoff related signaling to mobility agents such as SMAG and SLMA.

Packet Loss Rate. Figure 5 depicts the packet loss rate in terms of network size and the velocity of sensor nodes in proxy domain. We can see that the packet

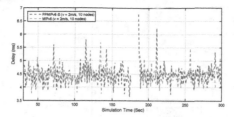

Fig. 2. handoff delay

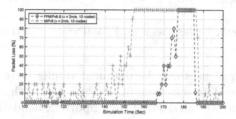

Fig. 3. Packet loss ratio

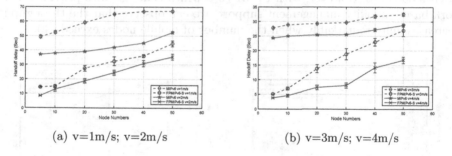

(a) v=1m/s; v=2m/s   (b) v=3m/s; v=4m/s

Fig. 4. Average handoff delay: FPMIPv6-S vs. MIPv6

loss rate for the two protocols decreases when the MN velocity slightly increases. The reason is that the MN with a slightly higher speed that does not change the average number of handoffs per node, has less handoff time and therefore less time to establish the new connection.

As illustrated in Fig. 5a, MIPv6 suffers from a serious packet loss when the node speed is 1 m/s. It is observed that the packet loss rate is greater than 30% when the node speed is 1 m/s and network size is 10 nodes. This rate increases to 42% for the same node speed and a network size equal to 50 nodes.

Even then, we see that FPMIPv6-S experiences the best packet loss rate for all MN speeds compared with MIPv6. Obviously, given that FPMIPv6-S tries to minimize as possible the handoff, it anticipates the interruption of packet transmission by sending an Associate Request message to associate with the new AP as soon as possible and therefore maintains its connectivity to the corresponding node(s).

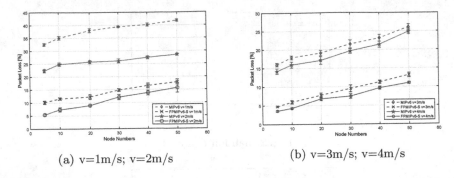

(a) v=1m/s; v=2m/s

(b) v=3m/s; v=4m/s

Fig. 5. Packet loss rate: FPMIPv6-S vs. MIPv6

Throughput. Figure 6 presents the obtained results in terms of the average throughput that is the data sent from 6LoWPAN MN to the CN. As packet loss affects the throughput, we can see that the important handoff delay with MIPv6 has affected the average throughput mainly when sensor speed is equal to 1 m/s. Also, we can see also the sudden decrease of throughput when sensor number reaches 50 nodes. However, with FPMPv6-S which is designed to provide a network based mobility management support, we can observe that the throughput decreases quite remarkably when the number of mobile nodes exceeds 40.

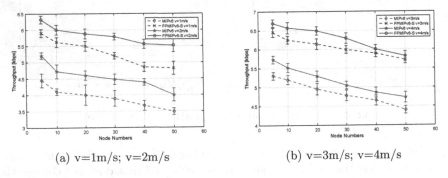

(a) v=1m/s; v=2m/s

(b) v=3m/s; v=4m/s

Fig. 6. Average throughput: FPMIPv6-S vs. MIPv6

5   Conclusion

In this paper, we have proposed a new fast proxy-based mobility management protocol. Based on performance results, FPMIPv6-S seems to provide a reasonable solution to manage mobility in wireless sensor networks. The proposed protocol has been evaluated via NS-3 simulations. Results obtained show significant performance improvement with respect to delay, packet loss, and throughput when compared to MIPv6. Our results also show, that when the node speed is 1 m/s and the number of mobile nodes exceed 40 nodes, throughput and packet loss ratio degrade significantly. Our next step is to deploy an experimental testbed and validate obtained simulation results.

References

1. Kushalnagar, N., Montenegro, G., Schumacher, C.P.: IPv6 over low-power wireless personal area networks, RFC 4919, RFC editor, August 2007. http://www.rfc-editor.org/rfc/rfc4919.txt
2. Berguiga, A., Youssef, H.: A fast handover protocol for 6LoWPAN wireless mobile sensor networks. Telecommun. Syst. 1–20 (2017)
3. Berguiga, A., Youssef, H.: Efficient mobility management in 6LoWPAN wireless sensor networks. In: Proceedings of The Ninth International Conference on Wireless and Mobile Communications (ICWMC 2013), Nice, France, vol. 2126, pp. 244–250 (2013)
4. Berguiga, A., Youssef, H.: A fast handover scheme for proxy-based mobility in wireless sensor networks. In: Proceedings of the 10th ACM International Symposium on Mobility Management and Wireless Access, pp. 139–142. ACM (2012)
5. Johnson, D.B., Perkins, C.E., Arkko, J.: Mobility support in IPv6, RFC 6275, July 2011. http://www.rfc-editor.org/rfc/rfc6275.txt
6. Soliman, H., Castelluccia, C., El Malki, K., Bellier, L.: Hierarchical mobile IPv6 mobility management (HMIPv6), RFC 5380, RFC editor, Fremont, August 2008
7. Montavont, J., Roth, D., Noel, T.: Mobile IPv6 in internet of things: analysis, experimentations and optimizations. Ad Hoc Netw. **14**, 15–25 (2014)
8. Shin, M.-K., Kim, H.-J.: L3 mobility support in large-scale IP-based sensor networks (6LoWPAN). In: 2009 11th International Conference on Advanced Communication Technology, ICACT 2009, vol. 2, pp. 941–945. IEEE (2009)
9. Islam, M.M., Huh, E.-N.: Sensor proxy mobile IPv6 (SPMIPv6)-a novel scheme for mobility supported IP-WSNs. Sensors **11**(2), 1865–1887 (2011)
10. Gundavelli, S., Leung, K., Devarapalli, V., Chowdhury, K., Patil, B.: Proxy mobile IPv6, RFC 5213, RFC editor, August 2008. http://www.rfc-editor.org/rfc/rfc5213.txt
11. Petajajarvi, J., Karvonen, H.: Soft handover method for mobile wireless sensor networks based on 6LoWPAN, pp. 1–6 (2011)
12. Kim, J.H., Hong, C.S., Shon, T.: A lightweight nemo protocol to support 6LoWPAN. ETRI J. **30**(5), 685–695 (2008)
13. Levis, P., Clausen, T., Hui, J., Gnawali, O., Ko, J.: The trickle algorithm (6206). http://www.ietf.org/rfc/rfc6206.txt
14. Marchetta, P., Botta, A., Katz-Bassett, E., Pescapé, A.: Dissecting round trip time on the slow path with a single packet. In: Faloutsos, M., Kuzmanovic, A. (eds.) PAM 2014. LNCS, vol. 8362, pp. 88–97. Springer, Cham (2014). https://doi.org/10.1007/978-3-319-04918-2_9

Distributed Systems and Architectures

Collaborative State Estimation and Actuator Scheduling for Cyber-Physical Systems Under Random Multiple Events

Lei Mo[1](✉), Angeliki Kritikakou[1], and Xianghui Cao[2]

[1] Univ Rennes, Inria, IRISA, CNRS, 35042 Rennes, France
lei.mo@inria.fr, angeliki.kritikakou@irisa.fr
[2] School of Automation, Southeast University, Nanjing 210096, China
xhcao@seu.edu.cn

Abstract. The design of fast and effective coordination among sensors and actuators in Cyber-Physical Systems (CPS) is a fundamental, but challenging issue, especially when the system model is a priori unknown and multiple random events can simultaneously occur. We propose a novel collaborative state estimation and actuator scheduling algorithm with two phases. In the first phase, we propose a Gaussian Mixture Model (GMM)-based method using the random event physical field distribution to estimate the locations and the states of events. In the second phase, based on the number of identified events and the number of available actuators, we study two actuator scheduling scenarios and formulate them as Integer Linear Programming (ILP) problems with the objective to minimize the actuation delay. We validate and demonstrate the performance of the proposed scheme through both simulations and physical experiments for a home temperature control application.

Keywords: Cyber-Physical Systems · Gaussian Mixture Model
Event estimation · Actuator scheduling

1 Introduction

Cyber-Physical Systems (CPS) bridge the cyber world to the physical world through a network of sensors and actuators. Sensors measure the environment, while actuators control the environment based on sensors' information. Wireless sensing and control facilitate the design of mobile systems, enabling closed-loop control of mobile devices, such as automated guided vehicles, mobile robots, and unmanned aerial vehicles. CPS are becoming a promising technology for a wide range of application domains, such as smart building [3], intelligent transportation [7], power grid [6], and industrial control [4].

The sensors are low-cost devices and they are usually largely deployed in the environment. The sensors usually have limited capabilities in terms of power,

© Springer Nature Switzerland AG 2018
N. Montavont and G. Z. Papadopoulos (Eds.): ADHOC-NOW 2018, LNCS 11104, pp. 267–279, 2018.
https://doi.org/10.1007/978-3-030-00247-3_24

communication and computation. Each sensor has a fixed sensing range and its position is usually static. The actuators, based on the state estimation deriving from the sensors' measurements, apply corresponding actions in order to control the environment. Therefore, the actuators have higher capabilities than the sensors. The measured data of the sensors provide only partial information of the physical world, especially when the Region Of Interest (ROI) is large. Therefore, it is unreliable to make actuator decisions based only on a small number of sensors' measurements. In addition, the measurements can be correlated and each measurement may reflect the overlapped effect of multiple events, making difficult to distinguish and localize the different events in the ROI.

Most of the existing works on state estimation and actuator scheduling problems usually assume that the system model is fixed and given in advance, i.e. the position of the events is a priori known [13]. However, when the events occur randomly, the system model cannot be known. It is time-varying and it is determined by the characteristics of events, e.g., the distances among the events and the distances among the sensors and the events. An example of such an unknown system model is the detection and extinction of fires in a given area. There is no priori knowledge when and where the fires will occur, i.e. fires are random occurring events. In case a fire breaks out somewhere, the actuators should be scheduled to the relevant area to handle this event as soon as possible. For the single-event case under unknown system model, state estimation can be performed by applying the Maximum Likelihood Estimation (MLE) method [10]. However, this method is hard to be extended to the multi-event case, since multiple events can be seen as a linear combination of single-events and the weighs of the linear combination cannot be obtained from the MLE. For the multi-event case, the physical field caused by the events forms a surface. Hence, the data fitting methods [11] can be used to estimate the surface function. However, these methods usually require to determine in advance the function order limiting the applicability of these methods.

In this paper, we focus on systems with unknown model where multiple random events can occur simultaneously. We address the challenges of *(1) How to identify, localize and evaluate the occurred events, and (2) How to schedule appropriate actuators to perform fast and effective actions against these events.* Both the event processing delay and the actuation delay should be low, otherwise an event may grow to an urgent level before a certain action takes place. We propose an novel state estimation and actuator scheduling scheme. Our main contributions are:

1. A Gaussian Mixture Model (GMM)-based method to identify, localize and estimate the states of possible multiple events. The proposed method is based on the characteristics of physical field of random events, e.g., the physical filed of a random event, such as fire, follows Gaussian distribution [10]. Then, a virtual sampling method is proposed to improve the estimation accuracy.
2. We consider two possible scenarios based on the number of actuators and the number of identified events and we formulate them as Integer Linear Programming (ILP) problems. The first scenario considers that the number

of actuators is no less than the number of events. Hence, the actuator, which resides nearest to the events, is scheduled to act. The second scenario considers the case when the number of actuators is less than the number of events. Thus, the available actuators should be scheduled to handle the events with high priorities. We propose an approach to predict the change of priority level based on historical date and we propose a predicted-priority-based method to schedule the actuators.

3. We evaluate the performance of our approach by both simulations and experiments based on a physical testbed.

The remainder of this paper is organized as follows. The proposed event estimation and actuator scheduling scheme is described in Sects. 2 and 3, respectively. Simulations and experiments are conducted in Sect. 4. Finally, Sect. 5 concludes this paper.

2   Event Estimation Scheme

We consider a CPS for environmental monitoring and control of a spatial area called Region Of Interest (ROI). We are interested in utilizing l sensors $S_1, \ldots, S_l$ and m actuators $A_1, \ldots, A_m$ to monitor and control the state of n Points Of Interest (POIs) $t = [t_1, \ldots, t_n]'$, e.g., temperature and illumination, within a given threshold $t^* = [t_1^*, \ldots, t_n^*]'$. We consider that the location of the POIs is not fixed and assume that an event e_i occurs at POI$_i$, if $t_i \geq t_i^*$. Since the information exchange among the sensors and the actuators is carried out by the discrete wireless packets [8], we have the following measurement model:

$$z(k) = Ct(k) + \nu(k), \tag{1}$$

where $z(k) = [z_1(k), \ldots, z_l(k)]'$, $z_i(k)$ is the measurement of the sensor S_i at the kth step, C and ν are the measurement matrix and the noise (Gaussian, white and zero-mean) vector with appropriate dimensions, respectively.

To deal with the events in the ROI, two key issues should be addressed: (1) How to estimate the state and the location of the POIs based on the sensor measurement $z(k)$, and (2) How to schedule the actuators to handle the occurring events. (1) shows that the measurement matrix C plays an important role on the estimation of the system states $t(k)$. Usually, the matrix C is determined by the network structure, such as the sensing range of the sensors and the distances between the sensors and the POIs. Most of the existing works are based on the assumption that the matrix C is fixed and given in advance [13]. In contrast to existing approaches, we focus on random events, where the matrix C is unknown.

2.1   Gaussian-Based Physical Field Distribution

We focus on monitor and control of physical variables, whose physical field can be described by Gaussian models, such as temperature and illumination [5,10,12]. Denote (x_i, y_i) as the location of the sensor S_i, and $\tilde{z}_i$ as the normalized value of

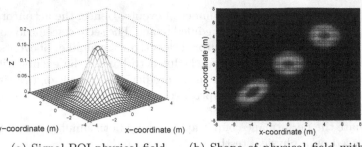

(a) Signal-POI physical field.   (b) Shape of physical field with μ
and σ varying.

Fig. 1. Single-POI case.

sensor S_i's measurement z_i, expressed as $\tilde{z}_i = \frac{z_i - z_{\min}}{z_{\max} - z_{\min}}$, where $z_{\min} = \min_i\{z_i\}$ and $z_{\max} = \max_i\{z_i\}$. When $l \to \infty$, we obtain a complete Gaussian model, as shown in Fig. 1(a) for a single POI.

An intuitive way to estimate the state and the location of the POI is to compare the sensors' measurements $\{z_1, \ldots, z_l\}$ and select the maximum value $z_j = \max_i\{z_i\}$ as the state of the POI and the location of sensor s_j (x_j, y_j) as the location of the POI. However, as the number of sensors is limited, we have to use the limited data set $\{x_i, y_i, z_i\}$ to estimate the state and the location of the POI. With two-dimensional random variables χ, the Gaussian model of Fig. 1(a) is formulated by

$$\mathcal{N}(\chi|\mu, \sigma) = \frac{1}{2\pi (\det \sigma)^{1/2}} \exp\left\{ \frac{(\chi - \mu)' \sigma^{-1} (\chi - \mu)}{-2} \right\}, \qquad (2)$$

where

$$\mu = \begin{bmatrix} \mu_1 \\ \mu_2 \end{bmatrix}, \sigma = \begin{bmatrix} \sigma_1^2 & \rho\sigma_1\sigma_2 \\ \rho\sigma_1\sigma_2 & \sigma_1^2 \end{bmatrix}, \det \sigma = \sigma_1^2\sigma_2^2(1 - \rho^2).$$

Substituting the sensor S_i's location (x_i, y_i) into (2), we obtain the normalized sensor S_i's measurement $\tilde{z}_i = \mathcal{N}((x_j, y_j)|\mu, \sigma)$.

For a fix Gaussian model, its mean μ and covariance σ are constant. The location and the shape of Gaussian model changes with the values of μ and σ. As shown in Fig. 1(b), the Gaussian models of the POIs in $(0, 0)$, $(4, 4)$, $(-4, -4)$ are with the parameters $\{\mu_1 = 0, \mu_2 = 0, \rho = 0, \sigma_1 = 1, \sigma_2 = 1\}$, $\{\mu_1 = 4, \mu_2 = 4, \rho = 0, \sigma_1 = 1, \sigma_2 = 1\}$ and $\{\mu_1 = -4, \mu_2 = -4, \rho = 0.5, \sigma_1 = 1, \sigma_2 = 1\}$, respectively. Hence, the mean μ and the covariance σ determines the location and the shape of Gaussian model, respectively. Since l sensors are deployed in the ROI, we obtain a set of sensor data $\{x_i, y_i, z_i\}$ $(1 \le i \le l)$. Therefore, if the Gaussian parameters μ and σ are estimated from the data set $\{x_i, y_i, z_i\}$, we can use μ and $\mathcal{N}(\mu|\mu, \sigma)$ to describe the location and the state of the POI, respectively. For the single-POI case, MLE is an efficient method to estimate the values of μ and σ [10]. For the multi-POI case, as shown in Fig. 2(a), a linear combination of several Gaussians can characterize the data set. However, the MLE is no

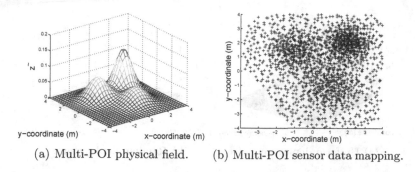

(a) Multi-POI physical field.   (b) Multi-POI sensor data mapping.

Fig. 2. Multi-POI case.

longer suitable for this case since the weights of the linear combination cannot be obtained by MLE. The next section presents our approach to estimate the values of $\{\mu_1, \sigma_1, \ldots, \mu_n, \sigma_n\}$ through the sensor data $\{x_1, y_1, z_1, \ldots, x_l, y_l, z_l\}$ for the multi-POI case.

2.2 Virtual Sample Method

In order to estimate the values of mean μ and covariance σ, we need to plot enough two-dimensional samples $\{s_i^x, s_i^y\}$, which reside within the ellipses that represent the distribution [2]. However, from the sensor measurements, we only obtain a set of three-dimensional data $\{x_i, y_i, z_i\}$. Therefore, we propose a virtual sample method to map the available data $\{x_i, y_i, z_i\}$ to the desired two-dimensional samples $\{s_i^x, s_i^y\}$:

1. The ROI is divided into several grids, such that each grid g_i has the same size and contains at most one sensor S_i.
2. Under a given constant $\mathcal{K}$, $M_i = \mathcal{K}\tilde{z}_i$ virtual samples $\{s_{i,j}^x, s_{i,j}^y\}$ $(1 \leq j \leq M_i)$ are uniformly deployed in the grid g_i.

Denote $s = \{s_1^x, s_1^y, \ldots, s_N^x, s_N^y\}$ as the total virtual samples, where $N = \sum_{i=1}^l M_i$ is the total number of the virtual samples. The virtual samples of the sensor data in Fig. 2(a) are shown in Fig. 2(b). From this figure, we observe that compared with the original data $\{x_i, y_i, z_i\}$, the virtual samples $\{s_i^x, s_i^y\}$ are much more suitable for clustering, processing, and analyzing, due to the adjustable parameter $\mathcal{K}$.

During the state estimation, the estimation accuracy is influenced by the number of the sensors. The more sensors are deployed in the ROI, the better is the estimation accuracy. Moreover, the sensors can be either uniformly or randomly deployed. Plotting the sensor data $\{x_i, y_i, z_i\}$, we obtain a non-smooth or incomplete mixed-Gaussian model, as shown in Fig. 3(a) and (b). Comparing Fig. 3(a) and (b) with Fig. 2(a), we observe that in the uniform deployment case, there exists a large gap between the real and the estimated system states; while in the random deployment case, some information is missing since there are some

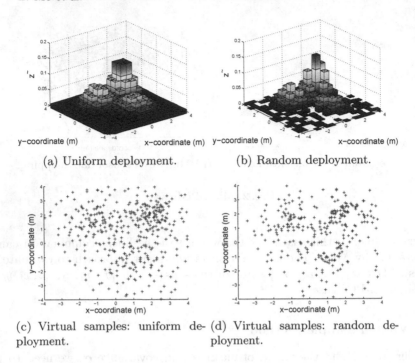

(a) Uniform deployment.   (b) Random deployment.

(c) Virtual samples: uniform de- (d) Virtual samples: random deployment.   ployment.

Fig. 3. State estimation with a limited number of sensors.

grids that are not covered by the sensors. Using the virtual sample method, we derive a set of spare and incomplete virtual samples, as shown in Fig. 3(c) and (d). Finally, through the GMM, we obtain $\{\hat{\varepsilon}_i, \hat{\boldsymbol{\mu}}_i, \hat{\boldsymbol{\sigma}}_i\}$ $(1 \leq i \leq n)$, where $\hat{\varepsilon}_i$, $\hat{\boldsymbol{\mu}}_i$ and $\hat{\boldsymbol{\sigma}}_i$ are the estimations of the weight, the mean and the covariance of the ith Gaussian model, respectively. Due to page limitations, the interested reader can find the details of GMM in [2].

Figure 4 shows the average estimation errors of (1) the states of the POIs, i.e., $E_s = \frac{1}{n} \sum_{i=1}^{n} |t_i - \hat{t}_i|$, and (2) the positions of the POIs, i.e., $E_p = \frac{1}{n} \sum_{i=1}^{n} \|\boldsymbol{\mu}_i - \hat{\boldsymbol{\mu}}_i\|_2^2$, with the number of the sensors l and the number of the virtual samples N varying. $\hat{t}_i$ is an estimation of the system state t_i, $M_i = \lceil \mathcal{K}\tilde{z}_i \rceil = \lceil \frac{10000}{n_v}\tilde{z}_i \rceil$, $l \in [1000, 4000]$, and $n_v \in [10, 100]$. From Fig. 4, we observe that in both uniform and random sensor deployment: (1) if n_v is fixed, $E_s \propto \frac{1}{l}$, $E_p \propto \frac{1}{l}$, and (2) if l is fixed, $E_s \propto n_v$, $E_p \propto n_v$. This is because the virtual samples can be used to describe the Gaussian distribution. The more the virtual samples are, the better is the description of the Gaussian model. This characteristic implies that when the number of the sensors is small, we can increase the number of the virtual samples so as to improve the estimation accuracy.

At each step k, using the GMM, we obtain the estimations of the states of n POIs, i.e., $\{\hat{t}_1(k), \ldots, \hat{t}_n(k)\}$. In this paper, we introduce a function $\mathcal{F}$ to evaluate the priorities of the events, expressed by

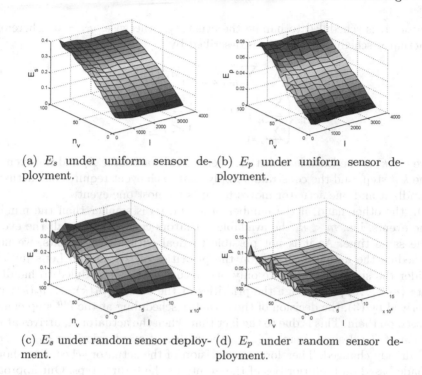

(a) E_s under uniform sensor deployment.

(b) E_p under uniform sensor deployment.

(c) E_s under random sensor deployment.

(d) E_p under random sensor deployment.

Fig. 4. State estimation accuracy of virtual sample method with l and N_v varying.

$$p_i(k) = \begin{cases} \mathcal{F}(\hat{t}_i(k)), & \hat{t}_i(k) < t_i^*, \\ 1, & \hat{t}_i(k) \geq t_i^*, \end{cases} \tag{3}$$

where $p_i(k)$ is the probability of the event e_i at the kth step, the function $\mathcal{F}$ is determined by the applications. It is given in advance and it can be calculated based on simulations or experiments. For instance, in forest fire detection and extinction, if the temperature of POI_1 exceeds $100\,°C$, we assume that a fire breaks out at the POI_1, i.e., $p_1(k) = 1$; if the temperature of POI_1 is below than $100\,°C$, e.g., $80\,°C$, we assume that $p_1(k) = 0.8$. Thus, we have $\mathcal{F}(\hat{t}_1(k)) = \frac{\hat{t}_1(k)}{100}$ and $t_1^* = 100$. Based on different application requirements, we define a priority threshold p_i^* for the event e_i and schedule an actuator to handle it, if $p_i(k) \geq p_i^*$.

3   Actuator Scheduling Scheme

We denote κ as the number of the events that need to be handled at the kth step. If the number of the actuators is higher than the number of the events, i.e., $m \geq \kappa$, the actuator scheduling problem is defined as how to move the actuators toward the events as soon as possible. In order to formulate the actuator scheduling problem, we introduce a $m \times \kappa$ binary matrix $Q = [q_{ij}]$. If $q_{ij} = 1$, the actuator A_i is scheduled to handle the event e_j, otherwise, $q_{ij} = 0$. Therefore, the actuator scheduling problem is described by

$$\min_{Q} \ J_1 = \sum_{i=1}^{m} \sum_{j=1}^{\kappa} d_{ij}(k) q_{ij} \tag{4}$$

$$\text{s.t.} \begin{cases} \sum_{i=1}^{m} q_{ij} = 1, \ 1 \leq j \leq \kappa, \\ \sum_{j=1}^{\kappa} q_{ij} \leq 1, \ 1 \leq i \leq m. \end{cases}$$

where $d_{ij}(k)$ is the Euclidean distance between the actuator A_i and the event e_j at the kth step, and the constraints imply that each event requires one actuator to handle it and one actuator moves towards at most one event.

On the other hand, if the number of actuators is smaller than the number of the events, i.e., $m < \kappa$, the available actuators cannot handle all the events at the same time. As it is not possible to deal with all the events, we need to schedule the actuators based on the priorities of the events. Let's initially consider the simple case, where only one actuator A_i is scheduled to handle r events $\{e_1, \ldots, e_r\}$. Although the priorities of the events $\{p_1(k), \ldots, p_r(k)\}$ can be derived by (3), the decision of the actuator scheduling at the kth step cannot be based on them. This is due to the fact that when the actuator A_i arrives at the location of the desired event, e.g., e_j, the values of event priorities $\{p_1, \ldots, p_r\}$ have already changed. Therefore, the decision of the actuator scheduling should be made based on the priorities of the events at the future steps. Our approach uses the Regression Algorithm (RA) [2] to predict the future priorities.

To illustrate the future priority prediction, we consider the estimation of $p_j(k)$. Suppose that $p_j(k)$ is not oscillating, and, thus, the target variable $p_j(k)$ can be given by a deterministic function ϕ_j with additive zero mean Gaussian noise ω_j, i.e., $p_j(k) = \alpha_j k^{\beta_j} + \gamma_j + \omega_j(\rho_j) = \phi_j(k) + \omega_j(\rho_j)$, where $\{\alpha_j, \beta_j, \gamma_j\}$ are the fitting parameters, and ρ_j is the inverse variance of Gaussian noise. Thus, we have $\mathcal{N}(p_j(k)|\phi_j(k), \rho_j^{-1}) = \frac{1}{\sqrt{2\pi\rho_j^{-1}}} \exp\left\{ \frac{(p_j(k)-\phi_j(k))^2}{-2\rho_j^{-1}} \right\}$. Denote ϑ as the window size of the estimation, and assume that the historical data $\{p_j(k - \vartheta), \ldots, p_j(k)\}$ are independent and identically distributed (i.i.d.). We obtain a likelihood function $\mathcal{L}(\boldsymbol{p}_j) = \prod_{i=k-\vartheta}^{k} \mathcal{N}(p_j(i)|\phi_j(i), \beta_j^{-1})$. Taking the derivative of $\ln \mathcal{L}(\boldsymbol{p}_j)$ with respect to $\{\alpha_j, \beta_j, \gamma_j, \rho_j\}$ and make them to 0, we derive the estimations of these parameters, i.e., $(\hat{\alpha}_j, \hat{\beta}_j, \hat{\gamma}_j, \hat{\rho}_j)$. Therefore, the priority $p_j(k)$ at the future step k' ($k' > k$) is estimated by $\hat{p}_j(k') = \hat{\alpha}_j(k')^{\hat{\beta}_j} + \hat{\gamma}_j + \omega_j(\hat{\rho}_j)$.

Denote v_i and Δ as the moving speed of actuator A_i and the system sampling period, respectively. The actuator scheduling process is summarized as follows:

1. At the kth step, based on the distance $d_{ij}(k)$ between the actuator A_i and the event e_j, we obtain the corresponding moving time $\frac{d_{ij}(k)}{v_i}$. Then, we estimate the future priorities of the events $\{\hat{p}_j(k + \frac{d_{ij}(k)}{v_i \Delta k})\}$, and schedule the actuator A_i to handle the event with the highest priority, e.g., event e_d, where $\hat{p}_d(k + \frac{d_{id}(k)}{v_i \Delta k}) = \max_j \{\hat{p}_j(k + \frac{d_{ij}(k)}{v_i \Delta k})\}$.
2. Step 1 is repeated to schedule actuator A_i to handle the residual $r - 1$ events.

Denote $p_{ij}(k)$ as the future priority of event e_j at the $(k + \frac{d_{ij}(k)}{v_i \Delta k})^{th}$ step, which is estimated at the kth step. Therefore, the actuator scheduling problem is formulated as follows:

$$\max_Q J_2 = \sum_{i=1}^{m} \sum_{j=1}^{\kappa} p_{ij}(k) q_{ij} \qquad (5)$$

$$\text{s.t.} \begin{cases} \sum_{k=1}^{m} q_{ij} \leq 1, \ 1 \leq j \leq \kappa, \\ \sum_{j=1}^{\kappa} q_{ij} = 1, \ 1 \leq i \leq m. \end{cases}$$

Note that the problems (4) and (5) are ILP, which can be solved by existing ILP algorithms [9]. As the proposed scheduling methods are event-driven, i.e., when a new event occur, the scheduling decision, which is given by the solution of problem (4) or (5), should be updated.

4 Performance Evaluation

We randomly deploy 4 actuators to 6 POIs in a 50 m × 50 m ROI, set $p_i^* = 0.5$, and assume that the priorities $\{p_1(k), p_2(k), p_3(k), p_4(k)\}$ are monotonic increasing, while the priorities $\{p_5(k), p_6(k)\}$ are monotonic decreasing. The dynamic change of the number of occurring events in time steps is shown in Fig. 5(a). From this figure, we observe that the scheduling decisions are divided into 3 periods based on the step k: [1, 6], [7, 35] and [36, 100]. Due to the number of occurred events, in the 1st and the 3rd periods we schedule the actuators based on the solution of problem (4). In the 2nd period, we schedule the actuators based on the solution of problem (5). Moreover, in the 2nd period, the actuators need to keep moving, as shown in Fig. 5(b). This is because the number of the actuators is smaller than the number of the events. When the actuator A_i finishes the assigned task in the current round, it will be scheduled again to handle another event in the next round. Figure 5(c) shows at which step the actuators arrive at the desired events. From this figure, we observe that each event is handled by at least one actuator. Figure 5(d) shows the corresponding objective function, which is a combination of J_1 and J_2. In the 1st and the 3rd periods, the aim is to minimize J_1 by scheduling the actuator A_i to the nearest event. While in the 2nd period, the aim is to maximize J_2 by handling the events with the higher priorities.

In order to evaluate the performance of proposed scheme, we build a testbed which consists of three main components: (1) base station, (2) LEGO Mindstorm NXT wheeled robot (Fig. 6(a)), and (3) OptiTrack system [1] (Fig. 6(b)). The OptiTrack system includes 6 cameras which are used to track the mobile targets in a 300 cm × 300 cm ROI. The base station is responsible for processing the data received from OptiTrack system, making the scheduling decision (Matlab), and sending the comments to the robot though a bluetooth connection.

The locations of POI_1, POI_2, POI_3 and POI_4 are set to $(-70, -50)$, $(30, 120)$, $(100, 25)$ and $(-100, 70)$, respectively. The initial location of actuator A_1 is set to $(0, -100)$, as shown in Fig. 6(a). In the base station, we simulate the dynamic

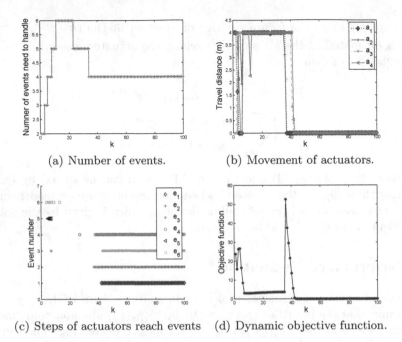

(a) Number of events.   (b) Movement of actuators.

(c) Steps of actuators reach events   (d) Dynamic objective function.

Fig. 5. Actuator scheduling.

(a) LEGO Mindstorm NXT robot.   (b) OptiTrack system.

Fig. 6. Overview of testbed.

changes of the priorities of the events $\{p_1(k), p_2(k), p_3(k), p_4(k)\}$ and assume that $p_1(k)$ is monotonic decreasing, while $\{p_2(k), p_3(k), p_4(k)\}$ are monotonic increasing. If the actuator A_1 arrives at POI$_i$, $p_i(k) = 0$ immediately. But after that, $p_i(k)$ increases gradually except $p_1(k)$, as it is monotonic decreasing. The base station is able to receive the information with respect to the robot position from the OptiTrack system. This information is recorded in a txt file for off-line analysis. The real robot trajectory and the changes in the probability of the events are shown in Fig. 7(a) and (b), respectively.

The experiment runs between 0–200 s, $p_i^* = 0.5$, and the system sample period $\Delta = 0.1$ s. Table 1 shows the scheduling sequence, where L_i, L_s, L_d, T_s, T_e are the

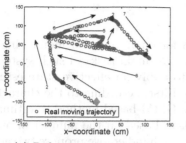

(a) Robot moving trajectory

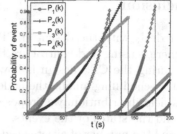

(b) Dynamic probability change under actuator influence

Fig. 7. Experimental results.

initial position, the desired position, the final position, the start moving time, and the stop moving time, respectively, and $*$ represents the idle operation. Based on Table 1, the whole scheduling sequence is divided into 8 periods. The moving details are analyzed as follows: at the beginning, $p_1 = 0.9$, the actuator A_1 spends 3 s to move towards the event e_1 and to handle it. Then, $p_1 = 0$. At the same time, p_2, p_3 and p_4 are increasing gradually during this period, and p_4 has the fastest growth rate. When $p_4 > 0.5$ at $t = 46$ s, the actuator A_1 moves towards the event e_4 and arrives there at $t = 54$ s. Then, $p_4 = 0$. When $t = 83$ s, we have $p_3 > 0.5$. The actuator A_1 starts moving towards the event e_3. During the movement, at $t = 91$ s, we have $p_2 > 0.5$. However, the actuator A_1 hasn't reached the position of e_3 yet, and, thus, the events e_2 and e_3 occur simultaneously. Therefore, we schedule actuator A_1 based on p_{12} and p_{13}. p_{ij} is the priority of event e_j at step $k + \frac{d_{ij}}{v_1 \triangle}$, which is estimated at current step k. Since p_2 grows faster, i.e., $p_{12} > p_{13}$, the actuator A_1 changes its direction and moves towards the event e_2. When $t = 100$ s, we have $p_4 > 0.5$, and, thus, the events e_2, e_3 and e_4 need to be handled simultaneously. In a similar way, by comparing p_{12}, p_{13} and p_{14}, the actuator A_1 goes back to the event e_4 and arrives at e_4 at $t = 116$ s. After that, the actuator A_1 moves towards the second highest probability event e_2, and it arrives there at $t = 131$ s. Since the events e_2 and e_4 have been handled, the remaining event is e_3. Therefore, the actuator A_1 moves towards the event e_3 immediately and arrives at e_3 at $t = 141$ s. The actuator A_1 stays at e_3 until $p_4 > 0.5$ at $t = 162$ s, and, then, the actuator A_1 moves towards the event e_4 and it arrives there at $t = 179$ s. Since the events e_1, e_2 and e_3 are smaller than 0.5 during the period $t = 179$–200 s, the actuator A_1 stays at e_4 until the experiment ends.

Table 1. Actuator moving sequence

	L_i	L_s	L_d	T_s	T_e		L_i	L_s	L_d	T_s	T_e		L_i	L_s	L_d	T_s	T_e		L_i	L_s	L_d	T_s	T_e
R_1	0	e_1	e_1	0	3	R_2	e_1	e_4	e_4	46	54	R_3	e_4	e_3	$*$	83	$*$	R_4	e_3	e_2	$*$	$*$	$*$
R_5	e_2	e_4	$*$	$*$	116	R_6	e_4	e_2	e_2	116	131	R_7	e_2	e_3	e_3	131	141	R_8	e_3	e_4	e_4	162	179

5   Conclusion

This paper deals with the design of CPS for environmental monitoring applications, where sensing and control are the two main tasks of such system. The challenge during the CPS design is how to apply an effective state estimation and actuator scheduling among the nodes. First, according to the characteristic of physical field distribution, we propose a GMM-based method to estimate the locations and the states of the events. Then, based on the number of available actuators and the number of events need to be handled, we propose two actuator scheduling schemes. Based on the relative distances between the events and the actuators, the former one schedules the nearest actuators to the event areas so as to fulfill the actuator relocation as soon as possible. The latter one predicts the priorities of the events through the regression algorithm, and follows priority-based sequence to handle these events with high priorities. Finally, simulations and experiments are conducted to illustrate the effectiveness of the proposed methods.

Acknowledgment. This research is funded by INRIA post-doctoral research fellowship program, and is partly sponsored by the National Natural Science foundation of China (Grant No. 61403340 and 61573103).

References

1. http://www.naturalpoint.com/optitrack/
2. Bishop, C.M.: Pattern Recognition and Machine Learning. Springer, New York (2006)
3. Cao, X., Chen, J., Xiao, Y., Sun, Y.: Building-environment control with wireless sensor and actuator networks: centralized versus distributed. IEEE Trans. Ind. Electron. **57**(11), 3596–3605 (2010)
4. Chen, J., Cao, X., Cheng, P., Xiao, Y., Sun, Y.: Distributed collaborative control for industrial automation with wireless sensor and actuator networks. IEEE Trans. Ind. Electron. **57**(12), 4219–4230 (2010)
5. Krause, A., Singh, A., Guestrin, C.: Near-optimal sensor placements in gaussian processes: theory, efficient algorithms and empirical studies. J. Mach. Learn. Res. **9**, 235–284 (2008)
6. Li, H., Lai, L., Poor, H.V.: Multicast routing for decentralized control of cyber physical systems with an application in smart grid. IEEE J. Sel. Areas Commun. **30**(6), 1097–1107 (2012)
7. Li, X., Qiao, C., Yu, X., Wagh, A., Sudhaakar, R., Addepalli, S.: Toward effective service scheduling for human drivers in vehicular cyber-physical systems. IEEE Trans. Parallel Distrib. Syst. **23**(9), 1775–1789 (2012)
8. Mo, L., Cao, X., Song, Y., Kritikakou, A.: Distributed node coordination for real-time energy-constrained control in wireless sensor and actuator networks. IEEE Internet Things J. 1–12 (2018). https://doi.org/10.1109/JIOT.2018.283903
9. Mo, L., Kritikakou, A., Sentieys, O.: Controllable QoS for imprecise computation tasks on DVFS multicores with time and energy constraints. IEEE J. Emerg. Sel. Top. Circuits Syst. 1–14 (2018).https://doi.org/10.1109/JETCAS.2018.2852005

10. Ota, K., Dong, M., Cheng, Z., Wang, J., Li, X., Shen, X.S.: ORACLE: mobility control in wireless sensor and actor networks. Comput. Commun **35**(9), 1029–1037 (2012)
11. Weiss, V., Andor, L., Renner, G., Varady, T.: Advanced surface fitting techniques. Comput. Aided Geom. D. **19**(1), 19–42 (2002)
12. Wen, Y.J., Agogino, A.M.: Control of wireless-networked lighting in open-plan offices. Lighting Res. Technol. **43**(2), 235–248 (2011)
13. Zhang, X.M., Han, Q.L., Yu, X.: Survey on recent advances in networked control systems. IEEE Trans. Ind. Inform. **12**(5), 1740–1752 (2016)

Game-Based Data Muling as a Service in Infrastructureless Area

Mohamed Jacem Guezguez[1(✉)], Slim Rekhis[1], and Noureddine Boudriga[1,2]

[1] Communication Networks and Security (CN&S) Research Lab.,
University of Carthage, Ariana, Tunisia
mohamed.jacem@gmail.com, slim.rekhis@gmail.com,
noure.boudriga2@gmail.com
[2] Computer Science Department,
University of Western Cape, Bellville, South Africa

Abstract. With the emerging of Internet of Things (IoT) concept, we are recently assisting to the proliferation of Wireless Sensor Networks (WSNs) around us in our daily life. However, such WSNs can be deployed far away from infrastructures to supervise unreachable areas such as countries' borders and natural preserves. Besides, the deployment of dedicated transport networks, the use of satellite communications or mobile 3G/4G networks can be expensive and complex to install in such areas. With the exponential development and ubiquity of smartphones, having powerful communication and computation capabilities, the concept of data muling can be beneficial by using these devices to provide low-cost and efficient communications for providers having WSNs deployed in infrastructreless areas.

This paper proposes a novel architecture providing data muling as a service where a set of data muling agents deployed on smartphones can be used to collect and forward sensing data from WSNs, deployed in infrastructureless areas, to remote servers. We design a QoS-aware game theory model to select best efficient data muling agents to perform data muling tasks with acceptable costs and adequate technical capabilities. Such a model encourages highly reputable and reliable agents to participate in data muling tasks by rewarding and updating their reputations. A simulation is also conducted to assess the efficiency of the proposed model.

Keywords: Data Muling · Smartphones · Broker · Trust level

1 Introduction

With the recent technological advancements of smartphones across the world, these smart devices are becoming the pioneers of mobile crowd-sensing. They are distinguished with high processing and storage capabilities, and they are able to connect simultaneously to several wireless networks such as IEEE 802.11 and mobile networks. With such capabilities, smartphones can be efficiently used to

© Springer Nature Switzerland AG 2018
N. Montavont and G. Z. Papadopoulos (Eds.): ADHOC-NOW 2018, LNCS 11104, pp. 280–292, 2018.
https://doi.org/10.1007/978-3-030-00247-3_25

collect and send data to remote servers in order to provide mobile crowd-sensing as a service in several fields such as healthcare [5], mobile networking [4], social media [1], and environmental monitoring [3].

WSNs are commonly widespread everywhere in order to provide a continuous monitoring of indoor and outdoor environments. However, in some cases, these wireless networks are far from the communication infrastructures, and mobile networks may be absent or their use to carry data can cause unnecessary financial costs [2]. Moreover, in the case of natural disaster, the network infrastructure can be damaged, depriving end users from several primordial voice and data services. For those reasons, the concept of data muling, which consists in using smartphones as data muling agents to collect and forward sensing data through cost-efficient and short range communications, becomes very important. In addition to that, such a mechanism ensures the monitoring of distant or unreachable areas having a poor mobile radio coverage to solve radio connectivity problems.

Several research works were developed in the literature and mainly focused on the benefits of crowd sensing and data muling through mobile phones. To the best of our knowledge, there is no prior study which shares our vision in performing QoS-aware selection of smartphones able to perform data muling tasks. However, there are some efforts which focus on data muling architectures using smartphones. The work [7] focused on the importance of using human-carried mobile phones as data muling agents and surveyed several motivating data muling applications. The work [2] provided a data muling model to collect healthcare information in highly disconnected environments. It also discussed data routing and prioritisation during the data forwarding procedure. However, the selection of data muling agents can be developed based on several Quality of Service (QoS) metrics such as their reputations and technical capabilities. The work [8] presented novel auction-based mechanisms to discourage free-riding and false reporting in crowdsourcing. They are also based on financial warranties and arbitration of third parties. With such mechanisms, both providers and mobile users have better to be honest to complete successfully their assigned tasks and to be rewarded. However, such a study [8] can be enhanced by recruiting honest mobile smartphones during a selection phase using QoS metrics and taking into consideration the agents' historical activities. The work [6] proposed a mechanism to select crowd-sensing mobile participants by guaranteeing a high Quality of Information (QoI) of the requested sensing tasks. Such a QoI can be satisfied by selecting efficient participants that perform sensing data collection in all sub-regions of a defined area. These mechanisms enable also an energy-aware selection to select participants having the smallest data rejection probabilities. Despite the great contribution of this work in selecting a set of participants which meet QoI requirements, it does not consider the historical behaviour of the agents, their ability in delivering the sensing data to remote base stations within the expected time period, and the cost of such an operation.

To cope with the aforecited issues, this paper proposes a novel data muling architecture for the monitoring of distant wireless sensor networks. It helps the provisioning of surveillance-based services by describing their specifications and requirements. It also proposes a game theoretic approach to efficiently select agents having best reputations, technical capabilities and offering lowest costs. Such a method helps also data muling agents to verify whether it is beneficial for them to participate or not in current data muling tasks.

The main contributions of this paper are presented in the following. First, our proposed approach does not impose any mobility model to the recruited data muling agents. It is based on a network of autonomous smartphones having the ability to perform data muling tasks within distant areas. We propose a game-based model that copes with the dynamic behavior of mobile subscribers. It optimally reward them for providing data muling services using their smartphones, depending on trustworthiness and their ability to meet the time delivery constraints. The second contribution consists in designing an optimal pricing model in a Cloud-based solution using self-reconfigurable smartphones. Such a model takes into consideration the functional cost of the mobile data muling agent, and the one proposed by the network side. The third contribution consists in providing a solution that can be exploited by Cloud-based surveillance applications working in infrastructureless area, such as the monitoring of countries' borders, supervision of wild-life preserves, and provision of public safety services.

In the remaining part of this paper, the requirements concerning the proposed architecture are discussed in Sect. 2. Such an architecture is detailed in Sect. 3. The designed game approach is described in Sect. 4. Section 5 presents the simulation results, and the last Sect. 6 concludes the work.

2   Requirements

We identify below the requirements related to the design of our proposed data muling architecture.

Ensuring the Localization of Data Muling Agents: Data muling agents can be smartphones of end users who perform a mutual agreement with a data muling broker. These agents can be also deployed on Unmanned Aerial Vehicles (UAV) in order to supervise distant areas. It is important to always locate them in order to be aware of their mobility and to have a global real time picture of all active data muling agents in the area. That is why, such agents are configured to periodically report their GPS positions. In case of absence of GPS signal, data muling agents can provide the SSID (Service Set IDentifier) of nearby public IEEE 802.11 networks and/or cell identifiers of the serving mobile network.

Reconfiguration of Data Muling Agents: The management of data muling agents is performed through their broker hosted in distant and secured areas. They always receive new or/and updated configurations in order to be aware of the potential WSNs to visit and the data muling tasks to perform. With such a procedure, data muling agents are dynamically configured to start collecting data from sink nodes, which belong to the predefined WSNs.

Selection Strategy: The WSN sink node performs a QoS-aware selection to select best agents able to transmit sensing data to the broker. Such a game selection is based on several criteria such as trust level score, storage capability, residual energy and the financial cost announced by each data muling agent. In addition to that, the data muling agent performs simultaneously another game to verify whether it is beneficial to it (i.e. getting financial reward and enhancing its trust level) to participate or not in the data muling task.

Reputation Raking of Data Muling Agents: In order to classify agents based on their data muling efficiency, the broker needs to set a reputation raking strategy on its agents. During each performed data muling task, the rank of an agent could be updated by incrementing it when the data delivery is successfully done (i.e. adherence to data delivery deadline), or decrementing it when the deadline is not met. In the case where a data muling agent is inactive for a long period of time, its trust level score is automatically decreased and the broker can notify and encourage it to contribute in data muling.

Strategy of Data Delivery: After selecting the best agents to perform data muling tasks, the sensing data is firstly processed and filtered by the sink node to compress and reduce its size. The obtained data can be classified into based on its priority level. In the case of high-priority information such as fire detection events, the information delivery process could be made more reliable by duplicating the data to send over several copies and transmitting them through different mobile agents. In the case of low-priority information, the delivery could be done through different muling agents having low trust levels.

3   Proposed Data Muling Architecture

We present in this section the proposed data muling architecture. The components of such an architecture, shown in Fig. 1, are detailed as follows:

- ***Service provider:*** Is composed of an application server and a sensing database that can be hosted and managed remotely by a cloud third-party. Such a provider is composed of:
  (a) Application Server: It directly interacts with users according to their access privileges (e.g. administrators or end users). It interacts also with the data muling broker to help administrators configuring data muling services and to also processing the collected sensing data stored into the data repository. Such a server can be also configured to send notifications in case of abnormal events.
  (b) Sensing Database: Is a repository dedicated to store and process sensing data received from the data muling broker. It is safely accessible by the application server to display and use sensing data based on the requests of end users. Such a repository can be hosted on a cloud computing platform to enhance its storage capacity and reduce its financial cost.
- ***Data Muling Broker:*** Is responsible of the management and configuration of data muling agents. It interacts also with the transport backbone to collect sensing data from the incoming agents and provides the requested output data to the service provider. Such a broker is composed of:

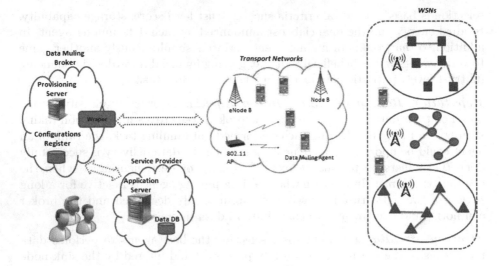

Fig. 1. The proposed data muling architecture

(a) Data Muling Agents: Represent client software installed on the smartphone of mobile subscribers after a mutual agreement with the broker. Such entities can be also carried by UAV to collect sensing data from remote areas. Based on the configurations received from their provisioning server and on their location with respect to the different WSNs, data muling agents will be in competition with each others in order to be selected by the sink node to perform data muling tasks. By achieving successfully such tasks, data muling agents will be rewarded by their broker and their reputations (i.e. trust level) will be improved.

(b) Provisioning Server: Its main role is to configure and manage data muling agents present in the network. It can also activate or deactivate them based on their locations and their approximate distances from WSNs. It also interacts with the wrapper to collect sensing data before processing and then storing them in the sensing Database. The performance of data muling agents is evaluated by the provisioning server which can update their trust levels based on their respect to delivery delays.

(c) Wrapper: Is a server behaving as a logical sink node which collects the sensing data from data muling agents through transport networks. It can be also modelled as a middleware between the WSNs, and the provisioning server.

- *Transport Backbone:* Is composed of PS (Packet Switching) networks such as 3G/4G or 802.11 networks which are used to transport sensing data from the incoming data muling agents to their broker.

- *WSNs:* Several WSNs can be deployed along the proposed architecture to provide surveillance-based services in remote areas. Each WSN contains a sink node able to perform a QoS selection in order to select and choose the best agents to perform data muling tasks and carry sensing data to the broker.

4   Game Theoretic Approach for Data Muling

The concept of game theory focuses on how different entities make decisions in conflicting situations. It uses several mathematical tools to model interactions between several entities based on gains or payoffs perceived by them. In this section, we describe the proposed theoretic game to efficiently select data muling agents and we describe the equilibrium status that satisfies both the WSN sink node and data muling agents.

4.1   Game Formulation and QoS-Aware Selection

In the following, we present the game formulation used by the sink node for a QoS-aware selection of efficient data muling agents, and by agents which are willing to be selected and to transmit the sensing data from the sink node to their broker. To this end, we consider that, at the time t, the sink node performs a QoS-aware selection to choose the efficient data muling agent from a list of N candidates in vicinity. A non-cooperative game is therefore proposed between such a sink node and the selected data muling agent, which may accept participating, or not, in the current data muling task. Each player has different set of pure strategies, where it selfishly selects the strategy that allows it maximizing its own utility. Thus, each data muling agent a_i uses the following parameters:

- Cov_{ai}: Is the average percentage of time of being covered by Packet Switching (PS) networks such as IEEE 802.11 and 3G/4G networks.
- Cap_{ai}: Is the storage space available on the data muling agent.
- $Cost_{ai}$: Is the financial cost of the agent a_i to perform a data muling task.
- $Price_{ai}$: Is the price proposed by an agent a_i for the data muling task.
- $Trust_{ai}$: Is a reputation score delivered and updated by the sink node to describe the historical performance of the agent a_i.
- $P_{del,ai}$: Is the perception of the probability of delivering data on time by agent a_i. Such a metric can be computed based on: (a) the mean speed of agent a_i depending on its type (e.g., a smartphone transported by a pedestrian, a computer embedded in a vehicle, a controller in an UAV); (b) the minimal distance between the agent a_i and the nearest location covered by PS network; and c) the maximal delay provided by the sink node to the agent a_i to deliver data to the nearest PS network.

The metrics (Cov_{ai}, Cap_{ai}, $Cost_{ai}$, and $Price_{ai}$) are self-calculated by the agent which securely sends them to the sink node. Whereas, the $Trust_{ai}$ is calculated by the broker which updates it after the accomplishment of each data muling task. The latter is encrypted and authenticated by a shared key known only by the broker and the WSN sink node. The $P_{del,ai}$ is calculated with the same manner by the sink node and the agent a_i after: (a) the agent a_i receives from the sink node the maximal allowed delay; and (b) the sink node receives from the agent its position in the network. In the remaining part of the paper, the perception of the probability of delivering data $P_{del,ai}$ will be denoted as p.

Algorithm 1. The proposed data muling gaming algorithm

$choose\_agent \leftarrow False$

$A = \{a_1, a_2, ..., a_N\}; \ L = \{a_i \epsilon A - Cov_{ai} > TH_{cov} \text{ and } Cap_{ai} > TH_{size}\}$

While ($Choose\_agent = False$ and L not empty)

$Trust_{a_k} = Max_{a_i \epsilon L}(Trust_{ai})$

If ($U_{sink} > U_{sink,TH}$)

If ($U_{a_k} > U_{a_k,TH}$)

$choose\_agent \leftarrow True$

Else $L = L \setminus \{a_k\}$ Endif

Else $L = L \setminus \{a_k\}$ Endif

Endwhile

For each block of data, the sink node performs a QoS-aware game selection to choose the best agent. The steps of this game are displayed in Algorithm 1.

From N data muling agents willing to participate in data muling tasks, the broker sets a list L containing agents having higher percentage of PS coverage and storage spaces than predefined thresholds TH_{cov} and TH_{size}, respectively. In the next step, the broker elects an agent a_k having the best trust reputation score. Then, the sink node calculates its utility function U_{sink} to verify whether it is convenient to work with agent a_k or not (i.e. its utility is higher than a threshold $U_{sink,TH}$). In the case where the sink node is not satisfied, it excludes the agent a_k from the list L and starts another selection. In the case it accepts this agent, the latter calculates its own utility function U_{a_k} to verify whether it is beneficial for it to participate or not (i.e. if it will be rewarded, its trust score will be improved and its utility function will be higher than a threshold $U_{a_k,TH}$). If the agent a_k accepts the offer, the sink node starts transmitting data to it, whereas the latter will be excluded from L and the game-based protocol is played again to choose another agent.

4.2   Utility Functions

After firstly selecting an agent, denoted by a_k, that have the best trust reputation, the sink node calculates its own utility function to verify whether it is suitable to work with that agent or not. We define the utility function of the sink node as:

$$U_{sink} = \alpha \times G_{sink} + \beta \times R_{sink}$$

where α and β are predefined coefficients. The variable G_{sink} describes the financial gain of the sink node and it is calculated as follows:

$$G_{sink} = \begin{cases} V - price_{a_k} & \text{with} \quad p \\ 0 & \text{with} \quad (1-p) \end{cases} \tag{4.1}$$

where V is the self financial estimation of the data muling task.

The variable R_{sink} details whether the sink node will be rewarded or penalised by the service provider. It is calculated as follows:

$$R_{sink} = \begin{cases} price_{prov} - V & \text{with } p \\ -\theta & \text{with } (1-p) \end{cases} \qquad (4.2)$$

where $price_{prov}$ is the price received by the sink node after successfully completing the data muling task, and θ is the penalty paid by the latter in the case of the non accomplishment of the data muling task.

The sink node accepts the agent a_k only when U_{sink} is higher than a self utility threshold denoted as $U_{sink,TH}$.

After notifying the first selection of the agent a_k, the latter calculates its utility function to verify whether it is beneficial for it to participate or not in the data muling task. Such a function is defined as follows: $U_{a_k} = \alpha' \times G_{a_k} + \beta' \times T_{a_k}$ where α' and β' represent predefined coefficients. The variable G_{a_k} describes the financial gain perceived by the agent a_k. It is calculated as follows:

$$G_{a_k} = \begin{cases} price_{a_k} - cost_{a_k} & \text{with } p \\ 0 & \text{with } (1-p) \end{cases} \qquad (4.3)$$

The second variable T_{a_k} describes the expectations of the trust score of the agent a_k whether it is improved or not. It is defined as follows:

$$T_{a_k} = \begin{cases} trust_{a_k} + \varepsilon & \text{with } p \\ trust_{a_k} - \gamma & \text{with } (1-p) \end{cases} \qquad (4.4)$$

where α and γ represent predefined offsets of trust level. The agent a_k accepts to participate in the data muling task only when U_{a_k} is higher than a self utility threshold denoted as $U_{a_k,TH}$.

4.3   Efficient Game Equilibrium

We form a game between the sink node and the selected data muling agent a_k. The strategies of the sink node are satisfaction (denoted by "S") or insatisfaction (denoted by "NS"). For the data muling agent, it can accept to deliver data (strategy denoted by "D") or not (denoted by "ND"). The different utilities of both the sink node and the data muling agent a_k are displayed on Table 1.

Table 1. Utilities of the sink node and the data muling agent

	S	NS
D	$p[\alpha(V - price_{a_k}) + \beta(price_{prov} - V)]$, $p[\alpha'(price_{a_k} - cost_{a_k}) + \beta'(trust_{a_k} + \varepsilon)]$	$-\beta(1-p)\theta, 0$
ND	$-\beta(1-p)\theta$, $\beta'(trust_{a_k} - \gamma) \times (1-p)$	$0, 0$

For the 2-tuples of Table 1, the first elements on the left are utilities of the sink node and the ones on the right are utilities of the selected data muling agent a_k. We assume that the strategy "S" of the sink node has more probability to occur than "NS". Based on Table 1, we translate the latter assumption by the following inequality:

$$p[\alpha(V - price_{a_k}) + \beta(price_{prov} - V)] - \beta(1 - p)\theta \geqslant -\beta(1 - p)\theta \qquad (4.5)$$

By solving it, we obtain the following condition on $price_{a_k}$ as follows:

$$price_{a_k} \leq V + \frac{\beta}{\alpha} \times (price_{prov} - V) \qquad (4.6)$$

Using the latter inequality, we obtain the maximum price $(price_{a_k})_{max}^{sink}$ by which the sink node accepts and selects the data muling agent a_k. Such a price is given by: $(price_{a_k})_{max}^{sink} = V + \frac{\beta}{\alpha} \times (price_{prov} - V)$.

Using the same analogy, we assume that the probability of the strategy "D" of the data muling agent is higher than "ND". We will look for the minimum price which satisfies the data muling agent denoted $(price_{a_k})_{min}^{agent}$. Based on Table 1, we obtain the following inequality:

$$p[\alpha'(price_{a_k} - cost_{a_k}) + \beta'(trust_{a_k} + \varepsilon)] + \beta'(trust_{a_k} - \gamma) \times (1 - p) \geq 0 \quad (4.7)$$

By solving the latter inequality, we obtain the following condition on $price_{a_k}$:

$$price_{a_k} \geq cost_{a_k} - \frac{\beta'}{\alpha'} \times [(trust_{a_k} + \varepsilon) + \frac{1}{p} \times (trust_{a_k} - \gamma)(1 - p)] \qquad (4.8)$$

Based on the latter condition, we conclude that the minimum price required by the data muling agent to participate in the task is equal to:

$$(price_{a_k})_{min}^{agent} = cost_{a_k} - \frac{\beta'}{\alpha'} \times [(trust_{a_k} + \varepsilon) + \frac{1}{p} \times (trust_{a_k} - \gamma)(1 - p)] \quad (4.9)$$

The equilibrium of the system is met by satisfying the following condition: $(price_{a_k})_{max}^{sink} \geq (price_{a_k})_{min}^{agent}$. In fact, the minimum price $(price_{a_k})_{min}^{agent}$ accepted by the data muling agent must be suitable for the sink node and should not exceed the maximum calculated value $(price_{a_k})_{max}^{sink}$. We obtain the following condition on $cost_{a_k}$ after several simplifications:

$$cost_{a_k} \leq price_{prov} + V \times (1 - \frac{\beta}{\alpha}) + \frac{\beta'}{\alpha'} \times [\frac{1}{p} \times (trust_{a_k} - \gamma) + \varepsilon + \gamma] \quad (4.10)$$

5   Simulation

In this section, we present the results of the simulations that we conducted to evaluate the performance of the proposed solution using MATLAB tool.

5.1   Simulation Model

We consider an area of $600 \times 600 \, \mathrm{m}^2$. The latter is half covered by a 4G network (i.e. an eNode B covers a surface of $300 \times 300 \, \mathrm{m}^2$). There are five WSN Sink Nodes (SNs) deployed in the border of the non covered area. Each one of them covers a surface of $20 \times 20 \, \mathrm{m}^2$. We assume that these SNs receive periodically notifications and configurations from the data muling broker (for example through broadcast downlink satellite service). The value of the Time Slot (TS) is set to three seconds and all the simulation lasts 1200 TS.

During the first TS, a variable number of data muling agents is randomly injected in the area. In each TS, every data muling agent remains at its place or moves randomly to an adjacent sub-square with a speed of $1 \, \mathrm{m/s}$. When there are a set of data muling agents near the WSN SN, the latter performs a QoS-aware selection to choose the best agent to carry sensing data. When the selected agent moves to the 4G covered area and delivers sensing data, its broker rewards it and enhances its trust level. The initial trust level of agents is set to 5 and each time it succeeds to deliver information on time, the latter value is incremented by a step equal to ε, whereas it is decremented by γ.

When a set of data muling agents are nearby the WSN SN, the latter firstly selects agents having the best trust level scores. Then, it calculates the maximum price to pay to each agent and the difference between the latter price and the one proposed by the agent. When such a difference, named Δ_{price}, is positive, the agent is selected to perform data muling tasks. Whereas, in case where it is negative, the game is played again to select another agent.

We assume that $price_{prov}$ is equal to 70, the private valuation V is equal to 60, α is equal to 0.6 and β is equal to 0.4, so that the maximum price which can be paid by the SN $(price_{a_k})_{max}^{sink}$ is equal to 90. In the other side, we assume that step offsets of trust level ε and γ are equal to 2 and 1, respectively. With respect to Inequality 4.10, coefficients α' and β' are set to 0.6 and -0.4, respectively. The minimum price accepted by the agent is therefore given by $(price_{a_k})_{min}^{agent} = cost_{a_k} + \frac{2}{3} \times (\frac{trust_{a_k}}{p} - \frac{1}{p} + 3)$. In these simulations, we evaluate the performance of the proposed game by analysing the ability of agents in delivering sensing data under different situations, and by studying the variation of $\Delta_{price} = (price_{a_k})_{max}^{sink} - (price_{a_k})_{min}^{agent}$ representing the difference between the price offered by the sink node and the minimal price that can be accepted by the agent a_k.

5.2   Simulation Results

We evaluate in Fig. 2a the variation Δ_{price} between the price proposed by the agent and the maximum one that can be paid by the SN with respect to the probability of displacement of agents, and also under different initial costs. In these simulations, we assume that selected agents have a perception to deliver data on time to their broker equal to 0.5 (i.e. $p = 0.5$). When the probability of displacement is between 0 and 0.1, the agents remain slightly fixed at their initial positions so that the agents, placed randomly nearby a WSN SN, will be selected but they will not be able to deliver data to their broker. As the probability of displacement becomes higher than 0.2, selected agents will deliver data to their broker so that their trust levels and their prices increase, leading to the decrease of Δ_{price}. We also notice that as initial costs of agents increases, their prices increase leading to the decrease of Δ_{price}. By having a probability of displacement equal to 0.7, the average delta is equal to 50.86, 45.84 and 40.87 for a set of initial costs equal to 35, 40, and 45, respectively. It is therefore recommended for the SN to select agents having lowest costs and highest probability of displacements.

In Fig. 2b, we study the variation of Δ_{price} with respect to the perception of data delivery probability under different initial costs of agents. As such a perception probability increases, the trust levels of selected agents and therefore their prices increase, leading to the decrease of Δ_{price}. Besides, selecting an agent, having the best data delivery perception probability, is a challenging task for the SN. In fact, such an agent will guarantee the well data delivery to the broker. However, the latter will be obliged to pay that selected agent more than other ones having lowest of data delivery perception. By having a data delivery perception equal to 0.1, Δ_{price} is equal to 66.90, 61.95 and 56.89 with initial costs equal to 35, 40, and 45, respectively.

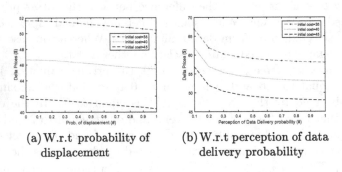

(a) W.r.t probability of displacement

(b) W.r.t perception of data delivery probability

Fig. 2. Assessment of Δ_{price}

We evaluate in Fig. 3a, the average buffered time in the SN with respect to the percentage of agents having acceptable prices under different agents' speeds. An agent having an acceptable price means that it has a price which satisfies the equilibrium relation ($\Delta_{price} > 0$). As the percentage of agents having acceptable prices increases, the average buffered time decreases because the WSN SN can select more quickly an adequate agent, leading to the decrease of its time of buffering data. With an agent's speed equal to 01 square per TS, and by having 10% of agents having acceptable prices, the average buffered time in the SN is equal to 336.30 TS which is higher than 49.66 TS in the case of having all agents with acceptable prices (i.e. 100%). By continuing to increase the agent's speeds up to 02 and 03 squares per TS and by having all agents with acceptable prices, this metric reaches 24.58 TS and 20 TS, respectively.

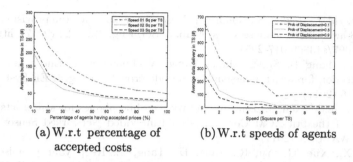

(a) W.r.t percentage of accepted costs   (b) W.r.t speeds of agents

Fig. 3. Average buffered time (left) and average data delivery (right)

Figure 3b shows the average data delivery delay with respect to the different speeds of selected agents. As the latter speeds increase, selected agents start to deliver data from the WSN SN to their broker with high performance. For a probability of displacement equal to 0.1 and by setting the agents' speed equals to 1 square per TS, the average data delivery is equal to 639.8 TS. By continuing to increase the agent's speed up to 10 squares per TS, the average data delivery is almost the sixth of the previous value. By keeping the latter speed and increasing the probability of displacement to 0.5 and 0.9, the average data delivery becomes equal to 21 and 18 TS, respectively.

6   Conclusion

In this paper, we proposed a novel data muling architecture for the monitoring of distant wireless sensor networks. A QoS-aware game theory is also proposed to select the best efficient data mulling agents having acceptable costs, good reputations and delivery rates. Such a model encourages honest and efficient data muling agents to participate by setting rewarding and updating their reputation after performing their data muling tasks. Simulations are conducted and results are presented to assess the performance of our proposed game theoretic model.

References

1. Cardone, G., et al.: Fostering participaction in smart cities: a geo-social crowdsensing platform. IEEE Commun. Mag. **51**, 6 (2013)
2. DeRenzi, B., Anokwa, Y., Parikh, T., Borriello, G.: Reliable data collection in highly disconnected environments using mobile phones. In: Proceedings of the Workshop on Networked Systems for Developing Regions, Kyoto, Japan (2007)
3. Devarakonda, S., Sevusu, P., Liu, H., Liu, R., Iftode, L., Nath, B.: Real-time air quality monitoring through mobile sensing in metropolitan areas. In: Proceedings of the 2nd ACM SIGKDD International Workshop on Urban Computing, Chicago, IL, USA. ACM (2013)
4. Guezguez, M.J., Rekhis, S., Boudriga, N.: Observation-based detection of femtocell attacks in wireless mobile networks. In: Proceedings of the Symposium on Applied Computing, Marrakech, Morocco. ACM (2017)

5. Guezguez, M.J., Rekhis, S., Boudriga, N.: A sensor cloud for the provision of secure and QoS-aware healthcare services. Arab. J. Sci. Eng. **42**, 1–24 (2017). https://doi.org/10.1007/s13369-017-2954-8

6. Liu, C.H., Zhang, B., Su, X., Ma, J., Wang, W., Leung, K.K.: Energy-aware participant selection for smartphone-enabled mobile crowd sensing. IEEE Syst. J. **11**(3), 1435–1446 (2017)

7. Park, U., Heidemann, J.: Data muling with mobile phones for sensornets. In: Proceedings of the 9th ACM Conference on Embedded Networked Sensor Systems, Seattle, WA, USA (2011)

8. Zhang, X., Xue, G., Yu, R., Yang, D., Tang, J.: Keep your promise: mechanism design against free-riding and false-reporting in crowdsourcing. IEEE Internet Things J. **2**(6), 562–572 (2015)

Distributed Computations in Wireless Sensor Networks by Local Interactions

Emna Taktak[1](✉), Mohamed Tounsi[1], Mohamed Mosbah[2],
and Ahmed Hadj Kacem[1]

[1] ReDCAD Laboratory, University of Sfax, Sfax, Tunisia
emna.taktak@redcad.org, {mohamed.tounsi,ahmed.hadjkacem}@fsegs.rnu.tn
[2] LaBRI, Bordeaux INP, Univ. Bordeaux, CNRS, Bordeaux Cedex, France
mohamed.mosbah@u-bordeaux.fr

Abstract. A Wireless Sensor Network (WSN) is an important wireless technology that is widely used in the Internet of things and that has wide variety of applications. In fact, a WSN consists of independent sensors, communicating with each other in a distributed way to monitor the environment. In this network, most of the existing distributed algorithms are designed without referring to a computations model. As a consequence, the study, the comparison and the proof of these algorithms become a difficult task. In this paper, we propose a new computations model based on local interactions. This model relies on Graph Relabelling System (GRS), a graph transformation model suitable for encoding distributed algorithms. We show that using our model simplifies the specification and the proof of distributed algorithms for WSN. We illustrate our proposed model through an example of distributed algorithm for WSN. Proofs are given in this paper to demonstrate the correctness of the selected algorithm.

Keywords: Wireless Sensor Network · Distributed computations
Graph relabelling system · Local interactions · Proofs

1 Introduction

The Internet of Things (IoT) includes a pervasive presence of sensors, actuators, and other devices deployed across large areas. The WSN is widely used as a wireless communication technology in the context of IoT. In fact, WSN has been designed to monitor physical and environmental conditions. Thus, a WSN consists of independent sensors, communicating with each other in distributed fashion to monitor the environment. Plenty of applications exist for WSNs. We are interested in the distributed applications for WSNs. We choose this type of applications because the distributed aspect allows to have scalability in the network i.e. to handle a large number of sensors.

In addition, we find that these applications are widely used for critical systems (health-care system, military system, fire detection system, volcanic eruption system, etc.). Consequently, before developing these applications, we should

© Springer Nature Switzerland AG 2018
N. Montavont and G. Z. Papadopoulos (Eds.): ADHOC-NOW 2018, LNCS 11104, pp. 293–304, 2018.
https://doi.org/10.1007/978-3-030-00247-3_26

be sure that the used algorithms are correct. Therefore, we need a computations model that expresses well our algorithms and allows to prove their correctness. Moreover, such a model makes the comparison between different algorithms possible and easy.

From the existing models, we tackle the population protocols model and its extensions. We find that they have many limits related to the communication description between sensors and to their use in critical systems.

In this paper, we propose a new distributed computations model for WSNs using local interactions. This model is based on the Graph Relabeling System (GRS) and, more generally, on local computations. The local computations are powerful models providing general tools for encoding distributed algorithms [1], for proving their correctness and for understanding their power [2]. Therefore, on one side, our local computations model allows to prove and ensure the correctness of the WSNs algorithms used in many systems including critical systems. On the other side, when using GRS, dealing with proofs becomes an easy task. In fact, with GRS we present an algorithm by a set of rules. Consequently, proofs can be conducted by analyzing the GRS rule by rule. Also, we can use induction to prove that the algorithm's invariants (properties that should be respected by the algorithms) are conserved by the rules. Our model is abstract enough to encode a diversity of WSN algorithms because it uses a high level encoding for distributed algorithms by means of GRS.

This paper details the proposed model through its different sections. In the second section, we start by presenting some basic concepts and definitions related to our work. In the third section, we detail our proposed model. The fourth section is dedicated for an example of distributed algorithm coded with our model and its proof. For the fifth section, it tackles some related work. The last section concludes the paper and gives some future directions.

2   Concepts and Definitions

In the first part of this section we recall the definition of the local computations model. As our work considers computations on two adjacent sensors in the network, we present, in the second part, the concept of local computations on edges (LCE). For the third part, it is dedicated for the definition of an algorithm correctness.

2.1   Local Computations Model

The local computations model makes the operating mode of a distributed system more explicit and more abstract. In this model, a network is represented by a graph whose nodes stand for processors and edges for (bidirectional) links between processors. At every time, each node and each edge is in some particular state, and this state will be encoded by a label. According to its own state and to the states of its neighbours, each node may decide to realise an elementary computation step. After this step, the state of this node, of its neighbours and of the corresponding edges may have changed according to some specific computation rules. We recall that graph relabelling systems satisfy the following requirements:

(C1) they do not change the underlying graph but only the labelling of its components (edges and/or nodes), the final labelling being the result,

(C2) they are local, that is, each relabelling changes only a connected sub-graph of a fixed size in the underlying graph,

(C3) they are locally generated, that is, the applicability condition of the relabelling only depends on the local context of the relabelled sub-graph.

For such systems, the distributed aspect comes from the fact that several relabelling steps can be performed simultaneously on far enough (non-overlapping) sub-graphs, giving the same result as a sequential realisation of them, in any order. A large family of classical distributed algorithms encoded by graph relabelling systems is given in [3].

2.2 Local Computations on Edges

Local computations on edges (LCE) are graph relabelling relations such that each relabelling step depends on and modifies only the labels of two adjacent nodes and the edge linking them. Let $\mathcal{L}$ be a recursively enumerable set. A network $\mathcal{G}$ can be defined as a pair $\mathcal{G} = (G, \lambda)$, where G is the *underlying graph*, and λ is the *labelling function*. λ associates with each processor and link a state in $\mathcal{L}$.

A LCE computation can be defined as a relation $R \subseteq \mathcal{L} \times \mathcal{L}$. A relabelling step consists of (1) choosing, in a non-deterministic way, an edge on which a rule can be applied, and (2) modifying the labels of this edge with respect to the rule. We write $\xrightarrow{R}$ for a relabelling step generated by the rule R, and $\xrightarrow{R^*}$ for the reflexive and transitive closure of $\xrightarrow{R}$.

2.3 Algorithm Correctness

An algorithm is correct if any relabelling sequence starting from initial states terminates. Moreover, any irreducible state reachable from an initial state determines a valid solution.

Let us consider for instance an algorithm S of spanning tree computation. Its correctness can be expressed as follows:

Let G be any simple, connected graph; for any initial state i,

– any rewriting sequence starting from i terminates, and
– any irreducible states reachable from i determines a spanning tree of G.

3   Distributed Computations for WSN by Local Interactions

GRSs have been introduced as suitable model for expressing and studying distributed algorithms on a network of communicating processors [4]. However, they do not capture the WSN particularity. For this reason, in this section we present our new model allowing to adapt the GRS for modelling the distributed algorithms used in a WSN, and proving their correctness. This model relies on a synchronisation algorithm that uses the local computations on edges (LCE) (i.e. communications occur between two nodes). Our local computations model can use other algorithms of synchronisation (after adaptation): LC1 and LC2 [11] where communications occur between more than two nodes. Moreover, this model can be used for designing algorithms working on critical systems because it is fault-tolerant. This important characteristic of fault-tolerance comes from the fact that the synchronisation algorithm LCE does not stop when a sensor is out of energy (disappears from the network).

3.1   Model Description

We recall that, in GRS, a state of a node/edge is encoded through several labels attached to it. This state is updated by a set of relabelling rules. Though, in the context of WSNs, the state of a node is changed in response to two types of events:

- **Internal events** resulting from a sensor's capture i.e. changes in the physical environment of a node. They are expressed through internal relabelling rules.
- **External events** resulting from communication between sensors. The external events are expressed by external relabelling rules.

As a result of this events' classification, we distinguish between the internal labels and the external labels of a sensor. The internal labels are modified by internal events. External labels can be modified by an internal or external event. Table 1 summarises the relation between the events, rules and labels in our model.

We illustrate the presented classification through the example detailed in [5]. This example supposes that we have equipped each bird in a particular flock with a sensor that can determine whether the bird's temperature is elevated or not. Our purpose is to know whether at least 5 birds in the flock are sick (have elevated temperatures).

We present an example for each type of event:

- *The internal event* is a result of changes in the temperature value of a bird. This event modifies the value of a label called **elevated** attached to a node (bird). The label **elevated** represents an internal label. It contains the value **true** if the temperature value of a bird is elevated and the value **false** if it is not elevated. In addition, if the temperature captured is elevated, this event increments an external label called **counter**. The **counter** contains the number of birds with elevated temperature. Hence this internal event concerns only the node concerned by the temperature change.

– *The external event* is a result of a synchronisation between two adjacent nodes. It is realised by an external rule that modifies an external label called **flockState**. The **flockState** contains initially the value: **not infected**. Its value is changed to **infected** for a node if it is synchronised with another node having the value **infected**. This event concerns the two synchronised nodes.

Table 1. Events' description

	Result of	Expressed by	Modify	Concern
Internal events	Capture	Internal relabelling rules	Internal and external labels	One node
External events	Synchronisation between two adjacent nodes	External relabelling rules	External labels	Two adjacent nodes

3.2 Model Formal Description

In this section we give a formal description of our new model. More precisely, we define the labelled graph, relabelling rule and graph relabelling system.

Definition 1. *Labelled graph: A wireless sensor network is represented by a labelled graph $G = (V, E, L_n, L_e, \lambda_s, \rho_s)$. V is a set of nodes which represents sensors. E is a set of edges that represents communication links between nodes. Nodes [resp. Edges] are labelled with labels from a possibly infinite alphabets L_n [resp. L_e]. We call state any pair s of two labelling functions λ_s: $V \rightarrow L_n$ and ρ_s: $E \rightarrow L_e$. The particularity of our model is that L_n is composed of two subsets: L_{n-in} and L_{n-ex}. $L_n = L_{n-in} \cup L_{n-ex}$. The subset L_{n-in} represents the internal labels of a node, whereas L_{n-ex} represents the external labels of a node. We note that these two subsets are disjoint: $L_{n-in} \cap L_{n-ex} = \phi$.*

Definition 2. *A relabelling rule: it is a triple $r = (G_r, S_r, S_{r'})$. (G_r, S_r) and $(G_r, S_{r'})$ are two labelled graphs. The labelled graph (G_r, S_r) is the left side of r and $(G_r, S_{r'})$ is the right side of r. We distinguish two types of rules: internal rules (r_i) and external rules (r_e).*

A relabelling rule r_e can be represented as a relabelling relation on the graph k2 (a ball of radius 2). It is triggered if there is a local synchronisation between two neighbouring nodes (Handshake) [6]. Formally, this rule is specified as follows:
r_e: $L_n \times L_n \times L_e \rightarrow L_n \times L_n \times L_e$. With this formalisation we describe a before/after relation between two adjacent nodes and their common edge. r_e can only update external labels.

A relabelling rule r_i depends and updates only labels of one node. It can update its internal and external labels. Formally, this rule is specified as follow:
r_i: $L_n \rightarrow L_n$.

Our work relies on the LCE model which is based on handshake synchronisations (between two nodes).

Definition 3. *A graph relabelling system: It is a quintuple* $S = \{L_n, L_e, R_e, R_i, I\}$ *encoding the following information:*

- *Two alphabets for labelling nodes and edges* (L_n, L_e). L_n *is decomposed into two sets* L_{n-ex} *and* L_{n-in}.
- *A set of external [resp. internal] relabelling rules* R_e *[resp.* R_i*]*.
- *A function I which associates to the graph a set* I_G *of initial states.*

4 Case Study: Dead Animals Detection

As an example of distributed algorithm for WSN, we cite an algorithm applied for a population of animals. In this population, a sensor is placed on each animal. This sensor allows to detect if the animal is alive or dead (by measuring its temperature for example). Animals in this example are always in the same place. Sensors placed on animals can communicate with each other in order to exchange information about dead animals. The execution of the algorithm allows to mark the alert state on all sensors if the number of dead animals reaches a threshold called **n**. **n** should be less than or equal to the total number of sensors.

The population of animals is represented by a static and complete graph (G). The sensors are represented by nodes (V). These sensors are connected through communication links represented by edges (E) in this graph.

- *Objective:* alert state if the number of dead animal reaches n.
- *Termination:* the diffusion of alert state on the whole graph if the number of dead animals reaches n.

4.1 Algorithm's Formalisation

The algorithm is coded with the following relabelling system: $S = \{L_n, L_e, R_e, R_i, I\}$:

- $L_n = \{L_{n-in}, L_{n-ex}\}$. $L_{n-in} = \{\text{animal\_state}\}$. We have, **animal_state** = {alive, dead}. $L_{n-ex} = \{\text{animals\_count, system\_state}\}$. **animals_count** is between 0 and **animals_number**, it is used for counting the number of dead animals. **system_state** = {normal, alert}. **system_state** becomes alert if the number of dead animals reaches the threshold n.
- $R_i = \{R1, R2\}$. $R_e = \{R3, R4, R5\}$. R_e and R_i are presented in Fig. 1. To simplify the figure, nodes with label **system_state** = alert are presented with empty (non coloured) nodes.
    - The rule R1 allows to change the label **animal_state** from alive to dead (after a capture done by the sensor). In this rule, the node is counted by the **animals_count** that contains the number of dead animals (**C**).

- The rule R2 does the same as R1 for the first and the second label. But, it expresses the exception of R1: when the **animals_count** reaches **n**, the node will be in alert state (non coloured node).
- The rule R3 allows to update the **animals_count** of two communicating nodes. It assigns the sum of the two **animals_count** to one of them and the **animals_count** of the other node will be set to zero.
- The rule R4 does the same as R3 for the first and second label. But, it expresses the exception of R3: when the sum of the two **animals_count** reaches n, the two nodes will be on alert state (non coloured node).
- The rule 5 expresses the spread of the alert state: when a node on alert state communicates with another node not informed by the alert state, the second will mark also the alert state (non coloured node).

- I = {alive, 0, normal}. Because initially, **animal_state** = {alive}, **animals_count** = 0 and **system_state** = normal for all nodes.

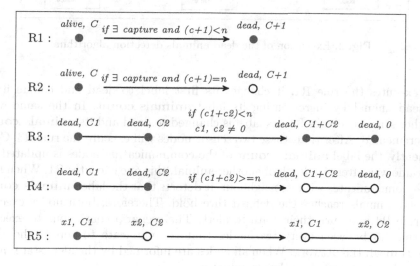

Fig. 1. Rules of dead animals detection algorithm

4.2 Algorithm Execution

We executed the dead animals detection algorithm with **n** = 3 (when a node detects that there are three dead animals, all nodes mark the alert state). The total number of animals **animals_number** = 5. Figure 2 presents the execution of the scenario. Note that nodes with bold and underlined labels execute a rewriting rule.

Initially, all nodes are alive, their labels **animals_count** are set to zero and they do not mark the alert state. After a capture event made by a sensor, this

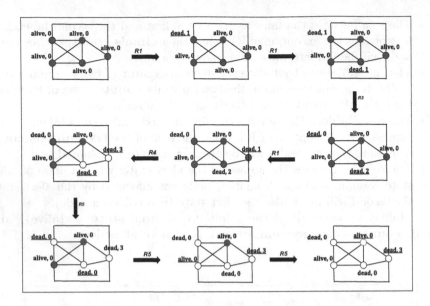

Fig. 2. Execution of the dead animals detection algorithm

one executes the rule R1: it changes its first label to dead and counts itself as dead animal by incrementing its label **animals_count**. In the same way, another sensor executes R1: its label is changed to dead and its **animals_count** is incremented. After that, these two sensor nodes will execute the rule R3. Consequently, the label **animals_count** of the communicating nodes is updated. In the same way after the death of another animal, this one executes R1. When this latter communicates with its neighbour, it detects that the label **animals_count** of dead animals reaches the defined threshold. Therefore, both nodes execute the rule R4 and turn their state to alert. The scenario continuous to execute the rule R5 between every two nodes that communicate to spread the alert state through the network. When all nodes are informed by the alert state (non-coloured nodes), the algorithm terminates.

4.3   Algorithm Proving

Lemma 1. *If the label* **system_state** *is alert then there are at least* **n** *dead animals.*

Proof: The label **system_state** is changed to alert by the rule R2, R4 and R5. For R2, the new value of the label **animals_count** indicates that there are exactly n dead animals. For R4, the new value of the label **animals_count** indicates that the number of dead animals is bigger or equal n, consequently, the number of dead animals is at least equal to n. R2 and R4 are rules that trigger the alert state. However, R5 represents a rule for the spread of the alert state in the network (the number of dead animals in the graph is not incremented). There is no rule that decrements the number of dead animals.

To conclude, if **system_state** is alert then there are at least **n** dead animals.

Lemma 2. *The label* **animals_count** *(C) does not exceed the total number of nodes* **animals_number**.

Proof: The rule R1 increases the **animals_count** C. We have $C + 1 < n$ and $n \leq$ **animals_number**, hence, the **animals_count** C will not exceed the total number of nodes after the application of R1 (by transitivity, we have $C + 1 <$ **animals_number**). The rule R2 increases the **animals_count** C. We have $C + 1 = n$ and $n \leq$ **animals_number**, hence, the **animals_count** C will not exceed the total number of nodes after the application of R2 (by transitivity, we have $C + 1 \leq$ **animals_number**). The rule R3 increases the **animals_count** C1 ($C1 = C1 + C2$). We have $C1 + C2 < n$ and $n \leq$ **animals_number**, hence, the **animals_count** will not exceed the total number of nodes after the application of R3 (by transitivity, we have $C1 + C2 <$ **animals_number**). For the rule R4 we make a proof by absurd: we suppose that $C >$ **animals_number** and we have $C = C1 + C2$. In case $C1 + C2 >$ **animals_number**, there are three possibilities. First, if $C1 >$ **animals_number** then the node should be on alert state because $n \leq$ **animals_number**. Giving that the node is not in alert state then C1 can not be greater than **animals_number**. Second, if $C2 >$ **animals_number** then the second node should be on alert state because $n \leq$ **animals_number**. Giving that this node is not on alert state then C1 can not be greater than **animals_number**. Finally, we consider the case when the sum is greater than **animals_number** $C1 + C2 >$ **animals_number**. Initially, the total number of dead animals in the graph is zero. This total is incremented only by R1 and R2. At maximum R1 or R2 is executed for each node. Thus, this total is at maximum equal to the **animals_number**. For these reason, $C1 + C2$ can not be greater than **animals_number**. The rule R5 does not change the label **animals_count** of the two concerned nodes.

To conclude, the label **animals_count** does not exceed the total number of nodes.

Lemma 3. *The label* **system_state** *can not be changed from alert to normal.*

Proof: The application of R2, R4, R5 changes the label **system_state** from normal to alert. The application of R1 and R3 does not change the label **system_state**.

To conclude, the label **system_state** can not be changed from alert to normal.

Lemma 4. *The system S is noetherian:*
A system is noetherian if it satisfies the property of termination i.e. no infinite sequence of rules exists.

Proof: Let φ be the function that associates to the labelling C of S a triplet $\varphi(C) = (|C|_{alive}, |C|_{td}, |C|_{normal})$. $|C|_{alive}$ is the number of nodes having the value alive for the label **animal_state**. $|C|_{td}$ is the total number of nodes animals_number **minus** the number of nodes having the value dead for the label **animal_state** and the value 0 for the value **animals_count**. $|C|_{normal}$ is the number of nodes having the value normal for the label **system_state**. The application of R1 decreases $|C|_{alive}$. However, it does not change $|C|_{td}$ and $|C|_{normal}$. The application of R2 decreases $|C|_{alive}$ and $|C|_{normal}$ (proved by Lemma 3). However, it does not change $|C|_{td}$. The application of R3 decreases $|C|_{td}$ and does not change $|C|_{alive}$ and $|C|_{normal}$. The application of R4 decreases $|C|_{normal}$ (proved by Lemma 3) and $|C|_{td}$. However, it does not change $|C|_{alive}$. The application of R5 decreases $|C|_{normal}$ (proved by Lemma 3). However, it does not change $|C|_{td}$ and $|C|_{alive}$.

Thus, $\varphi(C0) > \varphi(C1) > ... > \varphi(Ci)$. To conclude, the system S is noetherian.

5   Related Work

The population protocol is widely used for WSNs. It is proposed by Angluin et al. [7]. In fact, authors represent tiny objects (sensors) as agents with finite states and passively mobile. The movement pattern of the agents is usually the result of some natural phenomenon, for example river flow, wind, or sensors attached to some carrier. Agents in the population protocol communicate in pairs and form an asynchronous and anonymous network [5,8]. In this model, the agents forming the network are identically programmed and form a population of finite but unbounded size. The population protocol calculates a predicate or a function of the distributed entries that these agents have received from their environment. For example, the population protocol could be designed for a population of birds in order to decide whether the number of birds that are sick reaches a certain threshold [8]. The calculations are based on interactions between pairs. Two agents can communicate each time they are close to each other and also share a communication link. In this communication, an agent will play the role of initiator while the second will play the role of receiver. These two agents will exchange their current states. Consequently, each one will update its state according to its role, its current state, the received state, and the rules of the protocol. All possible interactions between pairs of agents are represented by the directed edges of the interaction graph whose nodes represent the agents of the population.

The computational power of the population protocol is ameliorated by Chatzigiannakis et al. [9]. They propose the mediated population protocol allowing the communication links (connecting agents) to have states. Another extension of the population protocol is the model PALOMA [10]. It allows agents to have a memory space more important instead of a constant memory space.

The strong point of these models is their computational power. However, we notice that they have several limits. First, the description of communications between agents is too abstract and it is based on strong hypothesis: authors suppose that each pair of agents will eventually meet and interact. Thus, they assume the interaction graphs are complete so that all pairs interactions are permissible. Second, these models are designed exclusively for passively mobile nodes. Additionally, they are based only on pairwise communications, eliminating networks where communications can occur between a ball of nodes. Finally, as mentioned in [5], authors do not address the issue of fault tolerance, which has an immense practical importance in real sensor networks. When an agent dies, say from an exhausted battery, many of the algorithms using the population protocols would not survive, especially those based on leader election. Although, 'WSN algorithms are widely used in critical systems where non-fault-tolerant algorithms should not exist.

Our proposed model is dedicated for asynchronous WSN. It is based on the local computation on edges (LCE) where communications are made between pair of nodes. Our local computations model can be combined with other algorithms of synchronization (after adaptation): LC1 and LC2 [11] where in both communications occur between more than two nodes but in a different way. The advantage of our model is that it relies on the local computation on edges that is fault-tolerant [12]. Consequently, when designing algorithms for critical system, our model is the adequate one. It is fault-tolerant and allows to easily prove the correctness of algorithms.

6   Conclusion and Future Work

In this paper we proposed a model for wireless sensor networks that is based on local computations and specifically on the graph relabelling system. We illustrated this model through coding an example of distributed algorithm. This algorithm allows to spread the alert state on all nodes when the number of dead animals reaches a defined threshold. We proved the functioning of this algorithm to ensure its correctness. As future work, we aim at proving algorithms coded with our model automatically with Event-B using the plateform Rodin [13]. Moreover, we notice that wireless sensors are commonly powered using batteries. The energy consumption is an important performance measure of a sensor network, although it has not yet been considered by the existing models. Therefore an appropriate energy model would be an interesting feature to import [14].

References

1. Bauderon, M., Métivier, Y., Mosbah, M., Sellami, A.: Graph relabelling systems: a tool for encoding, proving, studying and visualizing distributed algorithms. Electron. Notes Theor. Comput. Sci. **51**(Suppl. 1), 93–107 (2002). GETGRATS Closing Workshop
2. Litovsky, I., Sopena, É.: Graph relabelling systems and distributed algorithms. In: Handbook of Graph Grammars and Computing by Graph Transformation, pp. 1–56. World Scientific, Singapore (2001)

3. Bauderon, M., Métivier, Y., Mosbah, M., Sellami, A.: From local computations to asynchronous message passing systems. Technical report RR-1271-02, LaBRI (2002)
4. Métivier, Y., Sopena, É.: Graph relabelling systems: a general overview. Comput. Artif. Intell. 16(2), 167–185 (1997)
5. Angluin, D., Aspnes, J., Diamadi, Z., Fischer, M.J., Peralta, R.: Computation in networks of passively mobile finite-state sensors. Distrib. Comput. 18(4), 235–253 (2006)
6. Filou, V., Mosbah, M., Tounsi, M.: Towards proved distributed algorithms through refinement, composition and local computations. In: 2013 Workshops on Enabling Technologies: Infrastructure for Collaborative Enterprises, Hammamet, Tunisia, 17–20 June 2013, pp. 353–358. IEEE Computer Society (2013)
7. Angluin, D., Aspnes, J., Eisenstat, D., Ruppert, E.: The computational power of population protocols. Distrib. Comput. 20(4), 279–304 (2007)
8. Angluin, D., Aspnes, J., Diamadi, Z., Fischer, M.J., Peralta, R.: Computation in networks of passively mobile finite-state sensors. In: Proceedings of the Twenty-Third Annual ACM Symposium on Principles of Distributed Computing, PODC 2004, pp. 290–299. ACM, New York (2004)
9. Michail, O., Chatzigiannakis, I., Spirakis, P.G.: Mediated population protocols. Theor. Comput. Sci. 412(22), 2434–2450 (2011)
10. Chatzigiannakis, I., Michail, O., Nikolaou, S., Pavlogiannis, A., Spirakis, P.G.: Passively mobile communicating machines that use restricted space. Theor. Comput. Sci. 412(46), 6469–6483 (2011)
11. Métivier, Y., Saheb, N., Zemmari, A.: Randomized local elections. Inf. Process. Lett. 82(6), 313–320 (2002)
12. Fontaine, A., Mosbah, M., Tounsi, M., Zemmari, A.: A fault-tolerant handshake algorithm for local computations. In: 30th International Conference on Advanced Information Networking and Applications Workshops, AINA 2016 Workshops, Crans-Montana, Switzerland, 23–25 March 2016, pp. 475–480 (2016)
13. Abrial, J.R.: Modeling in Event-B: System and Software Engineering. Cambridge University Press, New York (2013)
14. Filippas, A., Nikolaou, S., Pavlogiannis, A., Michail, O., Chatzigiannakis, I., Spirakis, P.: Computational models for wireless sensor networks: a survey. In: 1st International Conference for Undergraduate and Postgraduate Students in Computer Engineering, Informatics, Related Technologies and Applications (Eureka!), October 2010

Testbeds and Real-World Deployments

SPHERE Deployment Manager: A Tool for Deploying IoT Sensor Networks at Large Scale

Xenofon Fafoutis[1,2](✉), Atis Elsts[1], George Oikonomou[1], and Robert Piechocki[1]

[1] Department of Electrical and Electronic Engineering, University of Bristol, Woodland Road, Bristol BS8 1UB, UK
{xenofon.fafoutis,atis.elsts,g.oikonomou,r.j.piechocki}@bristol.ac.uk
[2] DTU Compute, Technical University of Denmark, Richard Petersens Plads, 2800 Kongens Lyngby, Denmark
xefa@dtu.dk

Abstract. Internet of Things (IoT) technology has the potential to revolutionise several domains of everyday life, including the healthcare sector. In order to reach its full potential, IoT technology needs to be evaluated in the real world, beyond controlled environments, such as laboratories and test-beds. SPHERE is an experimental sensing platform for healthcare in a residential environment. Unlike other similar smart home health systems, SPHERE is deployed in a large number of properties of volunteers. Based on our experiences and lessons learned from SPHERE's large-scale deployments, this paper focuses on the challenge of effectively managing the sensor installation overhead, aiming at supporting our deployment technicians with achieving a satisfactory deployment throughput. In this context, this paper presents the SPHERE Deployment Manager: an open-source tool that facilitates the deployment of bespoke IoT networks by technicians that are not experts in IoT technology. We believe that the SPHERE Deployment Manager is a tool that can accelerate future IoT research deployments of similar nature and scale.

Keywords: Deployment tools · Sensor deployments
Internet of Things

1 Introduction

In the era of the Internet of Things (IoT), networked embedded sensing devices are going to be the foundational building block of several critical infrastructures of high societal and economic impact [1]. In this context, there is a growing interest in the academic community in evaluating IoT enabling technologies in

---

X. Fafoutis—Work done prior to joining DTU Compute.

© Springer Nature Switzerland AG 2018
N. Montavont and G. Z. Papadopoulos (Eds.): ADHOC-NOW 2018, LNCS 11104, pp. 307–318, 2018.
https://doi.org/10.1007/978-3-030-00247-3_27

the real world, rather than in controlled environments, such as laboratories and test-beds. At an infrastructure level, there is evidence that the environment plays a critical role in the performance of an IoT sensor network [21]. It is, therefore, vital to test these technologies in real environments in order to validate their effectiveness and robustness in a variety of contexts. At a data level, the robustness of machine learning models heavily depends on the quality of the training data. Indeed, models that are trained on input data that are based on small groups of participants, performing scripted activities, under ideal data collection conditions, tend to perform very well [10,20]. Yet, such models would be challenged in the wild, where the input data are imperfect (*e.g.* missing data, noise, etc. [14,19]) and derive from large groups of people performing free-living activities [3]. At an application level, several research hypotheses require input from dozens of individuals to be tested. This is particularly relevant for the health care domain. Indeed, there is increasing evidence that behaviour plays a critical role in the development of chronic health conditions, such as depression [18] and dementia [22]. In this context, large-scale IoT deployments have the potential to provide healthcare professionals with an unbiased and quantitative mechanism to assess the long-term behaviour of their patients.

SPHERE (a Sensing Platform for HEalthcare in a Residential Environment) is a multipurpose, multi-modal platform of non-medical home sensors that aims to provide data that would allow researchers to learn the behavioural patterns of the residents, and, enable them to conduct data-rich clinical studies [25]. Different to many other smart home health systems evaluated in controlled environments [13,15], the SPHERE platform is intended to be deployed in a large number of properties in the Bristol area for a period of up to 12 months (see SPHERE's 100 homes study[1]). At the time of writing, the SPHERE platform has been successfully deployed in the houses of 45 volunteers, and, indeed, the current rate of deployments is only constrained by the rate of recruiting. The purpose of the SPHERE deployments is three-fold. Firstly, a large number of IoT deployments in the wild, would allows us to understand and overcome the weakness and limitations of state-of-the-art IoT enabling technologies: for example, scheduling [6] and interference avoidance [4] in IEEE 802.15.4-2015 TSCH (time slotted, channel hopping) networks. Secondly, data collected from large-scale deployments in the wild, would enable the development of robust machine learning models that are able to operate effectively in real world situations and under missing data [14]. Thirdly, the produced dataset will be shared with medical professionals, enabling clinical research studies.

There are several challenges with IoT deployments of that scale. From software development to remote monitoring, the challenges of deploying IoT sensor networks in outdoor and indoor environments have attracted the interest of the research community over the last decades [2,12,17]. Leveraging experience and insight gain from the SPHERE deployments, our previous works discuss challenges, experiences and lessons learned from making SPHERE's bespoke IoT sensing platforms [7], as well as developing IoT networking software for them

---

[1] http://irc-sphere.ac.uk/100-homes-study.

[5]. Extending our previous work, the focus of this paper is on effectively managing the overhead of preparing IoT sensors for installation in a large-scale context.

Indeed, managing the overhead of preparation and installation is crucial for maintaining a satisfactory deployment throughput. In SPHERE, the preparation and installation of the IoT sensing platforms is conducted by a small number of deployment technicians that are not experts in the deployed IoT technology. To accelerate the deployment process and facilitate the job of the deployment technicians, we have designed and developed the SPHERE Deployment Manager. The SPHERE Deployment Manager is a tool that supports the deployment technicians with preparing bespoke IoT networks, tailored to the characteristics of each of the participating houses. The contributions of this paper can be summarised as follows. Firstly, we present requirements and challenges regarding the preparation of IoT sensors for deployment from the SPHERE perspective. We believe that IoT deployments of similar nature share the same challenges to a great extent. Secondly, we design, develop and present the SPHERE Deployment Manager: a supporting tool that facilitates the deployment of bespoke IoT networks by technicians that are not IoT experts. Lastly, with this paper, the SPHERE Deployment Manager is released as an open source project[2].

The remainder of the paper is structured as follows. Section 2 summarises the IoT embedded devices and networks of the SPHERE system, including details on security, configurability, and deployment requirements. Section 3 presents the SPHERE Deployment Manager. Lastly, Sect. 4 concludes the paper, providing deployment statistics.

2   The SPHERE System

In a nutshell, the SPHERE System has three distinct sensing modalities, namely environmental sensors, video sensors, and wearable sensors [25]. The focus of this paper is on the embedded IoT sensing devices of SPHERE, namely the environmental and wearable sensors. For further details on the video sub-system of SPHERE we refer the reader to [11]. The data generated from these sensing modalities is collected in a central server within each deployed house, named SPHERE Home Gateway, and stored in an encrypted solid state drive. Whilst sensor data are saved locally, monitoring data is transmitted over the cellular network to the University of Bristol for remote monitoring.

Each deployed house is uniquely identified in an anonymous manner with a 4-digit identifier, namely the House ID (HID).

2.1 IoT Embedded Devices and Networks

The IoT sub-system of SPHERE is composed of three types of embedded devices, namely the SPHERE Environmental Sensors (SPES-2), the SPHERE Wearable Sensors (SPW-2), and the SPHERE Gateways (SPG-2), as shown in Fig. 1b.

---

[2] http://www.github.com/irc-sphere/sphere-deployment-manager.

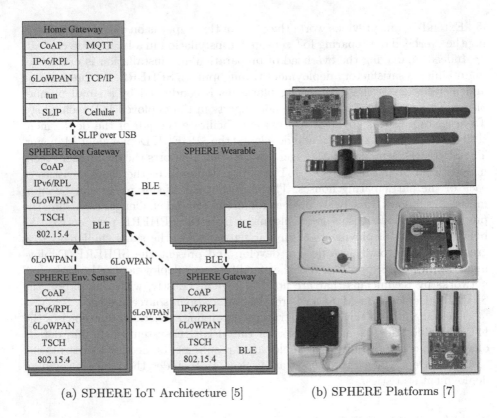

(a) SPHERE IoT Architecture [5]   (b) SPHERE Platforms [7]

Fig. 1. SPHERE IoT architecture [5]

The SPHERE Environmental Sensors are battery-powered devices and they are responsible for collecting environmental data, such as temperature, humidity, light levels, and mobility levels, at room-level granularity [8]. One of Environmental Sensors also hosts a water flow sensor [24]. The SPHERE Wearable Sensors are wrist-worn acceleration-based activity sensors [9]. One wearable sensor is provided to each resident of the house. Lastly, the SPHERE Gateways are mains-powered dual-radio nodes that form a backbone low power network that is responsible to collect the sensor data and forward them to the SPHERE Home Gateway for long-term storage.

In particular, the SPHERE Gateways form a 6LoWPAN (IPv6 over Low-Power Wireless Personal Area Networks) over IEEE 802.15.4 TSCH mesh network in each home [5], as shown in Fig. 1a. One of gateways is connected to the SPHERE Home Gateway, playing the role of the root gateway of 6LoWPAN. All the remaining gateways act as data forwarders. The SPHERE Environmental Sensors are connected directly to the 6LoWPAN network as leaf nodes. The SPHERE Wearable Sensors communicate the acceleration data by broadcasting Bluetooth Low Energy (BLE) non-connectable undirected advertisement packets periodically. The BLE advertisements are received by the secondary radio

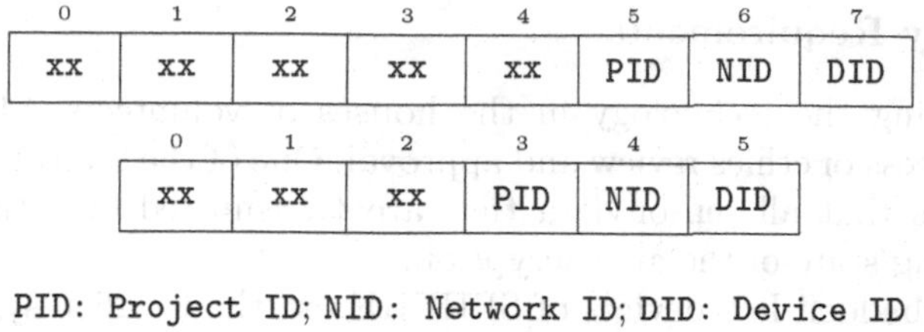

0	1	2	3	4	5	6	7
xx	xx	xx	xx	xx	PID	NID	DID

0	1	2	3	4	5
xx	xx	xx	PID	NID	DID

PID: Project ID; NID: Network ID; DID: Device ID

Fig. 2. Custom MAC addresses: IEEE 802.15.4 (top) and BLE (bottom).

of the SPHERE Gateways, which operates in BLE mode. Acting as gateways from the BLE to the 6LoWPAN network, the SPHERE Gateways forward the wearable sensor data to the SPHERE Home Gateway. Lastly, the system is leveraging the broadcasting nature of BLE advertisements to collect multiple copies of the wearable data packets. The signal strength of the advertisement packets, as received by multiple gateways, is leveraged for room-level indoor localisation.

A custom MAC (Medium Access Control) addressing scheme is adopted for the embedded devices of SPHERE. As illustrated in Fig. 2, the three least significant bytes of the BLE and IEEE 802.15.4 MAC addresses are modified as follows. The third-to-last byte is the Project ID (PID), allowing the same scheme to be used in future deployments; SPHERE uses PID = 0x00. The second-to-last byte is the Network ID (NID). The NID uniquely identifies each deployed house, *i.e.* the House ID (HID) is uniquely mapped to a NID. The least significant byte is the Device ID (DID). The DID uniquely identifies each embedded device, and it can also be used to identify the type of the device. In particular, the IEEE 802.15.4 radio of the SPG-2 is assigned a DID in [0x01-0x3F]; the BLE radio of the SPG-2 is assigned a DID in [0x40-0x7F]; the SPES-2 is assigned a DID in [0x80-0xBF]; and the SPW-2 is assigned a DID in [0xC0-0xFF]. The DID 0x01 is reserved for the root SPG-2 gateway.

The purpose of the custom addressing scheme is multifold. Firstly, MAC filtering is implemented to prevent external devices from joining the IEEE 802.15.4 TSCH network. This is particularly relevant in cases of overlapping TSCH deployments. Secondly, the custom MAC addresses are used to form the TSCH schedule and ensure that battery-powered devices operate as leaf nodes, *i.e.* do not forward traffic [6]. Thirdly, the custom MAC addresses are used as unique identifiers in the database. This ensures a logical coherence in the sensor data. For example, if a wearable sensor breaks and gets replaced, the same MAC address is used by the replacement and the sensor data from the two devices can be directly linked to each other. It is noted that, globally unique MAC addresses are considered personally identifiable information [16], whilst the custom MAC addresses of SPHERE are equivalent to pseudo-anonymous identifiers.

2.2 Security Requirements

Before deploying the technology in the houses of volunteers, SPHERE went through a process of ethics review and approval. One of the ethical commitments of SPHERE is that all sensor data that are transmitted over the air will be encrypted using state-of-the art encryption.

All the embedded IoT devices of SPHERE use the CC2650 system-on-chip, which incorporates hardware-accelerated AES (Advanced Encryption Standard) encryption. We implement this security commitment using hop-by-hop symmetric encryption, using the hardware-accelerated AES-128 module of CC2650 and one hard-coded encryption key per house. We consider that one encryption key per deployed house provides a sufficient level of security for the following reasons. Firstly, sensor data from the embedded IoT devices are transmitted using short-range wireless technology, and thus, can only be eavesdropped locally. Note that the location and identity of the participants are treated as highly confidential and kept secret even from the SPHERE researchers themselves. Therefore, the threat is limited to the direct neighbourhood of each deployment. Secondly, contrary to using a SPHERE-wide encryption key, a unique key per deployed house secures the confidentiality of the sensor data of participants from each other, should their identity is leaked via their social circles.

An interesting peculiarity of the SPHERE IoT network (see Sect. 2.1) is that the BLE network is unidirectional: the SPHERE Wearable Sensors communicate their data using non-connectable undirected BLE advertisements. The advantages of this approach are primarily energy-efficiency and efficient mobility support. However, as a result, the SPHERE Wearable Sensors are unable to receive any information. Hence, the encryption key must be installed to the device together with the firmware.

2.3 Configurability Requirements

Every house is different. The SPHERE houses differ in their building era (ranging from Victorian to contemporary), number of rooms (ranging from two-bedroom apartments to detached houses with more than ten rooms), number of floors (from one to four), materials used (different types of locally-sourced sandstone and limestone, bricks, or wood) and in other parameters. The number of SPHERE participants range from one to five per house. Some of SPHERE's houses are close to the centre of the city and receive interfering WiFi signals from a large number of nearby access points; others are in rural areas beyond the boundaries of Bristol.

This diversity makes it challenging to create one-fits-all software solution. In an embedded networking stack, there is a large number of configurable MAC-layer parameters that affect the performance of the system, and that ideally would be tuned for each house separately [23]. However, the large number of deployments makes such fine-tuning impractical in SPHERE. The solution used in SPHERE instead is to (1) enable runtime adaptations (for example, the

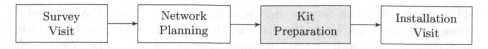

Fig. 3. Overview of the deployment process. The SPHERE Deployment Manager supports the highlighted *Kit Preparation* stage.

SPHERE TSCH networking stack automatically selects which wireless channels to use in order to minimise interference from external sources [4]) and (2) to pre-configure the number of sensor devices of each type to be deployed in a SPHERE house, and use that as a constant MAC-layer parameter. Knowing this number of devices of each type allows to statically reserve slots in the TSCH schedule in a fair manner and with no run-time overhead [6].

Technically, we achieve this per-house configurability though pre-building SPHERE firmware images for each possible type of configuration. This means that a large number of new firmware images are produced after each software update; it would be impossible to test all these images manually. Therefore we integrated a fully automated regression testing step in the build process. We use the Cooja network simulator for this testing step. As an example, the testing process verifies that for each configuration, the simulated network achieves 100% packet delivery rate in several different multihop network topologies.

In most cases, the deployment technicians do not need to explicitly configure MAC-layer parameters, since they are implied by the numbers of devices.

2.4 Deployment Process and Requirements

The deployment process, illustrated in Fig. 3, is summarised as follows. Upon successful recruitment, the SPHERE Deployment Officer arranges a Survey Visit, and assigns a randomly generated HID to the new participating house, as well as a letter (A, B, ...) to each resident of the house. During the survey visit, a SPHERE Deployment Technician creates a house plan, identifies a tentative location for the SPHERE Home Gateway, and identifies all available power plugs for the SPHERE Gateways, amongst other tasks that are out of the scope of this paper. The Network Planning stage follows next. In this stage, the technician plans the deployment, identifying the number of required embedded IoT devices and their location. The Kit Preparation stage follows. In this stage, the SPHERE Deployment Technician uploads the firmware on the embedded devices, installs the encryption key, and sets up the respective custom MAC address, as specified in Sect. 2.1. The IoT devices are then ready for the Installation Visit. During the installation of the devices, the SPHERE Deployment Technician marks the exact location of the deployed sensors. Lastly, the deployment technician gives to each participant their designated wearable sensor.

To facilitate their installation and future maintenance, all deployed embedded IoT devices must be easy to track by the deployment technicians in a quick and efficient manner. We address this requirement with QR (Quick Response) code labels that contain a unique identifier for each device, *i.e.* the custom MAC address for the Wearable Sensors, and the custom IPv6 address of Environmental Sensors and Gateways. Hence, by scanning the QR code label of an IoT device, the technicians can easily inspect relevant information about the device such its `DID` and `NID`. Moreover, they can directly query the contents of the QR code in the database, should they need to look deeper into the monitoring data and sensor data generated by the device. The labels for the wearable sensors also contain the letter identifier $(A, B, \ldots)$, assisting the participants with identifying their personal wearable sensor.

It is important to highlight that SPHERE is deployed in the private houses of participants, who are interrupting their everyday life to volunteer to a scientific experiment. It is therefore very important to keep both the duration and the number of the visits to the absolutely minimum. In addition, the time of the technicians is a very limited resource, and the efficient usage of their time is vital for sustaining a good deployment throughput.

3   The SPHERE Deployment Manager

The SPHERE Deployment Manager is a tool that primarily aims to assist the deployment technicians with *Kit Preparation* stage of the deployment, as described in Sect. 2.4. In addition, the SPHERE Deployment Manager is also used as a quick reference to the active `HIDs` and to the number of IoT devices deployed to each property. An illustration of the folder structure of the SPHERE Deployment Manager is provided in Fig. 4a.

In its current implementation, the SPHERE Deployment Manager supports up to 256 deployments. Indeed, during its installation, it generates a key file that contains 256 randomly generated 128-bit encryption keys. The key file itself is encrypted and password-protected.

The SPHERE Deployment Manager has three types of users, namely the *Researchers*, the *Deployment Officers*, and the *Deployment Technicians*.

3.1   Firmware, Table of Deployments, and Configuration Files

The researchers are responsible for creating and releasing new firmware versions. A new firmware version is released by adding a new directory under the `firmware` directory, titled after the release version number, as shown in Fig. 4a. The directory contains the raw images of each type of deployed device, including a different image for each static TSCH schedule (see Sect. 2.3). The version number is incremented for each new version, following a `major.minor` pattern – at the time of writing, the current deployed version is `elmer.4`. Old versions are not removed, allowing the deployment technicians to deploy a previous version if faults are identified in the newly released version of the firmware.

The deployment officer is responsible for maintaining a table of deployments that is named `sphere-network-id.csv`, as shown in Fig. 4a. This table is composed of four columns, namely the `NID`, the `HID`, and two binary fields that indicate whether the corresponding `HID` is allocated to a particular deployment,

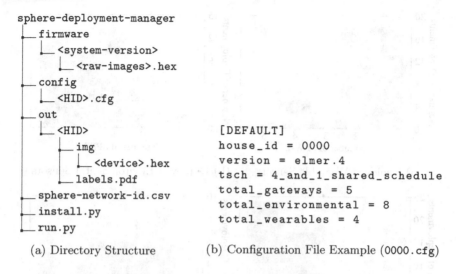

```
sphere-deployment-manager
├── firmware
│   └── <system-version>
│       └── <raw-images>.hex
├── config
│   └── <HID>.cfg
├── out
│   └── <HID>
│       ├── img
│       │   └── <device>.hex
│       └── labels.pdf
├── sphere-network-id.csv
├── install.py
└── run.py
```

```
[DEFAULT]
house_id = 0000
version = elmer.4
tsch = 4_and_1_shared_schedule
total_gateways = 5
total_environmental = 8
total_wearables = 4
```

    (a) Directory Structure   (b) Configuration File Example (0000.cfg)

Fig. 4. (a) Illustration of the SPHERE Deployment Manager's folder structure. (b) Example of a network configuration file for deployment HID = 0000.

and whether the deployment is active. The table has 256 rows that correspond to the NIDs: [0-255]. Each row implicitly corresponds to an encryption key in the key file. As highlighted in Sect. 2.4, following the recruitment of a new participant, the deployment officer randomly generates a unique HID for the new deployment and updates the table of deployments. In particular, the HID is assigned to an available NID and it is marked as allocated. Further to that, the deployment officer keeps the table up to date with updates in the status of the deployments. For instance, when a participant withdraws from the project, the NID is marked as inactive. This ensures that the same NID, and thus the same encryption key, will not be used in more than one deployment.

After the *Network Planning* stage of the deployment process (Fig. 3), the deployment technicians are responsible for preparing a configuration file for the deployment. This configuration file records the number of SPHERE Gateways, SPHERE Environmental Sensors, and SPHERE Wearable Sensors to be deployed. In addition, the file specifies the version of the firmware and the TSCH schedule to be used. An example configuration file for deployment HID = 0000 is shown in Fig. 4b.

3.2 Operation and Output

During the *Kit Preparation* stage of the deployment process (see Sect. 2.4) the deployment technicians execute the script run.py of the SPHERE Deployment Manager, providing the HID as input argument. The technicians also provide the password required to access the encryption key file.

The main purpose of the script is to prepare the firmware image for each IoT device to be deployed. To that end, a special 32-byte block is reserved in the flash

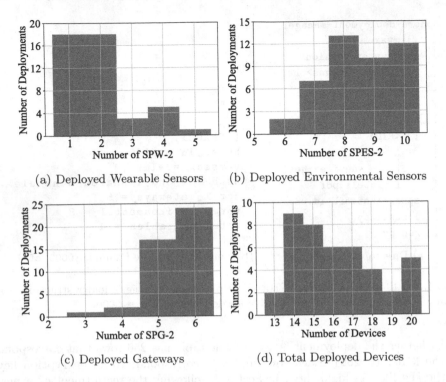

(a) Deployed Wearable Sensors   (b) Deployed Environmental Sensors

(c) Deployed Gateways   (d) Total Deployed Devices

Fig. 5. Deployment histograms extracted from the configuration files. In total, there are 706 deployed devices in 45 deployments: 88 deployed wearable sensors, 376 deployed environmental sensors, and 242 deployed gateways (April 12, 2018).

memory of the CC2650 System-on-Chip. A explicit instruction in the linker script ensures that this memory block would be free in the raw images (see Sect. 3.1). The SPHERE Deployment Manager execution script then operates as follows. First, it matches the provided HID to the NID using the table of deployments and extracts the corresponding encryption key from the key file. Then, for each device to be deployed, it generates the custom MAC address (see Sect. 2.1) and writes the address and the encryption key on the reserved flash memory block, effectively generating a bespoke image for each IoT device.

The SPHERE Deployment Manager execution script also generates labels for each device to be deployed. The label contains a QR code of the MAC or IPv6 address of the device, as well as the DID for quick access. The label of each wearable sensor also includes the respective letter identifier (see Sect. 2.4). The script then generates a LATEX source file that places all the labels in order, and compiles a label document (labels.pdf), ready to be printed on a 5 × 13 label paper. The outputs of the script are saved in out, as shown in Fig. 4a.

The deployment technicians prepare the IoT devices for installation by programming them with their corresponding generated image, mounting them inside their enclosures and sticking the corresponding label on the enclosure.

4   Deployment Statistics and Concluding Remarks

This paper presents SPHERE Deployment Manager, a tool for supporting large-scale deployments of IoT sensing platforms. Indeed, since December 2016, the SPHERE Deployment Manager is used to support the deployment of IoT sensing technology in the houses of 45 volunteers in Bristol, UK. For further information, Fig. 5 plots deployment statistics, extracted from the configuration files of the deployed properties, and serves as evidence that the SPHERE Deployment Manager can effectively support large-scale real-world IoT deployments. It is the authors belief that the SPHERE Deployment Manager has the potential to accelerate future research deployments of similar nature and scale.

Acknowledgement. This work was performed under the SPHERE (a Sensor Platform for HEalthcare in a Residential Environment) IRC funded by the UK Engineering and Physical Sciences Research Council (EPSRC), Grant EP/K031910/1.

The authors would also like to thank the SPHERE Deployment Technicians, Paddy Uglow and Russell Knights, for their valuable feedback during the development of the SPHERE Deployment Manager.

References

1. Al-Fuqaha, A., Guizani, M., Mohammadi, M., Aledhari, M., Ayyash, M.: Internet of things: a survey on enabling technologies, protocols, and applications. IEEE Commun. Surv. Tutorials **17**(4), 2347–2376 (2015)
2. Barrenetxea, G., Ingelrest, F., Schaefer, G., Vetterli, M.: The Hitchhiker's guide to successful wireless sensor network deployments. In: Proceedings of 6th ACM Conference Embedded Network Sensor Systems, pp. 43–56 (2008)
3. Diethe, T., Flach, P.: Smart-homes for ehealth: uncertainty management and calibration. In: NIPS Workshop on Machine Learning in Healthcare, December 2015
4. Elsts, A., Fafoutis, X., Piechocki, R., Craddock, I.: Adaptive channel selection in IEEE 802.15.4 TSCH networks. In: 2017 Global Internet of Things Summit (GIoTS), pp. 1–6 (2017)
5. Elsts, A., Oikonomou, G., Fafoutis, X., Piechocki, R.: Internet of things for smart homes: lessons learned from the SPHERE case study. In: Global Internet of Things Summit (GIoTS), pp. 1–6 (2017)
6. Elsts, A., Fafoutis, X., Pope, J., Oikonomou, G., Piechocki, R., Craddock, I.: Scheduling high-rate unpredictable traffic in IEEE 802.15. 4 TSCH networks. In: Proceedings of International Conference Distributed Computing in Sensor Systems (DCOSS), pp. 3–10. IEEE (2017)
7. Fafoutis, X., Elsts, A., Piechocki, R., Craddock, I.: Experiences and lessons learned from making iot sensing platforms for large-scale deployments. IEEE Access **6**, 3140–3148 (2018)
8. Fafoutis, X., Elsts, A., Vafeas, A., Oikonomou, G., Piechocki, R.: Demo: SPES-2 - a sensing platform for maintenance-free residential monitoring. In: Proceedings of International Conference Embedded Wireless Systems and Networks (EWSN), pp. 240–241 (2017)
9. Fafoutis, X., et al.: Designing wearable sensing platforms for healthcare in a residential environment. EAI Endorsed Trans. Pervasive Health Technol. **17**(12), 1–11 (2017)

10. Gao, L., Bourke, A.K., Nelson, J.: Evaluation of accelerometer based multi-sensor versus single-sensor activity recognition systems. Med. Eng. Phys. **36**(6), 779–785 (2014)
11. Hall, J., et al.: Designing a video monitoring system for AAL applications: the SPHERE Case Study. In: IET Conference Proceedings (2016)
12. Hnat, T.W., et al.: The Hitchhiker's guide to successful residential sensing deployments. In: Proceedings of 9th ACM Conference Embedded Networked Sensor Systems, pp. 232–245 (2011)
13. Islam, S.R., Kwak, D., Kabir, M.H., Hossain, M., Kwak, K.S.: The internet of things for health care: a comprehensive survey. IEEE Access **3**, 678–708 (2015)
14. Karadogan, S., Marchegiani, L., Hansen, L., Larsen, J.: How efficient is estimation with missing data? In: Proceedings of 2011 IEEE International Conference on Acoustics, Speech and Signal Processing (ICASSP), pp. 2260–2263. IEEE (2011)
15. Ko, J., Lu, C., Srivastava, M.B., Stankovic, J.A., Terzis, A., Welsh, M.: Wireless sensor networks for healthcare. Proc. IEEE **98**(11), 1947–1960 (2010)
16. Krishnamurthy, B., Wills, C.E.: On the leakage of personally identifiable information via online social networks. In: Proceedings of 2nd ACM Workshop on Online Social Networks, pp. 7–12. ACM, New York (2009)
17. Langendoen, K., Baggio, A., Visser, O.: Murphy loves potatoes: experiences from a pilot sensor network deployment in precision agriculture. In: Proceedings of 20th IEEE International Parallel Distributed Processing Symposium, pp. 1–8 (2006)
18. Livingston, G., Blizard, B., Mann, A.: Does sleep disturbance predict depression in elderly people? A study in inner London. Br. J. Gen. Pract. **43**(376), 445–448 (1993)
19. Marchegiani, L., Posner, I.: Leveraging the urban soundscape: auditory perception for smart vehicles. In: 2017 IEEE International Conference on Robotics and Automation (ICRA), pp. 6547–6554, May 2017
20. Maurer, U., Smailagic, A., Siewiorek, D., Deisher, M.: Activity recognition and monitoring using multiple sensors on different body positions. In: International Workshop on Wearable and Implantable Body Sensor Networks (BSN) (2006)
21. Mottola, L., Picco, G.P., Ceriotti, M., Gună, S., Murphy, A.L.: Not all wireless sensor networks are created equal: a comparative study on tunnels. ACM Trans. Sen. Netw. **7**(2), 15:1–15:33 (2010)
22. Pfeffer, R., Kurosaki, T., Harrah Jr., C., Chance, J., Filos, S.: Measurement of functional activities in older adults in the community. J. Gerontol. **37**(3), 323–329 (1982)
23. Strübe, M., Lukas, F., Li, B., Kapitza, R.: DrySim: simulation-aided deployment-specific tailoring of mote-class WSN software. In: Proceedings of 17th ACM International Conference Modeling, Analysis and Simulation of Wireless and Mobile Systems, pp. 3–11 (2014)
24. Vafeas, A., et al.: Energy-efficient, noninvasive water flow sensor. In: Proceedings of 4th IEEE International Conference Smart Computing (SMARTCOMP) (2018)
25. Woznowski, P., et al.: SPHERE: a sensor platform for healthcare in a residential environment. In: Angelakis, V., Tragos, E., Pöhls, H.C., Kapovits, A., Bassi, A. (eds.) Designing, Developing, and Facilitating Smart Cities, pp. 315–333. Springer, Cham (2017). https://doi.org/10.1007/978-3-319-44924-1_14

Constructing Customized Multi-hop Topologies in Dense Wireless Network Testbeds

Florian Kauer[iD] and Volker Turau[✉][iD]

Institute of Telematics, Hamburg University of Technology, Hamburg, Germany
{florian.kauer,turau}@tuhh.de

Abstract. Testbeds are a key element in the evaluation of wireless multi-hop networks. In order to relieve researchers from the hassle of deploying their own testbeds, remotely controllable testbeds, such as the FIT/IoT-LAB, are built. However, while the IoT-LAB has a high number of nodes, they are deployed in constraint areas. This, together with the complex nature of radio propagation, makes an ad-hoc construction of multi-hop topologies with a high number of hops difficult. This work presents a strategic approach to solve this problem and proposes algorithms to generate topologies with desired properties. The implementation is evaluated for the IoT-LAB testbeds and is provided as open-source software. The results show that preset topologies of various types can be built even in dense testbeds.

1 Introduction

The use of testbeds consisting of actual wireless hardware is of major importance for development and evaluation of algorithms and protocols for wireless networks. While analytical considerations and simulations come with less initial investment, they can only partly reproduce the real world. The main reason is that propagation of radio waves is highly complex and even the most complex models can only cover parts of the actual mechanisms and are computationally expensive. However, the deployment of wireless hardware comes with a high effort, especially when targeting large-scale multi-hop networks to be used in applications such as industrial plants [19, 22]. Instead of setting up a new testbed it is therefore often advisable to resort to existing testbeds that provide convenient remote control interfaces. One popular example is the FIT/IoT-LAB [1] that consists of multiple wireless network deployments ranging from 41 to 928 nodes of different types. These numbers are sufficient for many experiments. However, most deployments of the IoT-LAB span a comparatively small area where every transceiver can reach every other node in one hop, which does not allow evaluating complex routing algorithms, such as RPL [2], or data link layers such as IEEE 802.15.4 DSME [13]. The evaluation of such protocols requires dedicated topologies with specific properties. Furthermore, during debugging, very specific topologies can be very helpful. One obvious solution is to reduce

© Springer Nature Switzerland AG 2018
N. Montavont and G. Z. Papadopoulos (Eds.): ADHOC-NOW 2018, LNCS 11104, pp. 319–331, 2018.
https://doi.org/10.1007/978-3-030-00247-3_28

transmission power and receiver sensitivity of the transceivers or to select a sub-set of nodes to generate more sparsely connected networks. By this approach it is also possible to setup specific conditions to induce certain phenomena. This is especially interesting to provoke and debug weaknesses of protocols. Relevant topology properties include density – to regulate channel utilization and spatial reuse –, a high number of hops or the (non-)existence of weak or asymmetric links. Building long chains is interesting to model tunnels [6], grids for potato fields [14] or tree-like structures for large-scale data collection [17]. The main contribution of this paper is an approach to construct topologies in existing sensor network deployments satisfying given conditions for evaluating multi-hop protocols based on link quality measurements. The focus is on the construction of subgraphs with uniform density as illustrated in Fig. 1 as well as on tree-like topologies with specified depth and breadth. The implementation is published as open-source software [12] to enable other researchers to generate suitable topolo-gies for their experiments in the testbed of their choice. We present applications of our method for deployments in the FIT/IoT-LAB.

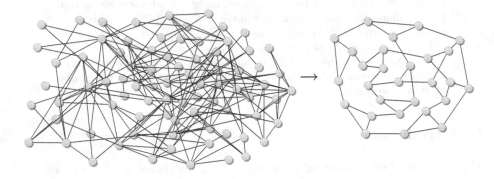

Fig. 1. Construction of an induced subgraph with uniform density.

1.1 Related Work

Building large-scale wireless sensor networks, especially outdoors, is a challeng-ing task. Successful examples include the Trio Testbed with 557 nodes in an area of $50000\,m^2$ [9] and CitySee [17] with 1196 nodes that build a multi-hop topology with up to 20 hops. Valuable overviews over the numerous problems that have to be solved are given in [4,14]. Therefore, multiple initiatives are made to build generic testbeds that can be controlled remotely by researches all around the world. These includes WISEBED [7], the MoteLab [28] and the FIT/IoT-LAB [1], providing convenient remote interfaces for software updates and debugging. Several publications cover channel characterization in the IoT-LAB [5,27], including work on the applicability of RSSI measurements for local-ization [11] and with the focus on the repeatability of experiments [20,21]. The latter covers many aspects relevant for this paper, including transmission power selection for controlling the density and the selection of quality radio links. For this, a strategic approach is important, because the topology has a large impact on the performance, for example on delivery ratio and energy consumption, as discussed in [8]. Outside the IoT-LAB, channel characterizations were conducted for example in complex factory environments [25] and by evaluating the influence of antenna, mutual alignment and distance on the transmission between wireless sensor nodes [18]. In the same publication, the influence of transmission power adjustment is discussed to minimize interferences. The adjustment of the transmission power for topology control is a broadly studied topic [15,23,24]. The latter also covers homogeneous transmission power adjustment for topology control and is therefore similar to the approach in this paper, though the objective is different.

2 Emulating Channel Conditions

One cornerstone of the proposed approach is the possibility to emulate different channel conditions by manipulating the transmission power and sensitivity of the transceivers. The primary node type in the IoT-LAB is the M3 Open Node. It consists of an ARM Cortex M3, an Atmel AT86RF231 [3], a 2.4 GHz chip antenna and several other peripherals. The transceiver can be configured with an output power from −17 dBm to 3 dBm and a reception sensitivity from −48 dBm to −101 dBm. The overall reduction of signal power between two nodes a and b is denoted as $\Lambda_{a,b}$ in the following. It depends on various losses and gains, including potential losses between the transceivers and the antennas, the gain of the antennas, which highly depends on the mutual alignment of the transceivers, and the path loss, which might also include fading effects, such as multi-path propagation. For example, given a link with $\Lambda_{a,b} = 63$ dB, a communication will be possible for a sensitivity setting of −66 dBm if the transmission power is chosen to be larger than −3 dBm. If the sensitivity is not reduced, reliable communication is even possible for the lowest transmission power of −17 dBm.

3 Topology Generation Procedure

In this section, the proposed procedure for generating multi-hop topologies is explained and exemplarily conducted for the Saclay testbed, more specifically the 12 M3 Open Nodes aligned in a 3×4 grid in the so called Digiteo 2 room. Compared to the other testbeds of the IoT-LAB it is relatively small and compact, so it allows for better traceability of the results in the following. Full results for the other testbeds are given in Sect. 4. The general procedure is as follows:

1. Measure $\Lambda_{a,b}$ between every pair of nodes.
2. Estimate the neighborhood graphs depending on the transmission power and sensitivity setting.
3. By means of these graphs, construct a topology by selecting a subset of the nodes and appropriate settings.
4. Verify this selection in the real testbed.

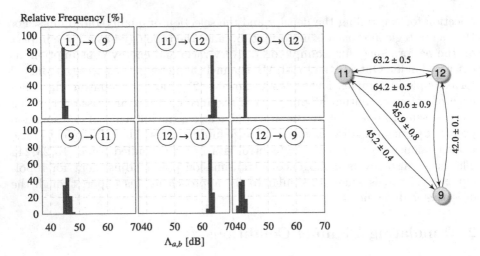

Fig. 2. The distribution of the pairwise RSSI measurements for three nodes. The right part shows the associated graph of the nodes together with the resulting mean and standard deviation of the measurements.

3.1 Pairwise $\Lambda_{a,b}$ Measurements

The RSSI is used in the following to estimate $\Lambda_{a,b}$ between each pair of nodes in the deployments of the IoT-LAB. Please be advised that wireless conditions change rapidly and are hardly reproducible, especially when the conditions change, such as a window or a door that is opened. Therefore, recent measurements will get better results, but still the topology generation algorithm itself has to take these fluctuations into account. The measurement is conducted as follows. Every node repeatedly sends out packets with full transmission power. To reduce the probability of collisions, random intervals between the transmissions are chosen and CSMA/CA is used according to the IEEE 802.15.4 standard. Every node in the neighborhood where the signal is strong enough to be received, measures the RSSI of the packet. By subtracting the RSSI from the constant and known transmission power, we get an estimate for $\Lambda_{a,b}$ between the respective nodes. This is repeated so that finally every node has sent at least 250 packets. It is important to measure on the same frequency channel as the one used in the final experiment. When multiple channels will be used such as in DSME [13], all relevant channels have to be taken into account. Figure 2 exemplarily shows the results for three nodes in the Saclay deployment. The left part of the figure depicts the distribution of the measured value for every pair of nodes, while the right part shows the mean and standard deviation of these measurements on the graph. Figure 3 shows a histogram over all links between the 12 M3OpenNodes and in Fig. 4 the losses over the distance between the respective nodes are plotted, showing only a slight correlation with a correlation coefficient of 0.38. This is also the reason why generating a topology by picking seemingly fitting nodes in the map of physical locations rarely works well.

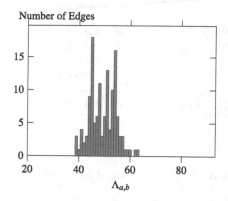

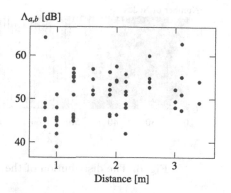

Fig. 3. The distribution of the measured $\Lambda_{a,b}$ for the Saclay testbed.

Fig. 4. Measured $\Lambda_{a,b}$ in relation to the euclidean distance between the nodes showing only a slight correlation (Pearson correlation coefficient 0.38).

3.2 Neighborhood Graphs

Based on the data from the last section, the existence of usable bidirectional links for various link budgets can be estimated. An edge is added to the neighborhood graph if the measured path loss between two nodes for both directions is smaller than the given link budget. This gives a family G of graphs $G_{\hat{\lambda}} = \left(V, E_{\hat{\lambda}}\right)$, with $\hat{\lambda}_{min} \leq \hat{\lambda} \leq \hat{\lambda}_{max}$ and $E_{\hat{\lambda}} = \left\{(a,b) \mid \Lambda_{a,b} \leq \hat{\lambda} \wedge \Lambda_{b,a} \leq \hat{\lambda}\right\}$. Here, $\hat{\lambda}_{min} = 31\,\mathrm{dB}$ is the smallest and $\hat{\lambda}_{max} = 104\,\mathrm{dB}$ the largest bound that is possible with the AT86RF231. Figure 5 shows the resulting graphs G_{42}, G_{46}, G_{50} and G_{104} for the Saclay testbed. Obviously, the number of edges increases with $\hat{\lambda}$. G_{104} is fully meshed, every node can reach every other node in a single hop. It is also apparent that there exist good links of long euclidean distance (e.g. $5 \leftrightarrow 12$), but also bad links with small euclidean distance (e.g. $11 \leftrightarrow 12$). Reasons for this include nonuniform antenna patterns, obstacles and reflections.

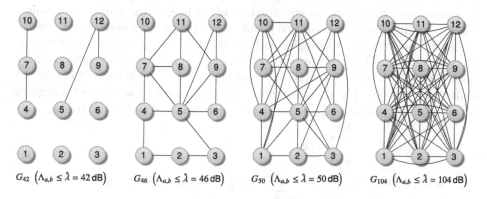

Fig. 5. Selected graphs from G for the Saclay testbed.

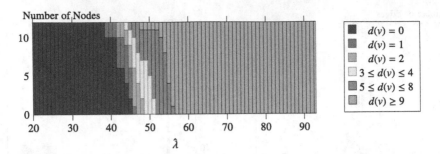

Fig. 6. The distribution of the node degree over the bound $\hat{\lambda}$.

The analysis of these graphs will finally help to decide which transmission power and which sensitivity should be chosen for a suitable topology for evaluation of multi-hop topologies. One approach to this task is the analysis of the degrees $d(v)$ of the nodes in the network. In Fig. 6, the distribution of the node degrees is shown for each $\hat{\lambda}$ for the Saclay testbed. Beyond $\hat{\lambda} = 56$, all nodes have at least 9 neighbors, while below $\hat{\lambda} = 39$, no edges exist. The intermediate section is the most interesting for our application. For example, in G_{46}, that is also shown in Fig. 5, one node has only one neighbor, five have 2 neighbors, four have degree 3 or 4, and for two it is between 5 and 8.

3.3   Constructing a Topology with Given Density

The task of this step is to decide for a subset of the nodes that form a topology suitable for the respective requirements at hand and a bound $\hat{\lambda}$, corresponding to the respective transmission power and sensitivity settings. While different settings per node may be feasible for some scenarios, we choose a homogeneous $\hat{\lambda}$ to simplify the final realization and to avoid unexpected effects from heterogeneous transmission powers. As stated in the introduction, the requirements for this selection can be very diverse. While very dense graphs with few hops can be realized easily by selecting as many nodes as possible and using high transmission power and sensitivity, the construction of the longest chain of nodes requires solving a well known NP-complete problem, referred to as *induced path* [10].

At first we consider topologies with constant node degree c, i.e., every node has c neighbors. This problem can be formulated and solved by integer linear programming (ILP). Let $\boldsymbol{x} \in \{0,1\}^{|V|}$ such that $\boldsymbol{x}(u) = 1$ if node u is selected and $\boldsymbol{x}(u) = 0$ if not. The set of neighbors of node u with a loss at most $\hat{\lambda}$ is given by $\mathcal{N}_{u,\hat{\lambda}} = \left\{ v \,\middle|\, (u,v) \in E_{\hat{\lambda}} \right\}$. For a given $\hat{\lambda}$, the ILP can be formulated as:

$$\underset{\boldsymbol{x}}{\text{maximize}} \quad \sum_{u \in V} \boldsymbol{x}(u)$$

$$\text{subject to} \quad c \cdot \boldsymbol{x}(u) \le \sum_{v \in \mathcal{N}_{u,\hat{\lambda}}} \boldsymbol{x}(v) \le c + m \cdot (1 - \boldsymbol{x}(u)), \forall u \in V.$$

Algorithm 1. Algorithm to construct a leveled subgraph for a given function κ

```
1: procedure MONITOREDBFS(V, E, v_0, λ̂, Δ, κ)
2:     V_sub(0) ← {v_0}, δ ← 0
3:     do
4:         V_sub(δ + 1) ← {}
5:         for all u ∈ V_sub(δ) do
6:             for all v ∈ N_{u,λ̂} do
7:                 if v ∉ ⋃_{i=0}^{δ+1} V_sub(i) then
8:                     if N_{v,λ̂+Δ} ∩ ⋃_{i=0}^{δ-1} V_sub(i) = ∅ then
9:                         V_sub(δ + 1) ← V_sub(δ + 1) ∪ {v}
10:        δ ← δ + 1
11:    while |V_sub(δ)| ≥ κ(δ)
12:    V_sub(δ) ← {}, δ_best ← δ − 1          ▷ remove partially filled layer
13:    return (δ_best, V_sub)
```

Here, $m = \max_{w \in V}\left(\left|N_{w,\lambdâ}\right|\right)$, so for $x(u) = 0$ the condition reduces to $0 \leq \sum_{v \in N_{u,\lambdâ}} x(v) \leq c + m$ and therefore always holds, while for $x(u) = 1$, it is equivalent to $\sum_{v \in N_{u,\lambdâ}} = c$. This ILP can be solved by a solver such as COIN-OR Cbc [16] that is interfaced with the Python PuLP frontend in our implementation. By iterating over the $\lambdâ$, we get a set of (not necessarily connected) subgraphs and can then select, for example, the largest connected component from these. Figure 7 shows a topology for the Saclay testbed that is generated by this procedure. Also Fig. 1 is the result of applying this technique to the largest connected component for $\lambdâ = 47\,\mathrm{dB}$ and $c = 3$ in the Lille testbed.

3.4 Construct a Tree Topology

For many evaluations, especially for analyzing tree routing techniques such as RPL, a tree topology with a large depth is useful. The following properties allow for a versatile, yet easy to compute, construction of such tree topologies.

1. The graph is connected.
2. A node v_0 is designated as root, e.g., to serve as a RPL DODAG root.
3. The number of nodes that are reachable from v_0 over exactly δ hops, referred to as breadth in this paper, is at least $\kappa(\delta)$, being a predefined function. For example, with $\kappa(\delta) = \delta + 1$, the number of nodes per level increases, while $\kappa(\delta) = 1$ also allows for linear topologies.
4. There exist no links with $\Lambda_{a,b} \leq \lambdâ + \Delta$ that would change the topology if the conditions change slightly; Δ is a margin to account for fluctuations.

Algorithm 1 finds subsets of nodes for given $\lambdâ$ and v_0 that lead to the largest number δ_{best} of hops towards v_0. In the algorithm, $V_{sub} : \mathbb{N}_0 \to \mathcal{P}(V)$ associates a depth value with the selected nodes of this depth. A node in $V_{sub}(\delta)$ may have several neighbors in $V_{sub}(\delta - 1)$ but none in $V_{sub}(l)$ with $l < \delta - 1$.

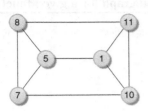

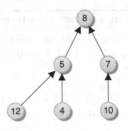

Fig. 7. Topology generated by the first technique with $\hat{\lambda} = 49\,\mathrm{dB}$ and $c = 3$. The positions do not represent the physical locations (cf. Fig. 5).

Fig. 8. RPL routing tree for a transmission power of $-17\,\mathrm{dBm}$ and a sensitivity of $-66\,\mathrm{dBm}$. Topology generated by the second technique.

Procedure MONITOREDBFS is basically a breadth-first search starting from v_0 and thus guarantees requirement 1 and 2. The condition in line 11 monitors the number of nodes per level and aborts the search when it can not be continued without violating requirement 3. Finally, line 8 ensures requirement 4 by excluding nodes that would have been visited earlier when $\hat{\lambda}$ would have been selected slightly larger. It has to be noted that this algorithm does not necessarily find *the* best possible topology, because it might be possible to generate subgraphs with a larger depth by removing nodes a priori. Though, this again would lead to the longest induced path problem. MONITOREDBFS is called for all values of $\hat{\lambda}$ and all nodes v_0 to get a set of subgraphs which can be used to select, for example, a subgraph with the largest depth. The total run-time of the algorithm is $O(nms)$, where s is the number of signal powers considered.

Node Reduction. Some applications require a large number of nodes, but usually it is advisable to reduce the size of the network to ease the analysis of a particular phenomenon as long as the behavior is unchanged. It should also not be forgotten that the FIT/IoT-LAB is shared with other researchers, so less nodes means less hindrance for others. Therefore, this section presents an optional procedure to reduce the number of nodes of the previously found subgraph, while still maintaining the requirements. It basically strips away all nodes that are not on a path to a higher depth with the additional constraint of maintaining $\kappa(\delta)$ nodes for depth δ. For a given generated layered subset of nodes V_{sub} with associated δ and $\hat{\lambda}$, this can again be specified as ILP where we want to

$$\underset{x}{\text{minimize}} \quad \sum_{u \in V} x(u)$$

$$\text{subject to} \quad \sum_{u \in V_{sub}(i)} x(u) \geq \kappa(i) \quad \forall 1 \leq i \leq \delta$$

$$\forall 1 \leq i \leq \delta, \forall u \in V_{sub}(i):$$

$$x(u) \leq \sum_{v \in V_{sub}(i-1) \cap \mathcal{N}_{u,\hat{\lambda}}} x(v).$$

3.5 Verification

The output of the algorithm is based on measurements of the pairwise RSSI values which are fluctuating due to changes in the environment. Therefore, current measurements are necessary if a high accuracy is required and it is important to verify that the constructed topology in fact fulfills the given requirements before starting the actual experiment.

For this, we use the RPL TSCH example for the IoT-LAB that is included in the IoT-LAB Contiki fork. A topology found for the given measurements of the Saclay testbed and $\kappa(\delta) = \delta + 1$ consists of the nodes $\{4, 5, 7, 8, 10, 12\}$ with root $v_0 = 8$ for the bound $\hat{\lambda} = 46\,\text{dB}$. Due to the constraint size of the testbed, it has depth $\delta_{best} = 2$. It can for example be achieved by choosing a transmission power of $-17\,\text{dBm}$ and a sensitivity of $-63\,\text{dBm}$, since $-17\,\text{dBm} - (-63\,\text{dBm}) = 46\,\text{dB}$.

It is, however, important to consider the transition region between perfect and no reception. Thus, it may be necessary to increase the transmission power slightly or to improve the sensitivity. For this evaluation, the sensitivity was improved to $-66\,\text{dBm}$. Finally, we get the routing tree by requesting the RPL parent for each node. This results in the tree shown in Fig. 8 fulfilling the given requirements. Links to candidate neighbors that are not parents are not shown.

4 Testbed Comparison

After focusing on the Saclay testbed we consider other testbeds in this section. Figure 9 shows the result for applying the second approach to all testbeds. The larger testbeds, Grenoble and Lille are in fact the only that are not fully meshed at full transmission power and sensitivity. With the previously stated requirements and $\Delta = 15$, the maximum achievable depth for $\kappa(\delta) = \delta + 1$ according to the measurements is $\delta_{best} = 8$ when setting $\hat{\lambda}$ to $74\,\text{dB}$ in Grenoble. With a reduced $\Delta = 5$, the depth increases to 15, but the topology is less robust. Also, with $\kappa(\delta) = 1$ more hops can be achieved. Finally, Fig. 10 shows a resulting RPL routing tree in the Lille testbed and Fig. 11 depicts the physical positions of the nodes in this experiment with some links that would not be obvious based on the locations, demonstrating the benefit of the presented approach.

Testbed	Nodes (available)		$\kappa(\delta) = \delta + 1$			$\kappa(\delta) = 1$		
			$\Delta = 15$	$\Delta = 10$	$\Delta = 5$	$\Delta = 15$	$\Delta = 10$	$\Delta = 5$
Grenoble	364	δ_{best}	8	13	15	15	37	38
		$\hat{\lambda}$	73-74	70	69-73	71	69	61
Lille	229	δ_{best}	5	7	8	8	10	12
		$\hat{\lambda}$	70-74	73-74	64-70	64-74	64-66	67-69
Paris	69	δ_{best}	2	3	4	3	5	9
		$\hat{\lambda}$	46-66	49-53	48-51	46-49	49	48
Strasbourg	63	δ_{best}	2	3	4	3	4	7
		$\hat{\lambda}$	48-74	50-57	49-56	50-53	46-52	51-52
Lyon	17	δ_{best}	-	2	2	2	2	4
		$\hat{\lambda}$		54-58	49-63	45-60	45-65	51
Saclay	12	δ_{best}	-	2	2	2	3	4
		$\hat{\lambda}$		46	46-51	45-51	46	46

Fig. 9. Maximal achievable depth δ and the associated $\hat{\lambda}$ range in dB for the different testbeds of the FIT/IoT-LAB. In Lyon and Saclay, no topologies with at least two hops are possible for $\Delta = 15$ and $\kappa(\delta) = \delta + 1$.

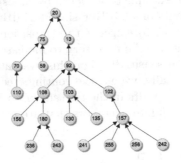

Fig. 10. A RPL routing tree with depth 5 at the Lille site for a transmission power of 3 dBm and a sensitivity of −81 dBm.

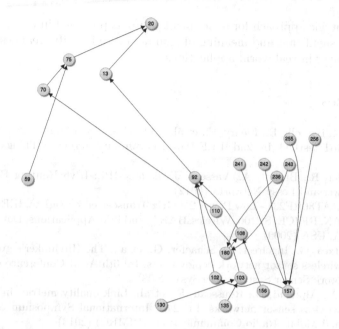

Fig. 11. The tree of Fig. 10 with the physical positions of the nodes.

5 Conclusion

The paper proposes an approach to generate multi-hop topologies in dense wireless network testbeds. The well-known fact that in common wireless sensor network settings, the received signal strength only correlates slightly with the distance can be verified for the FIT/IoT-LAB testbed. This makes it difficult to handpick reasonable nodes and settings for executing experiments. Therefore, channel condition measurements are conducted to estimate neighborhood graphs depending on the transmission power and sensitivity settings. As expected, the density of the resulting graph decreases with lower transmission power and reduced sensitivity.

These measurements form the starting point for a constructive algorithm to generate tree topologies with a custom minimum number of nodes per depth as well as an ILP for reducing the number of nodes afterwards. Finally, it is shown that by the proposed approach the number of hops can be increased significantly in contrast to the default settings, where - except for Grenoble and Lille - only single-hop topologies are possible.

The published toolset [12] is a convenient alternative for the conventional map based node selection in the FIT/IoT-LAB to be used by other researchers. Future work includes the development of alternative approaches for selecting nodes, for example to generate topologies appropriate for peer-to-peer experiments. Topologies can also be constructed based on application specific properties of links such as the nodes' roles (i.e., consumer or provider of information) [26].

Using a strategic approach for experiment setup as proposed in this paper helps to get more significant and meaningful results and to identify weaknesses before the deployment in real world applications.

References

1. Adjih, C., Baccelli, E., Fleury, E., et al.: FIT IoT-LAB: a large scale open experimental IoT testbed. In: 2nd IEEE World Forum on Internet of Things (WF-IoT) (2015)
2. Alexander, R., Brandt, A., Vasseur, J., et al.: RPL: IPv6 Routing Protocol for Low-Power and Lossy Networks (2012)
3. ATMEL: AT86RF231 - Low Power 2.4 GHz Transceiver for ZigBee, IEEE 802.15.4, 6LoWPAN, RF4CE, SP100, WirelessHART, and ISM Applications, Datasheet, San Jose, CA, USA (2009)
4. Barrenetxea, G., Ingelrest, F., Schaefer, G., et al.: The Hitchhiker's guide to successful wireless sensor network deployments. In: 6th ACM Conference on Embedded Network Sensor Systems (SenSys) (2008)
5. Bildea, A., Alphand, O., Rousseau, F., et al.: Link quality metrics in large scale indoor wireless sensor networks. In: 24th International Symposium on Personal Indoor and Mobile Radio Communications (PIMRC) (2013)
6. Ceriotti, M., Corrà, M., D'Orazio, L., et al.: Is there light at the ends of the tunnel? Wireless sensor networks for adaptive lighting in road tunnels. In: 10th ACM/IEEE International Conference on Information Processing in Sensor Networks (IPSN) (2011)
7. Chatzigiannakis, I., Fischer, S., Koninis, C., Mylonas, G., Pfisterer, D.: WISEBED: an open large-scale wireless sensor network testbed. In: Komninos, N. (ed.) Sensappeal 2009. LNICST, vol. 29, pp. 68–87. Springer, Heidelberg (2010). https://doi.org/10.1007/978-3-642-11870-8_6
8. Ducrocq, T., Hauspie, M., Mitton, N., et al.: On the impact of network topology on wireless sensor networks performances illustration with geographic routing. In: International Workshops on the Performance Analysis and Enhancement of Wireless Networks (2014)
9. Dutta, P., Hui, J., Jeong, J., et al.: Trio: enabling sustainable and scalable outdoor wireless sensor network deployments. In: 5th International Conference on Information Processing in Sensor Networks (IPSN) (2006)
10. Garey, M.R., Johnson, D.S.: Computers and Intractability: A Guide to the Theory of NP-Completeness, Freeman, New York (1979)
11. Heurtefeux, K., Valois, F.: Is RSSI a good choice for localization in wireless sensor network? In: 26th International Conference on Advanced Information Networking and Applications (AINA) (2012)
12. Kauer, F.: Toolset for Generating Multi-hop Topologies for the FIT IoT-LAB (2018). https://github.com/koalo/iotlab_topologies
13. Köstler, M., Kauer, F., Lübkert, T., et al.: Towards an open source implementation of the IEEE 802.15.4 DSME link layer. In: Scholz, J., Bodisco, A. (eds.) 15. GI/ITG KuVS Fachgespräch Sensornetze (2016)
14. Langendoen, K., Baggio, A., Visser, O.: Murphy loves potatoes: experiences from a pilot sensor network deployment in precision agriculture. In: 20th IEEE International Parallel & Distributed Processing Symposium (IPDPS) (2006)

15. Li, M., Li, Z., Vasilakos, A.V.: A survey on topology control in wireless sensor networks: taxonomy, comparative study, and open issues. Proc. IEEE **101**(12), 2538–2557 (2013)
16. Lougee-Heimer, R.: The Common Optimization INterface for operations research: promoting open-source software in the operations research community. IBM J. Res. Dev. **47**(1), 57–66 (2003)
17. Mao, X., Miao, X., He, Y., et al.: CitySee: urban CO_2 monitoring with sensors. In: 31st IEEE International Conference on Computer Communications (INFOCOM) (2012)
18. Myers, S., Megerian, S., Banerjee, S., et al.: Experimental investigation of IEEE 802.15.4 transmission power control and interference minimization. In: 4th IEEE Communications Society Conference on Sensor, Mesh and Ad Hoc Communications and Networks (SECON) (2007)
19. O'donovan, T., Brown, J., Büsching, F., et al.: The GINSENG system for wireless monitoring and control: design and deployment experiences. ACM Trans. Sens. Netw. **10**(1), 4:1–4:40 (2013)
20. Papadopoulos, G.Z., Gallais, A., Schrciner, G., et al.: Thorough IoT testbed characterization: from proof-of-concept to repeatable experimentations. Comput. Netw. **119**, 86–101 (2017)
21. Papadopoulos, G.Z., Gallais, A., Schreiner, G., et al.: Importance of repeatable setups for reproducible experimental results in IoT. In: 13th ACM Symposium on Performance Evaluation of Wireless Ad Hoc, Sensor, & Ubiquitous Networks (PE-WASUN) (2016)
22. Pfahl, A., Randt, M., Meier, F., et al.: A holistic approach for low cost heliostat fields. In: 20th International Conference on Concentrated Solar Power and Chemical Energy Technologies (SolarPACES) (2014)
23. Ramanathan, R., Rosales-Hain, R.: Topology control of multihop wireless networks using transmit power adjustment. In: 19th IEEE Conference on Computer Communications (INFOCOM) (2000)
24. Santi, P.: Topology control in wireless ad hoc and sensor networks. ACM Comput. Surv. **37**(2), 164–194 (2005)
25. Tang, L., Wang, K.-C., Huang, Y., et al.: Channel characterization and link quality assessment of IEEE 802.15.4-compliant radio for factory environments. IEEE Trans. Indus. Inform. **3**(2), 99–110 (2007)
26. Tsiropoulou, E.E., Paruchuri, S.T., Baras, J.S.: Interest, energy and physical-aware coalition formation and resource allocation in smart IoT applications. In: 51st Annual Conference on Information Sciences and Systems (CISS 2017) (2017)
27. Watteyne, T., Adjih, C., Vilajosana, X.: Lessons learned from large-scale dense IEEE802.15.4 connectivity traces. In: 11th International Conference on Automation Science and Engineering (CASE) (2015)
28. Werner-Allen, G., Swieskowski, P., Welsh, M.: MoteLab: a wireless sensor network testbed. In: 4th International Symposium on Information Processing in Sensor Networks (IPSN) (2005)

F-Interop Platform and Tools: Validating IoT Implementations Faster

Maria Rita Palattella[1]([✉]), Federico Sismondi[2], Tengfei Chang[3], Loic Baron[4],
Mališa Vučinić[5], Pablo Modernell[6], Xavier Vilajosana[6],
and Thomas Watteyne[3]

[1] Luxembourg Institute of Science and Technology, Esch-sur-Alzette, Luxembourg
mariarita.palattella@list.lu
[2] IRISA, Campus de Beaulieu, Rennes, France
federico.sismondi@irisa.fr
[3] Inria, Paris, France
{tengfei.chang,thomas.watteyne}@inria.fr
[4] Sorbonne Université, LIP6, Paris, France
loic.baron@lip6.fr
[5] University of Montenegro, Podgorica, Montenegro
malisav@ac.me
[6] Universitat Oberta de Catalunya, Barcelona, Spain
{pmodernell0,xvilajosana}@uoc.edu

Abstract. F-Interop allows implementors of IoT protocols to test compliance and interoperability of their implementation by connecting to a remote server in the cloud which contains and runs testing tools for different IoT standards. This paper provides an overview of the F-Interop Platform and the tools. Nowadays testing tools for CoAP, 6TiSCH, OSCORE and LoRaWAN standards are already available.

The F-Interop project, which has started as a H2020 project funded by the European Commission, is now supported by a large community of standard development organizations, small/large companies, academic institutions, and protocol designers and implementors. They all see the benefits of adopting the new Interoperability approach proposed by F-Interop, which allows to validate IoT implementation faster, reducing time to market, and standardization.

Keywords: IoT · Interoperability · Online tools · Standardization

1 Introduction

The principal barrier to massive IoT technology adoption is the lack of interoperability and the resulting segmented nature of the IoT market. The classical approach for checking conformance to a given standard, and interoperability

---

Supported by the H2020 F-Interop project (https://www.f-interop.eu/), and in particular the Open Call projects SORT, SPOTS, and F-LoRa.

N. Montavont and G. Z. Papadopoulos (Eds.): ADHOC-NOW 2018, LNCS 11104, pp. 332–343, 2018.
https://doi.org/10.1007/978-3-030-00247-3_29

with other products from different vendors, consists in organizing interoperability events, Face-to-Face (F2F) meetings where vendors meet and run interoperability tests. The F2F approach has a set of drawbacks, in term of cost to afford, and timeline to launch a standard-based and interoperable product on the market. Participants must cover engineering and travel costs, and this is often not possible for SMEs. During the event, there is usually not enough time for vendors to run all the tests, or to fix an implementation when a test fails. To test their product again, vendors must wait for the next event (which produce a delay in the time to market) and also invest new resources, to attend the new Interop meeting.

To overcome such drawbacks, the H2020 F-Interop project has fostered the development of online testing tools for emerging IoT standards and technologies, accessible remotely, on a cloud platform [1,2]. The shift in the Interoperability approach, from the classical F2F events to the online and remote ones, has several benefits: (i) ease the Interop procedure, using online tools, (ii) drastically reduce cost - no need to travel, only remote attendance, and (iii) faster the time to market, i.e., the production of standard-based and interoperable products.

In this paper, we describe the F-Interop Platform, and the integrated testing tools for different IoT technologies (CoAP, 6TiSCH, LoRaWAN, etc.). We share the lessons learned from the first F-Interop Interop events entirely run adopting the new approach.

2 F-Interop Platform

The F-Interop platform developed as a *platform as a service* offers remote online testing tools for IoT protocols. It has been designed with a modular and scalable architecture which allows easy integration of new testing tools. As illustrated in Fig. 1 it includes a set of core components, described hereafter, which communicate among them using an Event Bus.

Session Orchestrator: It is the core component of the architecture. It is in charge of provisioning (and tearing down) a virtual host per test session within the Event Bus in order to isolate the tests running suimultaneously. It is also responsible for supervising the processes associated with the testing tools, e.g. spawning and/or killing the testing tools containers on-demand, logging testing tool's log output, etc.

Resource Repository: It is the component responsible for the storage and retrieval of the resources used in the tests. These resources are selected by the user when launching the test session. Examples of resources include the user Implementation Under Test (IUT), virtual IUTs available on the Platform to run conformance tests, testbeds and related IoT devices, etc.

Result Repository: It is the component in charge of storing and retrieving the results generated during F-Interop test sessions.

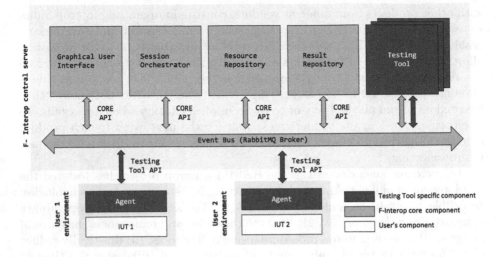

Fig. 1. F-Interop platform and CORE components.

Testing Tool: It is a protocol-specific component. It is responsible for the inter-action between the user components and the F-Interop platform during the test execution. It is also in charge of analyzing the network traffic exchanged between IUTs, and to issue a verdict based on the tests results. The Testing Tools communicates over the Event Bus, and the messages exchanged must comply with the defined API. F-Interop supports several testing tools for different IoT protocols (CoAP, 6TiSCH, OSCORE, LoRAWAN, etc.) as detailed in the following sections of the paper.

Graphical User Interface (GUI): It integrates the different components of the F-Interop platform together, offering to the end users an easy access through the web. Anyone with a web browser can create an account on the F-Interop Platform. Once logged in, the user can launch a new test session in three simple steps: (i) select the testing tool of interest, (ii) configure the tool according to the IUT features, and (iii) start the test session. Users can save the configuration setting in a JavaScript Object Notation (JSON) format for later re-use, during new test sessions. Once running, the testing tool sends messages to the GUI explaining to the user the steps to follow in order to complete the tests.

Agent: It is the proximity component of the Testing Tool which runs in the user environment close to the IUT. It can be a program which runs in the user's operating system, or a specific firmware which runs in a specific hardware platform.

Event Bus: It is the common medium used for exchanging all type of messages (control messages, raw data packets, logs, etc.), among the different components of the F-Interop platform. Each message sent over the Event Bus is composed of a routing key, properties and a body. The routing key indicates how to route a message to the relevant input queues of the listening components. The properties include a message identifier, a time-stamp defining the date and time when the message has been produced and a content-type specifying the use of the JSON format. It can also present a reply-to field and a correlation-id identifier in case of a request/reply exchange of messages. RabbitMQ is the underlying message-passing mechanism. It acts as a secure message broker between all the components through encrypted channels.

CORE API: It standardizes a set of messages which are sent over the Event Bus for providing the basic platform services such as "display message to user" (GUI), "save test results information" (Results Repository), and more. The complete feature set of the CORE API can be accessed online[1].

3   F-Interop Testing Tools

This section describes the testing tools currently integrated in the F-Interop Platform, addressing some of the most relevant IoT protocols: CoAP, 6TiSCH, OSCORE and LoRaWAN.

3.1   CoAP Testing Tool

The Standard: CoAP, the Constrained Application Protocol, standardized by the IETF CoRE working group, is the de-facto web transfer protocol for constrained devices. It is based on a request-response interaction model, and its basic architecture includes a CoAP client and a CoAP server.

CoAP runs on the connection-less unreliable transport protocol UDP. Therefore, it implements at application layer some lightweight reliable mechanisms for detecting duplication, re-ordering and acknowledging delivery. Orthogonal to these protocol features, CoAP defines also the GET, POST, PUT and DELETE methods in RFC7252. Then RFC7641 extends the feature set with the OBSERVE mechanism: CoAP clients can "observe" states of resources from CoAP servers (in other words it can retrieve the value of a resource, and get its updates over a given period of time).

The Test Description: All the aforementioned protocol features and mechanisms can be tested with the F-Interop testing tool. The CoAP reference interoperability Test Description, TD[2] has been integrated into F-Interop[3].

---

[1] doc.f-interop.eu#events-core-api.
[2] https://github.com/cabo/td-coap4.
[3] http://doc.f-interop.eu/testsuites/coap.

The Testing Tool: The CoAP Testing Tool offers to end users a controlled and feature-rich environment that eases the execution of the online and remote standard-based interoperability test procedure.

Figure 2 shows the setup for running a CoAP remote interoperability test between two IUTs. Two protocol-specific components (the Agent and the Testing Tool) have been implemented for supporting CoAP tests.

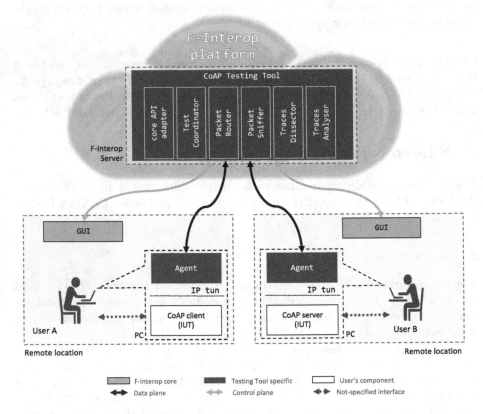

Fig. 2. CoAP remote user-to-user interoperability test setup.

The main components of the CoAP Testing Tool are:

1. `Packet Router and Agents`: establishes a VPN-like setup between IUTs. The controlled environment helps users bypass UDP-blocking firewalls and other middle boxes installed in their facilities. The setup creates IPv6 network interfaces bound to the VPN, therefore users can test their implementations over IPv6 regardless the IP version supported by their internet provider. The Packet Router is the middle-box between IUT1's interface and IUT2's interface, it can act as a lossy gateway for test scenarios which require simulating a lossy context.

2. `Test Coordinator`: coordinates the entire interoperability test. It iterates over the test steps described in the test description. It dispatches commands to users through the GUI, based on the TD (e.g. ``user1: CoAP Client is requested to send a GET request''). The user is guided to perform the test remotely.
3. `Packet Sniffer`: sniffs the traffic exchanged between IUTs and generates PCAP files records. The component enables the export feature for network traces so users can analyze the exchanged frames using tooling outside of F-Interop e.g. wireshark or some analysis scripts code.
4. `Traces Dissector`: dissects the exchanged messages between IUTs and provides a human readable representation of the packets. It provides a wireshark-like view to helps users find problems encountered during the interoperability test execution.
5. `Traces Analyzer`: analyzes the traffic exchanged between IUTs during a test case. The tool automatically issues PASS, FAIL, INCONCLUSIVE verdicts after each test case. The analysis is based on the CHECK steps of the test cases description.

F-Interop Integration: The `core API adapter` module handles the integration with F-Interop's core services such as GUI and Results Repository.

The integration enables two interoperability test use cases: (i) remote user-to-user interoperability session, as described in Fig. 2, and (ii) single-user sessions to test interoperability against reference implementations.

3.2   6TiSCH Testing Tool

The Standard: The 6TiSCH protocol stack, designed and standardized at IETF, glues together the IEEE802.15.4 PHY and MAC protocols with an IPv6-based upper stack. The latter includes the RPL routing protocol, the 6LoWPAN adaptation protocol, and the CoAP application protocol. Thanks to the Time Synchronized Channel Hopping (TSCH) scheme adopted at the MAC layer, 6TiSCH can offer low-latency, high reliability, scalability, and low power consumption, thereby meeting the requirements of Industrial Internet of Thing (iIoT) applications. 6TiSCH has defined the minimal configuration to run a 6TiSCH network (RFC8180), and a 6P sublayer that manages the allocation of MAC resources.

The Test Description: The first 6TiSCH Interoperability TD was prepared for the first 6TiSCH Plugtest organised by ETSI in 2015, at IETF93 [3]. Since then, the TD has been updated several times, for each new ETSI Plugtest and Interop event organised in the framework of the F-Interop project. The latest version of the TD is available online[4] and includes four classes of tests: SYN tests (testing the synchronization status of device), MINIMAL tests (testing the

---

[4] http://openwsn-builder.paris.inria.fr/job/td-6tisch%20builder/lastSuccessfulBuild/artifact/6tisch_plugtest_td_june_2018.pdf.

minimal configuration of 6TiSCH), **6LoRH** tests (testing IP packets in 6LoRH format, according to RFC8138), and **6P** tests (testing format and behaviors of the 6P sublayer).

The Testing Tool: The 6TiSCH testing tool is composed of three main protocol-specific components:

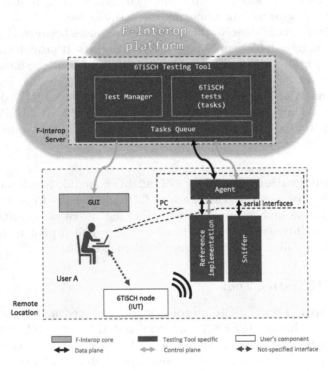

Fig. 3. 6TiSCH remote conformance test (IUT vs reference implementation) set up.

1. **Test Manager:** It is the brain of the 6TiSCH testing tool. To start the 6TiSCH manager, the user needs to select the 6TiSCH suite on the web GUI and start a session. Once it is running, the manger sends a message to the GUI asking which specific 6TiSCH test the user would like to execute. An AMQP consumer is up and running and listens to the choice made by the user. Once this information is received, the manager creates a test context which includes the sequence of steps required by that specific test, according to TD.

2. **6TiSCH Tests (tasks):** It is the component dispatching STIMULI actions to users (start/shut-down IUT), controls to the packet sniffer (start/stop), and handling CHECK steps analysis after the test execution, using the Wireshark dissector.

3. `Task Queue`: It is in charge of executing the tasks generated by the manager and/or the 6TiSCH Tests (tasks) component. Once a task is received, the task queue assigns it to one of its workers that is currently idle and marks it as busy. Hence multiple tasks can be assigned at the same time using several workers. Once the task is completed, then the worker can get back to the idle status. The Task Queue is implemented in Celery[5].

F-Interop Integration: Figure 3 shows the general setup for running a 6TiSCH conformance test using the F-Interop Platform. While running a test, the Manager generates three types of tasks for the Task Queue: `step start, step end, testcase verdict`. For all the tests, besides the specific feature for which interoperability is checked, the user has to perform some generic steps: turn on all the devices (the IUTs, and the packet sniffer); wait until the devices enter into a stable state; issue a stimulus to let the device perform a given action. As final step, to check the result of the test, the user uploads the Wireshark packet capture (pcap) file, which is analyzed by the Wireshark dissector. If the packet is found in the pcap file, and all the check fields are correctly dissected, then the manager gives a PASSED verdict. If the packet cannot be found or dissected, the test fails. The specific reasons why the test failed are shown inside the red bottom verdict.

In future developments of the 6TiSCH tools, an `Agent` component will be integrated to interact with the IUT and automatize some steps of the test session. This includes the initial execution of the stimulus (e.g. send a 6P ADD packet), and the final upload of the pcap file. Currently, these operations are executed manually by the end user.

3.3   OSCORE Testing Tool

The Standard: The Object Security for Constrained RESTful Environments (OSCORE) is a mechanism that provides application-layer security of CoAP. OSCORE secures CoAP by authenticating and encrypting the CoAP message and its payload, and by cryptographically bounding responses to requests. OSCORE excludes from cryptographic processing parts of the CoAP message that are supposed to be read or modified by a proxy. As a consequence, OSCORE enables CoAP to be used through untrusted intermediaries. This contrasts with the use of (D)TLS to secure CoAP, where any such intermediary needs to terminate the secure connection, and has full access to the exchanged data. OSCORE also enables the use of secure CoAP for group communication.

OSCORE relies on a pre-established security context between a client and a server. This security context encompasses cryptographic key(s) and initialization vectors, as well as application-level identifiers. The OSCORE security context can also be agreed upon dynamically, through an independent key exchange protocol.

---

[5]   http://www.celeryproject.org/.

OSCORE has been specifically designed for constrained IoT devices. It is therefore very efficient in terms of message overhead, and is an appealing solution for providing a secure end-to-end channel. As such, OSCORE has been adopted as a key security component in the IETF 6TiSCH protocol stack. Apart from securing CoAP application exchanges, in a 6TiSCH network, OSCORE also secures the "join" process of a new node.

The standardization work around OSCORE has first started in late 2014, and the specification is currently in the last stage before being published as an Internet Standard. There are multiple implementations of the draft standard available, including 2 in Python, 1 in C# and 2 in embedded C. As part of the F-Interop project, OSCORE has also been implemented within Wireshark, to facilitate packet analysis.

The Test Description: The core OSCORE team has released several versions of the OSCORE Test Description[6], used during F2F plugtest events held in the past, typically co-located with IETF meetings. In the framework of the SPOTS project, funded by the F-Interop Open Call, the TD has been redesigned to facilitate automated testing.

The OSCORE test description encompasses a total of 16 tests. These tests are divided into 3 categories: setup tests verifying the interoperability of the underlying CoAP implementation; correct usage tests, covering basic OSCORE functionality; incorrect usage tests, covering error handling behavior.

F-Interop Integration: The OSCORE testing tool has already been integrated in the F-Interop Platform. A video demonstration of an OSCORE test is available online[7]. It complements the 6TiSCH testing tool. From the point of view of an F-Interop user, the steps described in Sect. 3 are followed as in case of any 6TiSCH test: queries prompting for different configuration parameters, test stimuli, and the upload of a pcap file of a test execution. In case a user selects an OSCORE test, the GUI simply prompts the user for additional OSCORE-specific parameters, such as the application identifiers and cryptographic keys. This implementation method enables the testing of OSCORE on top of the 6TiSCH protocol stack, as well as any other generic OSCORE implementation whose packet capture the user can obtain. In the latter case, the 6TiSCH specific parameters are simply bypassed during the configuration prompt.

The OSCORE test suite relies on the Wireshark implementation to decrypt and dissect the packet(s). The Wireshark output is parsed and compared to the values expected by the test case semantics. For example if the decryption and authentication code verification of an OSCORE message was successful. Ongoing implementation work focuses on the integration of the OSCORE suite with the CoAP testing tool, in order to make it possible to launch an OSCORE test from the CoAP testing tool, leveraging the VPN-like tunneling provided by the Agent component.

---

[6]   https://github.com/EricssonResearch/OSCOAP.
[7]   https://youtu.be/05-MTLrFSrg.

3.4   LoRaWAN Testing Tool

The Standard: LoRaWAN is one of the most adopted Low-Power Wide Area Networking (LPWAN) technologies, with a simple network architecture that offers a multi-km communication range provided by the robustness of a LoRa physical layer. In the LoRaWAN network architecture, end devices communicate with application servers using gateways and a central network server, in a star-of-stars topology. The end devices communicate with the gateways using a single hop LoRa radio link. The gateways forward the received messages to the network server using, for example, an IP network.

Although the communication is bi-directional, uplink communication from the end devices to the network server is privileged. Three end device classes are defined: A, B, and C. The selection of the device class is based on a compromise between energy consumption and latency. Class A devices, mandatory to implement per the current LoRaWAN specification, defines two downlink reception windows after every successful uplink transmission in which the device will listen for downlink messages.

The LoRa PHY layer uses pseudo-random channel hopping and each frame is transmitted using a Spreading Factor (SF) in a trade-off between communication range and the time-on-air of the frames. The network server is in charge of the configuration of the different communication parameters in order to comply with the duty-cycle regulations of the used frequency band.

LoRaWAN implements a two-layer security mechanism. One key is used for the end-to-end encryption of the messages exchanged between the end device and the application server (this key is not known by the network). A second key is used for integrity checking and the encryption of the MAC commands exchanged by the end device and the network server. The MAC commands are used by the network server to configure the communication parameters of the nodes (e.g., selected data rate, delay of the downlink reception windows, data rate used in the reception windows).

The Testing Tool: Considering the LoRaWAN network architecture, the F-LoRa testing tool is designed to play the role of the Network Server and Application Server while interacting with an end device. As shown in Fig. 4, the end device is running the LoRaWAN Implementation Under Test (IUT) and the user must provide a compliant LoRa gateway running a packet forwarder.

The Test Description: A test description has been defined for testing the main specification of the LoRaWAN protocol. The tests are classified into different groups, based on the type of features they aim to verify: (i) ACT, device activation, (ii) FUN, basic functionalities and timing, (iii) SEC, security, encryption and integrity check, (iv) MAC, MAC commands. The different activation mechanism, Activation By Personalization (ABP) and Over the Air Activation (OTAA) can be tested. In addition to the basic joining message exchange of the OTAA, new data rate, reception windows delay, and frequencies are configured using the Join Accept message to test the implementation of this feature.

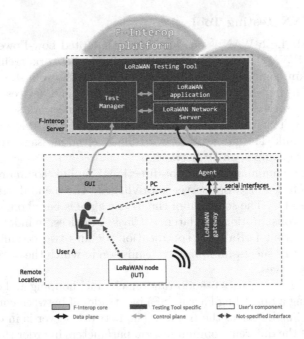

Fig. 4. LoRaWAN remote interoperability test set up.

Regarding security, end-to-end encryption with the configured keys can be tested and the Message Integrity Code calculation can be verified. Between the different messages exchanged with the IUT, new configuration parameters are set using MAC commands to check that the IUT behaves as expected.

F-Interop Integration: The user interacts with the F-LoRa testing tool using the F-interop GUI. After the selection of the F-LoRa LoRaWAN testing tool, instructions are provided on how to download, run, and configure the Agent module on the user's side. The ABP credentials of the IUT (security keys, short address, device EUI) can be configured and then the user selects a group of tests to be performed.

The Agent serves as an interface between the gateway's packet forwarder and the testing tool. The user must configure the gateway to send all the packets to the Agent component. Once the test session has started, all interactions are handled by the testing tool. The testing application running on the device with the IUT responds as defined by the testing protocol. A detailed description of the test verdict, indicating the errors found in any failing step is shown to the user in the GUI after all tests are completed.

4 From F2F to Online Remote Interop Events

The SORT project, funded by the 1st F-Interop Open Call, has largely promoted the adoption of the F-Interop Platform and testing tools, organizing two

F-Interop 6TiSCH Interop events. During the first event, organized in July 2017, and co-located with IETF99-Prague, the IETF community was informed about the H2020 F-Interop project and the possibility to run Interop tests online, using the F-Interop Platform. The use of the Platform was demonstrated with the set of 6TiSCH tools available at that time. Members of standard development organizations, small/large companies, academic institutions, and protocol designers and implementors, showed interest in adopting the F-Interop Platform, and run the tests online. This was confirmed by their attendance of the 2nd F-Interop 6TiSCH Interop event, held in Paris in June 2018. 15 people from 10 different organizations attended each of the two F-Interop event. Participants could test their implementations and validate the results of the tests, uploading a pcap file on the F-Interop platform. Participants run not only 6TiSCH tests, but also CoAP and OSCORE tests. The adoption of the F-Interop Platform by a wide Interop community (6TiSCH, CoAP, OSCORE) shows the feasibility of the initial F-Interop project industrialization plan.

6LoRITT-P&F and CoAP-P&F are two newly founded projects by the 2nd F-Interop Open Call which will kick-off during the second half of 2018. In the same spirit of the SORT project, they will organize remote Interop events for CoAP and 6LoWPAN. Participants located in different places around the globe will be connecting to F-Interop plaform to run Interop tests. To cope with the difference in working hours between different geographical locations, the Interop events will take place in a series of time slots, time-shifted between each occurrence in an efficient way for covering all participants local times requirements.

As already proved by the first F-Interop Interop events, IoT academic and industrial players, including SMEs, will benefit from the F-Interop Platform, as they will be able to check compliance and interoperability of their products in a shorter timeframe, and with highly reduced cost.

References

1. Leone, R., Sismondi, F., Watteyne, T., Viho, C.: Technical overview of F-Interop. In: Mitton, N., Chaouchi, H., Noel, T., Watteyne, T., Gabillon, A., Capolsini, P. (eds.) InterIoT/SaSeIoT - 2016. LNICST, vol. 190, pp. 11–17. Springer, Cham (2017). https://doi.org/10.1007/978-3-319-52727-7_2
2. Eunsook, E.K., Ziegler, S.: Towards an open framework of online interoperability and performance tests for the internet of things. In: Global Internet of Things Summit (GIoTS), Geneva, Switzerland (2017)
3. Palattella, M.R., Vilajosana, X., Chang, T., Reina Ortega, M.A., Watteyne, T.: Lessons learned from the 6TiSCH plugtests. In: Mandler, B., et al. (eds.) IoT360 2015. LNICST, vol. 170, pp. 415–426. Springer, Cham (2016). https://doi.org/10.1007/978-3-319-47075-7_46

Author Index

Printed in the United States
By Bookmasters